CANINE OREGON

WHERE TO PLAY AND STAY WITH YOUR DOG

Lizann Dunegan

FULCRUM PUBLISHING

Golden, Colorado

Library of Congress Cataloging-in-Publication Data

Lizann Dunegan
  Canine Oregon : where to play and stay with your dog / Lizann Dunegan.
    p. cm.
  ISBN 1-55591-328-8
  1. Travel with dogs—Oregon—Guidebooks. 2. Oregon—Guidebooks.
I. Title.
  SF427.4574.C6 H56 2001
  917.8804'34—dc21

                         2001001235

Printed in the United States of America
0 9 8 7 6 5 4 3 2 1

Editorial: Daniel Forrest-Bank, Laura Carlsmith
Cover design: Nancy Duncan-Cashman
Interior design: Rosanne Pignone, Pro Production
Cover photographs (clockwise from top left): Levi at Lost Lake; happy dog at
    Wilsonville's Memorial Park; Sadie at Smith Rock State Park; Levi near Mount Bachelor.
    All photographs by Lizann Dunegan.
Maps: Jim Miller, Fennana Design

Fulcrum Publishing
16100 Table Mountain Parkway, Suite 300
Golden, Colorado 80403
(800) 992-2908 • (303) 277-1623
www.fulcrum-books.com

To Sage—
May you always have
something to herd and someone to kiss.

To Levi—
May your indomitable spirit
lead you to big sticks, cool waters,
and new adventures.

My two traveling partners, Sage and Levi.

Contents

Acknowledgments

Thanks to all the forest service, state park, city and county officials, and business owners who took the time to share their knowledge and insights. Thanks to all of Levi's and Sage's buddies and their adventurous owners, who posed for photos and kept me company on hiking trails in the outback. Thanks to the folks at Fulcrum Publishing for making this book a reality.

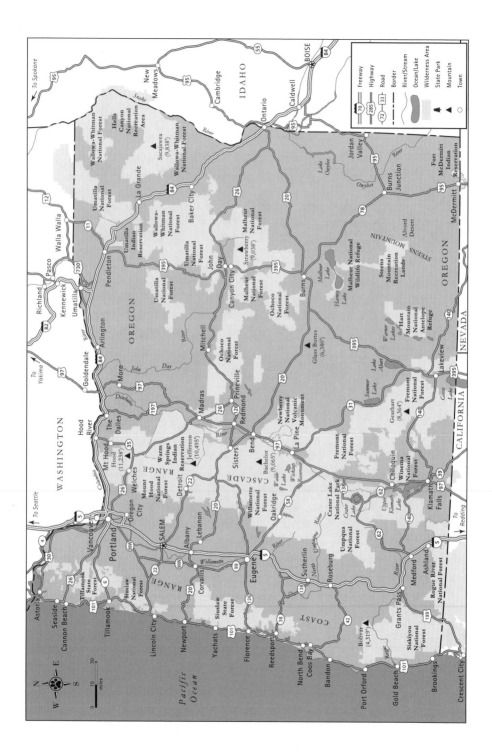

Introduction

Traveling with your canine pal is fun and rewarding. Dogs love to travel and discover new places, just like you do. In my case, I've got two adventurous Border Collies that travel with me everywhere I go in Oregon. At age 12, Levi is the older and wiser of the two. He is a big-boned, rough-coated, black-and-white Border Collie/Australian shepherd cross; his goals in life are to find and chew up big sticks, wallow in any water he can find, and fetch Frisbees and soccer balls. He loves other dogs and people, and has won the hearts of many on our travels throughout Oregon. Sage is a 7-year-old, tri-color Border Collie who is hard-wired to herd anything in sight. Since I don't own a flock of sheep, her mission in life is herding Levi and any other moving object wherever we go. She is a herding natural—she circles, stalks, and keeps everyone together, all on her own. Sage's other passion is people. She loves to kiss and snuggle with anyone who will let her (I just wish she loved her canine cousins as much). Both dogs are independent, like me, and love new adventures, just like I do.

In this book, we have tried to help you discover the best places in Oregon from a canine perspective. You'll find dog-adventure hotspots and tips for hiking, mountain biking, cross-country skiing, paddling, or just hanging out with your furry friend. You'll learn where to find leash-free parks, accommodations, campgrounds, dog events, dog-friendly stores, doggie daycare facilities, dog washes, clubs, veterinarians, and shelters. You'll also find tips on trail and park etiquette, dog gear and accessories, and an overview of canine first-aid.

You'll find out where dogs aren't welcome, and get an overview of dog regulations in Oregon's cities, state parks, state forests, national forests, Bureau of Land Management (BLM) lands, and national parks and monuments.

This book is organized into seven main parts, corresponding to Oregon's different regions: the Willamette Valley, the Columbia River Gorge/Mount Hood, Central Oregon, Northeast Oregon, Southeast Oregon, Southwest Oregon, and the Oregon Coast. Each section contains a map and the following information:

THE BIG SCOOP

In each section, The Big Scoop gives you an overview of the region or city and at-a-glance recommendations for what to see and where to stay with your dog. It covers highlights of the canine culture, where the leash-free parks are, what areas are closed to dogs, and other canine regulations. If you aren't sure where to get started, be sure to read this section.

PAW-APPROVED HIKES AND PARKS

With my two traveling partners, Levi and Sage, I've had great adventures exploring Oregon's parks and trails. Swimming in a cool stream, playing fetch at the beach, and meeting other dogs in a leash-free park are some of the activities my two trail hounds experienced while helping me research this book.

 Hikes and parks are given a paw-approval rating from 1 to 4 (4 is the best rating). This canine rating system is based on the amount of drinking water available, the availability of shade, whether your dog can be off leash, the presence of other dogs and their owners on the trail, scenic beauty, the trail's length, and the elevation gain. Use these recommendations to get started if you are new to the area, and by all means let me know if you find other canine-friendly hikes and parks I can add to future editions of *Canine Oregon*. Reach me at lizanndunegan@hotmail.com.

CYCLING FOR CANINES

Cycling with your canine pal is a great way to get a workout while enjoying Oregon's beautiful trails. Most trails listed have shade and water available. Before heading out on a really long trail, be sure your dog is in shape, and on the trail, take plenty of rest breaks. For your dog, the greatest trail hazards when he's running bike-side are footpad injuries and heatstroke. Consider dog boots to keep your best friend's feet happy on really long trails. (See the *Appendix: Gearing Up Your Pup*)

POWDERHOUNDS

Oregon is a paradise for snow adventures. This section lists areas to ski with your best friend. Most snow-park areas (i.e., parking areas that are plowed) in Oregon require that a Sno-Park permit be displayed in your vehicle's front window between November 15 and April 30. Daily permits are $3, three-day permits are $7, and annual permits are $15. Permits are sold at all Oregon Department of Motor Vehicle offices and by permit agents in resorts, nearby sporting goods stores and other retail outlets, and Forest Service offices. These agents may add a fee to the cost of each permit they sell.

Some high-use winter trails do not allow dogs. See individual chapters for restrictions.

Remember that plowing through the snow is a lot more work for your canine partner than it is for you. Dog boots provide protection for his feet against ice and

Dog boots are recommended for trail hounds.

snow buildup that can cause sores and eventual lameness. (See the *Appendix: Gearing Up Your Pup*) If you don't have dog boots, apply petroleum jelly to the bottom of your dog's feet to help prevent ice and snow buildup between his toes. Another way to protect his feet is to wrap them with a stretchy bandage. Just don't wrap it too tightly or it will cut off circulation to his feet. Short-coated dogs may also appreciate a dog coat. (See the *Appendix: Gearing Up Your Pup*)

PADDLEHOUNDS

Nothing beats a day with your pooch on a beautiful alpine lake or a slow, meandering river. Here you'll find recommended creeks, lakes, and rivers where you and your best friend can spend some quality time. All lakes and rivers listed in this section allow motorized traffic except where noted. Be sure your dog is fitted with a portable flotation device before you head out on your water adventure. (See the *Appendix: Gearing Up Your Pup*)

OTHER PLACES TO HOUND AROUND

This section spotlights unique canine sights or destinations that don't fit in any other category, such as dog art and restaurants that welcome dogs on their outdoor patios.

CANINE COMFORT ACCOMMODATIONS

From humble hotel rooms to fireplace suites with ocean views, listings include a description of the accommodation and any special amenities for canines such as treats, pet sheets, or outdoor pet washing areas. For each listing, "Dog Policy" describes added charges for your dog as well as other pet-specific policies (e.g., dogs can be left unattended in a room only if crated, or allowed only in specific areas of the hotel). *Policies, prices, or regulations are subject to change. Just because you read it here doesn't mean a detail is set in stone. It's best to call ahead, especially for lodging, to confirm that your dog is indeed welcome.*

The following price symbols are based on a standard room for two people per night:

$ = up to $49
$$ = $50–$99
$$$ = $100–$149
$$$$ = $150 and up

CAMPGROUNDS

Oregon has hundreds of campgrounds that welcome dogs. Best of all, many are close to hiking and biking trails or to prime paddling lakes and rivers. Individual campground site fees range from $5 to $30, depending on the time of year, the campground location, the type of campsite (hook-ups versus a primitive tent site), and the number of vehicles per party. Included is information on facilities available (water, restrooms, picnic tables, etc.), dates the campground is open, and a short description of the campground and nearby activities. Dogs must be leashed in all established campgrounds (except primitive camping sites on BLM land). Dogs are not allowed to stay in yurts, tepees, camper wagons, or cabins in state park campgrounds but are welcome in RV and tent sites.

DOG EVENTS

Here you'll get the lowdown on offbeat canine happenings such as fun runs, howling contests, owner and dog lookalike contests, dog shows, and pet fairs.

CANINE-APPROVED SHOPPING

This section lists stores that carry canine gear, apparel, food, supplies, and gifts for dogs as well as dog lovers.

DOGGIE DAYCARE

Sometimes, your dog can't join in on the fun. When you want to venture offshore for whale watching on the Oregon Coast, catch a tourist train in the Columbia River Gorge, or shop in downtown Portland, it's nice to know places that will board your dog for the day. Most of the doggie daycares listed require that you make advance reservations and provide proof that your dog's vaccinations are up-to-date. Some daycare providers also require that your dog's social skills be evaluated before he is allowed to stay for the day. If you don't find a doggie daycare listed for the area you are visiting, look at the *Canine ER* section. Many veterinary clinics offer day and overnight boarding services for your pooch.

DOG WASHES

Self-service dog washes make it easy to get your pooch spic-and-span. These wonderful places provide a large tub, shampoo, apron, grooming tools, and blow dryers. And the best part is the staff cleans up your mess! Some dog washes will trim your dog's nails and clean his ears for an additional charge, or, if you don't want to attempt bathing your dog on your own, wash your dog while you wait.

CANINE CLUBS

Have you ever wanted to take an agility class with your dog or learn more about skijoring? (Skijoring is a sport in which a dog in a harness is tethered to a waist harness worn by a cross-country skier. The dog pulls the skier through the snow, much like a sled dog pulls a sled.) This section lists canine clubs that sponsor classes, clinics, and seminars that you and your traveling partner may want to participate in.

DOG MEDIA

Specialty newspapers for canine-lovers give you the local scoop on dog issues and canine-related businesses, training tips and advice, and travel destinations that welcome furry friends.

CANINE ER

Whether on the road or on the trail, it's nice to know where the closest veterinarian is located. In larger cities, only those clinics that provide twenty-four hour emergency services are listed. In smaller communities, listings include clinics that provide high-quality veterinary care for dogs as well as service after-hours. Most veterinary clinics also stock food and other canine supplies and offer day and overnight boarding.

LOST AND FOUND (ANIMAL SHELTERS)

One of the scariest things when you are traveling is losing your dog. If this happens, consult this section to find the nearest animal shelter. Call it as soon as possible to see if your dog has been found. Carry a picture of your dog so you can make and post "Lost Dog" flyers. If you are at a trailhead and your best friend gets lost, leave your car there or camp there if allowed. Your dog may come back to look for you even after he has been lost for several hours. If your dog is gone for several days, visit the closest animal shelter every day. You can also put an ad in the local paper with a description of your dog and where he was lost.

LAND-USE POLICIES

Following are general dog-related guidelines for different public lands in Oregon. Specific locations within a region may have more restrictive rules. (See the individual chapters.)

Bureau of Land Management (BLM) Land

Your dog is not required to be on leash on BLM land (except established boat ramps and campgrounds) but he must be under voice control. The BLM has a liberal dog policy because most BLM land is in remote areas with few people.

City, County, and State Parks

The majority of city and county parks and all Oregon state parks require that your dog be leashed except within designated leash-free areas. All state park campgrounds allow dogs, although dogs are not allowed to stay in park yurts, tepees, camper wagons, or cabins. Dogs are not permitted to swim in designated swimming areas in any of the state parks. Most Oregon state parks require a pass, either a $3 day-use pass or a $30 annual pass. If you and Rover are traveling the Oregon Coast for several days, you can save money by purchasing an Oregon Pacific Coast Passport. It is valid for entrance, day-use, and vehicle parking fees at all state and federal fee sites along the entire Oregon portion of the Pacific Coast Scenic Byway (U.S. Highway 101), from Astoria to Brookings. An annual passport, valid for the calendar year, is $35. A five-consecutive-days passport is $10. Call 1-800-551-6949 to purchase an Oregon State Park Pass or Oregon Pacific Coast Passport.

National Forests and Wilderness Areas

Dogs are required to be on leash in all developed recreation sites in Oregon's national forests and wilderness areas, including campgrounds, picnic and day-use areas, trailheads, snow parks, boat ramps, interpretive sites, and swimming beaches. Dogs are also restricted from some high-use trails in certain wilderness and national scenic areas. In all undeveloped national forest areas, dogs can be off leash if they are under voice control. Many national forest trailheads in Oregon require a Northwest Forest Pass. A day pass is $5, or you can buy an annual pass for $30, good at all participating national forests and scenic areas in Oregon and Washington. For a list of participating national forests and locations that sell the Northwest Forest Pass, call 1-800-270-7504, or log on to www.naturenw.org.

National Parks and Monuments

Oregon has four designated national parks or monuments. Leashed canines are welcome on all trails and campgrounds at the Newberry National Volcanic Monument, and on all trails in the John Day Fossil Beds National Monument. The bad news is that dogs are not allowed on any of the trails in Crater Lake National Park or the Oregon Caves National Monument. As long as your dog is leashed, he is welcome at picnic areas, rest areas, viewpoints, and campgrounds at these two parks, but if you are planning to hike or backpack, Rover will have to stay at home.

The Clean-Up Routine

No matter where you visit with your canine friend, clean up after him! While some urban parks and trailheads provide poop-pick-up baggies, many don't, so carry your own supply. Plastic grocery store and newspaper bags make great pooper-scoopers. When on the trail in a national forest or other remote area, take your dog off the trail to do his business and then bury his waste.

Hunting Season

When fall arrives in Oregon, so does hunting season. The deer and elk-hunting season begins September 28 and can last through December 8, depending on the region of the state. (The exception is the bow-hunting season, which begins August 24 and ends September 22.) Game bird hunting season begins September 1 and can extend through January 31, depending on the region of the state. During hunting season, use caution when hiking with your dog on National Forest lands, and in some wilderness areas and wildlife refuges.

To make it easy for your dog to be seen by hunters, purchase an inexpensive bright orange reflective vest for him. For protection designed especially for dogs, Ruff Wear offers the Lab Coat, a reflective, urethane-coated vest. (See *Gearing Up Your Pup* in the *Appendix* for contact information) For specific information about hunting seasons, contact the Oregon Department of Fish and Wildlife at 503-872-5268 (www.dfw.state.or.us).

CANINE ETIQUETTE 101– PLAIN OL' DOG SENSE

Use common sense on the trail with your dog. Always keep him under control, allow him to visit others only by invitation, leash him on heavily used trails, and clean up after him by picking up or burying his waste.

Sage had a tough time with the "approach others only on invitation" rule. She absolutely loves people and nine times out of ten, she gets a warm welcome. But some folks just don't appreciate her advances or, in rare cases, are terrified of dogs. Sage now receives her visiting cues from me.

COMMUNICATIONS– SKILL BUILDING

Taking an obedience class is a great way to enhance your dog's relationship with other dogs, other people, and you. Dogs really appreciate knowing the rules of the road and where they stand in any relationship. Classes are usually offered through community colleges or by dog trainers.

Once you and your pooch have mastered basic commands such as "Sit," "Lie down," "Stay," and "Come," you are better prepared for Oregon's outdoors. Another helpful command is "Get back." Use it on narrow hiking trails. When other hikers approach, have your dog follow behind you with a quick "Get back." Nothing is more bothersome than an enthusiastic dog who runs back and forth on the trail, disrupting the peace for others. Or, when you see other trail users approaching, give them the right of way by quietly stepping off the trail and making your dog lie down and stay until they pass. This skill is necessary for herding dogs like Levi and Sage, whose instinct is to hold their ground with other moving objects. Luckily, Levi's first lesson with bikes was from a nimble mountain biker who managed to avoid a collision. Levi now makes good use of his "Heel" or "Get back" commands when joggers and bikers approach.

GETTING YOUR DOG IN TAIL-WAGGING SHAPE

Just like you, your pooch needs to get in shape before heading out on long outings. Luckily, he can get in shape with you. Take your furry friend on your daily walks or runs. If there is a park near your house, hit a tennis ball or play Frisbee with him. Another option is to ride a bicycle with your pal in tow. If you choose biking, make sure he is used to jogging next to a bicycle and that you ride on a soft surface such as a dirt road or trail, which is easier on his paws. Swimming is also an excellent way to get your water dog in shape. If your dog likes the water, have him retrieve a tennis ball or stick. Gradually build his stamina up over a period of several weeks.

HEALTH CHECK-UP

Before you leave for your outdoor adventure with your pal, make sure he has had his annual health checkup. Your veterinarian will make sure his joints and limbs are sound, listen to his heart for murmurs or arrhythmia, make sure his lungs are clear, take his temperature, check his ears for infection or foreign bodies, examine his eyes for any abnormalities or vision problems, look in his mouth for signs of broken teeth or swollen gums, check his toenails to be sure they aren't too long, and check his coat and skin for signs of skin allergies or parasites. Make sure your dog's shots are up-to-date, and before you leave the vet's, grab a copy of your dog's vaccination history. Doggie daycare centers and other overnight boarding facilities require this information.

LEASH/COLLAR/IDENTIFICATION

The most important pieces of equipment for Rover are a sturdy leash and collar with identification. For my dogs, I use a six-foot lead with a flexible, stretchy handle that is easy on my hands and arms. Flexi-leads work well for hiking because they allow freedom to explore but still leave you in control.

My dogs wear nylon, adjustable collars. I like nylon collars because they are strong and durable, and come in a variety of colors and designs. Make sure your pooch's identification includes your name, address, and veterinarian's phone number. A quick way to obtain an identification tag is through an automated ID tag machine available at most Petco stores.

Because ID tags can be lost, you may want to consider using a microchip to ensure your dog is always identifiable. In this procedure, a rice-sized silicon microchip is inserted into the loose skin on the back of the dog's neck using a specially designed implanting device. Your dog does not have to be sedated because the procedure takes only about ten seconds and causes only about as much discomfort as a vaccination. The microchip stays in place throughout your dog's lifetime. Information on it usually includes the dog's name; the owner's name, address and phone number; and a record of the dog's vaccinations. When an animal shelter finds your dog, he is scanned using a special scanner; low-frequency waves activate the microchip, allowing your dog's information to be read. When your dog is microchipped, he is also issued a special ID tag for his collar, which alerts anyone who finds him that he has a microchip. This procedure usually costs from $30 to $50. Each microchip is encoded with a unique number that is kept in a national database. Two companies supply microchips: American Veterinary Identification Devices (AVID®) and HomeAgain®; each has its own codes and databases.

Tattoos are another form of permanent identification. This procedure is more costly than the microchip (prices range from $100 to $200) and risky because your dog needs to be completely anesthetized. In this procedure, on the inside flank of the dog's back leg is tattooed the dog's registration ID number or another form of identification that is not likely to change, such as the owner's driver's license number or social security number. Phone numbers or home addresses are not recommended because they will most likely change during your dog's lifetime.

DOGGIE BACKPACKS
Why should you carry all of your dog's gear when he can carry it himself in his

Cool pooch!

own backpack? Teach your dog to wear a backpack by placing an empty pack on his back and adjusting the straps to fit his body's contours. Let him wear the pack while you supervise. Don't leave him alone because he may decide this foreign object needs to be chewed off! Soon enough, your canine pal will view the pack as a prelude to fun and not a foreign enemy.

Slowly increase the pack weight and your outing distance. For water-loving dogs, pack food items in waterproof bags in case an irresistible swimming hole appears. As a general rule of thumb, his load should not exceed 25% to 30% of his body weight. For example, a 60-pound dog should carry a maximum of 15 to 18 pounds. A dog's age, physical fitness, and frame size are other factors that influence how much weight he can carry. See the *Appendix: Gearing Up Your Pup* for information on types of packs and where to purchase them.

PADDLING
Most dogs are natural swimmers and love to play in the water. When you and your buddy are on a lake or river where the shoreline is a long way off, he needs a flotation vest. (See the *Appendix: Gearing Up Your Pup*) Vests are especially important when boating in river rapids, lakes, or the always-frigid Pacific, where the water temperature can quickly sap his strength. Before embarking on a long paddle trip, prepare your dog with short trips that allow him to get his sea legs. Canoes require some extra training, because a nervous dog can easily upset a canoe. Train your dog to keep his weight low in the canoe, and slowly introduce him to sensations of moving water. Never tie your dog into a boat—if the boat flips, your dog can drown.

BIKE TRAILERS
Like to go on long or multi-day bike rides and don't want to leave Rover behind?

Pulling your dog in a bike trailer is a great way to explore Oregon's outback. Photograph by Ken Skeen

Bring your buddy along in a bicycle trailer designed to hold children. For his comfort, replace the seat with a nylon-covered foam pad, cut to fit snugly in the bottom of the trailer.

Begin by training your pup to jump into the trailer. If he won't, gently lift him in and praise him. Let him sit there for short periods of time. Once he will sit quietly in the trailer without trying to jump out, pull the trailer without the bike a short distance down a sidewalk, with a second person walking beside to provide reassurance to your dog. Slowly increase the length of your walks while pulling the trailer.

Once he can sit in the trailer for ten to fifteen minutes without any attempts to jump out, hook the trailer up to your bike and try a short ride on a bike path or quiet dead end street. As you ride, look back and praise him for his good behavior. If he tries to jump out, stop, and make him get back in the trailer. Try it again. Never tie your dog into the trailer—if he tries to jump out while the trailer is in motion, he can choke himself or flip the trailer over. Once your pal will safely stay in the trailer, increase the distance and time of your rides over a period of several weeks. Before you head out on a multi-day ride,

take a practice trip with all of your gear. This trial trip is not only good practice for your partner but also helps you get used to pulling a fully loaded trailer and bike, which can be a very humbling experience! You can stow dog gear underneath the foam pad in the trailer and pack your gear in bike panniers. With a lot of patience and praise, most dogs will begin to view the trailer as an opportunity for a new adventure, and will soon love riding in it. I use a Burley D'lite trailer for my two dogs, available from Burley Design Cooperative (4020 Stewart Rd., Eugene, OR 97402, 541-687-1644, www.burley.com).

FIRST-AID KIT CHECKLIST

Carry a first-aid kit in the car and on the trail so you are prepared for unforeseen injuries to your traveling partner. A good canine first-aid kit should include:

Adhesive tape
Antibiotic ointment
Antihistamine liquid
Aspirin
Cotton
Eyewash
Gauze rolls or pads
Gloves
Hemostats
Hydrocortisone ointment
Hydrogen peroxide
Insect sting relief medicated pads
Rectal thermometer
Scissors, preferably with rounded tips
Stretchy leg wrap
Syringe (without the needle) for giving
    medications by mouth
Tweezers
Veterinarian's phone number
Veterinary first-aid manual

TIPS FOR CAR TRAVEL

- If your furry friend isn't used to riding in the car, take several short practice rides before you leave on a long trip. Praise him after each car ride so he gets the idea that traveling is fun.

- Make sure Rover travels on an empty stomach. Don't let him eat within two hours of your departure.
- Consider a canine restraint device to keep your dog safe in the car. Or help your pal feel more secure by having him travel in a crate, which is also handy if your dog is going through a chewing phase.
- Avoid letting your pooch stick his head out the window. Pollen, dirt, and road debris can get into his eyes, causing irritation.
- Once your four-legged friend is used to longer trips, be sure to stop every few hours so he can stretch his legs and take a potty break. Be sure he is leashed during these rest stops so he can't run in the road and get hit. I once made the mistake of letting Sage out of the car unleashed on an icy November day at a rest stop perched on a high cliff with a scenic view of the Columbia River Gorge. For some unknown reason, she immediately jumped up onto the concrete railing on the side of the cliff (maybe to get a better view!). To my horror, there was ice on the railing and she went sailing over the other side. Luckily, she only dropped about four feet onto a small shelf, and I was able to pull her over the top and snap her leash on with no further incident. However, she could have lost her life due to my lapse in judgment. No matter how well you know your dog, always leash him at rest stops or other unfamiliar places.
- Never leave your dog unattended in your vehicle. Even on a cloudy day, your car can heat to over 100°F within minutes and this can kill your dog.

CANINE TRAVEL CHECKLIST

Bags
Blanket
Bowls, regular or collapsible, for water and food
Brush/Comb
Coat
Collar with identification
Crate
Dog boots
Dog pack or protective vest
First-aid kit
Flea/tick powder or spray
Food stored in resealable plastic bags
Leash
Medication
Mosquito repellent
Nail trimmers
Photograph of your dog
Portable flotation device
Sunscreen
Tie-out cable
Toothbrush/toothpaste
Towels (to wipe down dirty, wet dogs)
Toys
Treats
Vaccination records from your veterinarian
Water

CANINE FIRST-AID

Learn to recognize common canine trail injuries and potential dangers and how to treat them.

Giardia

When your pup drinks from a river or stream (which is often unavoidable), even those that look pristine and clear, he may pick up the protozoan parasite Giardia lamblia. This parasite is carried in the feces of domestic and wild animals in a cyst form; when they defecate in a stream, lake, or river, the parasite spreads throughout the water source. Once ingested, by dogs or humans, the Giardia cysts can cause diarrhea, vomiting, and weight loss. Signs usually occur about a week after ingestion. If you notice these symptoms, take your dog to the nearest veterinarian for a fecal test. If the result is positive, Giardia can be treated with a prescription drug. A vaccine is also available to help prevent giardiasis. Two vaccinations are given three weeks apart, with a yearly booster thereafter.

Heat Stroke

If you are hiking on a hot day, watch your dog for signs of heat stroke. Your dog may pant excessively, have an increased heart rate and temperature (above 104°F), act anxious, have bright red gums, vomit or have diarrhea, lie down and refuse to get up, or act lethargic and disoriented.

If your four-legged friend shows any of these signs on the trail, have him lie down in the shade. If you are near a stream, pour cool water over his entire body to help bring his body temperature down. Encourage him to drink and stay put until his symptoms begin to subside. Once he is stabilized, take him to a veterinarian for assessment.

Heartworm

Dogs can get heartworm from mosquitoes, which carry the disease in the prime mosquito months of July and August. Talk to your veterinarian about recommended preventative treatments for this condition.

Hypothermia

If you and your buddy are in cold and windy weather or your dog has been swimming in cold water, conditions are ripe for hypothermia. Symptoms include shivering, stiff muscles, low pulse and respiration rate, low temperature (below 97°F), and lethargy. To treat hypothermia, wrap him in warm blankets, a coat, or a sleeping bag and move him to a sheltered area. Give him a warm sugar solution by mouth and transport him to a veterinarian as soon as possible.

Insects

Bees, Wasps, and Mosquitoes

If a bee or wasp stings your dog, remove the stinger by scraping at the base of the stinger with a small piece of cardboard (a matchbook works well). Avoid removing the stinger with tweezers because this can release more poison into the skin. Clean the area with an antiseptic wipe and apply hydrocortisone cream. Try to distract your dog so he won't lick off the cream.

Dealing with pesky mosquitoes is a fact of life if you are traveling to high mountain lakes, streams, or marshy areas in Oregon. You can protect your dog from mosquitoes with the same mosquito repellent products you use. If you are applying repellent to your dog's face, don't spray it on his face. Instead, spray the repellent on a small towel and wipe it gently on his face and nose. Avoid the area around his eyes so they don't become irritated.

Ticks and Fleas

Ticks can give your dog Lyme disease; an infectious disease that affects dogs and humans and is found less commonly in cats, cattle, and horses. This disease is caused by a bacterial organism, Borrelia burgdorferi, that is transferred from host to host primarily by bloodsucking Ixodes ticks, which migrate throughout the environment via deer and other large mammals, and are most often found in heavily wooded areas, meadows, and near lakes and rivers.

Ticks spread Lyme disease to dogs when they attach to the dog with their mouthparts and feed on the dog's blood. The most common symptom of Lyme disease in dogs is arthritis of the joints. Joints become warm, swollen and very painful, resulting in lameness and a reluctance to move. Other symptoms include fever, loss of appetite, and swollen lymph nodes. A blood test can test for Lyme disease. Affected dogs often improve when treated with antibiotics.

Highest risk areas in the United States are coastal states from Maine to North Carolina, and New Hampshire and Pennsylvania. Dogs in Wisconsin, Minnesota, Michigan, Illinois, Missouri, Iowa, California and Oregon are considered to have a mild risk of contracting Lyme disease. The rest of the states are considered to have a minimal risk for Lyme disease.

There is a vaccine that helps prevent Lyme disease. The first dose is via injection, with a booster shot in three weeks. The vaccine is then given once a year thereafter. The cost is $18 to $25 per dose.

After every hike, check your dog from head to toe for ticks. Ticks are more commonly found on the head (especially around the ears) and neck, stomach, and other exposed skin areas. If your dog has ticks, treat him with a tick spray or powder or pour-on treatment. Give these products time to work, and the ticks should drop off. If the ticks do not drop off, then you'll have to remove them. First, apply petroleum jelly to the tick, which often causes it to loosen its grip. Use a pair of tweezers and a firm grip on the tick's head, and gently twist the tick in a back and forth motion to loosen its grip. Once you loosen its grip, remove the tick with a steady pulling motion. Afterwards, clean the affected area with an antiseptic wash and apply an antibiotic ointment. Wash your hands after you are finished. Sometimes when you try to remove a tick with tweezers, the body comes off easily but the head remains embedded under your dog's skin, which can cause an infection. If this happens, take your dog to your veterinarian for further treatment.

Fleas are small, black, biting insects that can cause itching and skin irritation and carry tapeworm eggs. Before you hit the trail, treat your trail hound with a flea and tick spray or powder. Ask your veterinarian about a once-a-month pour-on treatment that repels fleas and ticks.

Plant Hazards

In Oregon, one of the biggest plant hazards for canines is foxtail, a grass whose pointed seed heads bury themselves in dogs' fur, between their toes, and even in to the ear canal. If left unattended, these nasty seeds can work their way under the skin and cause abscesses and infections. Foxtails are a problem in the summer and fall, when grass seed heads mature. If you have a long-haired dog, consider trimming the hair between his toes and giving him a summer haircut to help prevent foxtails from attaching to his fur. After every hike or bike ride, inspect your dog—especially between his toes and his ears. If your dog shakes his head frequently or digs at his ear, he most likely has a foxtail in his ear canal. If you can't see the offending seeds, take your dog to a veterinarian to have them removed.

Other plant hazards include burrs, thorns, and thistles. If you find burrs or thistles on your dog, remove them as soon as possible before they transform the fur into an unmanageable mat. Thorns can pierce a dog's foot and cause a great deal of pain. If you see that your furry friend is limping, check his feet for thorns.

Oregon doesn't have poison ivy, but its evil cousin, poison oak, is ubiquitous. Dogs are immune to poison oak but they can pick up the sticky, oily substance from the plant and transfer it to you. Check at a ranger station or in a hiking guide so you can learn what poison oak looks like. After hiking in areas where you see poison oak, give your dog, and yourself a shower as soon as possible.

Paw Injuries

Be sure to keep your dog's nails trimmed. If you discover your trail partner has a torn nail, trim the broken toenail and stop the bleeding with Kwik Stop powder or flour. Gently apply the Kwik Stop powder or flour to the affected area and apply gentle pressure with a gauze pad until the bleeding stops. Apply cotton or gauze to the affected area and wrap with a stretchy bandage. If your dog develops a limp, check to see if his paws are torn or abraded. If so, wrap the affected paw with soft cotton or gauze and cover with a stretchy bandage and call it a day. You can protect Rover from these common injuries by using dog boots. (See the *Appendix: Gearing Up Your Pup*)

Porcupine Quills

If your dog has a penchant for porcupines (like my dogs do) you may find that he

xix

may decide to take a nip at one of these innocent-looking creatures, and before you know it, he is full of quills. You can try to remove a quill that is not set too deeply in the skin by grasping the quill at its base with a pair of needle nose pliers or hemostats and pulling it straight out. Clean the wound with antiseptic and apply an antibiotic ointment. If quills are lodged deep inside the dog's mouth or other parts of his body, take him to a veterinarian so he can be sedated and the quills removed.

Snake Bite

Oregon's only poisonous snake is the western rattlesnake, which is found in all parts of the state except the Oregon Coast, the Coast Mountain Range, and the northern portion of the Willamette Valley.

If your dog is bitten, try to identify the snake. Western rattlesnakes are two to four feet in length, have a diamond-shaped head, and are brown, with large, rounded blotches along the back, and black-and-white crossbars on the tail. A rattle is also present on the end of the tail. These snakes prefer dry, sunny locations such as sagebrush-covered grasslands, rocky habitat in creek and river canyons, and open pine forest.

If your dog is bitten by a rattler, put on a pair of gloves and wash the wound. Be sure not to cut the wound, and don't, contrary to old wives' tales, try to suck out the venom. Also, do not put ice on the wound or use a tourniquet. Keep your dog quiet and transport him to a veterinarian as soon as possible.

Sunburn

If your dog has lightly pigmented skin, he is an easy target for sunburn on his nose and other exposed skin areas. Apply sunscreen to exposed skin areas. Use a sunscreen made for sensitive skin that is rated 30 SPF or greater.

> "He is your friend, your partner, your defender, your dog. You are his life, his love, his leader. He will be yours, faithful and true, to the last beat of his heart. You owe it to him to be worthy of such devotion."
> —Author unknown

Willamette Valley

*O*n the western side of the Cascade Mountains, the Willamette Valley dominates the northern part of the state with its miles of fertile farmland, orchards, and wineries. Carved by the Willamette River, the valley's rich soil was an oasis to early pioneers who settled here to farm. The Willamette Valley is Oregon's most populated region and is host to four of its largest cities, which include Portland, Salem, Corvallis, and Eugene. All of these cities are located along the banks of the meandering Willamette River and have riverfront parks where canines have plenty of opportunities to explore. The Willamette Valley is also host to many scenic state parks that have fun hiking and biking trails and plenty of paddling opportunities. State parks we recommend visiting are Champoeg State Heritage Area, Willamette Mission State Park, and Elijah Bristow State Park.

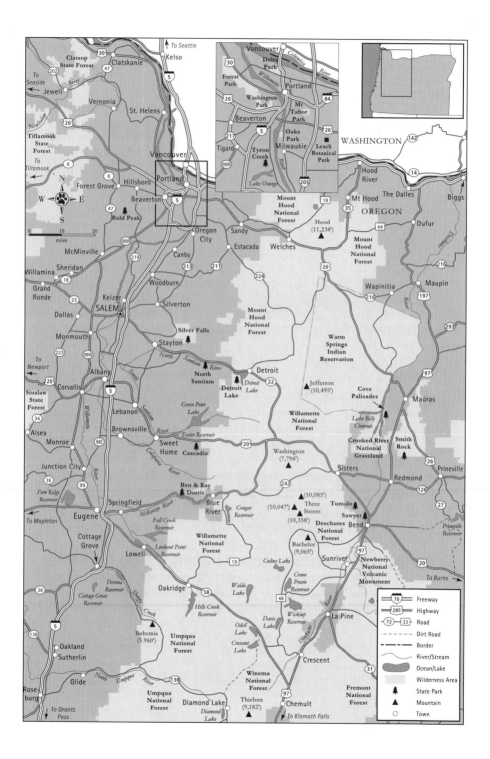

Portland and Vicinity

THE BIG SCOOP

Portland's adventures await you and your pooch around nearly every corner. It's also a great base for exploring Oregon's wilder areas, as it's just thirty minutes to the scores of waterfalls in the Columbia River Gorge, a National Scenic Area; an hour to the hikes, lakes and snow on Mount Hood; and ninety minutes to the beaches of the Oregon Coast.

Portland is separated into five different districts (North, Northeast, Northwest, Southeast, and Southwest) by the north-south running Willamette River and east-west running Burnside St. Also known as Bridgetown, Portland is home to many historic bridges. A great way to begin exploring the city with Rover is to head to downtown's Waterfront Park; it's connected via a 3.5-mile loop to the East Bank Esplanade, a riverside walkway that offers incredible city views and great people (and dog) watching. (See *Paw-Approved Hikes and Parks*) If you do the loop on a weekend from April to December, stop at the Saturday Market (held Saturdays and Sundays underneath the Burnside Bridge, downtown). This outdoor market features unique, handcrafted items made by local artisans as well as good food and live music.

Check out canine chic at Urban Fauna, a boutique at 338 NW 6th Ave. in Northwest Portland's Pearl District, a newly gentrified warehouse district. If you are looking for more outdoorsy duds for your pooch, step over to Oregon Mountain Community at 60 NW Davis St. This high-end outdoor shop carries a good selection of canine gear and, best of all, lets you bring Fido in the store (as long as he is leashed) to try on gear.

Portland is home to 5,000-acre Forest Park, with miles and miles of trails for you and your hound to explore. A fine hike is the Lower Macleay Park to Pittock Mansion hike. This 4-mile out-and-back hike winds moderately uphill through a tall, Douglas fir forest along the banks of bubbling Balch Creek. The route then charges steeply uphill to historic Pittock Mansion, built in 1914 by a local newspaper baron. At the mansion, drinking fountains and a water bowl for your dog greet you before you walk out to the rear lawn to soak in the incredible views of Portland, Mount Hood and Mount St. Helens.

Other recommended hikes around town include Hoyt Arboretum, Tryon Creek State Park, Oaks Bottom Wildlife Refuge, Powell Butte Nature Park, Warrior Rock Lighthouse on Sauvie Island, the Riverside Trail, and the Clackamas River Trail. (See *Paw-Approved Hikes and Parks* for details)

If you're inclined to sample one of Portland's fine microbrews, head over to the east side to the Lucky Labrador at 915 SE Hawthorne Blvd. This brewpub caters to canines by allowing you to sit with your leashed dog on the outdoor patio while you sip a pint of Lucky Lab Stout or Dog Day IPA.

For finer fare, visit the Berlin Inn at 3131 SE 12th St. This German restaurant and bakery has a special menu just for Rover. You can dine with your dog in their outdoor beer garden and he can select tantalizing delicacies from the Pooch Platter menu. (See *Other Places to Hound Around* for more details)

For more hiking action keep heading east and check out Mount Tabor Park. This park, an extinct volcanic cinder cone, is a favorite hangout for Portland canines. On its miles of trails, your dog is sure to make many new friends.

Portland even has its own paper, *The Dog Nose News*, dedicated to news and events about our four-legged friends. Portland is also host to dozens of accommodations (from posh downtown suites to bed and breakfast inns) that welcome your best pal (see *Canine-Approved Accommodations*).

Dogs must be leashed in all Portland area public spaces and parks except those designated as off-leash areas, such as Chimney Park, Gabriel Park, East Delta Park, West Delta Park, Lake Oswego's Luscher Farm Park, and Wilsonville's Memorial Park. State parks with off-leash areas include Rooster Rock (located in the Columbia River Gorge, east of Portland off I-84), Mary S. Young in Lake Oswego, Molalla River in Canby, Milo McIver outside Estacada, and Champoeg State Heritage Area (located 30 minutes south of Portland off I-5). Metro area parks that do not allow dogs include Oxbow Regional Park, Blue Lake Regional Park, Howell Territorial Park on Sauvie Island, Sauvie Island Boat Ramp, Smith and Bybee Lakes Wildlife Area, Beggars-tick Wildlife Refuge, Chinook Landing Marine Park, M. James Gleason Memorial Boat Ramp, and Glendoveer Golf Course Fitness Trail.

PAW-APPROVED HIKES AND PARKS

Portland—North

 Chimney Park
Contact: Portland Parks & Recreation, 1120 SW Fifth Ave., Suite 1302, Portland, OR 97204, 503-823-PLAY, www.parks.ci.portland.or.us
Paw-Approval Rating: 3 paws
Leashes Required? No

Frisbee is a favorite canine activity at Chimney Park.

Fees/Permits: None
Season: Year-round
Getting There: From the intersection of I-84 and I-5, head 4.3 miles north to exit 306B, Columbia Blvd. Head about 4.5 miles west on Columbia Blvd. to Chimney Park located on the left side of the road.
Description: Your dog will enjoy playing Frisbee, ball, and running to his heart's content at this leash-free park, located off busy North Columbia Blvd. in North Portland. The park features picnic tables and a gently sloping, large grassy area shaded by red cedar and blue spruce trees. The park is partially fenced along North Columbia Blvd.

 East Delta Park
Contact: Portland Parks & Recreation, 1120 SW Fifth Ave., Suite 1302, Portland, OR 97204, 503-823-PLAY, www.parks.ci.portland.or.us
Paw-Approval Rating: 2 paws
Leashes Required? Yes (except in the leash-free area)
Fees/Permits: None
Season: Year-round, though the leash-free area may be closed in winter due to flooding

Getting There: From the intersection of I-84/I-5, drive 5.5 miles north to exit 307, 99E/Delta Park/Marine Dr. Follow signs for Marine Dr. East/Portland Airport. After 0.6 mile, you'll arrive at a stop sign. Turn right toward Delta Park. Go 0.2 mile and arrive at East Delta Park. Park your vehicle on the right side of the road. The signed leash-free area is located on the left side of the road.

Description: This expansive park covers 86 acres and is most well known for its soccer tournaments. If your dog is a soccer fan he may enjoy being a spectator, or, if he wants to get in on more action he can practice his soccer moves in the fenced, leash-free area.

West Delta Park
Contact: Portland Parks & Recreation, 1120 SW Fifth Ave., Suite 1302, Portland, OR 97204, 503-823-PLAY, www.parks.ci.portland. or.us
Paw-Approval Rating: 2 paws
Leashes Required? No
Fees/Permits: None
Season: Year-round
Getting There: From the intersection of I-405 and I-5 in Portland, head north 4.5 miles and take exit 306B, Expo Center. At the end of the off-ramp, turn left and go under the freeway. At the T-intersection take North Expo Dr. toward the Portland International Raceway. Go 0.2 mile and turn left onto North Broadacre, then pull into the gravel parking area on the right side of the road. The off-leash area is the large grassy field adjacent to the parking area.

Description: This off-leash area is opposite the entrance to the Portland International Raceway. It is not fenced, so make sure you take your dog away from the road.

Portland—Northeast

Fernhill Park
Contact: Portland Parks & Recreation, 1120 SW Fifth Ave., Suite 1302, Portland, OR 97204,

503-823-PLAY, www.parks.ci.portland. or.us
Paw-Approval Rating: 2 paws
Leashes Required? Yes
Fees/Permits: None
Season: Year-round
Getting There: This park is located at the intersection of NE 37th St. and Ainsworth Ave. in Northeast Portland.

Description: Your pal will love this open, grassy 24-acre park with its small rolling hills and shade trees. You're sure to meet the local canines and their owners who frequent this park.

Marine Drive Hike
Contact: Portland Parks & Recreation, 1120 SW Fifth Ave., Suite 1302, Portland, OR 97204, 503-823-PLAY, www.parks.ci.portland. or.us
Paw-Approval Rating: 3 paws
Leashes Required? Yes
Length: 7.6 miles out and back
Difficulty: Easy
Fees/Permits: None
Season: Year-round
Getting There: From the intersection of I-5 and I-84 in Portland, travel 4.2 miles north on I-5 to exit 307, 99E/Delta Park/ Marine Dr. After 0.4 mile turn right toward Marine Dr. East and the Portland Airport. Go 0.3 mile to a T-intersection and stop sign. Turn left and follow signs for Marine Dr. East. At the next four-way junction, continue straight, following signs for Marine Dr. East. Go 3 miles east on Marine Dr. and park in a dirt pullout on the left side of the road just before a flashing yellow light at a bike crossing. If this dirt parking lot is full, continue east on Marine Dr. and pull into a large dirt parking area on the right side of the road just past the flashing yellow light.

Description: You and your pup can soak in Columbia River views from this paved multi-use path that parallels the river. Pups love chasing sticks and cooling off in the river. As an added bonus, snap pictures of

5

your best friend against the magnificent backdrop of 11,245-foot Mount Hood. From the parking area, walk east on the paved path for 3.8 miles until you reach a paved parking area just before the I-205 freeway. Dogs are not permitted on Broughton Beach, the beach located at the trailhead, but you can take him swimming in the river once you pass this beach.

Portland—Northwest

Leif Erikson Hike

Contact: Portland Parks & Recreation, 1120 SW Fifth Ave., Suite 1302, Portland, OR 97204, 503-823-PLAY, www.parks.ci.portland.or.us
Paw-Approval Rating: 2 paws
Leashes Required? Yes
Length: 11 miles one way.
Difficulty: Easy
Fees/Permits: None
Season: Year-round. This hike can be muddy during winter.
Getting There: From I-405 in downtown Portland, take the Highway 30 West/St. Helens exit (exit 3). At the end of the off-ramp, stay in the right lane, which turns into NW Vaughn St. At the first stoplight, turn left on NW 23rd Ave. Go one block and turn right on NW Thurman St. Go 1.4 miles to the end of Thurman St. and park near the green metal gate. Leif Erikson Dr. starts at the green metal gate.
Description: Your dog can get to know other Portland canines on this popular gravel, hiking/biking road that winds through the green expanse of 5,000-acre Forest Park. The road winds gently uphill with an elevation gain of 410 feet through a Douglas fir and big leaf maple forest for over 11 miles until it ends at Germantown Road. Handy mileage markers help you track your progress. Beware of mountain bikers who may buzz you and your dog on this trail. If you need to quench your thirst, there is a drinking fountain at the trailhead.
Option: A 5-mile loop option you may want to try explores some of the park's singletrack trails. To complete this loop, walk on Leif Erikson Dr. for 0.2 mile. Turn left onto the signed Wild Cherry Trail. Head uphill through a fern-filled forest until you reach the intersection with the signed Wildwood Trail at 0.9 mile. Turn right on the Wildwood Trail and follow this scenic trail as it winds along the ridge and ducks in and out of side canyons for 1.6 miles. At the intersection with Alder Trail, turn right and head on a fun, twisting downhill for another mile to the intersection with Leif Erikson Dr. Turn right on Leif Erikson Dr. and go another 1.5 miles back to the trailhead. Wild Cherry, Wildwood, and Alder Trails can be muddy during the winter months.

Lower Macleay Park to Pittock Mansion Hike

Contact: Portland Parks & Recreation, 1120 SW Fifth Ave., Suite 1302, Portland, OR 97204, 503-823-PLAY, www.parks.ci.portland.or.us
Paw-Approval Rating: 4 paws
Leashes Required? Yes
Length: 4 miles out and back
Difficulty: Difficult
Fees/Permits: None
Season: Year-round. This hike can be muddy during winter.
Getting There: From I-405 north in downtown Portland, take the Highway 30 West/St. Helens exit (exit 3). At the end of the off ramp, stay in the right lane, which turns into NW Vaughn St. Go 0.6 mile west on Vaughn St. Turn left on NW 28th St. and travel one block. Turn right on NW Upshur Street and proceed 0.2 mile to a parking area at the road's end at Lower Macleay Park.
Description: This trail winds steeply for over 600 feet through a tall, Douglas fir and maple forest through Balch Creek Canyon. The trail starts out at Lower Macleay Park, where you'll find a restroom and small parking area. Your pooch will love this trail because there are plenty of

opportunities for him (and you) to splash and cool off in Balch Creek. After 0.9 mile, the trail turns away from the creek and switchbacks steeply to another parking area. To continue to Pittock Mansion, walk through the parking area, cross Cornell Road and pick up the trail on the other side as it switchbacks steeply up the hill through a magnificent Douglas fir and fern-filled forest. After you have hiked 0.1 mile from Cornell Road you'll come to a trail intersection. Stay right and follow the trail for another 0.4 mile until you come to another trail intersection. Stay right again and follow the trail another 0.5 mile as it switchbacks steeply to the Pittock Mansion parking lot. There is a restroom and drinking fountain adjacent to Pittock Mansion, and usually a drinking bowl for your canine friend next to the drinking fountain. If it's clear, be sure to walk down the paved path to a viewpoint with a picnic table at the rear of the mansion. After you've soaked up the gorgeous view of downtown Portland and the mountains, head back to the trailhead on the same route.

Oak Island Hike

Contact: Oregon Department of Fish and Wildlife, Sauvie Island Wildlife Area, 18330 NW Sauvie Island Rd., Portland, OR 97231, 503-621-3488, www.dfw.state.or.us
Paw-Approval Rating: 3 paws
Leashes Required? Yes
Length: 2.9-mile loop
Difficulty: Easy
Fees/Permits: $3.50. Permits can be purchased at Sam's Cracker Barrel Store and Reeder Beach RV Park and Store. Sam's Cracker Barrel Store is located on the left, just after crossing the Sauvie Island Bridge. The Reeder Beach RV Store is located on the right after traveling 6.6 miles on NW Reeder Road.
Season: May through September. The trail is closed October 1 through mid-April for hunting season.

Getting There: From I-405 in Portland, take the Highway 30 West/St. Helens exit and follow the signs for St. Helens. Travel 9.3 miles north on Highway 30 until you see a sign indicating "Sauvie Island Wildlife Area." Exit to the right, at the stoplight, and cross the bridge to the island. After crossing the bridge, follow Sauvie Island Road north for 2.2 miles to the junction with Reeder Road. Turn right on Reeder Road and go 1.3 miles to the junction with Oak Island Road. Turn left on Oak Island Road and travel 3 miles to a road junction. Continue straight (left) and arrive at the trailhead in 0.4 mile.
Description: This route explores Oak Island—a small peninsula that shoots northward into Sturgeon Lake on the northwest end of Sauvie Island. This grassy peninsula is covered with thick white oak woodlands. Small mammals live and feed in the tall wild grasses, and the gnarled branches of the oaks provide shelter for jays, warblers, sparrows, kinglets, chickadees, and nuthatches. Northern harriers sail over the open fields hunting for small mammals, and bald eagles can be seen roosting high in the oak trees from December through March.

Begin by walking around a metal gate and walking on an old roadbed. Pick up a trail brochure (available in English and Spanish) that explains the history and natural features of the area. Walk a short distance to a road junction and turn right. The route continues through a thick white oak woodland. The doubletrack trail is often overgrown with tall grass (it is recommended you wear long pants on this hike) and blackberries line the trail in a tumbled mass. You can taste the delicious, sweet, purplish berries as they begin to ripen in mid-August. After 0.3 mile, turn right to begin the loop portion of the trail. At 0.6 mile, you'll arrive at Sturgeon Lake, a haven for geese, ducks, blue herons, swans, and sandhill cranes. A short side trail leads to the edge of the lake where Mt. St. Helens looms in the background.

The grassy doubletrack road skirts the edge of the lake for another 0.9 mile. The remaining portion of the loop takes you past grassy fields and oak woodland filled with the chatter of squirrels and songbirds. After 2.6 miles, the loop portion of the route ends. Continue straight (right) and go 0.3 mile to the trailhead. Be sure to check your hiking partner for ticks after this hike! For information on paddling Sturgeon Lake, see the *Paddlehounds* section.

Wallace Park
Contact: Portland Parks & Recreation, 1120 SW Fifth Ave., Suite 1302, Portland, OR 97204, 503-823-PLAY, www.parks.ci.portland.or.us
Paw-Approval Rating: 3 paws
Leashes Required? Yes
Fees/Permits: None
Season: Year-round
Getting There: This park is located at the intersection of NW 25th St. and NW Raleigh St.
Description: This 4.5 acre park is a favorite gathering place for Northwest Portland residents and their canines. It features large grassy fields with shade trees, walking paths, a playground, benches, a picnic shelter, a basketball court, horseshoe pit, and softball and soccer fields. It is also adjacent to Chapman Elementary School's open grassy fields and two tennis courts. It is also not far from a trendy shopping district located on NW 23rd Ave. Water and trash-cans are available (bring your own bags!)

Warrior Rock Lighthouse Hike
Contact: Oregon Department of Fish and Wildlife, Sauvie Island Wildlife Area, 18330 NW Sauvie Island Rd., Portland, OR 97231, 503-621-3488, www.dfw.state.or.us
Paw-Approval Rating: 4 paws
Leashes Required? Yes
Length: 6 miles out and back
Difficulty: Easy

Lander eyeing the best stick on the beach.

Fees/Permits: $3.50 permit required. See the *Oak Island Hike* for details.
Season: Year-round, though the trail may be flooded during winter
Getting There: From I-405 in Portland, take the Highway 30 West/St. Helens exit and follow the signs for St. Helens. Travel 9.3 miles north on Highway 30 until you see a sign indicating "Sauvie Island Wildlife Area." Exit to the right at the stoplight, and cross the bridge to the island. After crossing the bridge, continue straight (north) on NW Sauvie Island Road for 2.3 miles. Turn right on NW Reeder Road, and go 13.2 miles until it dead ends at a gravel parking area. The last 2.2 miles of this road are gravel.
Description: Take a journey through a thick cottonwood forest to the northern tip of Sauvie Island. Start hiking on the singletrack trail located next to a wood trail sign adjacent to the parking area. At 0.5 mile, turn right on a smooth double-track road that continues north through the forest. Proceed 100 yards and stay to the right at the road junction. You'll have to go through a blue metal gate after 1.4 miles. (Close the gate or you may let the cows out!) Continue on the double-track road for another mile and then take

a right at the road junction. At 3 miles (the trail's turnaround point) you'll arrive at a sandy beach at the tip of the island where you can climb around the base of Warrior Rock Lighthouse. Look in the nearby woods for the remains of the lighthouse-keeper's home. While your pal is cooling off in the river, keep an eye out for freighters, tugs, and other ships sailing up the Columbia to the Port of Portland. You can return via the same path or take the beach route back to the parking area.

Portland—Southeast

 East Bank Esplanade Hike
Contact: Portland Parks & Recreation, 1120 SW Fifth Ave., Suite 1302, Portland, OR 97204, 503-823-PLAY, www.parks.ci.portland.or.us
Paw-Approval Rating: 3 paws
Leashes Required? Yes
Length: 3.4 miles out and back (3.7-mile loop option)
Difficulty: Easy
Fees/Permits: None
Season: Year-round
Getting There: From I-5 south in Portland, take exit 300B and get in the left lane. Follow the brown OMSI (Oregon Museum of Science and Industry) signs that take you to SE Belmont Ave. where you'll head east. Turn right (south) on 7th Ave. and drive to the intersection with SW Clay St. Turn right (west) on Clay St. and drive to the intersection with SE Water Ave. Turn left (south) on Water Ave. and proceed to OMSI. Once you reach OMSI, continue driving south on Water Ave. for another 0.3 mile to the intersection with SE Caruthers St. Turn right on Caruthers and park where it dead-ends.

From Interstate 5 north in Portland, take exit 300, I-84/The Dalles/Portland Airport. Get in the right lane and exit at a sign that indicates OMSI/Central Eastside Industrial District. Turn right (south) on SE Water St. Proceed 0.7 mile. (You'll

pass the Oregon Museum of Science and Industry [OMSI] after 0.4 mile) to the intersection with SE Caruthers St. Turn right on Caruthers and park where the street dead-ends.
Description: Portland's Eastbank Esplanade is an urban adventure that gives a different perspective of Portland's vibrant waterfront. This 1.5-mile-long promenade hugs the east bank of the Willamette River. Located between the historic Hawthorne and Steel Bridges, this walking and biking path gives you an unobstructed view of Portland's downtown skyline, boasts unique art sculptures that celebrate Portland's history, and offers a 1,200-foot floating walkway that takes you and your hound down to the river's edge. Walkways on the two bridges tie the Esplanade to downtown's Waterfront Park, on the west side of the river, allowing you to do a loop.

To begin this urban walk, head north on the Esplanade. After 1.2 miles, turn left at the Ash St. sign, walk down a ramp, and follow the path as it continues north. You are now walking on a floating ramp (the longest floating ramp in the United States). You'll reach the Steel Bridge after 1.7 miles (your turnaround point).
Loop Option: Complete the entire 3.7-mile loop by crossing the Steel Bridge and walking south through Waterfront Park. On weekends from April through December, check out the Saturday Market located underneath the Burnside Bridge. This open-air market features unique handcrafted items and good food. From the Burnside Bridge, continue south along the wide concrete promenade and follow the path up and onto the newly painted Hawthorne Bridge. After crossing the Hawthorne Bridge, turn right on the East Bank Esplanade and return to your starting point

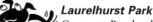 **Laurelhurst Park**
Contact: Portland Parks & Recreation, 1120 SW Fifth Ave., Suite 1302, Portland, OR 97204,

503-823-PLAY, www.parks.ci.portland.or.us
Paw-Approval Rating: 3 paws
Leashes Required? Yes
Fees/Permits: None
Season: Year-round
Getting There: From I-84 east, take the 39th Ave. exit. Head south on 39th Ave. for 0.7 mile. Turn right on SE Ankeny St., a small street one block south of the stoplight at East Burnside Ave. Turn right (west) on Ankeny and park on the street. The park is on your left.
Description: This picturesque and historic 34-acre city park features walking paths that take you through a forested setting and past large, grassy open areas. The park also has a large duck pond where your four-legged friend will be amused by hundreds of ducks.

 Mount Tabor Park
Contact: Portland Parks & Recreation, 1120 SW Fifth Ave., Suite 1302, Portland, OR 97204, 503-823-PLAY, www.parks.ci.portland.or.us
Paw-Approval Rating: 4 paws
Leashes Required? Yes
Fees/Permits: None
Season: Year-round. Trails can be muddy in winter.
Getting There: From downtown Portland, head 5.5 miles east on I-84 toward The Dalles. Exit at 82nd Ave. (exit 5). At the stop sign at the end of the off-ramp, turn right. Go one block to a stoplight and the intersection with NE 82nd Ave. Turn left (south) on 82nd Ave. and travel 1.1 miles to the intersection with SE Yamhill St. Turn right on Yamhill St. and proceed 0.3 mile west to the intersection with SE 76th St. Turn right on 76th St. and then take an immediate left on Yamhill St. and continue heading west for 0.3 mile to the intersection with SE 69th St. Turn left on 69th St., go one block, and turn right on an unmarked paved road at the base of Mount Tabor Park. Continue 0.2 mile to a parking area on the right side of the road.
Description: Mount Tabor Park is one of the premier Portland canine hangouts. This 200-acre forested park is located on a prominent volcanic butte with phenomenal city views from its 643-foot summit. Dozens of trails wind through the park, though most dogs and their owners hang out on its west side, just above the reservoir. The dog traffic has caused a bit of controversy because in wet months it turns the grass above the reservoir into mud, creating runoff problems. Portland Parks has reseeded this area many times; try to keep your dog off this grassy area. You'll also notice that although leashes are required, most dogs are not leashed.

 Oaks Bottom Wildlife Refuge Hike
Contact: Portland Parks & Recreation, 1120 SW Fifth Ave., Suite 1302, Portland, OR 97204, 503-823-PLAY, www.parks.ci.portland.or.us
Paw-Approval Rating: 4 paws
Leashes Required? Yes
Length: 3.6 miles out and back
Difficulty: Easy
Fees/Permits: None
Season: Year-round. This hike can be muddy during winter.

Rags cooling off at Oaks Bottom.

Getting There: Take exit 297 off I-5 South in Portland and turn south on SW Terwilliger Blvd. Drive 0.9 mile on Terwilliger Blvd. to the intersection with SW Taylors Ferry Road. Turn left on Taylors Ferry Road and drive one mile to the intersection with SW Macadam Ave. (Highway 43). Turn right (south) on Highway 43 and drive 0.5 mile to the Sellwood Bridge. Head east across the Sellwood Bridge. After crossing the bridge turn left on SE 7th St. Continue approximately 0.5 mile on 7th St. to the parking lot on the left side of the road at Sellwood Park.

Description: This out-and-back route passes through the expanse of Oaks Bottom Wildlife Refuge in Southeast Portland. On this hike you and your pooch will enjoy watching the wildlife that abounds in this riparian ecosystem. Start walking on the dirt path that starts next to the Oaks Bottom Trailhead sign. Head down a series of switchbacks past huge thickets of blackberries that ripen in mid-to-late August. At 0.3 mile, you'll arrive at an unsigned T-intersection. Turn right (north) and continue hiking next to the swampy marsh of Oaks Bottom through a canopy of black cottonwood, dogwood, and elderberry trees. Be on the lookout for Canada geese, mallard ducks, and blue herons that feed in the reeds and rushes of the marsh. Cross a series of wood footbridges at 0.6 mile, at 0.7 mile, and 1.4 miles. There are also several good wading holes along this section where Rover can cool off. At 1.5 miles, you'll arrive at a trail intersection in an open grassy meadow scattered with small trees. Turn right and walk up a wide, graveled path to the SE Milwaukee St. trailhead at 1.8 miles. From this trailhead, retrace your route back to your starting point at 3.6 miles at Sellwood Park.

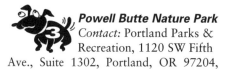

Powell Butte Nature Park
Contact: Portland Parks & Recreation, 1120 SW Fifth Ave., Suite 1302, Portland, OR 97204, 503-823-PLAY, www.parks.ci.portland.or.us

Paw-Approval Rating: 3 paws
Leashes Required? Yes
Fees/Permits: None
Season: Year-round. Trails may be muddy during winter.

Getting There: From Interstate 205 (I-205) in Southeast Portland take exit 19, and head east on SE Division St. Go 3.5 miles and turn right on SE 162nd Ave. Continue 0.7 mile on 162nd Ave. to the entrance of Powell Butte Nature Park. Proceed 0.3 mile to a large parking area and the trailhead.

Description: This 570-acre park is located on an extinct volcano that features diverse habitats and wildlife. Your best pal will love roaming on over nine miles of trails that wind through open grassy meadows, old fruit orchards, and thick woodlands of western red cedar, Douglas fir, alder, and big leaf maple. His sniffer will also appreciate the fact that he's sharing the trail with his equine friends. From the 630-foot summit are spectacular views of Mount Hood to the east. Beware of mountain bikers on blind corners. Trail maps, restrooms, and water are present at the trailhead.

Portland—Southwest

Gabriel Park
Contact: Portland Parks & Recreation, 1120 SW Fifth Ave., Suite 1302, Portland, OR 97204, 503-823-PLAY, www.parks.ci.portland.or.us

Paw-Approval Rating: 4 paws
Leashes Required? Yes, except in the leash-free area
Fees/Permits: None
Season: Year-round. The off-leash area is sometimes closed during winter due to flooding.

Getting There: From downtown Portland, head four miles west on U.S. 26. Take exit 69A, Highway 217/Beaverton/Tigard. Travel south on Highway 217 1.6 miles and take exit 2A, Highway 8 and Highway 10. After exiting the freeway, continue straight, following signs for Raleigh Hills. At the intersection with Highway 10, turn left and proceed 2.5 miles east on Highway 10 to the intersection with SW Oleson Road Turn right on Oleson Road and travel 0.6 mile to SW Vermont Road. Turn left and continue on Vermont Road to the intersection with SW 45th. Turn right on 45th and travel about a 0.25 miles to a paved parking area on the left adjacent to the tennis courts.

Description: This 90-acre park features rolling grassy hills, pockets of Douglas fir trees, and a leash-free area behind the tennis courts. Your dog can sniff to his heart's content and meet new friends at this grassy, fenced area. After Rover's romp, head across the bridge and into the trees to explore the park on a paved path that circles the entire park.

Hoyt Arboretum
Contact: Hoyt Arboretum, 4000 SW Fairview Blvd., Portland, OR 97221, 503-228-TREE, www.hoytarboretum.org
Paw-Approval Rating: 4 paws
Leashes Required? Yes
Fees/Permits: None
Season: Year-round. Trails may be muddy during winter.
Getting There: From downtown Portland, head 1.8 miles west on U.S. 26 toward Beaverton. Take exit 72, Oregon Zoo and the World Forestry Center. At the end of the off-ramp, turn right on SW Knights Blvd. and continue past the Zoo parking lot and the Forestry Center to the intersection with SW Fairview Blvd. Turn right on Fairview and continue 0.1 mile to the Arboretum Visitor Center and parking area on the right.
Description: This beautiful tree museum covers 185 acres in Portland's West Hills and boasts a collection of 1,100 species of plants and trees. Over 12 miles of trails wind through open meadows, beside a

bubbling creek, and through shady forest. Before you start exploring, pick up a trail brochure at the Arboretum Visitor Center. The $2 fee is well worth it because the brochure will help you navigate through the arboretum's maze of often unsigned trails. The visitor center has a water bowl marked with a bronze plaque dedicated to canine hiking partners.

Marquam Nature Park to Council Crest Hike
Contact: Portland Parks & Recreation, 1120 SW Fifth Ave., Suite 1302, Portland, OR 97204, 503-823-PLAY, www.parks.ci.portland.or.us
Paw-Approval Rating: 3 paws
Leashes Required? Yes
Length: 3.2 miles out and back
Difficulty: Difficult
Fees/Permits: None
Season: Year-round. This hike may be muddy during winter.
Getting There: From I-405 north in downtown Portland, take the 4th Ave. exit (1B) and proceed 0.2 mile north. Turn left on SW College St. Proceed one block and turn left on SW 5th Ave. Get in the right lane and go 0.3 mile on 5th Ave. Turn right on SW Caruthers St. Go one block and turn left on SW 6th Ave. Travel 0.3 mile on 6th Ave. to a stoplight at the intersection with SW Terwilliger Ave. Continue straight on SW Sam Jackson Park Road (6th Ave. ends here) for 0.2 mile. Just past a large water tower, turn right into the Marquam Shelter parking area.
Description: This trail takes you and your dog on a city escape through the fern-filled forested canyons of Marquam Nature Park. From the parking area, head uphill and to the right on the signed "Council Crest" trail. Follow the Council Crest signs all the way to the summit. You'll cross three paved roads before you reach the summit of Council Crest (SW Sherwood Dr. at 0.6 mile, SW Fairmont Dr. at 1.1 miles, and SW Greenway Dr. at 1.4 miles). Fido will love the big leaf maple

and Douglas fir trees that provide welcoming shade, and you'll be amazed at this seemingly remote wilderness set in the heart of the city. You'll ascend 420 feet in 1.6 miles to the spectacular 1,043-foot summit of Council Crest, the highest point in the city, and your turnaround point. Drinking fountains provide a welcome watering hole and the inviting grassy expanse is a great place for a Frisbee break before heading back down the trail. On a clear day you'll enjoy spectacular views of Portland and mounts Hood, Adams, St. Helens, Jefferson, and if it's really clear, Rainier.

Portland State University and South Park Blocks

Contact: Portland Parks & Recreation, 1120 SW Fifth Ave., Suite 1302, Portland, OR 97204, 503-823-PLAY,www.parks.ci portland.or.us
Paw-Approval Rating? 2 paws
Leashes Required? Yes
Fees/Permits: None
Season: Year-round
Getting There: From I-405 North in Portland, take exit 1C, 6th Ave. After exiting, stay in the left lane and park on the street

Coquille taking a stroll in Portland's South Park Blocks.

at the intersection of SW 6th Ave. and SW Harrison St.
Description: You and your dog can promenade on concrete paths that lead through grassy lawns, flowerbeds, and hundred-year-old elms right in the heart of downtown Portland. Historic statues and cafes with outdoor seating complete the scene in this "cathedral of trees with a simple grassy floor." To reach the South Park Blocks, walk west on SW Harrison St. and cross SW Broadway. Continue walking west through the Portland State University Campus for about a block, turn right (north), and walk on the paved promenade of the South Park Blocks for about 12 blocks.

Tryon Creek State Park

Contact: Oregon State Parks and Recreation, Suite 1, 1115 Commercial St. NE, Salem OR 97301-1002, 503-636-9886 or 1-800-551-6949, www.oregonstateparks.org
Paw-Approval Rating: 4 paws
Leashes Required? Yes
Fees/Permits: None
Season: Year-round. This hike may be muddy during winter.
Getting There: Take exit 297 off I-5 in Portland and turn south on SW Terwilliger Blvd. Continue on Terwilliger Blvd. for 2.7 miles following signs to Lewis and Clark College and Tryon Creek State Park. Turn right at the Tryon Creek State Park entrance sign. Proceed 0.2 mile on the entrance road to the parking area adjacent to the Nature Center.
Description: This 645-acre state park features eight miles of hiking trails and three miles of equestrian trails that wind through a spectacular red cedar, Douglas fir, and big leaf maple forest. Pick up a park brochure at the nature center and pick out your adventure for the day. If you're not sure where to start, head out on the shady Old Main Trail and then hook up with the Red Fox Trail that takes you down to Tryon Creek and Red Fox Bridge. From here, you have your choice

of completing a short or long loop. Your canine buddy will enjoy splashing in meandering Tryon Creek and will also appreciate the horse snacks available on the equestrian trails in the park.

Waterfront Park

Contact: Portland Parks & Recreation, 1120 SW Fifth Ave., Suite 1302, Portland, OR 97204, 503-823-PLAY, www.parks.ci.portland.or.us
Paw-Approval Rating: 3 paws
Leashes Required? Yes
Fees/Permits: None
Season: Year-round
Getting There: From I-5 South in Portland, get in the right-hand lane and take the OMSI/City Center exit. Stay in the right lane in this two-lane exit. Go 0.3 mile and exit to the right toward Morrison St./City Center. Cross the Morrison Bridge over the Willamette River. Stay in the right lane and take the Front Ave. exit. Turn right (south) onto Front Ave. (also called Naito Parkway) and go 0.1 mile and turn right on SW Morrison St. Park your vehicle in one of the metered parking areas along Morrison St. The park is located across Front Ave. (Naito Parkway) next to the Willamette River.
Description: This scenic riverside park features a mile-long promenade along the west bank of the Willamette River in downtown Portland. Great views of Portland's bridges, the river, and the downtown skyline can be seen from this unique urban park, which, believe it or not, used to be the site of a freeway. People-watching doesn't get any better, and on hot summer days kids and canines cool off in the Salmon Street Springs fountain at the south end of the park, just north of the Hawthorne Bridge.

Wildwood Trail to Pittock Mansion Hike

Contact: Portland Parks & Recreation, 1120 SW Fifth Ave., Suite 1302, Portland, OR 97204, 503-823-PLAY, www.parks.ci.portland.or.us
Paw-Approval Rating: 3 paws
Leashes Required? Yes
Length: 7 miles out and back
Difficulty: Difficult
Fees/Permits: None
Season: Year-round. This hike can be muddy during winter.
Getting There: From downtown Portland, head 1.8 miles west on U.S. 26 toward Beaverton. Take exit 72, Oregon Zoo/World Forestry Center. At the end of the off-ramp, turn right on SW Knights Blvd. and proceed through the Oregon Zoo parking area, following signs to the World Forestry Center. After 0.4 mile, you'll pass the World Forestry Center on your left. At 0.6 mile, turn right into a parking area directly across from the Vietnam Memorial at the intersection of Knights Blvd. and Kingston Blvd.
Description: This hilly singletrack route takes you and your canine pal on the Wildwood Trail—Portland's longest hiking trail—through the tree museum of Hoyt Arboretum and then on a twisting uphill route that climbs over 200 feet to the historic Pittock Mansion.

Taking a break on the Wildwood Trail in Forest Park.

Begin hiking on the Wildwood Trail across Knights Blvd. from the parking area. You'll stay on the Wildwood Trail the entire length of this route. Don't get dazed and confused by the trail junctions; just keep your eyes peeled for the Wildwood Trail signs. The route begins in the Arboretum, where you'll pass a grove of dawn redwoods, one of Earth's oldest tree species. While your best friend may not be too impressed by these rare trees, he will appreciate the shade on this route. Eventually the trail heads downhill to busy West Burnside St. After crossing Burnside, you'll both get a workout as you hike uphill through shady forest to your turn-around point at Pittock Mansion. Be sure to check out the amazing views of Portland and the mountains from the mansion's rear lawn. A drinking fountain and water bowl for dogs are part of the mansion's charms. Tours are available, but for humans only.

Estacada

Clackamas River Hike

Contact: Mount Hood National Forest, Estacada Ranger Station, 595 NW Industrial Way, Estacada, OR 97023, 503-630-8700, www.fs.fed.us
Paw-Approval Rating: 4 paws
Leashes Required? No
Length: 8 miles one way
Difficulty: Moderate
Fees/Permits: $5 Northwest Forest Pass. Purchase by calling 1-800-270-7504 or online at www.naturenw.org.
Season: April through November
Getting There: From I-205, take exit 12A toward Clackamas and Estacada. Head east for 3.4 miles and then bear right on Highway 224 toward Estacada. You'll reach Estacada in 15.6 miles. From Estacada, continue 15.3 miles east on Highway 224 to the turnoff for Fish Creek Campground. Turn right on Fish Creek Road (unsigned) and go 0.3 mile to a large parking area on the right. This is the end (or turnaround point) for the hike. If you are doing a shuttle, leave a bike or car at this trailhead.

To continue to the upper trailhead, turn left out of the parking area on Fish Creek Road. Go 0.3 mile. Turn right (east) on Highway 224 and go 6.8 miles. Turn right on unsigned Forest Road 4620 toward "Indian Henry Campground." Travel 0.6 mile on Forest Road 4620 and turn right into the trailhead parking area opposite the entrance to Indian Henry Campground.

Description: This beautiful river trail takes you and your dog on a mystical journey through pockets of mossy old growth forest that will amaze you. The hike provides a good workout with over 300 feet of elevation gain. Begin hiking on the singletrack trail at a wood trail sign. Almost immediately, you'll need to turn right as the trail passes through a cool mossy forest. In the first 2.9 miles, the trail has many ups and downs that take you through astounding old-growth red cedar and Douglas fir trees. As you and your buddy hike along the trail, you'll enjoy great views of the Clackamas River at several different points, where the trail drops down to almost river level. Keep an eye on your dog along sections of the trail that have steep drop-offs. At 4.4 miles, you'll have to slow down and cross Pup Creek over a rock path. Your dog will love lying down in the cool water on a hot summer day. Just after you cross the creek, you have the option of turning left and walking 200 yards up a side trail to view the feathery cascade of Pup Creek Falls. At 7.3 miles, you'll pass a tantalizing sandy beach that may tempt you and your dog to stop and take a swim. At 8 miles, the trail intersects Fish Creek Road. If you are completing your trip with a car or bike shuttle, cross Fish Creek Rd. to the trailhead parking area. Otherwise, this is your turnaround point.

Milo McIver State Park

Contact: Oregon State Parks and Recreation, Suite 1, 1115 Commercial St. NE, Salem

OR 97301-1002, www.oregonstateparks. org

Paw-Approval Rating: 3 paws

Leashes Required? Yes, except in the dog off-leash area

Fees/Permits: None

Season: Year-round

Getting There: From the intersection of I-5 and I-84 in Portland, head 5 miles east on I-84 to the junction with I-205. Take exit 6 signed for Salem and merge south onto I-205. Go 10.9 miles to exit 10, Oregon Highway 213, toward Park Place/ Molalla. Stay to the right at the fork in the off-ramp. Merge onto Oregon Highway 213 and go 0.6 mile to the junction with Redland Road. Turn right on Redland Road and continue 12.4 miles to the junction with Springwater Road. Turn right on Springwater Road and proceed to the signed campground entrance.

Description: This state park has good access to the Clackamas River where your dog can cool off on a hot summer day. It also features a forested campground (see *Campgrounds*) and many enticing smells in the designated off-leash area.

Forest Grove

Hagg Lake Hike

Contact: Washington County Parks, Facilities Management Division, Support Services Department, 111 SE Washington St., Hillsboro, OR 97123, 503/846-3692, www.co. washington.or.us

Paw-Approval Rating: 3 paws

Leashes Required? Yes

Length: 15.1-mile loop

Difficulty: Moderate

Fees/Permits: $4 day-use fee during summer

Season: Year-round

Getting There: From Portland, head 21 miles west on U.S. Highway 26 to the intersection with Highway 6. Turn left on Highway 6 (toward Banks, Forest Grove, and Tillamook) and go 2.5 miles to the intersection with Highway 47. Turn south

Keeping cool in Hagg Lake.

and proceed 12.5 miles to the junction with Scoggins Valley Road. Turn right (west) on Scoggins Valley Road and head 3.1 miles to the Henry Hagg Lake/Scoggins Valley Park entrance. Go 0.3 mile past the entrance booth to the junction with West Shore Dr. Turn left on West Shore Dr. and travel 0.9 mile to a gravel parking area with restrooms (no water) on the right side of the road.

Description: This trail weaves in and out of oak woodlands and fir forest and offers plenty of rolling hills; it has 100 feet of elevation gain. Great swimming holes and juicy blackberries (ripe in mid-August) are some of the many distractions waiting for you and your best friend. Watch out for mountain bikers blazing this route. To pick up the singletrack trail from the gravel parking area, turn right (west) and walk on the paved shoulder of West Shore Dr. You'll soon leave the pavement behind and begin hiking on the signed singletrack trail on the right side of the road after 0.2 mile.

Lake Oswego

Luscher Farm Park

Contact: Lake Oswego Parks & Recreation, 380 A Ave., Lake Oswego, OR 97034, 503-636-9673

Paw-Approval Rating: 3 paws

Leashes Required? No

Fees/Permits: None

Season: Year-round

Getting There: This park is located at the intersection of Stafford Road and Overlook Dr. in Lake Oswego.

Description: This popular off-leash area is in a large grassy field that allows canines of all shapes and sizes to romp and play. Beware of gopher holes that may trip your dog up. Bring your own water.

Mary S. Young State Park

Contact: Oregon State Parks and Recreation, Suite 1, 1115 Commercial St. NE, Salem, OR 97301-1002, 1-800-551-6949, www.oregonstateparks.org

Paw-Approval Rating: 3 paws

Leashes Required? Yes, except in the off-leash area

Fees/Permits: None

Season: Year-round

Getting There: This park is located 9 miles south of Portland off Oregon Highway 43.

Description: This forested park is located on the southwest bank of the Willamette River and features many hiking trails that wind through cool Douglas fir, big leaf maple, and alder forest, as well as a trail that takes you to the river's edge. The park has a designated off-leash area where your pal can hound around.

Molalla

Molalla River State Park

Contact: Oregon State Parks and Recreation, Suite 1, 1115 Commercial St. NE, Salem, OR 97301-1002, 1-800-551-6949, www.oregonstateparks.org

Paw-Approval Rating: 3 paws

Leashes Required? Yes, except in the pet exercise area

Fees/Permits: None

Season: Year-round

Getting There: From Portland head south on I-5 for approximately 15 miles to exit 282A, toward Canby/Hubbard. Continue to the intersection with Hubbard Cutoff Road. Continue straight on Hubbard Cutoff Road to the junction with Arndt Road. Turn left onto Arndt Road. Continue to the junction with Knights Bridge Road. Continue straight on Knights Bridge Road until you reach the junction with Holly St. in downtown Canby. Turn left on Holly St. and go 2.3 miles to the signed state park entrance.

Description: This 566-acre state park is located at the confluence of the Pudding, Molalla, and Willamette Rivers, creating a wetland and forest that are prime wildlife habitat. The park has been home to a large blue heron rookery since 1910. Ducks, geese, and double-breasted cormorants can be seen in the wetlands. You may also see bald eagles perched high in the trees above the Willamette River. You and Rover can explore a gravel hiking trail that heads 0.75 mile upstream along the Willamette. You can also hike a 0.75-mile trail that heads around a pond ecosystem. In the pet area, your dog can run untethered.

Wilsonville

Champoeg State Heritage Area

Contact: Oregon State Parks and Recreation, Suite 1, 1115 Commercial St. NE, Salem OR 97301-1002, 1-800-551-6949, www.oregonstateparks.org

Paw-Approval Rating: 4 paws

Leashes Required? Yes, except in the dog off-leash area

Fees/Permits: $3 day-use fee

Season: Year-round

Getting There: Champoeg State Heritage Area is between Portland and Salem, just west of Wilsonville. From Interstate 5, take exit 278 for "Donald/Aurora/Champoeg State Park." Turn west, and drive 3.5 miles on Ehlen Road/Yergen Road. Turn right on Case Road. Continue for 1.3 miles on Case Road and turn left on Champoeg Road. Proceed 0.8 mile on Champoeg Road to the entrance.

Description: Located on the south bank of the Willamette River, this state heritage area features white oak woodlands, open grassy meadows, an off-leash area, hiking and biking trails, a large campground (see *Campgrounds*), historic buildings, and a large visitor center.

Native peoples lived here 6,000 years before white settlers arrived. They burned the area in order to maintain the open white oak savanna, which allowed the growth of native plants and made it easier to hunt game. One of the largest tribes of Native Americans in the valley, the Calapooya, hunted small game, fished in the Willamette, and harvested camas roots. The camas, an onion-like plant, grows in open, sunny meadows and has a two-foot-long stem that has 10 to 30 bluish-purple blooms. When cooked, the bulbs taste like sweet potatoes.

In 1811, hunters and fur traders of the Hudson's Bay Company arrived on the scene. A warehouse, mill, and town were built, and Champoeg became an important site for trading beaver pelts and wheat. The word *Champoeg* is thought to be derived from the French word *champ* ("field") and the Native American word *pooich* ("root"). While the white settlers prospered, the Native American population was decimated due to introduced diseases. Before the white settlers arrived, the Native American population was over 13,000; by the mid-1800s, their numbers had plummeted to around 2,000.

In May of 1843, a provisional government was established at Champoeg, the first American government on the Pacific Coast. Although the provisional government moved to Oregon City in 1844, Champoeg continued to grow; by 1850 the population swelled to over 200 and the settlement contained over 30 buildings. In 1861, the mood of the Willamette River turned foul and a disastrous flood almost destroyed the community. By 1892, another record-breaking flood turned the area into a ghost town.

Memorial Park

Contact: Wilsonville Parks and Recreation, Wilsonville, OR, 503-570-1523, www.ci.wilsonville.or.us
Paw-Approval Rating: 3 paws
Leashes Required? No
Fees/Permits: None
Season: Year-round
Getting There: From I-5, south of Portland, take exit 283, Wilsonville. Turn east on Wilsonville Road toward downtown Wilsonville. Go 0.5 mile on Wilsonville Road and turn right on Memorial Dr. Continue 0.1 mile and turn left on to the entrance road for Memorial Park. Travel 0.2 mile on the entrance road to a T-junction. Turn left toward the signed "Pet Exercise Area." Proceed 0.2 mile and turn left into a gravel parking area.
Description: From the parking area, walk down the gravel trail about 75 yards to the 3-acre fenced, leash-free field on the right. This grassy field promises plenty of action for your dog. A walking trail circles the field's perimeter. If you want to explore other areas of the park, be sure your pup is leashed. The park has acres of grassy lawns, tennis courts, a skateboard park, basketball courts, and baseball diamonds.

CYCLING FOR CANINES

Banks/Vernonia State Park Trail

Contact: Oregon State Parks and Recreation, Suite 1, 1115 Commercial St. NE, Salem OR 97301-1002, 1 800-551-6949 or 503-324-0606, www.oregonstateparks.org
Paw-Approval Rating: 3 paws
Leashes Required? Yes
Length: 20 miles one way
Difficulty: Moderate
Fees/Permits: None
Season: Year-round. This route can be muddy during winter.
Getting There: From I-405 in Portland, head west on U.S. 26 toward Beaverton/Ocean Beaches. After approximately 28 miles, turn

Pam and Casper getting ready to ride on the Banks/Vernonia State Park Trail.

right on Fisher Road. Go 0.7 mile, passing through the small town of Buxton. Turn right on Bacona Road and proceed 0.7 mile to the entrance road to the Buxton Trailhead, which is marked by a State Park sign. Turn right and go another 0.1 mile to a large parking area and trailhead.

Description: When you and your pooch want to get away from it all, you'll enjoy the smooth graded surface on this 20-mile multi-use trail under a serene forest canopy. The trail has a moderate elevation gain of about 580 feet over its length. From the Buxton Trailhead, you have the option of heading 14 miles north or 6 miles south as the trail follows an old railroad line. You and Fido share the trail with equestrians and hikers—but more than likely you'll have the trail to yourself. Restrooms are available at the trailhead (no water).

Leif Erikson Drive (Portland)

Contact: Portland Parks & Recreation, 1120 SW Fifth Ave., Suite 1302, Portland, OR 97204, 503-823-PLAY, www.parks.ci.portland.or.us
Paw-Approval Rating: 3 paws

Leashes Required? Yes
Length: 11 miles one way
Difficulty: Easy
Fees/Permits: None
Season: Year-round. This route can be muddy during winter.
Getting There: From I-405 in downtown Portland, take the Highway 30 West/St. Helens exit (exit 3). At the end of the off-ramp, stay in the right lane, which turns into NW Vaughn St. At the first stoplight, turn left on NW 23rd Ave. Go one block and turn right on NW Thurman St. Go 1.4 miles to the end of Thurman St. and park near the green metal gate. Leif Erikson Dr. starts at the green metal gate.
Description: This gravel, multi-use trail winds through Portland's Forest Park for over 11 miles and 410 feet until its ending point at Germantown Road. This route is very popular, so keep your pup on a long lead while you ride. The many fire lanes shooting off this main track provide lots of choices for loops. If you left your bike at home, nearby Fat Tire Farm (2714 NW Thurman, 503-222-3276) rents mountain bikes.

Riverside Trail (Clackamas County)

Contact: Mount Hood National Forest, Estacada Ranger Station, 595 NW Industrial Way, Estacada, OR 97023, 503-630-8700, www.fs.fed.us
Paw-Approval Rating: 4 paws
Leashes Required? No
Length: 8.4 miles out and back
Difficulty: Moderate
Fees/Permits: $5 Northwest Forest Pass
Season: April through November
Getting There: From I-205 in Southeast Portland, take exit 12A, Highway 212/Highway 224/Clackamas/Estacada. Head east 3.5 miles and then bear right on Highway 224 toward Estacada. You'll reach Estacada in about 14 more miles. From Estacada, continue 25 miles to a road junction right after you cross the Oak Grove Fork of the Clackamas River. Continue

right toward Detroit/Bagby Hot Springs on Forest Road 46. Immediately after making this right turn, bear right into Rainbow Campground. Continue 0.3 mile through the campground to the trailhead at the end of the campground loop road.

Description: If you love to mountain bike with your dog, you'll love this riverside trail, which parallels the Oak Grove Fork of the Clackamas River and then takes you along the beautiful main channel of the Clackamas River. The trail winds through an immense red cedar and Douglas fir forest, with many whoop-dee-doo hills that combine short intense climbing with fast, twisty downhills. The route has about 130 feet of net elevation gain, which can be deceiving because of its many ups and downs. Numerous side creeks and the very chilly Clackamas River offer plenty of cool-off opportunities. The trail's other virtue is its near 100% shade. The many side trails lead to great viewpoints of the Clackamas River.

The trailhead is located at the far end of Rainbow Campground loop road. Ride on the singletrack trail south for 2.6 miles and stay to the right at the trail fork. Continue another 1.6 miles to your turnaround point at Riverside Campground. Rainbow and Riverside Campgrounds (see *Campgrounds*) have shady campsites with river views.

PADDLEHOUNDS

George Rogers Park to Willamette Park
Contact: For George Rogers Park: Parks & Recreation, 380 A Ave., Lake Oswego, OR 97034, 503-636-9673, www.ci.oswego.or.us. For Willamette Park: Portland Parks & Recreation, 1120 SW Fifth Ave., Suite 1302, Portland, OR 97204, 503-823-PLAY, www.parks.ci.portland.or.us
Paw-Approval Rating: 3 paws
Leashes Required? Yes, when your dog is not in the boat.

Length: 5 miles
Fees/Permits: $2 day-use fee at Willamette Park
Season: Year-round
Getting There: George Rogers Park is located on McVey Ave. just off Highway 43 (State St.) in downtown Lake Oswego. The takeout point is at Willamette Park, located at SW Macadam St. (Highway 43) and SW Nebraska St. in Portland.
Description: The Willamette River is one of the only major rivers in the United States that flows south to north. This float starts at George Rogers Park in Lake Oswego and takes you north (downriver) to Willamette Park in Portland. After almost two miles of casual floating, take a break at Elk Rock Island, named because of the Native American practice of herding elk off its cliffs in order to slaughter them. This small island is home to a 15-acre natural area that supports a large variety of wildlife. Look west, across the river, to the cultivated gardens of the Bishop's Close. From here, continue another 3 miles downstream to the Willamette Park boat ramp on the left bank.

Sturgeon Lake on Sauvie Island
Contact: Oregon Department of Fish and Wildlife, Sauvie Island Wildlife Area, 18330 NW Sauvie Island Rd., Portland, OR 97231, 503-621-3488, www.dfw.state.or.us
Paw-Approval Rating: 3 paws
Leashes Required? Yes, when your dog is not in the boat.
Fees/Permits: $3.50 day-use fee. Permits can be purchased at Sam's Cracker Barrel Store, located on the left side of the road immediately after crossing the Sauvie Island Bridge.
Season: This area is closed October 1 to April 15 for hunting season.
Getting There: From I-405 in Portland, take the Highway 30 West/St. Helens exit and follow the signs for St. Helens. Travel 9.3 miles north on Highway 30 to a sign:

"Sauvie Island Wildlife Area." Turn right at the stoplight and cross the bridge to Sauvie Island. After crossing the bridge, follow NW Sauvie Island Road north for 2.5 miles to the junction with NW Reeder Road. Turn right on Reeder Road and go 1.2 miles to the junction with NW Oak Island Road. Turn left on Oak Island Road, travel 3.8 miles and bear right after passing Webster Pond. Continue 0.5 mile east to the boat ramp.

Description: This is one of several paddling opportunities on Sauvie Island. The put-in is at the Oak Island Boat Ramp, giving access to beautiful Sturgeon Lake.

Spring Paddle Fest at Vancouver Lake Park, Vancouver, Washington

Canine paddlers will enjoy testing different types of canoes and kayaks at this annual event held the third weekend in April. Over fifty canoes, sea kayaks, and a few whitewater kayaks are available to test-paddle.

The event features free kayak clinics, classes, and demonstrations. Although dogs are not usually allowed at Vancouver Lake Park from April through October, they are welcome at this event.

To get to Vancouver Lake Park, take the 4th Plain exit off I-5 in Vancouver, Washington. Travel west 5.5 miles to the park entrance. Festival hours are 10 a.m.–5 p.m., Saturday; 9 a.m.–3 p.m., Sunday.

Getting ready to paddle at the Spring Paddle Festival on Vancouver Lake.

For information, contact the Paddle Fest's sponsor, Alder Creek Canoe and Kayak, 250 NE Tomahawk Island Dr., Portland, OR 97217, 503-285-0464, www.aldercreek.com

OTHER PLACES TO HOUND AROUND

The Berlin Inn
3131 SE 12th, Portland 503-236-6761, www.berlininn.com

This restaurant/bakery serves delicious German-style fare for humans and canines. You and your doggie date can dine on the flower-lined outdoor patio. He'll drool over the all-homemade offerings from the Pooch Platters Menu, like the Mutt Mix Platter: two grilled hotdogs and a side of veggie bones. Or, if he's really hungry, he may want to order the Chow Hound Platter: sautéed spätzle smothered in Jäger sauce, served with a side of dog biscuits.

Dogs with a sweet tooth will be tempted by the peanut butter/oatmeal cookies, honey carob chippers, or snicker poodles (all made especially for dogs by the Good Dog Bakery). Oh, and for humans, you'll enjoy this restaurant's delicious schnitzel and sauerkraut dishes, fondue, and other entrees such as Käse Garlic Spätzle and Smoked Salmon Potato Cakes. Be sure to save room for desserts like Poppyseed-Lemon Strudel, Apricot Marzipan, Caramel Walnut Torte, or Grand Marnier Truffle. Excellent German beers and wines accompany all this good stuff. Be sure to call ahead to reserve an outdoor table (there are only seven). Open for lunch 11:30 A.M.–2:30 P.M., Wednesday, Thursday and Friday; breakfast and lunch 10 A.M.–2:30 P.M., Saturday and Sunday; dinner 5 P.M.–8:30 P.M., Wednesday and Thursday, and 4:30 P.M.–9 P.M., Friday, Saturday, and Sunday.

Lucky Labrador Brew Pub
915 SE Hawthorne Blvd., Portland 503-236-3555

Dog lovers dig this unpretentious warehouse-style pub, where outside picnic tables allow your pooch to hang with you while you sip your brew. The only stipulation is that you keep your pal on a leash.

Although Rover can't go inside, you might appreciate the décor: big wood beams, hardwood floors, and long wood tables with mismatched chairs, accented by pictures of cool Labradors and photos of loyal patrons wearing their Lucky Lab T-shirts and caps at locations worldwide.

Beer brewed here is strong and tasty. Some favorites are the Hawthorne Bitter and the Lucky Lab IPA. A strong dark stout is a meal in itself. For lunch and dinner, try the veggie or chicken curry rice bowl or a deli sandwich with chips. You'll find veggie sandwiches here as well as the Vegetarian's Nightmare: a sandwich packed with different deli meats, cheeses, lettuce, tomatoes and your choice of condiments. You may want to give your carnivorous pal a bite to see what he thinks. A place that loves dogs, serves great beer for a decent price, and you can wear whatever you want. What more could you ask for?

Open 11 A.M.–midnight Monday to Saturday, and noon–10 P.M. Sunday.

CANINE COMFORT ACCOMMODATIONS

Unless otherwise stated, dogs should not be left unattended in the room and must be leashed on hotel property.

Portland—Downtown

$$-$$$ Four Points Sheraton

50 SW Morrison St., 503-221-0711/1-800-899-0247, www.fourpointsportland.com

This hotel features 140 dog-friendly rooms. The hotel staff mentioned that "not only do we take dogs, but once we had a ten foot python in the hotel." Rooms have river and city views. Amenities include coffeemaker with assorted coffee and teas, iron and ironing board, TV and remote, pay per view movies, hair dryer, and data ports.

The hotel has a riverview restaurant and bar, and offers guests complimentary use of Bally's Total Fitness Gym adjacent to the hotel and a USA Today or Wall Street Journal Monday through Friday. Take poochie for a stroll in adjacent Waterfront Park on the Willamette River.

Dog Policy

No extra fees are charged for dogs.

$$-$$$ Mark Spencer Hotel

409 SW 11th Ave., 503-224-3293/1-800-548-3934, www.markspencer.com

If you and your best buddy want to stay in luxurious European-style surroundings, check out the posh Mark Spencer Hotel in downtown Portland. All 101 guest rooms and one-bedroom suites are canine-friendly, with dog dishes and furniture covers provided on request. Rooms come equipped with kitchens, cable TV, and movie rentals. The hotel also has a reading library and rooftop garden with a gorgeous view of the city. A continental breakfast of cereal, muffins/pastries, toast, fruit, coffee, tea, orange juice and milk is included with your stay.

Dog Policy

A one-time $25 fee is charged for dogs staying one to seven nights. Dogs must be secured in a travel crate or taken out of your room when the staff is servicing your room.

$$-$$$ Marriott Residence Inn– Portland

Downtown Riverplace, 2115 SW River Parkway, 503-552-9500, www.residence inn.com, riverplace@innventures.com

All 258 studio, one bedroom, and two bedroom suites with fully furnished kitchens are pet-friendly. This hotel is adjacent to the Willamette River, downtown Portland, and Waterfront Park. When you check in, your friend gets a bag of canine treats. Your stay also includes a buffet-style breakfast and evening reception, complimentary grocery shopping service (this means bones for Rover!), a complimentary newspaper, and shuttle service. You also have access to a heated pool and sauna, and exercise room.

Dog Policy

A $10 fee per night per dog is charged. The hotel asks that you don't bring your dog into the lobby during breakfast or the hospitality reception—but he is welcome any other time as long as he is leashed. No dogs in the pool area. If you leave your dog loose in the room while you are gone, the hotel asks that you notify housekeeping.

$$$-$$$$ Portland 5th Avenue Suites Hotel

506 SW Washington St., 1-800-711-2971, www.5thavenuesuites.com

This hotel features deluxe guest rooms and one-bedroom suites. It is located within walking distance of Waterfront Park and other downtown activities.

Dog Policy

Dogs stay for free! Dogs can be left unattended in the room if they are well behaved.

$$$-$$$$ RiverPlace Hotel

1510 SW Harbor Way, 503-228-3233/1-800-227-1333, www.riverplacehotel.com

This entire European-style waterfront resort is dog-friendly. According to management, "All accommodations are oversized. All rooms come with a complimentary continental breakfast either in the dining room or through our twenty-four hour room service. You have a choice of a morning newspaper; have use of the RiverPlace Athletic Club, twice daily maid service, use of the private in-house spa [by appointment], and direct access to Waterfront Park and the Willamette River. All rooms have an iron and ironing board, umbrella, terry robe, feather beds, Nintendo games, on demand movies, and jetted tubs (available in some rooms). Dogs get a welcome gift along with food and water bowls and blankets."

Dog Policy

A one time non-refundable $45 fee is charged per room (not per dog!).

Portland—North

$-$$ Best Western Inn at the Meadows

1215 N. Hayden Meadows Dr., www.bestwestern.com

When we asked the Best Western Inn to describe their hotel Tessa Lepley, Sales Administrator, responded, "Whether you would like to enjoy a glass of wine in our vaulted lobby featuring a beautiful salt-water fish tank, take a soak in our large all-season spa, or relax in our warmly decorated guestrooms, the Best Western Inn at the Meadows will accommodate your desires for the best imaginable stay. You and your dog are welcome in all of our 146 guestrooms, as well as in our complimentary shuttle, which can take you to and from the Portland International Airport, as well as the surrounding areas, including the new dog-friendly section of Delta Park adjacent to the hotel."

Included is a complimentary continental breakfast, a coffeemaker, iron and ironing board, and hairdryer, newspaper, and free shuttle service to/from airport, and surrounding restaurants. Large outdoor spa. Free local phone calls. Complimentary day passes to a nearby full-service gym. Oven-fresh cookies three nights a week. Manager's wine and cheese reception every Thursday. Petco is adjacent to the hotel.

Dog Policy

There is a non-refundable pet fee of $21.80. Terry also said, "The only restriction is that housekeeping will not enter your room if your dog is loose. Your dog must be crated, or the room will not be cleaned. Other than that, we have had everything from seven pound terriers to 215 pound mastiffs."

$$ Days Inn

9930 North Whitaker Rd., 1-800-DAYS-INN, www.the.daysinn.com

The hotel is located in the vicinity of East Delta Park, which features a leash-free area, and the Marine Drive Multi-use

Path (see *Paw-Approved Hikes and Parks*). The hotel is also located only five miles north of downtown Portland. It features 211 pet-friendly rooms. After a day of adventure, your dog will be glad to know he will get a treat at check-in. This hotel features amenities including complimentary deluxe continental breakfast; twenty-four hour coffee, tea, and cocoa; free local calls, free HBO; guest laundry services; exercise room; pay per view movies; and games.

Dog Policy
The hotel charges a $15 pet fee.

Portland—Northeast

$$ Sullivan's Gulch B&B
1744 NE Clackamas St., 503-331-1104, www.sullivansgulch.com

This friendly B&B was built in 1907 and is located in the historic Sullivan's Gulch neighborhood in Northeast Portland. The innkeeper's say they are "totally dog-friendly" and the resident lab/shepherd mix Shonka agrees. It describes itself as "Not Laura Ashley–more like Frank Lloyd Wright meets Buffalo Bill." The four rooms are decorated in contemporary and western themes; two rooms share a bath, and two have private baths. Additional amenities include a cozy reading library, sitting room, and summer garden. Sullivan's Gulch is within walking distance of the eclectic NE Broadway shopping district and the MAX light rail. An expanded continental breakfast is also included with your stay.

Dog Policy
Well-behaved dogs are allowed at no extra charge.

$$-$$$ Residence Inn–Lloyd Center
1710 NE Multnomah, 503-288-1400

This hotel features pet-friendly rooms that have a fully equipped kitchen with a full size refrigerator, stove, dishwasher, and microwave. Additional amenities include continental breakfast buffet, Monday through Thursday evening reception

with complimentary hors d'oeuvres and refreshments, complimentary morning newspapers, data ports in rooms, two line phone with voicemail, laundry facilities, and a seasonal heated pool.

Dog Policy
The hotel charges a $50 non-refundable cleaning fee for pets.

$$-$$$$ La Quinta Inn
431 NE Multnomah, 503-233-7933

This is a modern, two-story hotel that has a heated indoor pool, a fitness room, free underground parking, and complimentary local calls. A free breakfast buffet is also included with your stay.

Dog Policy
There is a $10 per night pet fee.

Portland—Northwest

$$ La Quinta Inn and Suites
4319 NW Yeon, 503 497-9044

This pet-friendly hotel is located in the heart of Northwest Portland, not far from 5,000-acre Forest Park.

Dog Policy
The hotel charges a one-time pet fee of $7.

Portland—Southeast

$ Motel 6
2104 SE Powell Blvd., 503-238-0600
Dog Policy
Well-behaved dogs are permitted for no extra charge.

Gresham

$$ Carlton Inn
1572 NE Burnside St., 503-665-9545/1-888-422-9545, www.carltoninn.com

This no-nonsense motel offers a deluxe continental breakfast, complimentary in-room coffee, and free local calls.

Dog Policy
A $10 pet fee is charged. You may leave your dog unattended in your room if he is crated.

Hillsboro

$$-$$$ West Coast Hillsboro Hotel
3500 NE Cornell Rd., 503-648-3500/1-800-325-4000, www.westcoasthotels.com/hillsboro

This well-equipped hotel prides itself on its dog-friendly 123 guestrooms and suites. You and Rover are guaranteed to be comfy with the following amenities: complimentary in-room coffee service, newspaper, hair dryer, iron and ironing board, computer workspace, refrigerator, and microwave. This hotel also has a fitness area and heated swimming pool.

Dog Policy
A $5 fee per dog is charged, with a two-dog limit per room. You may leave your dog unattended in your room if he is crated.

Tigard

$ Motel 6
17950 SW McEwan Rd., 503-620-2066
Dog Policy
Well-behaved dogs are permitted for no extra charge.

Troutdale

$ Motel 6
1610 NW Frontage Rd., 503-665-2254
Dog Policy
Well-behaved dogs are permitted for no extra charge.

Tualatin

$$-$$$ La Quinta Inn & Suites
7640 SW Warm Springs St., 503-612-9952, www.nw-hotels.com

Built in 2000, this modern, clean hotel has 59 rooms on three levels. There are standard rooms with one king or two queen beds, kitchenettes, mini-kitchens, two-room suites, and spa suites. Rooms include deluxe breakfast bar, free local calls, free local and long distance FAX service, free HBO, free *USA Today*, free fresh-baked cookies every evening, twenty-four hour laundry facility, twenty-four hour gift shop, twenty-four hour indoor pool, spa, and fitness center. The hotel has a dog-friendly room available for each room type.

Dog Policy
There is a $5 fee charged per dog per day. The hotel management requests that your dog not be left unattended in your room unless he is crated.

CAMPGROUNDS

Champoeg State Heritage Area
Contact: Oregon State Parks and Recreation, Suite 1, 1115 Commercial St. NE, Salem OR 97301-1002, 1-800-551-6949 (information), 1-800-452-5687 (reservations), www.oregonstateparks.org
Season: Year-round
Facilities: 12 full-hook-up sites, 67 electrical sites, 6 yurts, 6 cabins, 3 group-tent areas, group RV area, hiker/biker camp, piped water, flush toilets, showers, fire rings, picnic tables, off-leash area, playground, ADA sites, and RV dump station
Getting There: Champoeg State Heritage Area is about a 30-minute drive southwest of Portland and northwest of Salem. From I-5, take exit 278, Donald/Aurora/Champoeg State Park. Turn west, and drive 3.5 miles on Ehlen Road/Yergen Road. Turn right on Case Road. Continue for 1.3 miles on Case Road and turn left on Champoeg Road. Continue on Champoeg Road to the signed entrance.
Description: On the banks of the Willamette River, this campground is located in a picturesque setting of Oregon oak and ash trees. You can take your dog on a walk along the river and explore the park's many other trails. Your pooch may also enjoy a romp in the park's off-leash area. While your pooch naps, you can tour the park's visitor center, Newell House museum, and Pioneer Mothers Log Cabin museum.

Indian Henry
Contact: Mount Hood National Forest, Estacada Ranger Station, 595 NW

Industrial Way, Estacada, OR 97023, 503-630-8700, www.fs.fed.us
Season: Mid-May through Labor Day
Facilities: 86 sites (no electrical hook-ups), picnic tables, fire rings, piped water, restrooms, sanitary disposal station
Getting There: From I-205 in Southeast Portland take exit 12A toward Clackamas and Estacada. Head east 3.4 miles and then bear right on Highway 224 toward Estacada. You'll reach Estacada in 15.6 miles. From Estacada, continue 22 miles east on Highway 224 to the turnoff for Indian Henry Campground. Turn right on unsigned Forest Road 4620 and travel 0.6 mile to a left turn into the campground entrance road.
Description: This campground offers many beautiful forested sites and is located adjacent to the Clackamas River and the Clackamas River Trail (see *Paw-Approved Hikes and Parks*).

Milo McIver State Park

Contact: Oregon State Parks and Recreation, Suite 1, 1115 Commercial St. NE, Salem OR 97301-1002, 1-800-551-6949 (information), 1-800-452-5687 (reservations), www.oregonstateparks.org
Season: Year-round
Facilities: 9 primitive tent sites, 1 hiker/biker site, 44 electrical hook-up sites, off-leash area, boat launch, ADA site, RV dump station, piped water, flush toilets, showers, picnic tables, fire rings, 18-hole Frisbee disc golf course, and a playground
Getting There: From the intersection of I-5 North and I-84 in Portland, head 5 miles east on I-84 to the junction with I-205. Take exit 6 signed for Salem and merge south onto I-205. Go 10.9 miles south to exit 10, Oregon Highway 213, toward Park Place/Molalla. Stay right at the fork in the off-ramp. Merge onto Oregon Highway 213 and go 0.6 mile to the junction with Redland Road. Turn right on Redland Road and continue 12.4 miles to the junction with Springwater Road. Turn right on Springwater Road and proceed to the signed campground entrance.

Description: This forested camping area is close to Portland and provides good access to the Clackamas River. Your dog will enjoy the many enticing smells in the designated pet area.

Rainbow

Contact: Mount Hood National Forest, Estacada Ranger Station, 595 NW Industrial Way, Estacada, OR 97023, 503-630-8700, www.fs.fed.us
Season: Mid-May through Labor Day Weekend
Facilities: 16 sites (no electrical hook-ups), picnic tables, fire rings, restrooms, no water
Getting There: From I-205 in Southeast Portland, take exit 12A, Highway 212/Highway 224/Clackamas/Estacada. Head east 3.5 miles and then bear right on Highway 224 toward Estacada. You'll reach Estacada in about 14 more miles. From Estacada, continue 25 miles to a road junction right after you cross the Oak Grove Fork of the Clackamas River. Continue right toward Detroit/Bagby Hot Springs on Forest Road 46. Almost immediately after making this right turn, bear right into Rainbow Campground.
Description: This cool, shady campground has some sites located on the shores of the Oak Grove Fork of the Clackamas River. It is also the starting point for the Riverside Trail that heads 4.2 miles north along the Oak Grove Fork and then the main tributary of the Clackamas River to Riverside Campground. This trail is open to mountain bikers. (See *Cycling for Canines*)

Riverside

Contact: Mount Hood National Forest, Estacada Ranger Station, 595 NW Industrial Way, Estacada, OR 97023, 503-630-8700, www.reserveusa.com
Season: Mid-May through Labor Day weekend
Facilities: 16 sites (no electrical hook-ups), picnic tables, fire rings, well water, restrooms

Getting There: From I-205 in Southeast Portland take exit 12A, Highway 212/ Highway 224/Clackamas/Estacada. Head east 3.5 miles and then bear right on Highway 224 toward Estacada. You'll reach Estacada in about 14 more miles. From Estacada, continue 25 miles to a road junction right after you cross the Oak Grove Fork of the Clackamas River. Turn right toward Detroit/Bagby Hot Springs on Forest Road 46 and go about 2.5 miles to the campground entrance.

Description: This small, forested campground has 16 sites, many of which are located along the banks of the Clackamas River. This campground also provides access to the supreme Riverside Trail, which heads 4.2 miles south along the Clackamas River and then along the banks of the Oak Grove Fork of the Clackamas River to Rainbow Campground. This trail is one of the few river trails still open to mountain bikers and their canine buddies within striking distance of Portland. (See *Cycling for Canines*)

DOG EVENTS

Bark in the Park

PGE Park, 1844 SW Morrison, Portland, 503-241-0825, www.pgepark.com

On the third Friday in August, take Fido out to the old ball game! Cheer and bark for the Portland Beavers at PGE Park in downtown Portland. Dogs are admitted for half price; if your dog is one of the first 1,000 dogs in, he gets a free tennis ball. The Oregon Humane Society offers dogs for adoption and canines can enjoy the acrobatic feats of Skyhoundz Disc Dogs at half time. The game starts at 7 P.M.

Dog Day in the Park

Rooster Rock State Park, I-84 East (Exit 25), 503-695-2261, Ext. 228

This annual event is held the third Saturday in August and features a dog walk, a leash-free area where your best friend can meet and greet other canines,

and an agility course. Multnomah County Animal Control offers pets for adoption, issues free pet ID tags, and sponsors a microchip and rabies clinic. Other canine activities happen throughout the day; prizes are awarded. The dog walk begins at 10 A.M.; registration at 9:30 A.M. All other activities are open 9:30 A.M.– 4 P.M.

Dog Daze of Summer

Clackamas Aquatic Park, 7300 SE Harmony Rd., Milwaukie, 503-557-7873, www.co.clackamas.or.us

For one day in mid-September, before the park drains the pools for annual maintenance, your dog can take the plunge at this multi-pool indoor aquatic park! The Fresh Water Session is from 12 P.M.–2 P.M. and the Semi-Fresh Water Session is from 3 P.M.–5 P.M. Fees are: $5 per dog or $7 multiple dog family. The Not-So-Fresh Water Session is held from 6 P.M.–8 P.M. Fees for this session are: $4 per dog or $6 multiple dog family. Clackamas County Dog Control will be selling and renewing dog licenses during this event. The date changes each year; call ahead.

K103 FM Doggie Dash

5005 SW Macadam Ave., Portland, OR 97201, 503-295-8587, www.k103fm.com

This annual event is held the third weekend in May at Portland's Waterfront Park; proceeds benefit homeless dogs at the Oregon Humane Society. Over 1,300 dogs (and 3,000 humans in tow) participate in a 2-mile fun run, walk, and parade. Additional events include a dog and owner lookalike contest, silly pet tricks, and recognition of the largest and smallest canine participants as well as the best parade entry. Canine-related information booths are also featured.

Northwest Pet & Companion Fair

Portland Exposition Center, Hall D, 2060 N. Marine Dr., Portland, OR 97217, 503-287-7541, www.expocenter.org

This annual event for pet lovers is held the second weekend in April. It features hundreds of exhibits and vendors promoting pet products and services. Other happenings are pet adoptions, bird performances, an agility course demonstration, obedience and grooming workshops, and seminars on healthcare, selecting the right pet, and legal issues of pet ownership.

Pug Crawl

3517 SE Salmon St., Portland, OR 97214, 503-515-1269, www.pugcrawl.org

This annual event for canines and their pals is held in downtown Portland the third weekend in May. For a $10 donation, you and your best friend get to eat and drink, listen to live music, and have chances to win prizes from many different drawings. Events include a pug costume contest and a best amateur pet tricks contest. All proceeds benefit the Oregon Humane Society.

Rose City Classic
Dog Show

Portland Expo Center, Portland Exposition Center, 2060 N. Marine Dr., Portland, OR 97217, 503-736-5200, www.expo center.org

This annual four-day event is held in mid-January and features a series of all-breed shows and obedience trials.

Walk for the Animals

Southwest Washington Humane Society, 2121 St. Francis Lane, Vancouver, WA 98660, 360-693-4746

This annual 1.5 or 3-mile dog walk is held the second Saturday in May to raise money for the Southwest Washington Humane Society. The walk starts at Esther Short Park, located between Esther and Columbia Streets, and the course takes you and your bud along the banks of the Columbia River. Water is provided for both species. Depending on the amount of money you raise, you can earn prizes such as a Frisbee, T-shirt, bandanna, cap, or sweatshirt.

CANINE-APPROVED SHOPPING

Portland—North

Petco

1132 N. Hayden Meadows Dr., 503-735-1778, www.petco.com

This Petco is conveniently located near the leash-free areas in East Delta Park and West Delta Park and the Marine Drive multi-use path (see *Paw-Approved Hikes and Parks*). Open 9 A.M.–9 P.M., Monday to Friday, 10:00 A.M.–8 P.M., Saturday and Sunday.

REI

1798 Jantzen Beach Center, 503-283-1300, www.rei.com

This favorite outdoor store stocks high quality gear for trail hounds including Ruff Wear and Granite Gear dog packs, flotation vests, food and water bowls, trail boots, food carriers, sleeping pads, collars, leashes, Zukes Hip Action Snacks and Trail Treats, Cool Pooch water bottles, and Chuck-It ball throwers. Leashed dogs are welcome to enter the store and try on any of this gear. REI also has skiing, canoe, and kayak rentals. Open 10 A.M.–9 P.M., Monday to Friday; 10 A.M.–9 P.M., Saturday; 10 A.M.–6 P.M., Sunday.

Portland—Northeast

Family Pet Center

12419 NE Glisan St., 503-254-5490

Open 10 A.M.–7 P.M., Monday to Saturday; 10 A.M.–6 P.M., Sunday.

Pets On Broadway

2762 NE Broadway St., 503-282-5824

You and your buddy will enjoy shopping in this friendly store that carries leashes, collars, toys, chews, beds, water bowls, food dishes, and high quality dog food (including holistic brands). Open 10 A.M.–7 P.M., Monday to Saturday; 11 A.M.–6 P.M., Sunday.

Townhouse Pet Care Center

2965 NE Sandy, 503-230-9596, www. townhousepetcare.com

This boarding facility and retail store carries leads, collars, harnesses, toys, grooming products, beds, blankets, dog coats, Iams, and Science Diet dog food. Open 7:30 A.M.–6:00 P.M., Monday to Friday; 7:30 A.M.–5 P.M., Saturday.

Portland—Northwest

Oregon Mountain Community

60 NW Davis St., 503-227-1038

You and your dog can gear up here for your next outdoor adventure. This outdoor shop carries exceptional quality outdoor clothing brands like The North Face, Royal Robbins, Gramicci, and Patagonia. The focus is mountaineering, rock climbing, hiking, backpacking, and cross-country skiing. They feature gear for all these pursuits as well as a large inventory of topographic maps and guidebooks. Oregon Mountain Community also remembers that our canine pals need good outdoor gear—they stock dog packs and other canine gear made by Ruff Wear. They don't even mind if you bring your pooch in with you to try on the gear—just remember to keep him on a leash! Open 10 A.M.–7 P.M., Monday to Friday; 10 A.M.–6 P.M., Saturday; 12 P.M.–5 P.M., Sunday.

Urban Fauna

338 NW 6th Ave., 503-223-4602, www. urbanfauna.com

This upscale pet shop is the Rodeo Drive of pet supplies in Portland. The 5,000-square foot shop carries high-end collars, leashes, bowls, beds, toys, and other unique pet supplies. In stock are premium dog foods, including Nutro, Natural Choice, Solid Gold, Innova & California Naturals, Wellness, Royal Canine, Sensible Choice, Precise, Premium Edge, and Canidae. Doggie daycare and a full-service grooming salon too. Open 10 A.M.–7 P.M., Monday to Friday; and 9 A.M.–6 P.M., Saturday.

Portland—Southeast

Healthy Pets Northwest

1402-A SE 39th, 503-236-8036, www. healthypetsnw.com

This top-quality natural pet store carries holistic/natural foods, herbal and homeopathic remedies, and natural treats. In addition, the store stocks quality backpacks, coats, reflective gear, toys, collars, leashes, shampoos, and grooming tools. The store gives back to the dog community by providing natural pet health seminars for a small donation fee. All proceeds from the seminars go to Portland shelters and rescue programs. Your leashed dog is welcome. Open 10 A.M.–6 P.M., Monday to Saturday; 12 P.M.–5 P.M., Sunday.

Petco

14410 SE Division St., 503-761-0553, www.petco.com

Bring your pal shopping at this huge pet store that has all of the food, toys, and gear a dog could ever want. Open 9 A.M.–9 P.M., Monday to Saturday; 10 A.M.–7 P.M., Sunday.

Portland Pet Supply

4242 SE Hawthorne Blvd., 503-233-3866

Your best friend is welcome to browse the aisles of this store where you'll find a great selection of over thirty brands of specialized dog and cat foods, toys, crates, doggie backpacks, coats, life vests, and dog boots by Muttluk and Ruff Wear. Open 9:30 A.M.–6 P.M., Monday to Friday; 9:30 A.M.–5 P.M., Saturday.

R Pet Shop

4429 SE Woodstock Blvd., 503-775-3520

Open 9 A.M.–7 P.M., Monday to Wednesday; 9 A.M.–6 P.M., Thursday to Saturday; 11 A.M.–5 P.M., Sunday.

Portland—Southwest

Great Dog Bakery
7535 SW Barnes Rd., #112, 503-292-1111

This canine-loving bakery features freshly baked cheesecakes, chicken pup pies, tarts, carob muffins, and personalized cakes for your dog. The store also carries specialty merchandise for all breeds of dogs. Open 10 A.M.–6 P.M., Tuesday to Saturday; and 12 P.M.–5 P.M., Sunday.

The Pet Loft
6333 SW Macadam, #104, 503-244-9546

Bill LaPolla, Manager, says, "We specialize in holistic super premium pet foods like Wellness, Innova, California Natural, Canidae, Natural Balance, and Wysong. We also go out of our way to carry high quality, locally made products such as dog beds, pet jackets, toys, chews, and leashes. We also have a full freshwater fish room, some birds, and small animals. From the day we opened, we have been involved with animal rescue. We have a cat adoption program with the Oregon Humane Society where up to four cats come to live at the store and we are certified to approve new homes. To date, we have placed almost 500 cats from the shelter." Leashed dogs are welcome to check out all the great products at this store. Open 10 A.M.–7 P.M., Monday to Friday; 9 A.M.–6 P.M., Saturday; 11 A.M.–5 P.M., Sunday.

Western Pet Supply
6908 SW Beaverton/Hillsdale Highway, 503-297-6644, westernpet.citysearch.com

This 19,000-square foot store carries a large selection of sporting dog supplies, canine backpacks, car and van barriers, custom dog kennels, and premium dog foods such as Iams, Science Diet, and Nature's Recipe. Open 9 A.M.–7 P.M., Monday to Friday; 9 A.M.–6 P.M., Saturday; 11 A.M.–5 P.M., Sunday.

Beaverton

Petco
4037 SW 117th Ave., Suite C, 503-644-6558, www.petco.com

Open 9 A.M.–9 P.M. Monday through Saturday; 10 A.M.–7 P.M. Sunday

Petsmart
12375 SW Walker Rd., 503-644-7901, www.petsmart.com

This store carries all the dog gear known to man, including leashes, ID tags, collars, beds, toys, grooming tools, high quality dog food, apparel, and dog boots. This store is located next door to the Banfield Pet Hospital (503-644-1100), which accepts walk-in appointments. Open 9 A.M.–9 P.M., Monday to Saturday; 10 A.M.–7 P.M., Sunday.

Clackamas

Holistic Pet Center
15599 SE 82nd Dr., 1-800-788-PETS, 503-656-5342, www.holisticpetcenter.com

This store's motto is "The Health Food Store for Pets." It carries all-natural dog and cat foods such as Precise, Natural Life, Wellness, Canidae, Felidae, Innova, California Natural, Solid Gold, Halo Spot's Stew, and Wysong. Also available are food-grade vitamins and supplements for dogs and cats, organic flea control products, flower essences, herbs, homeopathic remedies, hypoallergenic treats, and books. Chip Sammons, owner of Holistic Pet Center, discusses pet nutrition and news on Saturday mornings from 10 A.M.–11 A.M. on 1290 AM, K-PRAISE.

West Linn

Healthy Pet
2220 Salamo Rd., 503-722-0200

Take your pup to browse the aisles of this friendly store which stocks healthy pet foods and supplements, natural treats, canine backpacks, carriers, training devices, boots, sweaters, coats, toys, and much more. Open 9 A.M.–7 P.M., Monday to Friday; 10 A.M.–6 P.M., Saturday; 12 P.M.–5 P.M., Sunday.

Tail Wagging Bakery

2460 Michael Dr., 503-704-2884 or 888-269-8525, www.tailwaggingbakery.com

This bakery caters to canines by offering organic dog biscuits in a variety of flavors. You can order the biscuits online or by phone.

DOGGIE DAYCARE

Portland—North

It's A Dog's Life

8709 N. Lombard St., 503-286-2668

This facility in Portland's St. John's neighborhood offers twenty-four-hour pet care and features indoor climate-controlled play areas with rubber matted floors for safety. An outside fully fenced play area is also available. The day care also offers obedience training and has a small inventory of freshly baked treats, toys, and other canine accessories. Open 6:30 A.M.–6:30 P.M., Monday to Friday; Saturday 9 A.M.–5 P.M.; Sunday 10 A.M.–4 P.M.

Portland—Northeast

Daycare for Doggie

11931 NE Sumner, 503-251-9001, www.daycarefordoggy.com

This facility has 2,000 square feet of indoor play area with lots of toys, and features supervised group play sessions. Charges are $20 per day for one to two days; $17 per day for three to four days; $15 per day for five days. Additional services include grooming and nail trims, pick ups and drop-offs (in some locations), and overnight stays ($30 per night). A Certified Veterinary Technician is on site. Open 7 A.M.–7 P.M., Monday to Friday.

Happy-Go-Lucky
Dog Training & Playcare

1642 NE Sandy Blvd., 503-731-8774, www.happygoluckydog.com

This daycare charges $22 per day, and offers discounts if your dog attends the daycare on a weekly basis. Two or more dogs merit a 10% discount. Your pooch must be evaluated for a $15 fee before you can bring him to the facility. This popular daycare often has a waiting list. Evening training classes are also offered. Open 7:15 A.M.–6 P.M., Monday to Friday.

Portland—Northwest

Urban Fauna

338 NW 6th, 503-223-4602, www.urbanfauna.com

This daycare features 2,500 square feet of space with three different play areas. Dogs are walked daily and get to play with other dogs of the same temperament. $25 per day per dog. Open 7 A.M.–7 P.M., Monday to Friday; 9 A.M.–6 P.M., Saturday.

Portland—Southeast

Family Dogs Northwest

6817 SE 52nd, 503-774-6126

This daycare charges $20 per day per dog, with a ten percent discount for multiple dogs. If you purchase a ten-visit card, the rate is $15 per day, good for daycare or overnight boarding. This daycare has a 3,000-square foot play area with protective rubber matting. Dogs will enjoy an upstairs room complete with palm tree décor. Sleeping pens are 64 square feet, and dogs can be crated by request. Dogs must be current on all shots, and dogs older than seven months must be spayed or neutered. Family Dogs Northwest also runs an Adoption Center. Open 7 A.M.–7 P.M., Monday to Friday; 9 A.M.–6 P.M., Saturday; 9 A.M.–5 P.M., Sunday.

Howliday Inn Doggie Daycare

3425 SE Yamhill St., 503-230-1050

This daycare charges $20 per day, $18 per day for five visits, $17 per day for ten visits, or $16 per day for 20 visits. Your dog will have a ball playing in the 3,000 square foot upstairs loft space. The daycare also features a fenced outdoor patio and offers overnight boarding for $28 per twenty-four hour period. The owners ask that your dog pass a free evaluation before he can stay. Open 7 A.M.–6 P.M., Monday to Friday.

See Spot Play—
Doggie Daycare and Training
3303 SE 20th, 503-234-0155

This facility offers a huge inside and outside play area, and training classes (including agility).

Portland—Southwest

Arf 'n Bark Doggie Daycare
3433 SW Multnomah Blvd., 503-245-7003, www.arfnbark.com

This daycare has large exercise areas with toys and a cozy snooze room. Your canine pal will receive daily brushings and scheduled potty breaks. Charges run $20 per day with discounts given for dogs signed up for five-week packages. Open 7 A.M.–6 P.M., Monday to Friday.

Lexi Dog Boutique & Social Club
6767 SW Macadam, 503-245-4363

This doggie daycare offers supervised play with other dogs, and has a boutique where you can purchase distinctive accessories and gifts for your dog.

Daycare hours: 7 A.M.–7 P.M., Monday to Friday; 9 A.M.–2 P.M., Saturday. Boutique hours: 10 A.M.–7 P.M., Monday to Friday; 10 A.M.–6 P.M., Saturday. Open 12 A.M.–4 P.M., Sunday.

Gresham

Kountry Kanine DayKare
125 NW 2nd St., 503-465-6819, www.kountrykanine.com

This day care features over 3,300 square feet of matted indoor play space, a huge outdoor play area with doggie pool, and cageless boarding. Charges are $19 per day per dog, with discounts if you purchase a multi-day pass. Overnight cageless boarding is $25 per dog per night. A second dog in the same family is $15 per night.

Hillsboro

Schroeder's Den
2110 NW Aloclek Dr., Suite 620, 503-614-9899, www.schroedeersden.com

Your dog will have tons of fun at this doggie daycare that features 3,000 square feet of rubber matted play space. Open 6:45 A.M.–6:30 P.M., Monday to Friday.

Tigard

4 Paws Dog Daycare
9740 SW Tigard St., 503-639-8897, www.4pawsdogdaycare.com

This facility has 3,000 square feet of secure play space, and offers overnight cageless boarding. All dogs are screened before they can stay. Rates for daycare are one day a week, $20; more than one day a week, $18 per day; half day (six hours), $14; less than 6 hours, $2 per hour; monthly, $280 ($14 per day); or you can purchase a 12-visit punch card for $180 ($15 per day). Two dogs from the same family are $28 day. Open 7 A.M.–6 P.M., Monday to Friday.

Tualatin

Doggone Fun
Doggy Daycare Center
8972 SW Tualatin Sherwood Rd., 503-691-9796

This facility has a large, indoor play area and offers training classes. Open 7 A.M.–6 P.M., Monday to Friday.

DOG WASHES

Portland—Northeast

Beauty for the Beast–
Pet Launderette

3832 NE Sandy Blvd., 503-288-5280, www.beautyforthebeast.com

Prices range from $9–$18 depending on the size of your dog. All tubs have a tie-down to secure your pet in place. A wash includes your choice of shampoo, scrub brush, apron, towels, grooming tools, and blow dryer. For an additional charge you have your choice of medicated or oatmeal shampoos, conditioners, electric clippers, and cologne. Open 8 A.M.–8 P.M., Monday through Friday; 9 A.M.–6 P.M., Saturday; 11 A.M.–6 P.M., Sunday.

Pups & Cups Dog Wash & Café

4516 NE 42nd Ave., 503-493-4000, www.pupsandcups.com

This unique dog wash lets you wash your pup in an elevated claw foot tub and provides all the shampoo and grooming tools to get him smelling fresh and looking top notch. A self-service wash, $15 for any size dog, includes aprons and your choice of four all-natural shampoos, conditioner, scrubbing brushes, grooming tools, toe nail trimmers, towels, professional dryer, electric clippers, ear cleaner, dog cologne, and dog treats. If you don't feel like washing your pup, let the experts do it for $30. The full-service wash includes a pre-wash brushing, shampoo, conditioner, drying, post-wash brushing, and ear cleaning. This full-service dog wash is first come, first serve, with up to an hour wait on weekends. Enjoy the free coffee while you wait. Open 10 A.M.–7 P.M., Monday and Tuesday; 10 A.M.–7 P.M., Thursday and Friday; 9 A.M.–5 P.M., Saturday; 10 A.M.–5 P.M., Sunday.

Portland—Southeast

Connie's U-Wash Dog Wash

8001 SE King Rd., 503-788-4152

Prices are $10 for dogs 35 pounds and under; $12 for dogs 36–65 pounds; $14 for dogs 66–100 pounds; $16 for dogs 101 pounds and over. Includes shampoo, the use of brushes, and a blow dryer. Open 11 A.M.–7 P.M., Tuesday to Friday; 9 A.M.–6 P.M., Saturday; 11 A.M.–5 P.M., Sunday.

Happy Tails Grooming
and Self-Service Pet Wash

6111 SE 82nd, 503-774-4135

Prices are based on your dog's height, and range from $8 to $17. This price includes all the shampoo and grooming tools you need to get your furry friend squeaky clean. Open 11 A.M.–6:30 P.M., Wednesday to Friday; 11 A.M.–5:30 P.M., Saturday; 11 A.M.–4:30 P.M., Sunday.

Pawsatively Clean

3962-D SE Hawthorne Blvd., 503-232-5037

Open 10 A.M.–8 P.M., Wednesday to Friday; 9 A.M.–8 P.M., Saturday. 12 P.M.–8 P.M., Sunday.

Portland—Southwest

All Paws Full & Self Service Pet Wash

6325 SW Capitol Highway, 503-452-7023

Prices for self-service pet wash (which includes shampoo and grooming tools) range between $9–$15 depending on the size of your dog and his coat length. Open 11 A.M.–7 P.M., Monday, Thursday, and Friday; 9 A.M.–6 P.M., Saturday; 10 A.M.–6 P.M., Sunday.

Wiggles & Wags

6141 SW Macadam Ave. #105, 503-977-1775

Get your dog smelling good and looking great at this popular self-service dog wash. Prices range from $12–$20 based on your dog's weight. This price includes your choice of seven types of shampoo, a tub, grooming brushes, towels, and blow dryer. The staff will trim your dog's nails for you as well as show you how to clean his ears. You can rent clippers for $8. Professional grooming services are also available. Open 8 A.M.–7 P.M., Tuesday to Friday; 10 A.M.–7 P.M., Saturday; 10 A.M.–6 P.M., Sunday.

Beaverton

Aqua Dog
16155 NW Cornell Rd. #350, 503-533-4396, www.aquadog.com

Prices for self-service pet wash (includes shampoo and grooming tools) range between $12–$18 depending on the size of your dog and his coat length. Open 9 A.M.–8 P.M., Tuesday to Thursday; 9 A.M.–6 P.M., Friday and Saturday; 12 P.M.–5 P.M., Sunday.

Pup-a-Razzi
16300 SW Hart Rd., 503-259-8978, www.pup-a-razzi.com

This self-service dog wash has raised tubs, professional sprayers, three types of shampoos, towels, professional grooming tables, brushes, combs, toenail clippers, and forced-air (unheated) dryers. Prices are $10 for small dogs, $12 for medium dogs, $14 for large dogs, and $16 for extra large dogs. Open 10 A.M.–8 P.M., Monday, Wednesday, Friday and Saturday; 10 A.M.–6 P.M., Sunday.

CANINE CLUBS

Columbia Agility Team
7193 SE Brehaut, Milwaukie, OR 97222, 503-224-4755, www.columbiaagility.org

This agility club hosts training clinics and competitions throughout the year.

Mixed Breed Dog Club of Oregon
2373 NW 185th Ave, Hillsboro, OR 97124, 503-649-3855, www.mbdca.org

This club offers workshops, training sessions, and competitions for mixed breed dogs. Dogs can earn titles in obedience, conformation, tracking, and other events.

Northwest Stockdog Association, Inc.
2499 Donegal Ct., West Linn, OR 97068, 503-656-6051, www.effectnet.com/dickinson

This club trains and works with stock dogs for recreational and practical purposes and provides information about herding organizations, herding events, and training resources.

The X-Fidos Flyball Team
1095 NE 25th Ave. Space L, Hillsboro, OR 97124, 503-359-4220 or 503-693-6205, www.flyball.com/x-fidos

This flyball club allows any breed of dog with flyball experience to join. Flyball is a racing event where a dog runs down a racing lane (against dogs in other lanes) with four low hurdles to jump. When the dog reaches the end of the lane, he hits a pedal on a box to release a tennis ball. The dog catches the ball and runs back, leaping over the four hurdles to the starting point and finish line. Instructional classes and practice sessions are offered. The club competes in tournaments throughout the Pacific Northwest two to four times per year.

Willamette Valley Herding Club
26515 NW Dairy Creek Rd., North Plains, OR 97133, 503-647-2081, Mapruitt2000@yahoo.com

Members can practice herding livestock, attend club sponsored events and trials, and learn about other herding events and organizations in Oregon.

DOG MEDIA

Dog Nose News
5519 NE 30th Ave., Portland, OR 97211, 503-281-2041, www.dognosenews.com

This monthly newspaper serves the canine community in Portland and surrounding areas. It features articles about dog events, trainers, businesses, and individuals who work with dogs. Find upcoming canine happenings in the events calendar, access cool used dog stuff in the classified ads, and read about dogs who need homes. The paper is viewable online and is available free at many Portland businesses that cater to canines. For locations that distribute this paper, visit www.dognosenews.com and click on the "Find" link.

CANINE ER

Portland

Animal Poison Control
1-888-426-4435

Dove Lewis Emergency Animal Hospital
1984 NW Pettygrove; 503-228-7281, www.dovelewis.org

This is the main emergency clinic for the entire Portland metro area. This hospital provides high quality emergency veterinary care and is open twenty-four hours a day, seven days a week. The clinic is also a resource for animal assisted therapy and offers grief counseling sessions.

Search and Rescue
503-618-0497 (voice mail) or 503-705-0258 (mobile phone)

ANIMAL SHELTERS

Hillsboro

Washington County Animal Services & Bonnie L. Hays Small Animal Shelter
2650 SE Tualatin Valley Highway, 503-846-7041

Open 12 P.M.–6 P.M., Monday to Friday; 11 A.M.–5 P.M., Saturday.

Oregon City

Clackamas County Dog Control
2104 Kaen Rd., 503-655-8628, www.co.clackamas.or.us

Open 11 A.M.–5 P.M., Monday to Saturday.

Portland

Oregon Humane Society
1067 NE Columbia Blvd., 503-285-7722, www.oregonhumane.org

Open 10 A.M.–7 P.M., Monday to Saturday; 12 P.M.–7 P.M., Sunday.

St. Helens

Columbia Humane Society and Columbia County Dog Control
2084 Oregon St., 503-397-4353 (Humane Society), 503-397-3935 (Animal Control).

Open 11 A.M.–5 P.M., Monday to Saturday.

Troutdale

Multnomah County Animal Control
1700 S. Columbia River Highway, 503-988-7387, www.multcopets.org.

Open 11 A.M.–6 P.M., Tuesday to Friday; 10 A.M.–2 P.M., Saturday.

Vancouver, Washington

Southwest Washington Humane Society
2121 St. Francis Lane, 360-693-4746, www.sw-wa-humanesociety.org

Open 12 P.M.–6 P.M., Monday to Friday; 9 A.M.–5 P.M., Saturday and Sunday.

Dog Art in the Park
If your canine friend appreciates a beautiful aesthetic, take him to the bronze water bowl in Portland's North Park blocks at NW Park and 9th St. Designed by William Wegman, the well-known Weimaraner photographer, this is a working drinking fountain for dogs. The Pearl Arts Foundation commissioned this one-of-a-kind piece of artwork in February 2002.

Salem and Vicinity

THE BIG SCOOP

Salem, an hour south of Portland on I-5, is Oregon's state capital and is located in the heart of the Willamette Valley farming country. It is surrounded by vast fields of crops and rolling hills covered with vineyards. The Willamette River flows through Salem's downtown district and serves as an important landmark for the city. While your pup may not be too interested in Salem's politics and history, he will appreciate roaming untethered at Salem's Minto Brown Island Park's leash-free area. Although his spirit can run free in this park, he must be leashed in Salem's other public spaces. Another park worth exploring, in the heart of downtown, is Bush's Pasture Park. This park hosts the annual Paws in the Park event held the first Saturday in September where you can take part in a dog walk and participate in other canine activities.

More adventures can be found in three state parks within a thirty minute drive: Champoeg State Heritage Area (see *Portland and Vicinity*), Silver Falls State Park, and Willamette Mission State Park (see *Paw-Approved Hikes and Parks*). Fifty miles east of Salem on Highway 22 is the small community of Detroit, gateway to the Mount Jefferson Wilderness, which boasts many scenic trails that take you to views of 10,497-foot Mount Jefferson and to high alpine lakes offering great swimming.

PAW-APPROVED HIKES AND PARKS

Salem

Bush's Pasture Park
Contact: Salem Parks Administration Recreation

Sage at Bush's Pasture Park in Salem.

Office, 3rd floor, City Hall, 555 Liberty St. SE, Room 300, Salem, OR 97301, 503-588-6261, www.open.org
Paw-Approval Rating: 3 paws
Leashes Required? Yes
Fees/Permits: None
Season: Year-round
Getting There: From I-5 in South Salem, take exit 252, Kuebler Blvd. Turn west onto Kuebler Blvd. and travel 2 miles. Turn right (north) on Commercial St. Continue north on Commercial St. 3.5 miles. (Note: after 3 miles it turns into Liberty St.) Turn right on Bush St. Continue 0.2 mile on Bush St. to a large paved parking area adjacent to the Bush House Museum, Barn Art Center and Gallery, and Rose Gardens.
Description: This 90.5-acre downtown park is filled with walking and jogging paths, picnic areas, play grounds, shady groves of oak trees, rhododendrons, azaleas,

and rose gardens. The park is named after Asahel Bush, pioneer banker and newspaper publisher, who lived here in a Victorian-style house built in 1877. This house is now home to the Bush House Museum. This park also hosts the Bush Barn Art Center and Gallery and the annual Paws in the Park Spay/Neuter Walk held the first weekend in September (see *Dog Events*). Bags are provided for waste removal.

Minto-Brown Island Park

Contact: Salem Parks Administration Recreation Office, 3rd floor, City Hall, 555 Liberty St. SE, Room 300, Salem, OR 97301, 503-588-6261, www.open.org
Paw-Approval Rating: 4 paws
Leashes Required? Yes, except in the leash-free area.
Fees/Permits: None
Season: Year-round. Some trails may be closed during winter due to flooding.
Getting There: From I-5 in South Salem, take exit 252, Kuebler Blvd. Turn west onto Kuebler Blvd. and travel 2 miles. Turn right (north) on Commercial St. Continue north on Commercial St. 3.5 miles. (Note: after 3 miles it turns into Liberty St.) Turn left on Bush St. Go 1 block and then turn left on Commercial St. heading south. Proceed to the next light and turn right on Owens St. Go 1.2 miles on Owens St. (Note: this turns into River Road), and then turn right onto Minto Island Road. Go 0.7 mile and turn left into a gravel parking area for the leash-free area.
Description: Your dog will love exploring this 900-acre park filled with orchards, large grassy areas, and pockets of forest, sloughs, and waterways. Originally, this park consisted of two islands in the Willamette River. Around 1900, the Willamette flooded, and when the waters receded, an abundance of topsoil was left behind, causing the two islands to join. The original homesteader on Brown Island

Meeting new friends at Minto-Brown Island Park in Salem.

was Isaac Whiskey Brown who grew tobacco and raised livestock there. John Minto, an early homesteader and legislator, purchased 247 acres and settled on neighboring Minto Island in 1867.

You and your partner can create your own adventure on the 20 miles of paved and unpaved pathways that provide grand views of the river. To top it off, the park boasts a huge, 20-acre leash-free area in a grassy field surrounded by deciduous trees. Your Frisbee arm will wear out long before Rover will in this huge outdoor playground. Bags and trash cans are provided for waste pick-up. No water is available at the leash-free area.

Willamette Mission State Park Hike

Contact: Oregon State Parks and Recreation, Suite 1, 1115 Commercial St. NE, Salem OR 97301-1002, 1-800-551-6949, www.oregonstateparks.org
Paw-Approval Rating: 2 paws
Leashes Required? Yes
Length: 2.3-mile loop
Difficulty: Easy
Fees/Permits: $3 day-use fee
Season: Year-round
Getting There: From I-5, take exit 263 toward Brooks and Gervais. This exit is

approximately 8 miles south of Woodburn and 9 miles north of Salem. At the end of the off-ramp, set your trip odometer to zero. Turn west on Brooklake Road and go 1.6 miles to the intersection with Wheatland Road. Turn right on Wheatland Road and drive 2.4 miles to the entrance to Willamette Mission State Park. Turn left into the park entrance road and drive 0.6 mile to the pay booth. Continue 1.2 miles (staying left at each road junction) to the Filbert Grove Day-use Area.

Description: You and your trusty pal can take a tour past the scenic Willamette River, Mission Lake, and what is thought to be the world's biggest black cottonwood tree at 26 feet circumference and 155 feet tall. Start walking on the trail adjacent to the restrooms located at the far northwest corner of the parking area. At 0.2 mile, turn right on the paved bike path that parallels the wide, lazy Willamette River. Walk on this for 1.2 miles. Turn right on a grassy double-track road. Soon you'll pass Mission Lake on your left. As you continue through a walnut orchard, stay left at all trail junctions until you reach a road and sign that points to the world's largest black cottonwood at 1.9 miles. Continue hiking on the paved road 0.4 mile–at the first road junction go left, and at the second road junction go right–back to the trailhead at 2.3 miles. A boat ramp is available if you want to paddle with your pooch on Mission Lake.

Detroit

Jefferson Park Hike

Contact: Willamette National Forest, Detroit Ranger District, HC73, Box 320, Mill City, OR 97360, 503-854-3366, www.fs.fed.us

Paw-Approval Rating: 4 paws
Leashes Required? No
Length: 11.6 miles out and back
Difficulty: Difficult

Fees/Permits: $5 Northwest Forest Pass. Purchase one by calling 1-800-270-7504 or logging on to www.naturenw.org. A wilderness permit is also required and is available from the Detroit Ranger District (see the Contact information above).

Season: Mid-July through mid-October

Getting There: From Salem, travel 61 miles east on Highway 22 to the junction with Whitewater Road. Turn left and continue 7.4 miles to the trailhead parking area.

Description: Mount Jefferson is the star attraction of this very popular wilderness trail that climbs over 1,800 feet into a pristine alpine lakes basin. The trail traverses through a shady Douglas fir forest and switchbacks uphill to a trail junction at 1.5 miles. Go right and continue climbing. Enjoy the stunning views of the mountain. At 3.9 miles, cross a bridge over Whitewater Creek. When you reach the junction with the Pacific Crest Trail at 4.2 miles, turn left and follow the path as it traverses Jefferson Park, a beautiful high alpine meadow filled with Indian paintbrush and lupine. From this junction, continue 1.6 miles on the Pacific Crest Trail to Russell Lake (located on the right side of the trail) and your turnaround point. Enjoy a dip in the lake and then retrace the same route back to the trailhead. The lake makes a great overnight backpack destination. If you decide to spend the night, you'll need a wilderness permit. Expect crowds during August weekends. If you want solitude, visit in September when summer crowds have thinned.

Pamelia Lake Hike

Contact: Willamette National Forest, Detroit Ranger District, HC73, Box 320, Mill City, OR 97360, 503-854-3366, www.fs.fed.us

Paw-Approval Rating: 4 paws
Leashes Required? Yes
Length: 4.4 miles out and back, with longer options
Difficulty: Easy to Pamelia Lake. Difficult if you continue to Hunts Cove or Grizzly Peak.

Fees/Permits: Due to high use, this trail requires a free limited use wilderness entry permit between Memorial Day and October 31, issued only at the Detroit Ranger Station in Detroit. A $5 Northwest Forest Pass is also required, available at 1-800-270-7504 or www.naturenw.org.

Season: May through November for the trail to Pamelia Lake; mid-July through October for the Hunts Cove and Grizzly Peak hikes.

Getting There: Head 62 miles east of Salem on the North Santiam Highway (Highway 22) to Pamelia Lake Road (Forest Rd. 2246). Turn left and travel 3.7 miles to the parking area and trailhead. Restrooms are available at the trailhead (no water).

Description: This magical trail takes you through towering old growth trees in the Mount Jefferson Wilderness. Mossy coated logs, wild rhododendrons, and picturesque Pamelia Creek are added bonuses to this near-perfect-10 trail—the only drawback is its popularity. After 2.2 miles, you'll arrive at the inviting shores of Pamelia Lake where you can hang out and let your dog go for a swim.

Trail Options: From the intersection with the lake at 2.2 miles, continue 4 more miles to secluded Hunts Cove. To get there, turn left and follow the trail as it winds around the left side of the lake. Ignore trails that peel off to the left toward the Pacific Crest Trail. Once you reach the other end of the lake, continue on the trail to Hunts Cove. You'll reach Hunts Cove at 6.2 miles. Once there, retrace your route back to your starting point, for a total of 12.4 miles.

Another option from the 2.2-mile lake intersection is to go right and continue 3 more steep miles to the summit of Grizzly Peak, where you'll have an incredible view of Mount Jefferson. Once you reach the summit, retrace the same route for a total mileage of 10.4. These two trails are not usually open until mid-July. Try to avoid this area during summer weekends. The best time is in mid-to-late September when summer crowds have thinned.

South Breitenbush Gorges Hike

Contact: Willamette National Forest, Detroit Ranger District, HC73, Box 320, Mill City, OR 97360, 503-854-3366, www.fs.fed.us

Paw-Approval Rating: 4 paws

Leashes Required? No

Length: 7.2 miles out and back (with a longer option)

Difficulty: Easy

Fees/Permits: None

Season: April through November

Getting There: From Salem, head about 50 miles east on Highway 22 to Detroit. In Detroit, turn left on Forest Road 46 signed for Breitenbush River. Go 11 miles to Breitenbush Campground (see *Campgrounds*). Once you reach the campground, continue 1.6 miles on Forest Road 46 to a gravel road number 050 on the right side of the road. Turn right and go 0.4 mile and park on the left side of the road.

Description: Start the hike by walking a short distance along the road to the trailhead on the left. Follow the forested path as it descends to the rumbling South Breitenbush River and passes through a shady, red cedar forest dotted with bright wild rhododendrons (they bloom in June). The trail winds through the forest, offering several different views of the river. You'll arrive at a trailhead and your turn-around point at 3.6 miles.

Option: You have the option of continuing on this trail for another 3 miles to the South Breitenbush Trailhead.

Silverton

Silver Falls State Park

Contact: Oregon State Parks and Recreation, Suite 1, 1115 Commercial St. NE, Salem OR 97301-1002, 1-800-551-6949, www.oregonstateparks.org

Paw-Approval Rating: 3 paws
Leashes Required? Yes
Fees/Permits: $3 day-use fee
Season: Year-round
Getting There: From I-5 in Salem turn east on Oregon Highway 22 toward North Santiam Highway/Stayton/Detroit Lake. Travel 5 miles east and take exit 7 on to Oregon Highway 214 toward "Silver Falls State Park." At the end of the off-ramp turn left on Oregon 214 and continue 4.5 miles to a stop sign. Turn left at the stop sign and travel 12.2 miles on Oregon 214 to the entrance to Silver Falls State Park. After entering the park, turn left at the South Falls turnoff. Proceed to the parking area and trailhead.
Description: You and your pooch will love exploring over 35 miles of trails at Oregon's largest state park. Your best friend is allowed on all trails in the park except the Canyon Trail. If you want to set up a base camp, you can stay at the park's large campground (see *Campgrounds*).

CANINE COMFORT ACCOMMODATIONS

Unless otherwise stated, dogs should not be left unattended in a room and should always be leashed on hotel property.

Detroit

$ All Seasons Motel

130 Breitenbush Rd., 503-854-3421, www. open.org

This motel near Detroit Lake and the Mount Jefferson Wilderness is located in 2.5 acres of forest with a seasonal creek. Pet-friendly rooms are available.
Dog Policy
No extra fees for dogs.

Salem

$ Motel 6

1401 Hawthorne Ave. NE, 503-371-8024
Dog Policy
Well-behaved dogs are permitted for no extra charge.

$$ Phoenix Inn

4370 Commercial St., NE, 503-588-9220 or 1-800-445-4498

This pet-friendly hotel has eighty-nine suites furnished with refrigerators, data ports, and cable TV. Additional amenities include a complimentary continental breakfast, pool, hot tub, exercise room, laundry facilities, and business services.
Dog Policy
A fee of $10 per day is charged for one or more dogs.

$$ Red Lion Inn

3301 Market St., 503-370-7888
Dog Policy
A fee of $10 per day per dog is charged.

$$-$$$ Holiday Inn Express

890 Hawthorne Ave SE, 503-391-7000
Dog Policy
A fee of $15 per day is charged for your dog.

CAMPGROUNDS

Silver Falls State Park

Contact: Oregon State Parks and Recreation, Suite 1, 1115 Commercial St. NE, Salem OR 97301-1002, 1-800-551-6949 (information), 1-800-452-5687 (reservations), www.oregonstateparks.org
Season: Year-round, except tent sites
Facilities: 54 electrical hook-up sites, 51 tent sites (these sites are closed October 31 through April 15), 3 group-tent areas, 2 group RV areas, 5 horse sites with corrals, 14 cabins, fire rings, picnic tables, piped water, flush toilets, showers, playground, RV dump station
Getting There: From I-5 in Salem, turn east on Oregon Highway 22 toward North Santiam Highway/Stayton/Detroit Lake. Travel 5 miles east and take exit 7 onto Oregon Highway 214, toward Silver Falls State Park. At the end of the off-ramp, turn left on Oregon 214 and continue 4.5 miles to a stop sign. Turn left and travel 12.2 miles on Oregon 214 to the Silver Falls

State Park entrance. Watch for campground signs.

Description: 8,700-acre Silver Falls State Park is Oregon's largest state park. It features numerous waterfalls and miles of hiking trails in a beautiful forested setting. The campground is located in a towering forest of Douglas fir, western hemlock, red cedar, alder, and maple trees. Dogs are not allowed on the Canyon Trail or in the park's cabins. Silver Falls is popular; sites fill up fast during summer.

CANINE-APPROVED SHOPPING

Salem

Petco

628 Lancaster Dr. N.E., 503-391-1828, www.petco.com

You and Rover are welcome to shop at this huge store that carries a wide assortment of canine supplies, gear, and food. Open 9 A.M.–9 P.M., Monday to Saturday; 10 A.M.–6 P.M., Sunday.

Petsmart

2925 Lancaster Dr. NE, 503-362-5325, www.petsmart.com

This pet superstore carries all the toys, treats, and gear your dog could ever want. Leashed dogs are welcome. This store is adjacent to the Banfield Pet Hospital (503-581-5899), which accepts walk-in appointments. Open 9 A.M.–9 P.M., Monday to Saturday; 10 A.M.–7 P.M., Sunday.

CANINE ER

Salem Veterinary Emergency Clinic

450 Pine St. N.E., Salem 503-588-8082

Open 5:00 P.M.–8:00 P.M., Monday to Friday; twenty-four hours Saturday, Sunday, and holidays.

ANIMAL SHELTERS

Humane Society of the Willamette Valley

4246 Turner Rd., Salem 503-585-5900, www.hswv.com

Open 12 P.M.–7 P.M., Monday to Friday; 12 P.M.–6 P.M., Saturday and Sunday.

Corvallis and Vicinity

THE BIG SCOOP

This friendly college town is home to Oregon State University. Its tree-lined streets and proximity to the Willamette River, Coast Range, Tillamook State Forest, and Siuslaw National Forest make it a wonderful base for explorations with your dog.

Corvallis boasts dozens of scenic parks, with leash-free areas in five parks: Bald Hill Park, Chip Ross Park, Walnut Park, Willamette Park, and Woodland Meadow Park (see *Paw-Approved Hikes and Parks*). If your trail hound loves waterfalls be sure to check out the Alsea Falls and Green Peak Falls hikes. Cycling canines may also want to explore the Mary's Peak ride, located in the scenic Siuslaw National Forest. Dogs must be leashed in all public areas within Corvallis city limits. Corvallis parks that do not allow dogs include Central, Chintimini, Franklin, Lilly and the upper level of Washington Park.

PAW-APPROVED HIKES AND PARKS

Alsea Falls and Green Peak Falls Hike

Contact: Bureau of Land Management, Salem District, 1717 Fabry Rd. SE, Salem, OR 97306, 503-375-5646, www.or.blm.gov
Paw-Approval Rating: 4 paws
Leashes Required? Yes
Length: 4.8 miles out and back
Difficulty: Moderate
Fees/Permits: None
Season: Year-round

Getting There: From Corvallis, travel 16 miles south on Highway 99W to Monroe. From Monroe turn right at a sign for Alpine and follow signs for Alsea Falls, 13.2 miles. Turn right into the Alsea Falls picnic parking area.
Description: Begin walking on a gravel path along the banks of the South Fork of the Alsea River. Fido may be tempted to take a dip in the cool water when you reach the river's edge. Turn left and walk a short distance to the shimmering 20-foot cascade of Alsea Falls. From here head back to the main path next to the river's edge and walk upstream under the cool canopy of a pine-scented forest. At 0.6 mile, cross the river on a footbridge and follow the path as it heads downstream. Go about a mile on this trail until it turns into a road. Continue walking on the road a short distance and look for the hiker symbol on the right. Continue to the right on the singletrack hiking trail as it travels next to Peak Creek until you reach the pleasant 60-foot cascade of Green Peak Falls. Retrace the route back to the trailhead. If you want to stay overnight you can stay at Alsea Falls Campground (see *Campgrounds*).

Avery Park

Contact: Corvallis Parks and Recreation Department, 1310 SW Avery Park Dr., Corvallis, OR 97333, 541-766-6918, www.ci.corvallis.or.us
Paw-Approval Rating: 3 paws
Leashes Required? Yes
Fees/Permits: None
Season: Year-round

Getting There: This park is located at 15th St. and Avery Ave.

Description: This 75-acre park features trails where you and your best friend can stroll through beautiful rose and rhododendron gardens and view the Mary's River.

Bald Hill Park

Contact: Corvallis Parks and Recreation Department, 1310 SW Avery Park Dr., Corvallis, OR 97333, 541-766-6918, www.ci.corvallis.or.us

Paw-Approval Rating: 3 paws

Leashes Required? Yes (except in the leash-free area)

Fees/Permits: None

Season: Year-round

Getting There: This park is located on Oak Creek Dr.

Description: This 284-acre park features trails that wind through many open natural areas. Bubbling Oak Creek borders the park. West of Bald Hill Park is an area where dogs are permitted off leash.

Chip Ross Park

Contact: Corvallis Parks and Recreation Department, 1310 SW Avery Park Dr., Corvallis, OR 97333, 541-766-6918, www.ci.corvallis.or.us

Paw-Approval Rating: 4 paws

Leashes Required? Yes (except in the leash-free area)

Fees/Permits: None

Season: Year-round

Getting There: In Albany, Oregon, take exit 234B off I-5. At the end of the off-ramp, follow Pacific Blvd. southeast for a mile until it turns into U.S. Highway 20. Continue following Highway 20 west toward Corvallis. After about 10 miles, turn right on Conifer Blvd. Proceed on Conifer Blvd. for 1.4 miles to Highway 99W. Turn left on Highway 99W and go 0.3 mile to the intersection with Walnut Blvd. Turn right on Walnut Blvd. and

travel 1.1 miles to NW Highland Dr. Turn right and proceed 0.9 mile to Lester Ave. Turn left and go 0.9 mile to the road's end at Chip Ross Park.

Description: Your dog will enjoy the sights and smells on the many trails that wind through white oak woodlands and Douglas fir forest. In the leash-free area, your pup can explore to his heart's content. Explore the 1.6-mile loop trail through the park, or hook up with Dan's Trail and head to the top of Dimple Hill for a 7.6-mile round trip hike.

Riverfront Commemorative Park

Contact: Corvallis Parks and Recreation Department, 1310 SW Avery Park Dr., Corvallis, OR 97333, 541-766-6918, www.ci.corvallis.or.us

Paw-Approval Rating: 3 paws

Leashes Required? Yes

Fees/Permits: None

Season: Year-round

Getting There: This park is located on First St.

Description: This 6-acre park features a paved bike and pedestrian path that follows the banks of the Willamette River.

Walnut Park

Contact: Corvallis Parks and Recreation Department, 1310 SW Avery Park Dr., Corvallis, OR 97333, 541-766-6918, www.ci.corvallis.or.us

Paw-Approval Rating: 4 paws

Leashes Required? Yes (except in the leash-free area)

Fees/Permits: None

Season: Year-round

Getting There: This park is located on Walnut Ave.

Description: An off-leash area is located in the southwest corner of this city park. Additional facilities include a walnut barn covered picnic shelter, volleyball courts, two horseshoe pits, two softball fields, a bike path, and a play area.

Willamette Park
Contact: Corvallis Parks and Recreation Department, 1310 SW Avery Park Dr., Corvallis, OR 97333, 541-766-6918, www.ci.corvallis.or.us
Paw-Approval Rating: 4 paws
Leashes Required? Yes (except in the leash-free area)
Fees/Permits: None
Season: Year-round
Getting There: This park is located on SE Goodnight Ave., in Corvallis off of Highway 99W.
Description: Covering 287 acres, this park is bordered by the Willamette River and has many trails and natural areas. Dogs are permitted off leash at the north end of the park, between the boat ramp and the north end of the soccer fields. This park also features a Frisbee golf course, restrooms, a boat ramp, and a camping area.

 Woodland Meadow Park
Contact: Corvallis Parks and Recreation Department, 1310 SW Avery Park Dr., Corvallis, OR 97333, 541-766-6918, www.ci.corvallis.or.us
Paw-Approval Rating: 4 paws
Leashes Required? Yes
Fees/Permits: None
Season: Year-round
Getting There: This park is located at Circle and Witham Hill Dr.
Description: Let Rover roam free in this park's leash-free area, located in the upper section of the park from the Corl House to the crest of a hill. This park also features a bike path, hiking trails, basketball courts and a meeting facility at the Corl House.

CYCLING FOR CANINES

 Mary's Peak
Contact Information: Siuslaw National Forest, Waldport Ranger District, 1094 SW Pacific Highway, Waldport, OR, 541-563-3211, www.fs.fed.us
Paw-Approval Rating: 3 paws

Leashes Required? No
Length: 13 miles out and back
Difficulty: Difficult
Fees/Permits: None
Season: June through October
Getting There: From Corvallis, drive west on U.S. 20/OR 34 to Philomath. Go through Philomath and stay on U.S. 20 toward Toledo/Newport. Soon after you cross Mary's River, you'll turn left on Forest Road 2005 (Woods Creek Road). Drive on Woods Creek Road for approximately 7.5 miles. At the intersection with Forest Road 112, park in the pullout on the left.
Description: Cycling canines will enjoy the challenge of this 13-mile singletrack ride that ascends over 2,300 feet to the top of Mary's Peak, the highest point in the Coast Range. Begin the ride by going around a gate and cranking uphill on Forest Road 2005. After about 3.5 miles, you'll reach another gate. Ride around this gate, then bear right onto East Ridge Trail. At the next intersection bear left, and continue on East Ridge Trail. Eventually, East Ridge Trail intersects with a gravel road. Turn left on the gravel road and ride to the summit of Mary's Peak. Follow the same route back to the trailhead. If you want to explore this area further, you can set up base camp at Mary's Peak Campground. (See the *Campgrounds* section in the *Oregon Coast* chapter)

CANINE COMFORT ACCOMMODATIONS
Unless otherwise stated, dogs should not be left unattended in the room and must be leashed on hotel property.

$ Jason Inn
800 NW 9th St., 541-753-7326 or 1-800-346-3291
Dog Policy
This hotel charges $4 per night per dog.

$$ Shanico Inn
1113 NW 9th St., 541-754-7474 or 1-800-432-1233, www.shanicoinn.com

Dog Policy

This hotel accepts dogs that weigh 25 pounds or less. They charge $10 per pet per night and require that you read and sign a pet policy agreement.

CAMPGROUNDS

Alsea Falls Campground

Contact: Bureau of Land Management, Salem District, 1717 Fabry Rd. SE, Salem, OR 97306, 503-375-5646, www.or. blm.gov
Season: Mid-May through September
Facilities: 6 sites (no electrical hook-ups), drinking water, barbecue grills, and vault toilets
Getting There: From Corvallis, travel 15 miles south on Highway 99W. Turn west on County Road 45120 and drive 5 miles to Alpine Junction. Continue on the South Fork Alsea Access Road 9 miles to Alsea Falls Campground.
Description: This campground is located in a forested setting adjacent to the South Fork of the Alsea River. For hiking opportunities, see the Alsea Falls and Green Peak Falls Hike in *Paw-Approved Hikes and Parks*.

DOG EVENTS

Paws in the Park

Humane Society of the Willamette Valley, 4246 Turner Rd. SE, Salem, OR 503-585-5900, www.hswv.com

You'll have a howling good time at this event held the first Saturday in September. The happenings include a dog walk, a mutt show (best costume, best trick, longest tail, fastest tail, smallest dog, biggest dog, pet lookalike), dog agility and flyball demonstrations, obedience training, a raffle, and the purr-tiest kitty photo contest. In the Kid's Furry Friends Fun Zone little ones can get their faces painted and participate in craft sessions. Registration is from 9 A.M.–10 A.M. The dog walk starts at 11 A.M. All other events are from 11 A.M.–2 P.M.

PetWalk and 4.5K Fun Run

Heartland Humane Society, 398 SW Twin Oaks Circle, 541-757-9000, www.heart landhumane.peak.org

PetWalk is an annual activity bringing pet-guardians, community members, and runners together to celebrate the human-animal bond and to raise funds for the Heartland Humane Society. The run and walk are held the second weekend in June in Willamette Park in Corvallis. Post PetWalk festivities include treats for both species, and canine contests for best personality, longest tail, shortest tail, most spots, dog/owner lookalike, best trick, and best Frisbee dog.

CANINE-APPROVED SHOPPING

Animal Crackers Pet Supply

949 NW Kings Blvd., 503-753-4559 or 1-800-641-4559, www.animalcrackerspet supply.com

This friendly pet store carries all the essentials your four-legged traveling partner will need, including high quality dog foods, treats, chews, collars, leashes, toys, training aids, bedding, flea treatments, grooming supplies, pet safety products, supplements, books, and much more. Open 10 A.M.–7 P.M., Monday to Friday; 9 A.M.–6 P.M., Saturday; 11 A.M.–6 P.M., Sunday.

Petco

2365 NW Kings Blvd., 541-766-8997, www.petco.com

Petco welcomes your leashed dog to browse its huge selection of dog gear, food, and toys. Open 10 A.M.–9 P.M., Monday to Saturday; 10 A.M.–7 P.M., Sunday.

DOG WASHES

Dirty Dog Self-Service Pet Wash

920 NW 9th St., 97330, 541-758-0764

This Corvallis dog wash has been in business fifteen years and gives you all the grooming tools and shampoo you need. The fee for dogs under seventy pounds is

Levi getting squeaky clean at a self-service dog wash.

$13, and dogs over seventy pounds is $15. A nail trim is $5, and a full body clip is $10. Dirty Dog also offers full-service grooming by appointment only. This shop sells grooming tools, dental products, treats, and specialty shampoos. Open 11:30 A.M.–7 P.M., Wednesday to Friday; 8 A.M.–6 P.M., Saturday; 12 P.M.–5 P.M., Sunday.

CANINE ER

Emergency Medicine and Critical Care Clinic

650 SW 3rd St., Corvallis, OR 541-753-2223

Open twenty-four hours a day, seven days a week.

LOST AND FOUND (ANIMAL SHELTERS)

Heartland Humane Society

398 SW Twin Oaks Circle, Corvallis, OR 541-757-9000, www.heartlandhumane. peak.org

Open 12 P.M.–7 P.M., Tuesday to Friday; 12 P.M.–6 P.M., Saturday.

Humane Society of the Willamette Valley

4246 Turner Rd. SE, Salem, OR 503-585-5900, www.hswv.com

Open 12 P.M.–7 P.M., Monday to Friday; 12 P.M.–6 P.M., Sunday.

Eugene and Vicinity

THE BIG SCOOP

Eugene

Eugene, home of the University of Oregon, offers many dog-friendly parks and green spaces. This environmentally-conscious community is located at the southern end of the Willamette Valley, and is about sixty miles east of the Oregon Coast. The Willamette River flows through the heart of downtown Eugene, with many parks and green spaces along its shores. Don't miss the Willamette River Hike, which takes you on paved walking and bike paths through downtown Eugene, and offers plenty of spots to get wet. In addition, traveling dogs will appreciate Eugene's four leash-free parks (Amazon, Alton Baker, Candlelight, and Morse Ranch) that allow road weary canines the opportunity to stretch their legs and meet new friends. Eugene also boasts beautiful forest paths on its Ridgeline trail system and a system of trails that wind through the Mount Pisgah Arboretum.

Springfield and the McKenzie River

Springfield, Eugene's sister city to the east, is the gateway to the McKenzie River Valley and the Willamette National Forest. East of Springfield on Highway 126 you'll find dozens of hiking and cycling opportunities in this vast national forest. One of the premier hiking and mountain biking trails is the McKenzie River National Scenic Trail (see *Paw-Approved Hikes and Parks*) that winds over twenty-six miles along the crystal clear waters of the McKenzie River. Other recommended hikes are French Pete Creek, and Sahalie and Koosah Falls.

Oakridge

The small community of Oakridge, about 40 miles southeast of Eugene on Highway 58, is a gateway to many shady, old growth trails in the adjacent Willamette National Forest. A recommended old growth hike is the Larison Creek Trail. Further east on Highway 58, you'll find pristine Waldo Lake—Oregon's second-deepest freshwater lake. Explore this gorgeous high mountain lake by boat, or hike or mountain bike around it on the 21-mile Waldo Lake Trail.

Cottage Grove

Cottage Grove, about 18 miles south of Eugene on I-5, is home to two trails worth exploring: the Row River Trail and the Brice Creek Trail. The Row River Trail is a multi-use trail that starts in Cottage Grove adjacent to rambling Mosby Creek. The paved trail follows the course of the Row River to the shores of Dorena Lake. As a bonus, you can view one of Oregon's famed covered bridges, the Mosby Creek Covered Bridge. If you love creek trails, the Brice Creek Trail is sure to please, as it follows Brice Creek through pockets of old growth forest, past serene waterfalls, and to awesome swimming holes.

PAW-APPROVED HIKES AND PARKS

Eugene

Alton Baker Park

Contact: Lane County Parks, 90064 Coburg Rd., Eugene, OR 97408, 541-682-4414, www.co.lane.or.us

Paw-Approval Rating: 4 paws
Leashes Required? No (in the off-leash area only)
Fees/Permits: None
Season: Year-round
Getting There: This park is off Leo Harris Parkway in Eugene.
Description: This city park on the banks of the Willamette River has a fenced, off-leash area for your pooch between the community gardens and research center. This park is also the starting point for the Willamette River Hike. The park has water and restrooms.

Amazon Park
Contact: Eugene Parks, 1820 Roosevelt Blvd., Eugene, OR 97401, 541-682-4800, www.ci.eugene.or.us
Paw-Approval Rating: 4 paws
Leashes Required? No (in the off-leash area only)
Fees/Permits: None
Season: Year-round
Getting There: Located adjacent to the intersection of 29th and Amazon Parkway in Eugene.
Description: This large city park has a fenced, off-leash area located near the skateboarding area as well as many hiking and jogging paths that parallel playful Amazon Creek.

Candlelight Park
Contact: Eugene Parks, 1820 Roosevelt Blvd., Eugene, OR 97401, 541-682-4800, www.ci.eugene.or.us
Paw-Approval Rating: 4 paws
Leashes Required? No
Fees/Permits: None
Season: Year-round
Getting There: This park is at the corner of Candlelight and Royal in Eugene.
Description: Your pal can be off leash in this large, unfenced field where he can meet new friends and stretch his legs to a game of fetch or Frisbee.

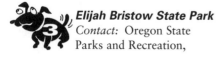
Elijah Bristow State Park
Contact: Oregon State Parks and Recreation,
Suite 1, 1115 Commercial St. NE, Salem OR 97301-1002, 1-800-551-6949, www. oregonstateparks.org
Paw-Approval Rating: 3 paws
Leashes Required? Yes
Fees/Permits: None
Season: Year-round. Some trails may flood during winter.
Getting There: From I-5 in Eugene, take exit 188A, Highway 58/Oakridge/Klamath Falls. Head east on Highway 58 for 10 miles to Wheeler Road. Turn left onto Wheeler Road at a sign for Elijah Bristow State Park. Go 0.3 mile and turn right into the park entrance road. Continue to the road's end and a large parking area.
Description: This state park covers 847 acres and has over ten miles of multi-use trails that wind through meadows, woodlands, and wetlands. Your dog will appreciate cooling off in Lost Creek or the Middle Fork of the Willamette River. During your day of adventure, you may see some local wildlife residents, including osprey, great blue heron, bald eagle, beaver, and the Western pond turtle.

Morse Ranch Park
Contact: Eugene Parks, 1820 Roosevelt Blvd., Eugene, OR 97401, 541-682-4800, www. ci.eugene.or.us
Paw-Approval Rating: 4 paws
Leashes Required? No
Fees/Permits: None
Season: Year-round
Getting There: Access and parking for the off-leash area is at 595 Crest Dr. in Eugene.
Description: This 27-acre park has natural and wooded areas to explore. It features a large fenced area where Rover can roam without a leash. The park's historic house and picnic shelter can be rented for large events. The Willamette Wildlife Rehabilitation Center is also located on park grounds. This privately run organization rehabilitates sick and injured birds and small mammals.

Mount Pisgah Arboretum Hike

Contact: Lane County Parks, 90064 Coburg Rd., Eugene, OR 97408, 541-682-4414, www.co.lane.or.us
Paw-Approval Rating: 3 paws
Leashes Required? Yes
Length: 4.7-mile loop
Difficulty: Moderate
Fees/Permits: None
Season: Year-round
Getting There: From I-5 at Eugene's southern city limits, take exit 189, 30th Ave.-South Eugene. At the end of the off-ramp continue straight 0.2 mile. Turn right on Franklin Ave. (a Texaco Station is on the corner) and go 0.4 mile to the intersection with Seavey Loop Road. Turn left on Seavey Loop Road, travel 1.5 miles, and cross a bridge over the Coast Fork of the Willamette River. After the bridge, continue 0.4 mile on a gravel road to a large gravel parking area. Proceed through the main parking area until you reach another parking area at the signed Mount Pisgah Arboretum.
Description: This scenic loop has an elevation gain of 700 feet and takes you and your hiking partner through the many landscapes of Mount Pisgah Arboretum. You'll travel through open oak woodlands and cool, shady Douglas fir forests. From the Arboretum Parking Area start hiking on the signed Riverbank Trail. At 0.3 mile turn left onto Quarry Road. At 0.5 mile go around a metal gate and continue straight. At 0.8 mile the trail turns to grassy singletrack. At 1.8 miles turn left at the trail fork, which is hard to distinguish. (This trail junction appears a few hundred yards after your last glimpse of the Coast Fork of the Willamette River.) At 1.9 miles ignore the faint trail that heads off to the right. At this point the trail heads uphill and becomes more obvious and bit rutted. At 2.8 miles cross gravel Trail 36 and continue straight under a set of power lines. At 4 miles turn left on the signed connector Trail 35. A

sign indicates "West Trailhead 0.7 mile." At 4.4 miles a trail joins the route from the left. Continue straight and head downhill. At 4.5 miles continue straight (ignoring the trail that heads right). At 4.6 miles turn right. At 4.7 miles arrive back at the trailhead.

Ridgeline Trail: Spencer Butte to Blanton Road Hike

Contact: Eugene Parks, 1820 Roosevelt Blvd., Eugene, OR 97401, 541-682-4800, www.ci.eugene.or.us
Paw-Approval Rating: 4 paws
Leashes Required? Yes
Length: 7.4 miles out and back
Difficulty: Moderate
Fees/Permits: None
Season: Year-round. This trail can be muddy during winter.
Getting There: From the intersection of 7th St. and Willamette St. in downtown Eugene, turn south on Willamette St. and travel 5.3 miles to Spencer Butte Park on the left side of the road. Look carefully for the small park sign indicating the entrance to the park—it's easy to miss!
Description: This shady forested route has an elevation gain of 290 feet and takes you and Rover on a journey through a thick Douglas fir forest right in the heart of Eugene. From the parking lot go around a set of yellow metal posts and then proceed on the middle path. At 0.5 mile, turn right at a 3-way intersection. At 1.2 miles, arrive at a 3-way intersection. Turn left. Continue heading downhill on a series of tight switchbacks. At 1.3 miles, cross a wood bridge. At 2.2 miles, arrive at a gravel parking area under a set of power lines. Head across the parking lot and then cross Willamette St. Turn right and walk parallel to Willamette St. for about 300 yards until you see a sign marking the continuation of the Ridgeline Trail. Turn left at the trail sign and continue on the singletrack trail as it hugs the ridgeline through a shady forest. At 3.7 miles, you'll arrive at

a gravel parking area at Blanton Road. From here, turn around and retrace the route back to the trailhead at Spencer Butte, for a total of 7.4 miles.

Ridgeline Trail: Spencer Butte to Fox Hollow Road Hike

Contact: Eugene Parks, 1820 Roosevelt Blvd., Eugene, OR 97401, 541-682-4800, www.ci.eugene.or.us
Paw-Approval Rating: 4 paws
Leashes Required? Yes
Length: 7-mile loop
Difficulty: Moderate
Fees/Permits: None
Season: Year-round. This trail can be muddy during winter.
Getting There: From the intersection of 7th St. and Willamette St. in downtown Eugene turn south on Willamette St. and travel 5.3 miles to Spencer Butte Park on the left side of the road. Look carefully for the small park sign indicating the entrance to the park—it is easy to miss!
Description: This forested city escape promises a good workout with 250 feet of elevation gain. It begins at Spencer Butte Park and takes you through pockets of old growth fir as it descends to Fox Hollow Road. After you cross Fox Hollow Road you'll complete a loop through more urban forest. If you and your dog like to run trails, this route promises a good workout. From the parking area go around a set of yellow metal posts and then proceed on the middle trail. At 0.5 mile, turn right at a 3-way intersection. At 1.2 miles, arrive at a 3-way intersection. Turn right toward Fox Hollow Road. At 1.9 miles, go across Fox Hollow Road. After crossing the road turn right and follow the guardrail that parallels the road for about 50 yards. Then turn left and continue on the unsigned single-track trail. Continue on the trail for about 100 yards and arrive at a small gravel parking lot. Traverse the parking lot and continue on the singletrack trail on the opposite side. Go another 25 yards to a

trail fork. Head right and begin ascending a short hill. At 2.7 miles, arrive at a trail fork. Go left and proceed 50 yards and then continue straight downhill. At this point you are on the signed mountain bike portion of the trail. At 3.4 miles, ignore the side trail that drops sharply to the right. Continue straight. At 3.5 miles you've completed the loop portion of the route. Retrace the route back to your starting point for a total of 7 miles.

Willamette River Hike

Contact: Eugene Parks, 1820 Roosevelt Blvd., Eugene, OR 97401, 541-682-4800, www. ci.eugene.or.us
Paw-Approval Rating: 3 paws
Leashes Required? Yes
Length: 7.7-mile loop
Difficulty: Easy
Fees/Permits: None
Season: Year-round
Getting There: From the intersection of 7th St. and Pearl St. in downtown Eugene, turn left on 7th St. and follow signs to Coburg Road. Go 0.5 mile and cross the Ferry St. Bridge over the Willamette River. After the bridge, turn right on Centennial Blvd. and go 0.2 mile to the intersection with Club Road. Turn right on Club Road and continue 0.1 mile and turn left into Alton Baker Park.
Description: This easy hike starts at scenic Alton Baker Park on the banks of the Willamette River in downtown Eugene. This park has a leash-free area, water, and restrooms. From the park, the route heads southeast along the banks of the Willamette. You'll walk under shady cottonwoods, with plenty of scenic river views. After two short miles, cross the Willamette on the Willy Knickerbocker Bike Bridge. From here, the route heads northwest. You and your doggie will walk through some business parks and a short distance on some quiet city streets before you meet the South Bank Trail at 3.3 miles. After you turn onto the South Bank

Trail, the route continues on its northwest journey along the Willamette. Hike past the large, grassy lawns of Skinner Butte Park and after 5.3 miles arrive at the Owen Rose Gardens. Colorful varieties of roses can be seen at the gardens, with the peak bloom in May and June. The park is home to a cherry tree thought to be over 100 years old. At 5.9 miles, continue across the Greenway Bike Bridge. (If you crave more mileage, don't cross the bridge here, but continue north on the bike path for about another 2.5 miles.) After crossing the bridge, the route turns southeast and takes you past Valley River Shopping Mall and continues along the shores of the Willamette until you return to Alton Baker Park at 7.7 miles.

Springfield and the McKenzie River

French Pete Creek Hike
Contact: Willamette National Forest, McKenzie Ranger District 57600 McKenzie Highway, McKenzie Bridge, OR 97413, 541-822-3381, www.fs.fed.us
Paw-Approval Rating: 4 paws
Leashes Required? No
Length: 3.4 miles (with longer options)
Difficulty: Easy
Fees/Permits: $5 Northwest Forest Pass. Purchase at 1-800-270-7504 or www.naturenw.org.
Season: April through mid-November
Getting There: Head about 45 miles east of Eugene on Highway 126 to Blue River. Travel 4 more miles east of Blue River and turn right (south) on Forest Road 19 (Aufderheide Dr.) and continue 0.4 mile to a road junction. Bear right toward the signed Cougar Reservoir and continue another 11 miles to a signed trailhead parking area on the left side of the road.
Description: This forest path leads you and your dog through an amazing old growth Douglas fir and red cedar forest in the Three Sisters Wilderness. The trail has

only 400 feet of elevation gain and travels through a thick undergrowth of Oregon grape, sword fern, and vine maple under towering trees until you arrive at French Pete Creek at 1.7 miles. Turn around here or wade through the creek and continue on this magical trail for another 8.1 miles through a picturesque forested valley. You'll have to cross the creek again at the 3-mile mark. If you want to spend the night in this area, be sure to check out the beautiful French Pete Creek Campground (see *Campgrounds*).

McKenzie River Hike
Contact: Willamette National Forest, McKenzie Ranger District, 57600 McKenzie Highway, McKenzie Bridge, OR 97413, 541-822-3381, www.fs.fed.us
Paw-Approval Rating: 4 paws
Leashes Required? No
Length: 5 miles out and back (with longer options)
Difficulty: Easy
Fees/Permits: $5 Northwest Forest Pass. Purchase at 1-800-270-7504 or www.naturenw.org.
Season: April through November
Getting There: Head 51 miles east of Eugene on Oregon Highway 126. Turn left into the trailhead parking area just before milepost 52.
Description: This route will dazzle you with its awesome singletrack trail, gorgeous old growth trees, and crystal clear river. The trail, with an elevation gain of 170 feet, weaves in and out of magical forest, and at several different points takes you near the river's edge until you reach Paradise Campground (see *Campgrounds*)—your turnaround point. If you and Rover feel energetic, continue on the trail for twenty-four more gorgeous miles! This trail makes a wonderful trail-running route and is open to mountain bikes for its entire length. If you are looking for a shorter loop that explores some of the falls on the river, check out the Sahalie and Koosah Falls Hike.

Sahalie and Koosah Falls Hike

Contact: Willamette National Forest, McKenzie Ranger District, 57600 McKenzie Highway, McKenzie Bridge, OR 97413, 541-822-3381, www.fs.fed.us

Paw-Approval Rating: 4 paws
Leashes Required? Yes
Length: 2.6-mile loop
Difficulty: Easy
Fees/Permits: $5 Northwest Forest Pass. Purchase at 1-800-270-7504 or www.naturenw.org.
Season: April through November
Getting There: From Eugene, drive approximately 50 miles east on Highway 126 to the small community of McKenzie Bridge. From McKenzie Bridge, head 19 miles east on Highway 126 and turn left into a signed parking area for Sahalie Falls.
Description: This hike explores some of the waterfalls that tumble over lava cliffs along the McKenzie River. Start by heading down to a viewpoint of impressive Sahalie Falls, which roars over a lava shelf into a churning, spring-fed pool. From the viewpoint, continue left, following signs for the Waterfall Trail. After 0.5 mile, soak in the views of the splashing cascade of Koosah Falls, then continue downstream (staying right at all trail junctions) until you reach a gravel road at 0.9 mile. Turn right on the gravel road as it parallels Carmen Reservoir. Continue until you see a signed spur trail that leads to the McKenzie River Trail. Once you reach the McKenzie River Trail, turn right and head upstream for more great views of the churning McKenzie River. At 2.2 miles, turn right and cross a footbridge over the river. After crossing the bridge bear right and continue 0.4 mile to the trailhead. The total elevation gain for this hike is 400 feet.

Oakridge

Goodman Creek Hike

Contact: Middle Fork Ranger District, Lowell Office, 60 South Pioneer St., Lowell, OR 97452, 541-937-2129, www.fs.fed.us
Paw-Approval Rating: 4 paws
Leashes Required? No
Length: 4 miles out and back (or 13.4 miles out and back to Eagles Rest)
Difficulty: Easy. (Difficult if you are hiking to the summit of Eagles Rest)
Fees/Permits: $5 Northwest Forest Pass. Purchase at 1-800-270-7504 or www.naturenw.org.
Season: March through November
Getting There: From I-5 in Eugene, take exit 188A, Highway 58/Oakridge/Klamath Falls. Head southeast on Highway 58 for about 21 miles to Lookout Point Reservoir. Park in a small parking area marked with a hiker sign on the right side of the road.
Description: This easy route ascends 300 feet and takes you and Rover through cool mossy forest and past prime swimming holes. From the parking area, start hiking on the forest path. At 0.2 mile, turn right onto the Goodman Trail. At 1.9 miles, turn left onto a side trail that leads to a nice swimming spot and small waterfall. Continue on the main trail until you reach a log bridge that spans Goodman Creek at 2 miles. This picturesque creek promises more wading as well as opportunities to find the perfect stick. Turn around here or continue as the trail parallels the creek another 2.2 miles and then climbs steeply to a viewpoint atop Eagles Rest Summit at 6.7 miles. If you decide to hike to Eagles Rest, be ready to tackle the 1,800 feet of elevation gain from here to the summit.

Larison Creek Hike

Contact: Middle Fork Ranger District, Lowell Office, 60 South Pioneer St., Lowell, OR 97452, 541-937-2129, www.fs.fed.us
Paw-Approval Rating: 4 paws
Leashes Required? No
Length: 10.2 miles out and back
Difficulty: Moderate

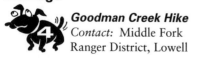

Fees/Permits: $5 Northwest Forest Pass. Purchase at 1-800-270-7504 or www. naturenw.org.

Season: May through October

Getting There: From I-5 in Eugene, take exit 188A, Highway 58/Oakridge/Klamath Falls. Head southeast on Highway 58 for about 36 miles to Oakridge. From the bridge crossing Salmon Creek in Oakridge, travel 1.4 miles east on Highway 58 to Kitson Springs Road (Forest Road 23) at the Hills Creek Dam sign. Turn right on Kitson Springs Road and travel 0.5 mile to Diamond Dr. (Forest Road 21). Turn right on Diamond Dr. and go 2.4 miles to a dirt parking lot and trailhead on the right side of the road. The trailhead is marked with a brown hiker sign.

Description: This gorgeous trail climbs over 700 feet as it sweeps up Larison Creek Canyon. Moss-coated logs, old-growth trees, and rocks create a glistening green canvas, and the soothing sounds of the creek invite your dog to cool off. Start the hike on the singletrack Larison Creek Trail. Follow it as it parallels the creek 5.1 miles to your turnaround point at a bridgeless creek crossing, where a huge log spans the creek. This trail is open to mountain bikes.

Middle Fork of the Willamette River Hike

Contact: Middle Fork Ranger District, Lowell Office, 60 South Pioneer St., Lowell, OR 97452, 541-937-2129, www.fs.fed.us

Paw-Approval Rating: 4 paws

Leashes Required? No

Length: 33.1 miles

Difficulty: Easy to Difficult

Fees/Permits: $5 Northwest Forest Pass. Purchase at 1-800-270-7504 or www. naturenw.org.

Season: June through November

Getting There: From I-5 in Eugene, take exit 188A, Highway 58/Oakridge/Klamath Falls. Head southeast on Highway 58 about 36 miles to Oakridge. From Oakridge, travel 1.4 miles east on Highway 58 to a

turnoff for Hills Creek Dam. Turn south and go 0.5 mile, and then turn right on Forest Road 21. Follow Forest Road 21 for 28.7 miles until you reach Indigo Springs Campground. Turn left into the campground and park in the hiker parking area. If you don't want to start from this trailhead, be on the lookout for other Middle Fork trailhead signs along Forest Road 21.

Description: This trail parallels the Middle Fork of the Willamette for over 33 miles. You and your pooch will love this beautiful river trail as it passes through cool, mossy forest and offers many opportunities for fantastic swim sessions and games of fetch. Begin the hike by walking out to Forest Road 21 and turning left. Continue a short distance and turn right at the Middle Fork Trail sign. Continue on a wide doubletrack trail until you see another trailhead sign on the right. Turn right on this spur trail until you reach the Middle Fork Trail. You have the option of turning right and following the trail 19 miles west, or, turning left to explore the trail as it continues east for about 14 miles. Let your dog decide when it is time to turn around. This trail is open to mountain bikes.

Salmon Creek Hike
(See *Cycling for Canines*)

Waldo Lake Hike

Contact: Middle Fork Ranger District, Lowell Office, 60 South Pioneer St., Lowell, OR 97452, 541-937-2129, www.fs.fed.us

Paw-Approval Rating: 4 paws

Leashes Required? No

Length: 4.6 miles out and back (with longer options)

Difficulty: Easy (Moderate if you hike around the entire lake)

Fees/Permits: $5 Northwest Forest Pass. Purchase at 1-800-270-7504 or www. naturenw.org.

Season: Late June through October

Getting There: From I-5 in Eugene, take exit 188A, Highway 58/Oakridge/Klamath Falls. Head southeast on Highway 58

about 36 miles to Oakridge. Continue about 24 miles east of Oakridge on Highway 58, and turn left on Forest Road 5897. Travel on Forest Road 5897 for 7 miles to the junction with Forest Road 5896. Turn left on Forest Road 5896 and continue about 2 miles to the boat ramp parking area at Shadow Bay Campground (see *Campgrounds*).

Description: Waldo Lake, the headwaters of the Middle Fork of the Willamette River, is in the Waldo Lake Wilderness. With a 410 feet maximum depth, Waldo Lake is the second deepest natural lake in Oregon (Crater Lake is the deepest), and is also one of the largest natural lakes in the state.

Hike along the shores of this pristine lake on the 21-mile long Waldo Lake Trail, which circles the entire lake. Pick the trail on the left side of the parking area and follow it as it skirts the edge of Shadow Bay and follows the lakeshore. Keep your eye open for good swimming holes. At 1.7 miles, you'll reach the South Waldo Lake Shelter. Continue right on your journey around the lake. At 2.3 miles, you'll reach a trail junction, your turnaround point, or continue on the trail as far as you want. This trail is open to mountain bikes for its entire length.

Cottage Grove

Brice Creek Hike

Contact: Umpqua National Forest, Cottage Grove District, Cottage Grove, OR, 541-942-5591, www.fs.fed.us

Paw-Approval Rating: 4 paws

Leashes Required? Yes

Length: 12.2 miles out and back (with longer options)

Difficulty: Easy

Fees/Permits: None

Season: Year-round

Getting There: From Eugene, travel about 18 miles south on I-5 to Cottage Grove. At Cottage Grove, take exit 174. At the end of the off-ramp, turn left (east) onto Row River Road and continue 4.3 miles to a

road junction with Shoreview Dr. Continue straight on Shoreview Dr. (Row River Road heads left) 7 miles to where it merges with Row River Road. Bear right and continue east on Row River Road 8.1 miles and then turn right onto Brice Creek Road (which turns into Forest Road 22). Proceed 3.4 miles on Forest Road 22 and park in the Brice Creek Trailhead pull-out on the left side of the road.

Description: This hike ascends 600 feet through a deep forest of towering old growth Douglas fir and red cedar along the banks of picturesque Brice Creek in the Umpqua National Forest. Follow the trail as it sweeps along the creek through a carpet of mossy rocks, logs, sword fern, Oregon grape, and oxalis. After 1.5 miles, you'll pass a side trail on the right that leads to Cedar Creek Campground. At 1.7 miles, stop for a refreshing swim at a small waterfall with a deep pool. At 4.7 miles, you have the option of turning left on a 2-mile loop trail that leads to the feathery cascade of Upper Trestle Falls. At 5.2 miles, turn left onto a side trail that leads you 0.3 mile to Lower Trestle Falls. After viewing this charming cascade, head back to the main trail, turn left, and continue 0.3 mile to the trail's end and your turnaround point. This trail is open to mountain bikes.

Row River Hike

Contact: Bureau of Land Management, Eugene District, Eugene, OR 541-683-6600, www.edo.or.blm.gov

Paw-Approval Rating: 3 paws

Leashes Required? Yes

Length: 10.6 miles out and back

Difficulty: Easy

Fees/Permits: None

Season: Year-round

Getting There: From Eugene, travel about 18 miles south on I-5 to Cottage Grove. At Cottage Grove, take exit 174. At the end of the off-ramp, turn left (east) on Row River Road. Drive one mile east on Row River Road and then turn right onto Currin

Conn Road. Immediately after this turn, take a quick left on Mosby Creek Road. Go 2 miles southeast on Mosby Creek Road and then turn left on Layng Road. Just after this turn, take a quick left into the Mosby Creek Trailhead parking lot.

Description: This rail-trail is managed by the BLM. The original rail line was built in 1902; steam engines carried logs, ore, supplies, and passengers along the route, which terminated at the town of Disston. This tour starts at the Mosby Creek Trailhead, which has restrooms and water, and ascends an easy 170 feet to your turnaround point at the Harms Park Trailhead.

From the parking area, this paved trail heads northeast. Just before crossing a picturesque bridge over Mosby Creek, check out the Mosby Creek Covered Bridge located just to the right. One of Oregon's historic covered bridges, it was built in 1920, with extensive restoration work completed in 1990. After 1.3 miles, you'll cross the Row River. This swift-moving river once was used to float logs to over 20 mills that operated along its banks. After crossing the river, the route turns southeast and takes you past oak woodlands, wetlands, and small farms. At 3.4 miles, you'll arrive at Dorena Trailhead, on the northwest edge of Dorena Lake, a reservoir. From here, check out the 150-foot-high earthen dam built to prevent floods and provide irrigation and recreation for the surrounding communities. Continue on the paved trail as it hugs the northern shore of Dorena Lake. You'll pass through a shady Douglas fir forest with many open areas to view the lake. Your turnaround point is the Harms Park trailhead at 5.3 miles. This trailhead has restrooms but no water.

CYCLING FOR CANINES

Springfield and the McKenzie River

McKenzie River Trail
(See *Paw-Approved Hikes and Parks*)

Oakridge

Larison Creek Trail
(See *Paw-Approved Hikes and Parks*)

Middle Fork of the Willamette River Trail
(See *Paw-Approved Hikes and Parks*)

 ### Salmon Creek Trail

Contact: Willamette National Forest, Middle Fork Ranger District, Lowell Office, 60 South Pioneer St., Lowell, OR 97452, 541-937-2129, www.fs.fed.us

Paw-Approval Rating: 4 paws
Leashes Required? No
Length: 7.6 miles out and back
Difficulty: Easy
Fees/Permits: None
Season: Year-round

Getting There: From I-5 in Eugene, take exit 188A, Highway 58/Oakridge/Klamath Falls. Head southeast on Highway 58 about 36 miles to Oakridge. From the bridge crossing Salmon Creek in Oakridge, travel 1.2 miles east on Highway 58 to Fish Hatchery Road. Turn left on Fish Hatchery Road, go 1.3 miles, and turn right on an obscure dirt lane that takes you to the trailhead. (You'll reach this turnoff immediately after you cross a bridge over Salmon Creek.)

Description: Your cycling hound will love this fast, easy route that ascends 140 feet through shady forest along the banks of cheery Salmon Creek. Begin the ride on a dirt path that quickly heads downhill and crosses a wood bridge. The path then widens and winds under a shady canopy of Douglas fir and big leaf maple. At 0.1 mile, stay left. At 0.4 mile, ignore a doubletrack road that heads left. At 0.9 mile, the route passes under a train trestle. At 1.3 miles, turn right on the signed Fitness Trail. At 2 miles, cross a doubletrack road and continue straight on the singletrack trail. At the next trail junction, turn right. At 2.5 miles, the trail narrows on a steep bank above the creek. Ignore a spur trail that heads left toward a paved road. At 2.6 miles, the trail turns into a doubletrack road. Go 200 yards and arrive at a road junction. Continue straight and ignore the doubletrack road that peels off to the right. At 3.3 miles, turn left at the trail junction. (The trail that goes right dead ends at a primitive campsite.) Go another 30 feet and then take a sharp right on an unmarked singletrack trail. At 3.4 miles, the trail intersects paved Salmon Creek Road. Turn right and ride on the dirt trail next to Salmon Creek Road. At 3.6 miles, turn right on the signed Salmon Creek Trail 4365. At 3.7 miles, turn right on a doubletrack road and follow this road 0.1 mile to a primitive camping area. Continue toward the creek and pick up a singletrack trail. At 3.8 miles, arrive at a picturesque wood bridge spanning Salmon Creek (your turnaround point). Retrace the route back to your starting point.

Waldo Lake Trail
(See *Paw-Approved Hikes and Parks*)

Cottage Grove

Brice Creek Trail
(See *Paw-Approved Hikes and Parks*)

Row River Trail
(See *Paw-Approved Hikes and Parks*)

POWDERHOUNDS

The Willamette Pass area, 67 miles southeast of Eugene off Oregon Highway 58, boasts seven distinct trail systems accessed via four different snow parks. To get started, check out Gold Lake Sno-Park, located about 1 mile west of Willamette Pass on the south side of Highway 58, which provides access to many trails. Dogs are not allowed on the groomed cross-country trails at Odell Lake.

To find out more about other snow parks and trails in the area, contact the Willamette National Forest Supervisor's Office, Federal Building, 211 East 7th Ave., P.O. Box 10607, Eugene, OR 97440, 541-225-6300, www.fs.fed.us. Another great resource is *Cross-Country Ski Routes: Oregon* by Klindt Vielbig.

PADDLEHOUNDS

Just west of Eugene, near the home of the Oregon Country Fair, lies the Fern Ridge Reservoir, whose warm waters make it a great place to let your dog paddle. This manmade lake has about 30 miles of shoreline and an average depth of only 11 feet. The Long Tom River feeds it from the north; several other creeks also flow into it. Over 250 species of birds inhabit the area during the various seasons, such as blue heron, duck, swan, geese, egret, osprey, bald eagle, and a variety of shorebirds. Launch your boat at Richardson Park. From I-5 in Eugene, take exit 194B, Highway 105/126. Head west 1.4 miles and take exit 2, Coburg Road/Downtown. Go 2 miles and follow signs for Highway 126 West/Florence. (You are now on 6th Ave.) Proceed 1 mile and then turn left on Garfield St. toward Veneta/Florence/Elmira. Go 0.4 mile and then turn right on Highway 126 West. Head west 4.3 miles and then turn right (north) on Green Hill Road. Travel 3.5 miles on Green Hill Road, turn left (west) on Clear Lake Road and then go 6.2 miles on Clear Lake Road to Richardson Park and Campground.

East of Eugene, the high mountain lakes in the Willamette National Forest, the Waldo Lake Wilderness, and the Three Sisters Wilderness offer water dogs wonderful mountain scenery. One of our favorite boating spots is Clear Lake. This beautiful 148-acre lake, the headwaters for the McKenzie River, is 175 feet deep. Launch your boat from Cold Water Cove Campground (see *Campgrounds*), 18 miles northeast of McKenzie Bridge off Highway 126.

Another favorite high mountain lake is Scott Lake with its gorgeous views of North, Middle, and South Sister mountains. This lake's 1.8-mile long shoreline makes it easy to explore. You'll also be assured of a peaceful paddle because motorized boats are not allowed here. Launch your boat at Scott Lake Campground. To get there, travel 3 miles east of McKenzie Bridge on Highway 126 to the junction with Highway 242. Follow Highway 242 for 14 miles east to the campground.

Waldo Lake, another high lake, should not be missed. Launch your boat from the boat launch at Shadow Bay Campground (see *Campgrounds*). The lake is about 2.5 miles wide and 6 miles long, with 21 miles of shoreline. It's worth spending a few days exploring; you can camp overnight at one of the many primitive sites around the lake. From I-5 in Eugene, take exit 188A, Highway 58/Oakridge/Klamath Falls. Head southeast on Highway 58 about 36 miles to Oakridge. Continue about another 24 miles east on Highway 58 and turn left on Forest Road 5897. Travel on Forest Road 5897 for 7 miles to the junction with Forest Road 5896. Turn left on Forest Road 5896 and continue about 2 miles to the boat ramp parking area at Shadow Bay Campground.

Another high lake gem is Gold Lake, where motorized boats are verboten. It's a great place to enjoy some peace and quiet with your dog. Gold Lake has a campground (see *Campgrounds*) with a boat launch, hiking trails, and a mountain biking trail nearby. Head south from Eugene on I-5 and take exit 188. Turn east on Oregon 58 and go about 62 miles to Gold Lake Road Turn left (north) on Gold Lake Road and travel 2 miles to the campground.

All of these high mountain lakes are generally not accessible until July. Mosquitoes are usually a problem during July and the first few weeks in August. Bring plenty of bug juice.

CANINE COMFORT ACCOMMODATIONS

Unless otherwise stated, dogs should not be left unattended in the room and must be leashed on hotel property.

Eugene

$-$$ Classic Residence Inn
1140 W. 6th Ave., 541-343-0730, www.classicresidenceinn.com

This hotel features air-conditioned rooms with cable TV/HBO, a mini-fridge, and microwave.
Dog Policy
The hotel charges $5.50 per dog per night.

$-$$ Courtesy Inn
345 W. 6th Ave., 541-345-3391 or 1-888-259-8481

This budget hotel has four dog-friendly rooms with cable TV and free HBO, and is located two blocks from a large park where you can walk your dog.
Dog Policy
The hotel charges a $10 fee per dog per night.

$$ Best Western Greentree Inn
1759 Franklin Blvd., 541-485-2727

All the rooms in this hotel are dog-friendly. Amenities include a pool, Jacuzzi, and exercise room. A continental breakfast is included. The hotel is within walking distance of jogging and biking paths along the Willamette River in downtown Eugene (see *Paw-Approved Hikes and Parks*).
Dog Policy
No additional fees are charged for your dog. Your dog cannot be left unattended in your room and must be leashed on hotel property.

$$ Best Western New Oregon Hotel
1655 Franklin Blvd., 541-683-3669

This hotel is located across from the University of Oregon in downtown Eugene. All rooms are dog-friendly. A pool, Jacuzzi, and exercise room are available, and a continental breakfast is included. The hotel is within walking distance of jogging and biking paths along the Willamette River in downtown Eugene (see *Paw-Approved Hikes and Parks*).

Dog Policy
No additional fees are charged for your dog. Your dog cannot be left unattended in your room and must be leashed on hotel property.

$$ Days Inn
1859 Franklin Blvd., 541-342-6383, www.daysinn.com
This hotel has sixty rooms in downtown Eugene. Amenities include a complimentary continental breakfast, hot tub, and sauna.
Dog Policy
Well-behaved dogs are allowed at no extra charge.

$$-$$$ Red Lion Hotel
205 Coburg Rd., 541-342-5201, www.redlion.com
This hotel is a mile north of Eugene's city center and fifteen minutes from the airport via complimentary hotel transportation. Its 137 rooms are furnished with telephones, data ports, hair dryers, irons and ironing boards, and cable TV. The hotel also has a restaurant and lounge, heated pool, and hot tub.
Dog Policy
Fido gets to stay free.

$$$-$$$$ Eugene Hilton
66 E. Sixth Ave., 541-342-2000
This comfortable hotel is located in downtown Eugene, within walking distance of the Willamette River, many downtown parks, and the University of Oregon. Amenities include a pool and hot tub, exercise room, and a restaurant and lounge.
Dog Policy
The hotel only accepts well-behaved dogs and charges a one-time $25 pet fee per dog.

$$$-$$$$ Valley River Inn
1000 Valley River Way, 541-687-0123, www.valleyriverinn.com
This four star hotel is adjacent to the Valley River Shopping Center in downtown Eugene as well as the Willamette River

running and biking paths. Many rooms and suites overlook the river. All rooms have hair dryers, coffee pots, irons and ironing boards, and complimentary morning newspapers. Additional amenities include Jacuzzi and sauna, seasonal outdoor pool, and bicycle rentals. All ground floor rooms are dog-friendly.
Dog Policy
Well-behaved dogs stay for free.

SPRINGFIELD AND THE MCKENZIE RIVER

Blue River

$-$$ Motel 6
3690 Glenwood Dr., 541-687-2395
Dog Policy
Well-behaved dogs are allowed at no extra charge. The hotel allows only one dog per room.

$$-$$$ Shilo Inn
3350 Gateway, 541-747-0332 or 1-800-222-2244, www.shiloinns.com
This hotel has 142 dog-friendly rooms. Some rooms are suites with full-service kitchens. Additional amenities include a complimentary *USA Today,* satellite TV with premium channels, VCR and movie rentals, outdoor seasonal pool, guest Laundromat, room service, and a restaurant and lounge.
Dog Policy
A one-time fee of $10 is charged for your dog.

$$$ Adventure River House
49701 McKenzie Highway, 1-888-547-5565
You and your dog will enjoy this vacation home rental that features open beam ceilings and a wood stove, and can sleep up to four people. It also has a TV/VCR, stereo, and sitting room. Dogs can stay in the house or in the fenced backyard with its 5' by 10' dog run.
Dog Policy
No fees are charged for your dog.

Cottage Grove

$$ Holiday Inn Express
1601 Gateway Blvd., 503-942-1000

This hotel, located at exit 174 off I-5 in Cottage Grove, has five dog-friendly rooms. Additional amenities include an indoor pool, spa, and exercise room. This hotel is located close to the Row River Trail (see *Paw-Approved Hikes and Parks*).

Dog Policy
The hotel charges $10 per dog per night.

Oakridge

$$ Best Western Oakridge Inn
47433 Highway 58, 541-782-2212

This hotel is located close to many hiking and biking trails in the Willamette National forest. Its forty guestrooms have cable TV with HBO, hair dryers, coffeemakers, irons, and ironing boards. Suites with kitchens are available. A seasonal swimming pool and year round hot tub are available. A complimentary continental breakfast is included.

Dog Policy
A $5 fee per night per dog is charged.

Vida

$$-$$$ McKenzie River B&B and Cabins
49164 McKenzie Highway, 541-822-6260, www.mckenzieriverinn.com

Hubertina and Bert de Klery are the owners of this wonderful resort, one of the oldest along the McKenzie River. If you stay in one of the lodge's three bedrooms, you'll receive a hot gourmet breakfast of salmon omelets or hazelnut pancakes. The lodge features a living room with cozy fireplace, sunroom with library, and dining room.

The three cabins have fully equipped kitchens and a TV/VCR. The Atrium cabin, which sleeps four, has a breathtaking view of the river, a walk-in shower and Jacuzzi, and a small courtyard. The Osprey cabin has a separate bedroom with a queen bed, a hide-a-bed, and a panoramic view of an osprey nest across the river. The River Otter cabin, which sleeps five, is a two-story guesthouse with a private deck.

Dog Policy
No extra fees are charged for your dog. Really large dogs and their owners are asked to choose a cabin instead of a room in the lodge. Doggie blankets for your best friend are provided.

$$-$$$ Wayfarer Resort
46725 Goodpasture Rd., 1-800-627-3613, www.wayfarerresort.com

This resort is located on ten acres on the banks of the spring-fed McKenzie River and glacier-fed Marten Creek. It has one dog-friendly, non-smoking cabin that has a full kitchen, cozy fireplace, and cable TV.

Dog Policy
A $10 fee per day is charged for your dog.

Willamette Pass Area

Odell Lake Resort
P.O. Box 72, Crescent Lake, OR 97425, 1-800-434-2540

This resort is located 6 miles east of Willamette Pass off Highway 58. Its dog-friendly cabins have a full kitchen, wood stove, propane heat, bathroom, and linens.

Dog Policy
A $5 fee per night per dog is charged. Only one dog is allowed per cabin. Dogs are not allowed on the groomed cross-country ski trails at the lake.

CAMPGROUNDS

Eugene

Richardson Park
Contact: Lane County Parks, 90064 Coburg Rd., Eugene, OR 97408, 541-682-4414 (information), 541-935-2005 (reservations), www.co.lane.or.us
Season: Mid-April through mid-October
Facilities: 88 electrical hook-up sites, showers, restrooms, picnic area, boat launch, RV dump station

Getting There: From I-5 in Eugene take exit 194B, Highway 105/126. Head west 1.4 miles and take exit 2, Coburg Road/Downtown. Go 2 miles and follow signs for Highway 126 West/Florence (you are now on 6th Ave.). Proceed 1 mile and then turn left on Garfield St. toward Veneta/Florence/Elmira. Go 0.4 mile and then turn right on 126 West toward Veneta/Florence/Elmira. Head west on Highway 126 for 4.3 miles and then turn right (north) on Green Hill Road. Travel 3.5 miles on Green Hill Road and then turn left (west) on Clear Lake Road. Go 6.2 miles on Clear Lake Road to Richardson Park and the campground.

Description: This mostly forested campground is adjacent to Fern Ridge Reservoir. (See *Paddlehounds*) A favorite activity is paddling on the reservoir.

McKenzie River Area

Cold Water Cove

Contact: Willamette National Forest, McKenzie Ranger District, 57600 McKenzie Highway, McKenzie Bridge, OR 97413, 541-822-3381, www.fs.fed.us
Season: Late May through mid-October
Facilities: 35 tent sites (no electrical hookups; 12 sites can be reserved), water, restrooms, fire rings, picnic tables, boat launch
Getting There: From McKenzie Bridge, travel 18 miles northeast on Highway 126 to the campground.
Description: This forested campground is located on the shores of Clear Lake—headwaters of the McKenzie River. From the campground you and your pup can enjoy a five-mile hike around the lake, or explore this beautiful lake by boat. The McKenzie River Trail is also nearby.

French Pete

Contact: Willamette National Forest, Blue River Ranger District, P.O. Box 199, Blue River, OR 97413, 541-822-3317, www.fs.fed.us
Season: Mid-May through mid-September

Facilities: 17 tent sites (no electrical hookups), water, restrooms, fire rings, picnic tables
Getting There: Travel about 5 miles east of Blue River (Blue River is about 45 miles east of Eugene) on Highway 126. Turn right (south) on Forest Road 19 (Aufderheide Dr.) and continue 10.5 miles to the campground.
Description: This pristine campground is located on the banks of the South Fork of the McKenzie River in a mossy forest of towering old trees. The campground is close to the French Pete Creek hike (see *Paw-Approved Hikes and Parks*).

Paradise

Contact: Willamette National Forest, McKenzie Ranger District, 57600 McKenzie Highway, McKenzie Bridge, OR 97413, 541-822-3381, www.fs.fed.us
Season: Mid-May through October 31
Facilities: 64 tent sites (no electrical hookups; 20 sites can be reserved), fire rings, piped drinking water, restrooms, picnic tables, boat launch, day-use picnic area
Getting There: From McKenzie Bridge (McKenzie Bridge is about 50 miles east of Eugene) head 4 miles east on Highway 126 to the campground.
Description: Sites at this campground are scattered among towering red cedars along the shores of the McKenzie River. You can access the 26.5-mile McKenzie River Trail from the campground. This national scenic trail takes you and your dog on an amazing journey along the crystal clear McKenzie. Mountain bikes are allowed the entire length of this trail. For the longest ride, head east on the trail from the campground.

Oakridge

Gold Lake

Contact: Middle Fork Ranger District, Lowell Office, 60 South Pioneer St., Lowell, OR 97452, 541-937-2129, www.fs.fed.us
Season: Late June through October

Facilities: 24 tent sites (no electrical hook-ups), 1 walk-in site, water, vault toilets, fire rings, picnic tables, ADA sites, recycle center, log shelter, boat launch

Getting There: To get to Gold Lake head south from Eugene on I-5 and take exit 188. Turn east on Oregon 58 and drive about 62 miles to Gold Lake Road. Turn left (north) on Gold Lake Road and travel about 2 miles to the campground.

Description: This forested campground is along the shores of Gold Lake. This lake allows only non-motorized boats, so it's a peaceful place to paddle with your pooch. If you are looking for a fun hike, check out the 3-mile hike to Bobby Lake, accessible from the campground. Cycling enthusiasts can also crank on some great singletrack on the 5.8-mile Maiden Peak Trail that climbs over 2,900 feet to the summit of Maiden Peak. This trailhead is located about 0.5 mile south of the campground on Gold Lake Road.

Shadow Bay at Waldo Lake

Contact: Middle Fork Ranger District, Lowell Office, 60 South Pioneer St., Lowell, OR 97452, 541-937-2129, www.fs.fed.us

Season: July through September

Facilities: 92 tent sites (no electrical hookups), water, restrooms, fire rings, picnic tables, recycle center, boat launch

Getting There: From I-5 in Eugene, take exit 188A, Highway 58/Oakridge/Klamath Falls. Head southeast on Highway 58 about 36 miles to Oakridge. Continue approximately 24 miles east of Oakridge on Highway 58 and turn left on Forest Road 5897. Travel on Forest Road 5897 for 7 miles to the junction with Forest Road 5896. Turn left on Forest Road 5896 and continue about 2 miles to Shadow Bay Campground.

Description: This campground is located on the southeast end of Waldo Lake and gives access to many hiking trails, including the Waldo Lake Trail (see *Paw-Approved Hikes and Parks*) that encircles

the lake. Swimming and paddling are also worthy afternoon pursuits. Mosquitoes are a problem during July and August. Bring plenty of bug juice.

DOG EVENTS
Eugene

Wag'n Trail Fun Walk and Run
Greenhill Humane Society, 88530 Green Hill Rd., 541-689-1503, www.green-hill.org

This annual event, held the third Saturday in July, features a 2K walk and 5K fun run at Alton Baker Park in downtown Eugene. Over 150 participants and their dogs help raise money for the Greenhill Humane Society.

CANINE-APPROVED SHOPPING
Eugene

Mini Pet Mart
974 W. 6th St., 541-344-9603

This friendly store carries a full line of toys, treats, food, and travel and home supplies for canines and other small pets. Brands of dog food include Nutro, Canidae, Avo, Nature's Recipe, Diamond, Sensible Choice, Kasco, Pedigree, Whiskas, and Purina. Open 9 A.M.–7 P.M., Monday to Saturday; 10 A.M.–6 P.M. Sunday.

Petco
1169 Valley River Dr., 541-485-7900, www.petco.com

Open 9 A.M.–9 P.M., Monday to Saturday; 10 A.M.–7:30 P.M. Sunday.

Petsmart
2847 Chad Dr., 541-683-3353, www.petsmart.com

Open 9 A.M.–9 P.M., Monday to Saturday; 10 A.M.–7 P.M. Sunday.

Zany Zoo Pets
3390 W. 11th St., 541-345-3430

This store carries a full line of dog supplies and Nutura dog foods. Grooming services are available. Your leashed dog is welcome. Open 10:30 A.M.–7:30 P.M., Monday to Saturday; 11 A.M.–6 P.M., Sunday.

DOG WASHES

Eugene

Suds Em Yourself
192 W. 11th Ave., 541-484-2239
Prices range from $7 for a small dog to $13 for an extra-large dog. This price includes your choice of shampoos (herbal flea or tearless), two towels, brushes and other grooming tools, apron, forced air dryers, and hand dryers. Have your dog's nails trimmed for an additional $2. Also available are Nutro Max food and treats, ID tags, breath freshener, joint supplements, Frontline Flea and Tick Control, and more. Open 10 A.M.–7 P.M., Tuesday to Friday; 8:30 A.M.–6 P.M., Saturday; 10 A.M.–6 P.M., Sunday.

CANINE ER

Springfield

Eugene/Springfield
Emergency Veterinary Hospital
103 W. Q. St., Springfield, 541-746-0112
Open 6 P.M.–8 A.M., Monday to Friday; 12 P.M. Saturday to 8 A.M. Monday.

Cottage Grove

Cottage Grove Veterinary Clinic
1221 East Main St., 541-942-9181
This clinic offers overnight boarding for $12 per dog per night.
Open 8 A.M.–6 P.M., Monday to Friday; 8 A.M.–1 P.M., Saturday.

LOST AND FOUND (ANIMAL SHELTERS)

Eugene

Greenhill Humane Society
88530 Green Hill Rd., 541-689-1503, www.green-hill.org
Open 11 A.M.–6 P.M., Friday to Tuesday.

Cottage Grove

Humane Society
of Cottage Grove
2555 Mosby Creek Rd., Cottage Grove, 541-942-3130

Columbia River Gorge/ Mount Hood

*A*dventurous canines will love the Columbia River Gorge National Scenic Area, just a thirty-minute drive east of Portland on I-84. This National Scenic Area, established in 1986, is home to one of the highest concentrations of waterfalls in North America, and stretches for sixty miles on both sides of the river, from Troutdale to The Dalles, Oregon, on the south, and from Camas to Lyle, Washington, on the north. Hundreds of miles of trails wind up cliffs and through side canyons, with cool shade and cold streams—the theme of most gorge trails.

Dogs are required to be leashed on all trails in both the National Scenic Area and in all state parks and campgrounds within the Gorge. The only state park that does not allow dogs is Dabney State Park on the Sandy River just east of Troutdale.

THE BIG SCOOP

Hood River
The Columbia River Gorge is home to the laid back and dog-loving town of Hood River. This town is an internationally known wind surfing and mountain biking mecca. Canines fit right into the outdoor groove here. If you are cruising through downtown Hood River on Oak Street, you'll find many eateries with outdoor patios where canines are welcome. Recommended are Andrews Pizza and Bakery (107 Oak St.) and Mike's Ice Cream (504 Oak St.). Gorge Dog (410 Oak St.) stocks gear and gifts that even the most discriminating Fido and Fifi will appreciate. Hood River is also the gateway to great hikes and bikes in the Hood River Valley and on Mount Hood. The Mount Hood National Forest features spectacular trails that wind along wild and scenic rivers and take you and your pup to scenic vistas and around high alpine lakes.

Dogs are required to be leashed within Hood River's city limits but can be unleashed on national forest trails as long as they are under voice control.

Mount Hood

As the tallest peak in Oregon at 11,235 feet, Mount Hood is a well-known landmark in Northwest Oregon and is the centerpiece of the immense 1.2 million-acre Mount Hood National Forest. At about 780,000 years old, Mount Hood is young compared to other Cascade peaks. Classified as a stratovolcano, the mountain has had four eruptive periods over the last 15,000 years. Evidence of recent volcanic activity is present at Crater Rock, a volcanic lava dome believed by geologists to be only 200 years old. The dome is located south of the summit and emits a steady outflow of sulfur gas and steam. Mountain dogs can explore many different trails that provide outstanding views of this gorgeous Cascade peak. Some of our favorites are Lost Lake, Cooper Spur, Mazama Trail #625, Mirror Lake, and McNeil Point.

The Dalles

Located a quick 15 miles east of Hood River on I-84 is the small, hard-working community of The Dalles. Established in 1857, The Dalles served for years as the center of trade and transport for goods transported via the Columbia River between western and eastern Oregon. Fur trappers congregated here before shipping their furs to Fort Vancouver, and The Dalles was the put-in for pioneers who braved the Columbia's once-fierce rapids on their trek to the Willamette Valley. While Fido may yawn at the area's history, you can learn more about it at the architecturally gorgeous Columbia Gorge Discovery Center and Wasco County Historical Museum (5000 Discovery Dr., The Dalles, OR 97058, 541-296-8600, www.gorge discovery.org). Fido (much to his delight) cannot tour the museum, but he can walk with you on the 1.3-mile paved Riverfront Trail that begins outside the museum and heads east along the Columbia.

The Dalles is gateway to many outdoor destinations you and your dog can explore. Don't miss Deschutes River State Park, which features a shady campground, hiking trails, and a multi-use hiking and mountain biking trail that follows a rail-line along the banks of the Deschutes (see Paw-Approved Hikes and Parks).

Dogs do not have to be leashed within The Dalles city limits or in other towns within Wasco County, though they must be under voice control. The only exceptions are some city parks in The Dalles, Deschutes River State Park, and White River Falls State Park, all of which require that dogs be leashed.

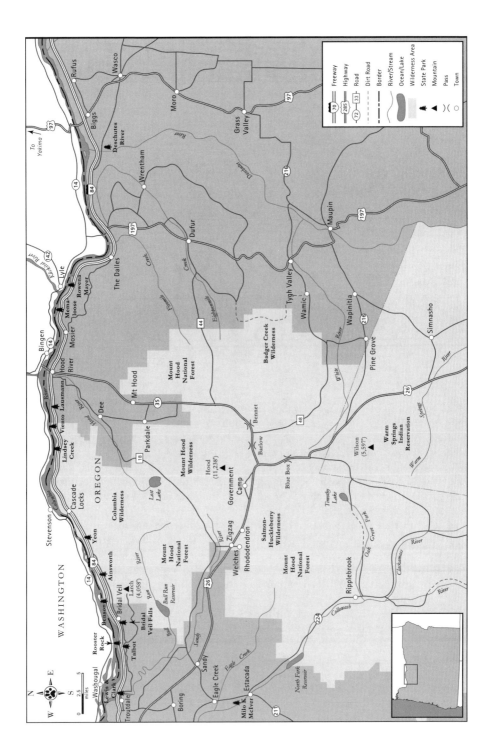

Columbia River Gorge

PAW-APPROVED HIKES AND PARKS

Hikes and parks in this section are listed in geographical order, starting on the west end of the Columbia River Gorge near Portland and heading east toward Hood River.

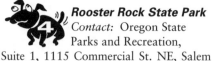

Rooster Rock State Park

Contact: Oregon State Parks and Recreation, Suite 1, 1115 Commercial St. NE, Salem OR 97301-1002, 1-800-551-6949, www.oregonstateparks.org
Paw-Approval Rating: 4 paws
Leashes Required? Yes except in the off-leash area.
Fees/Permits: $3 day-use fee payable at the entrance booth.
Season: Year-round.
Getting There: From the intersection of I-205 and I-84 in Portland, travel 15.5 miles east on I-84 to Rooster Rock State Park, exit 22. Go 0.5 mile to the entrance booth and pay a $3 entrance fee. For the off-leash area, drive past the entrance booth 0.1 mile to a T-junction. Turn left toward the signed Pet Exercise Area. Continue 0.4 mile to the parking area on the right. The pet exercise area is located across the paved entrance road from the parking area.
Description: This large state park on the banks of the Columbia River has two miles of sandy beach and is probably most well known for its nude beach—one of two officially designated nude beaches in Oregon. What the park isn't as renowned for is its off-leash area: a large, unfenced grassy area shaded by huge old growth oak and maple trees. Restrooms and water are not far away and trash cans are available.

In addition, the park features several large picnic areas, a 2-mile walking path at its east end, and a boat launch. Windsurfing is popular here.

Angels Rest Hike

Contact: USDA Forest Service, Columbia River Gorge National Scenic Area, 902 Wasco Ave., Suite 200, Hood River, OR 97031, 541-386-2333, www.fs.fed.us
Paw-Approval Rating: 3 paws
Leashes Required? Yes
Length: 4.4 miles out and back
Difficulty: Difficult
Fees/Permits: None
Season: Year-round. This trail can be icy during winter.
Getting There: From the intersection of I-205 and I-84 in Portland travel about 18.5 miles east on I-84 to Bridal Veil Falls, exit 28. Continue 0.4 mile to a stop sign at the intersection with the Historic Columbia River Highway. Turn right onto the Highway and then turn right into the Angels Rest trailhead parking area on the right side of the highway. If you are coming from the east, take exit 35 off I-84 and travel approximately 7.3 miles west on the Historic Columbia River Highway until you reach the Angels Rest parking area on the right side of the highway.
Description: This challenging route climbs over 1,500 feet through a fern-filled forest to a spectacular viewpoint of the Columbia River Gorge. Start the hike by heading to the west end of the parking lot and crossing the highway. Walk up a short set of stone steps and then begin hiking on the signed dirt path. After about 100 yards

you'll arrive at a T-intersection. Stay left and continue on the main trail (the trail going right heads toward the overflow parking lot). At 0.3 mile, the trail heads up an open, rocky slope with good views of the Columbia River. At 0.5 mile, stop and admire the sweeping cascade of Coopey Falls from a viewpoint on your left. After 0.6 mile cross a wood bridge over tumbling Coopey Creek. This is a good spot to stop and let your hound cool off before continuing the steep trek to the summit. After 1.4 miles you'll pass through an old burn area from the early 1990s. Near the summit, you'll walk through a large boulder field that is home to a colony of rabbit-like rodents called pikas. After 2.2 miles, turn left at the trail junction, climb a short set of boulders, and continue until you reach the summit viewpoint. Hang on tightly to your pooch because the viewpoint is on a cliff with a steep drop-off. Lounge at the summit, admire the views of the gorge, and then retrace the route back to your starting point.

Bridal Veil Falls State Park Hike

Contact: Oregon State Parks and Recreation, Suite 1, 1115 Commercial St. NE, Salem OR 97301-1002, 1-800-551-6949, www.oregonstateparks.org

Paw-Approval Rating: 3 paws

Leashes Required? Yes

Length: 1 mile

Difficulty: Easy

Fees/Permits: None

Season: Year-round

Getting There: From the intersection of I-205 and I-84 in Portland, travel about 18.5 miles east on I-84 to Bridal Veil Falls, exit 28. Continue 0.4 mile to a stop sign at the intersection with the Historic Columbia River Highway. Turn (right) west on the Highway and travel 0.8 mile to Bridal Veil State Park on the right side of the highway.

Description: This state park features a picturesque picnic area and two scenic hiking trails. You'll begin the hike on the Overlook Loop Trail, which passes through a thick undergrowth of wild raspberries, bright purple lupine, fern, vine maple, and other bright wild flowers.

After 0.1 mile, you'll pass an interpretive sign on the left that describes the native people who have lived here for over 10,000 years. The Columbia River allowed the Chinookan-speaking people to travel via canoe and was an important trade route between the coast and the central and eastern part of the state. Traders gathered here from all over the Northwest at large, fair-like gatherings that featured gambling, games, races, dances, and ceremonial displays. The Native Indians' primary food source was salmon. Their diet was supplemented with native plants including wapato, camas, nuts, berries, and wild game.

As you continue on this trail, you'll pass through one of the largest remaining meadows of camas in the western part of the Columbia River Gorge. This edible plant can grow to 6 to 24 inches tall and is identified by its beautiful blue flowers that bloom from mid-April to May. Its small bulb was baked by Native Americans in earth ovens and then pressed into cakes. Pioneers also dined on camas and took care not to confuse it with the white-flowered, toxic death camas.

Other wildflowers on this trail include Oregon iris, the bright orange globes of tiger lily, and cliff penstemon. As you continue you'll pass more viewpoints of the Columbia River Gorge. The Overlook Loop Trail ends at the parking lot after 0.3 mile. The route continues on the Bridal Veil Falls Trail that travels through thick stands of big leaf maple, sword fern, vine maple, yarrow, wild rose, bright purple lupine, and wild raspberry. At 0.4 mile the paved trail turns to gravel and descends 75 feet into a creek canyon. After 0.6 mile, you'll cross a bridge over a bubbling creek. Just after the bridge a side trail leads down to the creek, where your dog may enjoy cooling off. From here, continue up a series of stairs to a viewpoint of the billowy cascade of the Bridal Veil Falls. This popular hike can be crowded on summer weekends.

 Latourell Falls Hike
Contact: Oregon State Parks and Recreation, Suite 1, 1115 Commercial St. NE, Salem OR 97301-1002, 1-800-551-6949, www.oregonstateparks.org
Paw-Approval Rating: 3 paws
Leashes Required? Yes
Length: 2.3 miles
Difficulty: Moderate
Fees/Permits: None
Season: Year-round
Getting There: From the intersection of I-205 and I-84 in Portland, travel about 18.5 miles east on I-84 to Bridal Veil Falls, exit 28. Continue 0.4 mile to a stop sign at the intersection with the Historic Columbia River Highway. Turn (right) west on the Highway and travel 2.7 miles to the Latourell Falls parking area on the left side of the highway.

Description: This loop trail has an elevation gain of 600 feet and takes you and your hound on a gorgeous waterfall tour of upper and lower Latourell Falls in Guy W. Talbot State Park. The trail heads left from the parking area and takes you 0.3 mile to a viewpoint of the shimmering cascade of 249-foot Lower Latourell Falls. From the viewpoint continue about 0.5 mile through thick undergrowth of vine maple, wild raspberry, and sword fern to the 100-foot cascade of Upper Latourell Falls. From the upper falls, descend 0.5 mile to a scenic viewpoint of the Columbia River Gorge. From here, keep following the trail as it continues downhill to the highway. Cross the highway and follow a path through a picturesque picnic area. Bear right at the trail junction and follow the paved path as it heads under the highway and leads you along the edge of the creek to Lower Latourell Falls. This is a good spot for your pup to cool off in the creek. From here, continue back to your starting point at 2.3 miles. This hike can be crowded on summer weekends.

Sage checking out the sights at Lower Latourell Falls.

 Wahkeena Falls Hike
Contact: USDA Forest Service, Columbia River Gorge National Scenic Area, 902 Wasco Ave., Suite 200, Hood River, OR 97031, 541-386-2333, www.fs.fed.us/r6/columbia
Paw-Approval Rating: 4 paws
Leashes Required? Yes
Length: 4.9-mile loop (with a longer option of 13.6 miles round-trip to the summit of Larch Mountain)
Difficulty: Difficult
Fees/Permits: None
Season: Year-round for the Wahkeena Falls Hike; June through October for the Larch Mountain Hike
Getting There: From the intersection of I-205 and I-84 in Portland, head 21 miles east on I-84 to Multnomah Falls, exit 31. Park in the large paved parking area. To

reach the trailhead, go through the tunnel (under I-84) and follow the broad paved steps which lead you to the trailhead behind Multnomah Falls Lodge.

Description: This strenuous hike has over 1,600 feet of elevation gain and is filled with bouldery creeks and plenty of shade for hiking hounds. The trail begins at historic Multnomah Falls Lodge and takes you and your pooch on a steep uphill climb on a paved path to the top of spectacular Multnomah Falls. You'll have to weave in and out of the crowds that hike this trail for the first mile, but then you'll leave them behind. At the top of Multnomah Falls, you'll reach the crest of the hill and then the paved trail begins to descend a short distance until you arrive at a T-intersection. Continue left on the dirt path (the path that heads right leads to an overlook of Multnomah Falls). Cross a stone bridge over the creek. After crossing the creek, the route enters the gorgeous Multnomah Creek canyon, with its waterfalls, rocky outcrops, and fern-covered hillsides. At 1.1 miles, you'll arrive at a T-intersection. Go left on Larch Mountain Trail 441. The trail continues upward as it turns away from Multnomah Creek and winds its way across a ridge through a magnificent fir forest. At 1.7 miles, you'll arrive at a T-intersection with a sign that indicates Wahkeena Trail 420/Wahkeena Trailhead 2.7/Angels Rest 1.2. Head right and continue your uphill journey on Wahkeena Trail 420. At 2.7 miles, Devil's Rest Trail 420C joins the trail from the left. Continue straight. Continue about another 100 feet to a T-intersection. Turn right where a sign indicates Vista Point 419/Wahkeena 1/Columbia River Highway 1.9. At 3.2 miles, you'll cross Wahkeena Creek and then continue 100 feet to a trail intersection toward Columbia Highway/Wahkeena Falls Trailhead 1.2. Turn right and continue your steep descent on multiple switchbacks next to Wahkeena Creek. At 3.5 miles, you'll pass the cascade of Upper Wahkeena Falls on your right—be sure to let your dog cool off in its misty spray. At 3.7 miles, you'll arrive at a T-intersection. Go right and continue your descent on a series of switchbacks that skip back and forth across Wahkeena Creek. At 4.2 miles, the trail turns to a paved path. Proceed another 100 yards and soak in the views of Lower Wahkeena Falls on your left. You'll finish the loop by hooking up with a short dirt path at the Wahkeena Falls trailhead that takes you back to your starting point at Multnomah Falls. This hike can be crowded on summer weekends.

Trail Option: For a longer trek, hike over 3,800 feet to the top of Larch Mountain to a gorgeous viewpoint at Sherrard Point. To complete this challenging option, turn left at 1.7 miles onto Larch Mountain Trail 441 where a sign states "Larch Mountain 5." (Wahkeena Trail 420 heads right at this junction.) Follow the trail as it ascends at a fast pace next to mossy Multnomah Creek. At 3 miles the singletrack trail intersects with a doubletrack road. Continue a short distance on the doubletrack to another trail junction. Turn right onto a singletrack trail, where a sign states "Larch Mountain Trail 4 miles." At 3.3 miles continue straight (right). (Franklin Ridge Trail 427 goes left.) At 5 miles, turn right at the trail fork. At 5.5 miles, cross a doubletrack road and continue powering uphill. At 6.5 miles, turn left at the trail fork. At 6.6 miles, arrive at a paved parking area. Cross the parking area and pick up the paved trail toward Sherrard Point. At 6.8 miles, you'll arrive at the 4,056-foot summit of Larch Mountain at Sherrard Point. From this viewpoint you'll have phenomenal views (on a clear day) of Mount Rainier, Mount St. Helens, Mount Adams, Mount Hood, Mount Jefferson, and the Columbia River Gorge. Retrace the route back to your starting point. If you attempt this strenuous hike, be sure to bring a lot of water and food for you and your dog. There is no water available at the summit.

Horsetail-Oneonta-Triple Falls Hike

Contact: USDA Forest Service, Columbia River Gorge National Scenic Area, 902 Wasco Ave., Suite 200, Hood River, OR 97031, 541-386-2333, www.fs.fed.us

Paw-Approval Rating: 4 paws
Leashes Required? Yes
Length: 6.4 miles out and back
Difficulty: Difficult
Fees/Permits: None
Season: Year-round
Getting There: From Portland, head approximately 33 miles east on I-84 to the Ainsworth exit, 35. Travel 1.5 miles west on the Historic Columbia River Highway and turn right into the Horsetail Falls Parking area.
Description: This route's 1,140 feet of elevation gain takes you and your pooch on a tour past some of the Gorge's most beautiful waterfalls including Horsetail, Ponytail, Oneonta, and Triple Falls. As you start the hike you'll be able to see the swishing action of 176-foot Horsetail Falls. After a short jaunt of steep climbing, you'll arrive at the refreshing cascade of Ponytail Falls that plunges over a basalt ledge into a deep rock pool. As the trail continues you'll cross Oneonta Creek on a footbridge over stunning Oneonta Gorge and get a fantastic view of Oneonta Falls. After crossing the bridge, turn left and continue on a steep grade along Oneonta Creek past stunning canyon scenery. After 2.2 miles, you'll arrive at a log bridge that crosses the creek above Triple Falls. After crossing the bridge, you'll continue on the trail as it heads uphill through an astounding mossy green forest for another mile to a footbridge crossing Oneonta Creek (your turnaround point). This is a good spot to take a break and let your dog cool off in the creek before heading back to the trailhead on the same route. This hike can be crowded on summer weekends.

Wahclella Falls Hike

Contact: USDA Forest Service, Columbia River Gorge National Scenic Area, 902 Wasco Ave., Suite 200, Hood River, OR 97031, 541-386-2333, www.fs.fed.us

Paw-Approval Rating: 3 paws
Leashes Required? Yes
Length: 2.2 miles out and back
Difficulty: Easy
Fees/Permits: $5 Northwest Forest Pass. Purchase at 1-800-270-7504 or www.naturenw.org
Season: Year-round
Getting There: From Portland, head east on I-84 about 40 miles and exit at Bonneville Dam, exit 40. At the stop sign turn right (south) and pull into the gravel parking lot at the Wahclella Falls Trailhead.
Description: This route begins at the south end of the parking area. You and your furry friend will walk on a well-graded path next to Tanner Creek. At 0.8 mile stay left at the trail fork. (If you head right you'll continue on an optional loop section of the trail, where you and your buddy can cool off in the refreshing creek.) At 1.1 miles, you'll arrive at the impressive 620-foot cascade of Wahclella Falls, which plunges over a basalt shelf into a deep rock pool. After soaking in the view, retrace your route to the trailhead. This hike can be crowded on summer weekends.

Eagle Creek Hike

Contact: USDA Forest Service, Columbia River Gorge National Scenic Area, 902 Wasco Ave., Suite 200, Hood River, OR 97031, 541-386-2333, www.fs.fed.us

Paw-Approval Rating: 4 paws
Leashes Required? Yes
Length: 6 miles out and back
Difficulty: Moderate
Fees/Permits: $5 Northwest Forest Pass. Purchase at 1-800-270-7504 or www.naturenw.org

Season: Year-round. This trail can be icy during winter.

Getting There: From Portland, head east on I-84 about 41 miles. Take exit 41, Eagle Creek Recreation Area. At the stop sign, turn right and stay right toward the picnic area and trailhead. Drive about 0.5 mile to a paved parking area at the road's end.

From Hood River, head west on I-84 and take the Bonneville exit, 40. Get back on I-84 heading east. Take exit 41 for Eagle Creek Recreation Area. At the stop sign, turn right and stay right toward the picnic area and trailhead. Drive about 0.5 mile to a paved parking area at the road's end.

Description: This creek trail heads up Eagle Creek Canyon for an elevation gain of 485 feet and is filled with spectacular scenery and waterfalls. You'll begin the hike near creek level but soon the trail begins climbing high, promising gorgeous scenery around every bend. At 0.8 mile is a precipitous section where you'll need to hang on tightly to your pooch. At 1.5 miles, you can take a side trail to the short cascade of Metlako Falls. At 1.9 miles, head right on a side trail that descends 0.4 mile down to the creek bed and a viewpoint of the broad cascade of Lower Punchbowl Falls, which tumbles into a rocky, circular bowl. After cooling off in the creek, head back up to the main trail and turn right. It's not long before you reach another side trail that leads to a viewpoint of Upper Punchbowl Falls. At 3.5 miles, you'll reach a high suspension bridge that straddles the deep creek canyon and offers gorgeous views. Hang on tightly to your pup if he is skittish of bridges with see-through slats. This bridge is your turnaround point. If you want to soak in more canyon scenery, this incredible trail continues another 10.3 miles to Wahtum Lake, an excellent backpack destination. Expect crowds on this trail on summer weekends.

Historic Columbia River State Park Trail Hike

Contact: Oregon State Parks and Recreation, Suite 1, 1115 Commercial St. NE, Salem OR 97301-1002, 1-800-551-6949, www.oregonstate parks.org

Paw-Approval Rating: 3 paws

Leashes Required? Yes

Length: 9.2 miles out and back

Difficulty: Easy

Fees/Permits: $3 day-use pass

Season: Year-round

Getting There: Hood River West Trailhead: From the intersection of I-205 and I-84 in Portland, travel 54 miles east on I-84 toward Hood River and The Dalles. Turn off at exit 64, Hood River Highway 35/White Salmon/Government Camp. At the end of the off-ramp, turn right (south) toward Hood River. Continue 0.3 mile to a stop sign and a four-way intersection. Turn left (east) on the Historic Columbia River Highway. You'll see a sign indicating "Historic State Park Trail." Travel 1.3 miles on the Historic Columbia River Highway until you reach a parking area, visitor center, and the trailhead on the left side of the road.

Description: This 9.2-mile out and back hike follows an old section of the Historic Columbia River Highway between Hood River and Mosier. The entire route is paved and delivers spectacular views of the Columbia River Gorge. Be sure to stock up on water at the visitor center before heading out. Start by heading east on the paved trail adjacent to the visitor center where a trail sign indicates "Senator Mark O. Hatfield West Trailhead." On the first part of the route, you and your pup will walk through an ecosystem of fir mixed with big leaf maple and other deciduous tree species. In the spring, purple lupine and bright-yellow balsam root add splashes of color. As you head further east, the landscape changes to an open oak woodland sprinkled with ponderosa pine trees.

After 2.7 miles, you'll pass a viewpoint on your left. Be sure to stop and soak in the view of the Columbia River and cliff-lined gorge. At 3.5 miles, you'll enter the Mosier Twin Tunnels. From inside the tunnels you'll have opportunities to stop and check out more stunning views of the gorge through arched windows that were blasted out of the rock when the tunnels were built. At 3.7 miles, you'll exit the Mosier Twin Tunnels.

At 3.8 miles, be sure to check out the viewpoint on the left where you may catch glimpses to the north (on a clear day) of Mount St. Helens and Mount Adams.

At 4.4 miles, at a T-intersection and stop sign, turn right and head uphill to the East Mosier Trailhead. At 4.6 miles, you'll arrive at the Mosier trailhead and your turnaround point. This trailhead also has water, restrooms, and a phone.

Dog Mountain Hike
Contact: USDA Forest Service, Columbia River Gorge National Scenic Area, 902 Wasco Ave., Suite 200, Hood River, OR 97031, 541-386-2333, www.fs.fed.us
Paw-Approval Rating: 3 paws
Leashes Required? Yes

Joe Mullen, Sage, and Rhea at the summit of Dog Mountain.

Length: 6 miles out and back
Difficulty: Difficult
Fees/Permits: $5 Northwest Forest Pass. Purchase at 1-800-270-7504 or www.naturenw.org.
Season: Year-round
Getting There: This hike is on the Washington side of the Gorge. From Portland, travel 44 miles east on I-84 to exit 44, Cascade Locks. Cross the Bridge of the Gods toll bridge (the fee is 75 cents) over the Columbia River. At the intersection with Washington Highway 14 turn right (east). Travel 12 miles east to a large gravel parking area on the left side of the road signed for Dog Mountain.
Description: This challenging and popular hike takes you over 1,500 feet to the magnificent summit of Dog Mountain. The quickest and steepest route to the top is the trail at the far right-hand corner of the parking area. (The other option, the Augspurger Mountain Trail, is longer and climbs more gradually.) Follow the steeper trail through shady Douglas fir forest on the lower slopes and then past open hillsides covered with springtime blooms of yellow balsam root, purple lupine, and bright red Indian paintbrush. May and June provide the best color show. At 2.6 miles, turn right to continue to the summit. At 3 miles you'll reach the grassy summit, a perfect spot to eat and enjoy phenomenal views of the Columbia River Gorge. This is a hot, dry hike; bring lots of water. Beware of poison oak and ticks. No water is available at the trailhead.

CAMPGROUNDS

Ainsworth State Park
Contact: Oregon State Parks and Recreation, Suite 1, 1115 Commercial St. NE, Salem OR 97301-1002, 1-800-551-6949 (information), 1-800-452-5687 (reservations), www.oregonstateparks.org
Season: March to November
Facilities: 45 full-hook-up sites, 5 walk-in tent sites, piped water, flush toilets,

showers, fire rings, picnic area amphitheater with interpretive programs. No reservations are accepted.

Getting There: From the intersection of I-84 and I-205 in Portland head about 30 miles east on I-84 to exit 35, Historic Highway and Ainsworth State Park. Travel west on the Historic Columbia River Highway to the signed park entrance.

Description: This shady campground is a quick 30-minute drive east of Portland near many beautiful waterfalls and Columbia Gorge trails. The Nesmith Point Trail can be accessed from the campground. Due to its proximity to Portland, sites fill up fast on summer weekends.

Deschutes River State Park

Contact: Oregon State Parks and Recreation, Suite 1, 1115 Commercial St. NE, Salem OR 97301-1002, 1-800-551-6949 (information), 1-800-452-5687 (reservations), www.oregonstateparks.org

Season: Year-round

Facilities: 9 full-hook-up sites, 25 electrical sites, 25 primitive tent sites, 4 group RV/tent sites, 1 covered camper wagon, piped water, vault toilets, picnic tables

Getting There: From The Dalles travel 14 miles east on I-84 to exit 97, Highway 206/Celilo Park/Deschutes River State Park. Turn right at the end of the off-ramp and then take an immediate left on Highway 206. Head east 3.1 miles and turn right into the entrance for Deschutes River State Park. Proceed 0.4 mile on the paved road to the campground.

Description: This shady campground sits on the banks of the Deschutes River in the Columbia River Gorge. Hiking trails lead you and your pup along the banks of the river (see *Paw-Approved Hikes and Parks*). This campground is also the starting point for the Deschutes rail-trail. This double-track road travels over 17 miles into the river canyon following an old rail line. Your dog will love swimming in the river day and you'll have many opportunities to view the abundant wildlife.

Eagle Creek Campground

Contact: USDA Forest Service, Columbia River Gorge National Scenic Area, 902 Wasco Ave., Suite 200, Hood River, OR 97031, 541/386-2333, www.fs.fed.us

Season: June to September

Facilities: 20 tent campsites (no electrical hook-ups), fire rings, picnic tables, piped water, and flush toilets. No reservations are accepted.

Getting There: From Portland, head east on I-84 about 41 miles. Take exit 41, Eagle Creek Recreation Area and campground. From Hood River head west on I-84 and take the Bonneville exit, 40. Get back on I-84 heading east. Take exit 41 for Eagle Creek Recreation Area and campground.

Description: This campground is adjacent to the beautiful Eagle Creek hike (see *Paw-Approved Hikes and Parks*). Some sites have good Columbia River views and some are nestled in the trees. The only drawback to this scenic spot is the drone of cars on nearby I-84.

Viento State Park

Contact: Oregon State Parks and Recreation, Suite 1, 1115 Commercial St. NE, Salem OR 97301-1002, 1-800-551-6949, www.oregonstateparks.org

Season: March through November

Facilities: 57 electrical hook-up campsites, 18 tent campsites, piped water, restrooms, showers, day-use and picnic area, and an ADA site. No reservations are accepted.

Getting There: Travel 8 miles west of Hood River on I-84 and take exit 56; follow signs to the state park and campground.

Description: This campground has access to the Columbia River and is a popular area for windsurfing. Head to the day-use area and watch the windsurfers or hike on a one-mile trail that follows the historic highway to Starvation Creek.

Hood River/Mt. Hood

PAW-APPROVED HIKES AND PARKS

 Cooper Spur Hike
Contact: Mount Hood National Forest, Hood River Ranger District, 6780 Highway 35, Mt. Hood-Parkdale, Oregon 97041, 541-352-6002, www.fs.fed.us
Paw-Approval Rating: 3 paws
Leashes Required? No
Length: 7.6 miles out and back
Difficulty: Difficult
Fees/Permits: $5 Northwest Forest Pass. Purchase at 1-800-270-7504 or www.naturenw.org
Season: June through October
Getting There: From Hood River, travel 22.4 miles south on Oregon Highway 35 to the junction with Cooper Spur Road and a sign for Cooper Spur Ski Area. Turn right and continue 2.4 miles to Cloud Cap Road (Forest Road 3512). Continue straight (right) toward Cloud Cap and Tilly Jane Campground. Go about 8 miles to a road junction. Turn right toward Cloud Cap and continue 0.6 mile to the trailhead parking on the right.
Description: This strenuous hike climbs over 1,000 feet and takes you and your four-legged friend into the high country on the east side of Mount Hood. The route leads you to the top of Cooper Spur—a high ridge sandwiched between Eliot Glacier and Newton Clark Glacier. This trek promises grand views of the deep crevasses of Eliot Glacier and the majestic snow-covered summit of Mount Hood. Start the hike on Trail 600. Go about 100 yards and then bear left. The trail climbs steeply; after 0.8 mile you'll exit the forest and have a panoramic view of Mount Hood, Mount Rainier, and Mount Adams. After 1.2 miles you'll arrive at a trail junction. Continue straight (right) on the Cooper Spur Trail as it switchbacks steeply up the ridge. At 3.8 miles, you'll arrive at the end of the trail and a commemorative marker. Enjoy the views and retrace the route back to the trailhead.

 Lost Lake Hike
Contact: Mount Hood National Forest, Hood River Ranger District, 6780 Highway 35, Mt. Hood-Parkdale, Oregon 97041, 541-352-6002, www.fs.fed.us
Paw-Approval Rating: 4 paws
Leashes Required? Yes
Length: 3-mile loop
Difficulty: Easy
Fees/Permits: $5 Northwest Forest Pass. Purchase at 1-800-270-7504 or www.naturenw.org

Iko taking a rest break.

Season: Mid-May through October

Getting There: From the intersection of I-205 and I-84 in Portland, head east 7.2 miles on I-84 to exit 13, 238th Dr./Wood Village. Turn right on 238th Dr. and proceed 2.9 miles. Turn left on Burnside Road. Travel 1 mile on Burnside Road and then turn left (east) on U.S. Highway 26. Continue 27.5 miles east on Highway 26 to the town of Zigzag. At the Zigzag Store turn left (north) on East Lolo Pass Road. Travel 10.9 miles on East Lolo Pass Road to the intersection with the unsigned gravel Forest Road 1810 (McKee Creek Road), which is the first right turn after the signed Forest Road 828. Turn right on Forest Road 1810 and continue 7.5 miles until the road intersects with Forest Road 18. Proceed 7 miles on pavement to the intersection with Forest Road 13. Turn left on Forest Road 13 and travel 6 miles to the pay booth at Lost Lake. After the entry booth, stay right as the road parallels the lake. Continue past the general store to the road's end at a day-use picnic area.

From I-84 in Hood River take exit 62, West Hood River. Travel about a mile into Hood River and take a right on 13th St. Travel approximately 3.5 miles to Odell. Cross a bridge and turn right past Tucker Park and travel 6.3 miles. Stay right toward Dee. From the small town of Dee, travel 14 miles, following signs to Lost Lake. After the pay booth at the lake stay right as the road parallels the lake. Continue past the general store to the road's end at a day-use picnic area.

Description: This hike takes you and your hound around picturesque Lost Lake in the Mount Hood National Forest. Perks include spectacular views of Mount Hood, pockets of old growth forest, and opportunities for swimming. Begin hiking in a counterclockwise direction on Lakeshore Trail 656. There is also a large campground here if you want to spend a few days (see *Campgrounds*). For more comfortable accommodations, Lost Lake Resort rents canine-friendly cabins right on the lake.

Mazama Trail #625 Hike

Contact: Mount Hood National Forest Headquarters Office, 16400 Champion Way, Sandy, OR 97055, 503-622-7674, www.fs.fed.us

Paw-Approval Rating: 3 paws

Leashes Required? No

Length: 7.5 miles

Difficulty: Difficult

Fees/Permits: $5 Northwest Forest Pass. Purchase at 1-800-270-7504 or www.naturenw.org. A self-issue wilderness permit is also required and can be obtained at the trailhead.

Season: Late June through October

Getting There: From Hood River, travel south on Highway 35 about 13 miles to Woodworth Road. Turn west on Woodworth Road and travel 3 miles to Dee Highway. Turn right onto Dee Highway and travel about 5 miles to the Dee Hardwood plant. Turn left, and continue across a bridge. Stay left and follow signs to Lost Lake for about 7 miles to Forest Road 18. Turn left onto Forest Road 18 to continue to Forest Road 1810. Follow Forest Road 1810 to Forest Road 1811. Continue on Forest Road 1811 for 3 miles to the trailhead.

From Portland: From the intersection of I-205 and I-84 in Portland, head east 7.2 miles on I-84 to exit 13, 238th Dr./Wood Village. Turn right on 238th Dr. and proceed 2.9 miles. Turn left on Burnside Road. Continue about a mile and turn east onto Highway 26. Continue 27.5 miles east on Highway 26 to the town of Zigzag. Just after the Zigzag Store, turn left (north) on East Lolo Pass Road. Travel 10.9 miles on East Lolo Pass Road to an intersection with the unsigned gravel Forest Road 1810 (McKee Creek Road). Turn right and continue 5 miles to the junction with Forest Road 1811. Turn right onto Forest Road 1811 and travel 3 miles to the trailhead.

Description: The hike starts in a forested setting on a ridge above Ladd Creek and has spectacular views of majestic Mount

Hood in the Mount Hood Wilderness. The trail switchbacks steeply up a talus slope, and then up a high ridge. The route then follows Cathedral Ridge through pine-scented forest, and arrives at beautiful wildflower meadows near the junction with the Timberline Trail.

McNeil Point Hike

Contact: Mount Hood National Forest Head-quarters Office, 16400 Champion Way, Sandy, OR 97055, 503-622-7674, www.fs.fed.us

Paw-Approval Rating: 4 paws
Leashes Required? No
Length: 9 miles
Difficulty: Difficult
Fees/Permits: $5 Northwest Forest Pass. Purchase at 1-800-270-7504 or www.naturenw.org.
Season: Late June through October
Getting There: From the intersection of I-205 and I-84 in Portland, head east 7.2 miles on I-84 to exit 13, 238th Dr./Wood Village. Turn right on 238th Dr. and proceed 2.9 miles. Turn left on Burnside Road. Continue about a mile and turn east onto Highway 26. Continue east on Highway 26 to the town of Zigzag. Turn left (north) on East Lolo Pass Road and travel 4.2 miles to Forest Road 1825. Turn right on Forest Road 1825 and go 0.7 mile to a junction with Forest Road 1828. Go straight (left) and continue on FS 1828 for 5.6 miles to a road junction. Stay right (the road turns to gravel here) and continue on FS 1828 where a sign states "Top Spur Trail 788." Continue 1.6 miles to a parking area on the left side of the road.
Description: Intrepid dogs will love this strenuous hike's opportunities to cool off in high alpine creeks and pools; you'll enjoy gorgeous views of Mount Hood and the historic McNeil Shelter. This shelter was named after outdoor enthusiast Fred H. McNeil. McNeil moved to Oregon in 1912 and was a Mazama club member (a Portland mountaineering group) and a

A summer trail run in a high alpine meadow in the Mount Hood Wilderness. Photograph by Ken Skeen

well-known journalist for the *Oregon Journal.* He also took an active role in developing the Pacific Northwest Ski Association. Begin on a dirt path across from the parking area. After 0.5 mile turn right at a T-junction (the trail heading left leads to Lolo Pass). Continue about 60 yards and arrive at a three-way junction. Continue on the center trail toward "Pacific Crest Trail 2000/Timberline Trail 600." After a short distance you'll arrive at a self-registration station where you'll need to fill out a wilderness permit. At 0.8 mile, the trail heads out of the forest and passes the wildflower-filled slopes of Bald Mountain, with grand views of Mount Hood in front of you. At 1.1 miles, turn left onto an unmarked dirt path. Hike over a small ridge to where the trail joins unmarked Timberline Trail 600. Turn right onto Timberline Trail 600 and continue 0.2 mile to a trail fork. Go right toward Cairn Basin. At 3 miles turn left at the trail junction. Over the next 0.5 mile you'll cross a series of creeks where your trail hound may want to hunt for sticks or lounge in the cool waters. At 3.6 miles, bear left. At 3.7 miles you'll walk past two alpine pools where Rover may again be tempted to wallow. At

3.8 miles turn right at the trail junction (Mazama Trail 625 heads left). At 4.2 miles, head right. At 4.5 miles you'll arrive at McNeil Shelter. From here, enjoy the views of Mount Hood, Mount Adams, Mount Rainier, and Mount St. Helens. Retrace the route back to the trailhead.

Mirror Lake Hike

Contact: Mount Hood National Forest Headquarters Office, 16400 Champion Way, Sandy, OR 97055, 503-622-7674, www.fs.fed.us

Paw-Approval Rating: 4 paws

Leashes Required? No

Length: 3.2-mile loop

Difficulty: Easy

Fees/Permits: $5 Northwest Forest Pass. Purchase at 1-800-270-7504 or www.naturenw.org

Season: June through October

Getting There: From the intersection of I-205 and I-84 in Portland, head east 7.2 miles on I-84 to exit 13, 238th Dr./Wood Village. Turn right on 238th Dr. and proceed 2.9 miles. Turn left onto Burnside Road. Continue about a mile and turn left (east) onto Highway 26. Travel east on U.S Highway 26 to an unmarked trailhead between mileposts 51 and 52 on the right (south) side of the highway.

From Hood River, head south on Highway 35 to the junction with Highway 26. Turn right (west) onto Highway 26 and travel west to Government Camp. From Government Camp continue approximately 2 miles west on to an unmarked trailhead on the left (south) side of the highway between mileposts 51 and 52.

Description: This spectacular lake loop in the Mount Hood National Forest has plenty of shade and water fun that trail hounds will appreciate. Begin by walking across a footbridge across Camp Creek and then begin ascending the Mirror Lake Trail that takes you and your best friend on a series of switchbacks through a cool, shady forest. At 1.4 miles you'll arrive at a

Levi looking for the perfect swimming hole in Lost Lake.

T-intersection and the beginning of the signed Mirror Lake Loop trail. Turn right and circle the lake in a counter-clockwise direction. At the next trail junction, stay left and continue around the lake. Take time to smell the flowers–deep purple lupine and vibrant Indian paintbrush–and to cool off in the lake. After completing the lake loop and enjoying the Mount Hood views, retrace the route back to the trailhead. Expect crowds on summer weekends.

Salmon River Hike

Contact: Mount Hood National Forest Headquarters Office, 16400 Champion Way, Sandy, OR 97055, 503-622-7674, www.fs.fed.us

Paw-Approval Rating: 3 paws

Leashes Required? No

Length: 7.2-mile loop

Difficulty: Moderate

Fees/Permits: $5 Northwest Forest Pass. Purchase at 1-800-270-7504 or www.naturenw.org

Season: Year-round

Getting There: From Hood River, travel south on Highway 35 to the junction with Highway 26. Turn right (west) on Highway

26 and continue to the town of Zigzag. Turn left (south) on Salmon River Road and travel 4.9 miles to the parking area and trailhead on the left side of the road.

From the intersection of I-205 and I-84 in Portland head east 7.2 miles on I-84 to exit 13, 238th Dr./Wood Village. Turn right on 238th Dr. and proceed 2.9 miles. Turn left on Burnside Road. Continue about a mile and turn east onto Highway 26. Continue east on U.S. 26 to the town of Zigzag. Turn right (south) on Salmon River Road and travel 4.9 miles to the parking area and trailhead on the left side of the road.

Description: This beautiful river trail takes you and your dog on a tranquil journey through the Salmon River Canyon in the Salmon-Huckleberry Wilderness. Begin on the singletrack trail at the far end of the parking area next to the bridge. The trail travels close to the river through old growth cedar and Douglas fir. At 2 miles, cross a footbridge and arrive at a self-issue wilderness permit station. Fill out a permit and continue on your trek. At 3.4 miles, turn right to begin a short loop. At 3.5 miles, the route exits the trees onto a grassy ridge with grand views of the river canyon. Hang on to Fido on this section because there are many steep drop-offs. At 3.6 miles, turn left at a T-intersection. After 3.8 miles the loop portion of the trail ends. Stay right and retrace the route to the trailhead at 7.2 miles.

Tamanawas Falls Hike

Contact: Mount Hood National Forest Headquarters Office, 16400 Champion Way, Sandy, OR 97055, 503-622-7674, www.fs.fed.us

Paw-Approval Rating: 3 paws
Leashes Required? No
Length: 4 miles out and back
Difficulty: Easy
Fees/Permits: $5 Northwest Forest Pass. Purchase at 1-800-270-7504 or www.naturenw.org
Season: May through October

Getting There: From I-84 in Hood River, take exit 64. Turn south on Highway 35 and travel 25.3 miles to a gravel parking area at the trailhead on the right side of the road.

From Portland, head about 56 miles east on Highway 26 to the intersection with Highway 35. Turn north on Highway 35 and travel about 15 miles to a gravel parking area and the trailhead on the left side of the road (0.2 mile north of Sherwood Campground).

Description: Trail hounds will love this cool, shady hike that parallels bouldery Cold Spring Creek then travels to a viewpoint of Tamanawas Falls. Start by hiking on Tamanawas Falls Trail 650A. Cross a bouncy suspension bridge over the roaring East Fork of Hood River. After crossing the bridge, turn right toward Tamanawas Falls 2/Pollalie Campground. After 0.5 mile, the route descends to Cold Spring Creek. Cross a wood footbridge, then take a sharp left and continue walking on the shady forest path as it parallels Cold Spring Creek. At 1.5 miles, you'll arrive at a trail junction. Stay left and continue on Tamanawas Trail 650A. Proceed a short distance, and then you'll have to power up a steep rocky section of the trail for about 50 feet. The next section takes you around an old washout and a small boulder field. At 2 miles, you'll reach a good viewpoint of roaring Tamanawas Falls, your turnaround point. Head back to the trailhead on the same route.

CYCLING FOR CANINES

Crosstown-Wally's Tie-Skiway Trail

Contact: Mount Hood National Forest Headquarters Office, 16400 Champion Way, Sandy, OR 97055, 503-622-7674, www.fs.fed.us

Paw-Approval Rating: 4 paws
Leashes Required? No
Length: 6.1 miles out and back with a small loop

Great singletrack riding in the Mount Hood National Forest.

Difficulty: Easy
Fees/Permits: None
Season: June through October
Getting There: From the intersection of I-205 and I-84 in Portland, head 6.3 miles east on I-84 east to exit 13, 238th Dr./ Wood Village. Turn right on 238th Dr. and proceed 2.8 miles. Turn left on Burnside Road. Continue about 0.6 mile and turn left (east) onto Highway 26. Continue east on Highway 26 for 37.6 miles to the Summit Ski Area/Government Camp turnoff. Turn left and then take a quick right into a large paved parking area in front of the Summit Ski Lodge.
Description: Your cycling companion will drool over this smooth and zippy singletrack route that dashes over creeks and races through a shady mountain hemlock and Douglas fir forest in the Mount Hood National Forest. This route combines three popular cross-country ski trails—Crosstown Trail, Wally's Tie, and Skiway Trail. At the start of the ride, don't be deterred by two signs to the right of the Summit Ski Lodge that say "No Dogs" and "No Mountain Bikes." These signs refer to the ski lodge property and not to this trail. Start riding uphill on the signed Crosstown

Trail No. 755 singletrack trail located to the left of the blue Summit Ski Area Lodge. As you ascend, you'll have a view of Mt. Hood. At 0.1 mile, turn right onto a narrower singletrack trail marked by a brown hiker/ biker sign. At 0.2 mile, the trail curves sharply left, crosses a wide, doubletrack road, and then enters a deep forest corridor of Douglas fir, mountain hemlock, and red cedar. At 0.3 mile, continue straight at the four-way junction where a sign states "Crosstown Trail .75/Wally's Tie 1.5/ Glacier View Sno-Park 2.5." At 0.4 mile, cross a wood bridge over a small creek and begin to descend slightly. Over the next 0.5 mile you'll cross many more wood bridges over small creeks where your hound can lounge and cool off. At 0.9 mile, continue straight at the four-way junction on the signed Crosstown Trail. Begin descending at a moderate pace on zippy singletrack. After 1.6 miles turn right at the T-junction toward the signed Crosstown Trail. At 2.6 miles turn left at the T-junction and keep riding on the Crosstown Trail. At this point the forest becomes very lush with rhododendron, salal, and sword fern. After 2.8 miles, admire a large open meadow and small pond on the right side of the trail. At 2.9 miles, turn left at a T-junction. At 3 miles, the Crosstown Trail ends at the Glacier Snow-Park. Turn around and head back toward the Summit Ski Area on the Crosstown Trail. At 3.4 miles, turn right and continue riding on the Crosstown Trail. At 4.5 miles, turn right onto Wally's Tie Trail 755A. At 4.7 miles, turn left at the T-junction onto Skiway Trail 755B. Begin a steep ascent on a rocky, rutted doubletrack road. After 5.1 miles, turn right onto the Crosstown Trail at a four-way junction.

After 5.2 miles, continue straight on the Crosstown Trail at the 4-way junction. At 6.1 miles, arrive back at the trailhead.

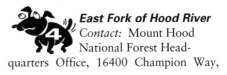

East Fork of Hood River
Contact: Mount Hood National Forest Headquarters Office, 16400 Champion Way,

Sandy, OR 97055, 503-622-7674,www.fs. fed.us
Paw-Approval Rating: 4 paws
Leashes Required? No
Length: 10.8 miles out and back
Difficulty: Easy
Fees/Permits: $5 Northwest Forest Pass. Purchase at 1 800-270-7504 or www. naturenw.org
Season: May through October
Getting There: From I-84 in Hood River take exit 64. Turn south on Highway 35 and travel 25.3 miles to a gravel parking area at the trailhead on the right side of the road.

From Portland, head about 56 miles east on Highway 26 to the intersection with Highway 35. Turn north on Highway 35 and travel about 15 miles to a gravel parking area and the trailhead on the left side of the road (0.2 mile north of Sherwood Campground.)
Description: This route takes you and your dog along the East Fork of Hood River, which rushes down the north side of Mount Hood into the Hood River Valley. Your dog will appreciate the shady forest canopy and river access that will keep him cool during your ride. Start this fast singletrack route by crossing the narrow wood bridge over the East Fork of Hood River. After you cross the bridge, turn left (south) on the singletrack trail 650. The trail sweeps along the ridge above the river. You'll have fun cranking up short hills with many curly fry turns and then blasting down the trail as it follows the ridge contours. At 3.9 miles, the trail is close to the river and can be sandy and soft in spots. At 5.1 miles, you'll sail through a thick forest and cross many wood ramps over marshy areas for the next 0.3 mile. At 5.4 miles, arrive at Robinhood Campground, your turnaround point. Here, give Fido water, take a break, and then reverse the trail directions back to the trailhead at 10.8 miles.

Levi snagging a stick in Timothy Lake.

Timothy Lake

Contact: Mount Hood National Forest Headquarters Office, 16400 Champion Way, Sandy, OR 97055, 503-622-7674, www. fs.fed.us
Paw-Approval Rating: 4 paws
Leashes Required? No
Length: 13.8 miles
Difficulty: Easy
Fees/Permits: None
Season: June through October
Getting There: From the intersection of I-205 and I-84 in Portland head east 7.2 miles on I-84 to exit 13, 238th Dr./Wood Village. At the end of the off-ramp, turn right on 238th Ave. and proceed 2.9 miles to the intersection with Burnside Road. Turn left on Burnside Rd. and proceed to the intersection with Highway 26. Turn left (east) on Highway 26 and go 51.4 miles to the junction with Forest Road 42 (Skyline Road). Turn right on Forest Road 42 and travel 8.3 miles to the junction with Forest Road 57. Turn right on Forest Road 57 and go 3.6 miles (passing four campgrounds on your right) and cross over the dam. After you cross the dam turn right and travel 0.1 mile to a road intersection. Turn right on a gravel road and drive

0.1 mile to the Timothy Lake Trail 528 trailhead parking area.

Description: Your pooch will love this mostly singletrack trail as it sails around Timothy Lake in the Mount Hood National Forest. Complete the entire loop, or ride an out and back section of this gorgeous lake trail with its many opportunities to view Mount Hood and cool off in the lake. The ride does have short sections of pavement. Be sure your dog is in shape before you attempt this ride.

Begin the route by riding in a clockwise direction on Timothy Lake Trail 528. At 1.1 miles, continue riding straight on Timothy Lake Trail 528. (Trail #526 for Meditation Point goes right at this junction.) At 3.3 miles, you'll reach a junction with a gravel road. Turn left and ride about 100 yards. Turn right and continue riding on the signed Timothy Lake Trail 528. At 4.2 miles, turn right and continue on Timothy Lake Trail 528. A sign states "Bicyclists dismount for 600 feet to Old 1916 Trail #537." At 4.3 miles, turn left on signed Old 1916 Trail 537. The sign indicates you will reach Forest Road 42 in 4 miles. (Pacific Crest Trail 2000 continues straight at this junction.) At 4.8 miles, cross a gravel road and continue on the singletrack trail. At 5.5 miles, cross Road 4280 and continue riding on Old 1916 Trail 537. The trail turns from singletrack to doubletrack road here. The doubletrack road is very rocky in spots. At 6 miles turn right on the signed Old 1916 Trail 537. The sign also indicates you'll reach Joe Graham Horse Camp in 3 miles. After 6.7 miles turn left on Old 1916 Trail 537. The sign also indicates "Skyline Road 2 miles." The trail turns to singletrack at this junction (this junction is easy to miss!) At 8.3 miles, cross a gravel road and continue on the singletrack trail. At 8.4 miles, turn right on a doubletrack road where a sign indicates "Trail 537." At 8.5 miles, turn left on signed Old 1916 Trail 537 (this sign is difficult to see!) After this junction the

trail turns back to fun singletrack. At 8.8 miles, turn right on the unmarked paved Forest Road 42 (be sure to leash your dog here). At 8.9 miles, turn right on paved Forest Road 57 toward Timothy Lake. After 9.5 miles, turn right on the single-track Miller Trail 534. At 10 miles, turn right on the signed Oak Fork Cutoff Trail 531. At 10.2 miles, the trail comes to a T. Turn left on Timothy Lake Trail 528. Over the next 3 miles you will follow this trail as it winds next to the lakeshore and passes through four campgrounds and boat ramps. At 13.4 miles, you'll pass a fishing dock on your right and then the trail turns to pavement. Ride about 100 yards on the paved trail and then turn right on the paved road that crosses the dam. At 13.5 miles, after crossing the dam, turn right on a paved road. At 13.7 miles, turn right on a gravel road. At 13.8 miles, you'll arrive at the trailhead parking area and your vehicle. Timothy Lake has many campgrounds (see *Campgrounds*) if you want to spend a few days. This lake is also a great place to spend a day on the water with your pooch.

POWDERHOUNDS

All cross-country ski trails in the Mount Hood National Forest are open to dogs except Teacup Lake. Dogs do not have to be leashed on any of the trails except on the Trillium Lake Loop Trail. Listed below are a few areas to start your snow adventures. For more areas to ski in the Mount Hood National Forest, visit www.fs.fed.us or call 503-622-7674. Another great resource is *Cross-Country Ski Routes: Oregon* by Klindt Vielbig.

 **Frog Lake**
Contact: Mount Hood National Forest Headquarters Office, 16400 Champion Way, Sandy, OR 97055, 503-622-7674, www. fs.fed.us
Paw-Approval Rating: 3 paws
Leashes Required? Yes

Length: 1.4 miles
Difficulty: Easy
Fees/Permits: $3 Sno-Park pass
Getting There: This route begins at the Frog Lake Sno-Park on U.S. 26, about 4 miles south of the junction of Highways 35 and 26 on Mount Hood.
Description: This easy route takes you to Frog Lake and offers some good views of Mount Hood. From the snow park, follow Road 2610 south for 0.4 mile to a junction. Go right and begin descending. At the next trail junction head right and ski to the west end of the lake.

Heather Canyon

Contact: Mount Hood National Forest Headquarters Office, 16400 Champion Way, Sandy, OR 97055, 503-622-7674, www.fs.fed.us
Paw-Approval Rating: 4 paws
Leashes Required? No
Length: 4.4 miles out and back
Difficulty: Moderate
Fees/Permits: $3 Sno-Park pass
Getting There: Hood River Meadows Sno-Park is 11 miles north of Government Camp off Highway 35.
Description: This gorgeous trail follows the course of Clark Creek and has awesome views of snow-capped Mount Hood. The route begins on the north side of the Hood River Meadows Sno-Park and heads into beautiful Heather Canyon. Look for avalanche warnings posted on the bulletin board at the trailhead before you head out.

White River Sno-Park West

Contact: Mount Hood National Forest Headquarters Office, 16400 Champion Way, Sandy, OR 97055, 503-622-7674, www.fs.fed.us
Paw-Approval Rating: 4 paws
Leashes Required? Yes
Length: Varies depending on trails selected.

Difficulty: Easy to difficult depending on the trails selected.
Fees/Permits: $3 Sno-Park pass
Getting There: From the intersection of I-205 and I-84 in Portland, head 6.3 miles east on I-84 east to exit 13, 238th Dr./Wood Village. Turn right on 238th Dr. and proceed 2.8 miles. Turn left on Burnside Road. Continue about 0.6 mile and turn left (east) onto Highway 26. Continue east on Highway 26 for 39.6 miles to the junction with Highway 35. Turn north onto Highway 35 and continue 4.2 miles to the White River Sno-Park West located on the left side of the road.
Description: This White River Sno-Park West gives you access to many ski trails that have phenomenal views of Mount Hood. From the north side of the snow park, you can ski 2 miles up the valley next to the White River.

For a short, advanced route, try the 1.9-mile Yellowjacket Loop. The trailhead for this loop is at the center of the west end of the large snow park area. You can also ski through a silvery forest on the Mineral Jane Trail. This signed trail starts across Highway 35 opposite the entrance to the snow park. For more details on the trails in this area, refer to *Cross-Country Ski Routes: Oregon* by Klindt Vielbig.

PADDLEHOUNDS

Paddle with your best friend at Lost Lake where no motorized boats are allowed (see *Paw-Approved Hike and Parks*), and Timothy Lake (see *Cycling for Canines*) in the Mount Hood National Forest. These picturesque mountain lakes offer phenomenal views of Mount Hood and quiet waters promising hours of paddling fun.

CANINE COMFORT ACCOMMODATIONS

Unless otherwise stated, dogs should not be left unattended in the room and must be leashed on hotel property.

Hood River

$-$$ Vagabond Lodge

4070 Westcliff Dr., 541-386-2992 or 1-877-386-2992, www.vagabondlodge.com

The Vagabond Lodge sits on a high bluff overlooking the Columbia River. Some of its 42 rooms are furnished with fireplaces, balconies, kitchens, fireplaces, and whirlpools.

Dog Policy

No extra fees are charged for your dog.

$$-$$$ Best Western Hood River Inn

1108 E. Marina Way, 1-800-828-7873 www.hoodriverinn.com

This dog-friendly hotel, located next to the Hood River Marina, has 149 rooms decorated in a casual Northwest style, with wonderful views of the Columbia River. Room amenities include coffeemaker, hair dryer, and cable TV. Web TV service, in-room movies, and music are available for a fee. The hotel also has its own restaurant and lounge, heated pool, spa, and exercise room. Walk your dog on paths along the Columbia River.

Dog Policy

A fee of $12 per night is charged for your dog.

$$-$$$ Lost Lake Resort

Hood River, OR 541-386-6366

This resort has 12 cabins with kitchenettes on Lost Lake.

Dog Policy

Call for the current canine policy.

$$$ Hood River Hotel

102 Oak St., 541-386-1900 or 1-800-386-1859, www.hoodriverhotel.com

This hotel has canine-friendly ground floor suites with their own private entrance. Each suite has a full size kitchen, and living area with queen sofa bed. The hotel is located in downtown Hood River, near shops and restaurants.

Dog Policy

A $15 per night pet cleaning fee is charged.

$$$$ Columbia Gorge Hotel

4000 Westcliff Dr., 541-386-5566 or 1-800-345-1921, www.columbiagorgehotel.com

The upscale hotel boasts forty unique rooms and suites. Your stay includes a delicious World Famous Farm Breakfast (you can sneak a few tidbits to your furry friend) that includes baked apples, apple fritters with sugar and spice, old-fashioned oatmeal, hash browns, farm-fresh eggs, bacon, smoked pork chops, maple flavored sausage, grilled Idaho Mountain Trout, biscuits, and buttermilk pancakes. You'll receive complimentary coffee service, a morning paper, an afternoon champagne and caviar social, gourmet chocolates (keep Fido away from the chocolate!), and a rose on your pillow. While Fido may not appreciate all these luxuries, he'll appreciate the fact that he can curl up on a thick carpet and be with you while you indulge yourself in your posh surroundings.

Dog Policy

Well-behaved dogs are allowed in selected rooms for a charge of $25 per dog per night.

Government Camp

$$$-$$$$ Mount Hood Inn

87450 E. Government Camp Loop, 1-800-443-7777, www.mthoodinn.com

This pet-friendly hotel is located in the heart of the skiing action; it's 6 miles from Timberline Ski Area, 12 miles from Mount Hood Meadows, and just across the highway from Ski Bowl. All of the hotel's 56 rooms and 4 suites are dog friendly and are furnished with satellite TV, refrigerator, and hot tub. The hotel also has complimentary ski lockers and a ski tuning room. A complimentary continental breakfast is included.

Dog Policy

The hotel charges $10 per dog per night.

Welches

$$$ The Old Welches Inn

26401 E. Welches Rd., 503-622-3754, www.lodging-mthood.com

This historic inn is located in the Welches Valley in the Mount Hood National Forest. Dogs are allowed in Lutie's Cottage. This cottage, located next to the inn, was built in 1901 and sits nestled under a 500-year-old Douglas fir. It features two bedrooms, one bathroom, a fully equipped kitchen, and a cozy river rock fireplace in the living room. Its yard is fenced. The inn provides towels and blankets for your dog to sleep on, with toys and treats also available to keep your four-legged friend happy. Explore the nearby Salmon River, within walking distance of the inn.

Dog Policy

No extra fees are charged for dogs. However, any dog-damage will be charged to your credit card. The managers ask that your dog be clean and on a flea program and that you dry him off after swimming sessions in the river.

CAMPGROUNDS

Gone Creek at Timothy Lake

Contact: Mount Hood National Forest Headquarters Office, 16400 Champion Way, Sandy, OR 97055, 503-622-7674, www.fs.fed.us

Season: Mid-June through September

Facilities: 50 RV/tent sites (no electrical hook-ups), fire rings, picnic tables, water, restrooms, boat launch

Getting There: From the intersection of I-205 and I-84 in Portland, head east 7.2 miles on I-84 to exit 13, 238th Dr./Wood Village. At the end of the off-ramp, turn right on 238th Ave. and proceed 2.9 miles to the intersection with Burnside Road. Turn left on Burnside Road and proceed to the intersection with Highway 26. Turn left (east) on Highway 26 and go 51.4 miles to the junction with Forest Road 42 (Skyline Road). Turn right on Forest Road 42 and travel 8.3 miles to the junction with Forest Road 57. Turn right on Forest Road 57 and go 1 mile to the campground.

Description: This campground has forested sites on the shores of Timothy Lake. Hike or mountain bike around the lake (see *Cycling for Canines*). This lake is also a great place to go swimming and paddling. A bonus is the phenomenal view of Mount Hood from the lakeshore.

Lost Lake

Contact: Mount Hood National Forest, Hood River Ranger District, 6780 Highway 35, Mt. Hood-Parkdale, Oregon 97041, 541-352-6002, www.fs.fed.us

Season: June through mid-October

Facilities: 125 RV/tent sites (no electrical hook-ups), picnic tables, fire rings, piped water, restrooms, ADA sites, RV dump station. No reservations are accepted.

Getting There: From I-84 in Hood River, take exit 62, West Hood River. Travel about a mile into Hood River and take a right on 13th St. Travel approximately 3.5 miles to Odell. Cross a bridge and turn right past Tucker Park and travel 6.3 miles. Stay to the right toward Dee. From the small town of Dee, travel 14 miles following signs to Lost Lake.

Description: From the campground you can access a 3-mile trail that circles the lake and has gorgeous views of Mount Hood. Paddle on the lake with your best friend or just hang out in camp and relax.

Summit Lake

Contact: Mount Hood National Forest Headquarters Office, 16400 Champion Way, Sandy, OR 97055, 503-622-7674, www.fs.fed.us

Season: Late June through September

Facilities: 5 tent sites (no electrical hook-ups), picnic tables, fire rings, restrooms, no water, boat launch

Getting There: From the intersection of I-205 and I-84 in Portland, head east 7.2 miles on I-84 to exit 13, 238th Dr./Wood

Village. At the end of the off-ramp, turn right on 238th Ave. and proceed 2.9 miles to the intersection with Burnside Road. Turn left on Burnside Road and proceed to the intersection with Highway 26. Turn left (east) on Highway 26 and go 51.4 miles to the junction with Forest Road 42 (Skyline Road). Turn right on Forest Road 42 and travel 12 miles to the junction with Forest Road 141. Turn west on Forest Road 141 (a rough dirt road) and go approximately 1 mile to the campground. *Description:* The small campground on Summit Lake is cozy and quiet. The high mountain lake does not allow motorized boats, which means hours of quiet paddling.

CANINE-APPROVED SHOPPING

Hood River

Gorge Dog

410 Oak St., (541) 387-3996, www.gorge dog.com

Gorge Dog is a novelty gift store for dogs and dog lovers. The store carries an array of items including collars, leashes, beds, bowls, clocks, books, picture frames, lamps, travel gear, coats, boots, backpacks, jewelry, wall decorations, gourmet treats, shampoos, supplements, cards, and tons of toys. Your leashed dog is welcome. Open 8 A.M.–6 P.M., Monday to Friday; 9 A.M.–5 P.M., Saturday.

Little Bit Ranch Supply

2727 W. Cascade Ave., 541-386-1299

This store has been in business for nineteen years and stocks canine gear, treats, toys, and premium diets. Your leashed dog is welcome. Open 8 A.M.–6 P.M., Monday to Friday; 9 A.M.–6 P.M., Saturday.

CANINE ER

Hood River

Columbia Gorge Veterinary Clinic

1208 Belmont, 541-386-7773

Established in 1990, this clinic offers complete small animal healthcare. The clinic will see walk-ins but prefers appointments. Wysong and Hills Prescription dog food, flea control products, and medicated shampoos are stocked. Board your dog for $6/day. The clinic also offers overnight boarding. Dogs under 30 pounds are $11 per night; dogs over 30 pounds are $12 per night. Emergency service is available. Call the regular clinic number and the doctor on call will be paged.

Open 8 A.M.–5 P.M., Monday to Friday; 8:30 A.M.–12 P.M., Saturday.

LOST AND FOUND (ANIMAL SHELTERS)

Hood River

Hood River Animal Control

309 State St., 541-386-2098

The Dalles

PAW-APPROVED HIKES AND PARKS

 Deschutes River Hike

Contact: Oregon State Parks and Recreation, Suite 1, 1115 Commercial St. NE, Salem OR 97301-1002, 1-800-551-6949, www.oregonstateparks.org

Paw-Approval Rating: 4 paws

Leashes Required? Yes

Length: 3.7-mile loop (with longer options)

Difficulty: Easy

Fees/Permits: $5 parking fee. Envelopes for the fee are available at the campground self-pay station.

Season: Year-round

Getting There: From The Dalles travel 14 miles east on I-84 to exit 97, Highway 206/Celilo Park/Deschutes River State Park. Turn right at the end of the off-ramp and then take an immediate left on Highway 206. Head east 3.1 miles and turn right into the entrance for Deschutes River State Park. Proceed 0.4 mile on the paved road through the campground to where it dead-ends at the trailhead sign.

Description: Rover will love this river romp along the scenic Deschutes River. Start by walking across a large grassy field paralleling the river. At 0.1 mile, you'll arrive at a wood trail sign that indicates the River Trail is to the right and the Middle and Upper Trails are to the left. Go right and continue on the smooth singletrack of the River Trail. Check out the many riverside swimming holes where your friend may want to cool off. At 0.6 mile, stay right on the River Trail (the Middle Trail goes left at this intersection). At 0.7 mile, cross several wood ramps over a marshy area. At 1.4 miles, go left toward Upper Trail/Middle Trail. Begin walking uphill on a rough, rocky trail. At 1.8 miles, you'll arrive at an overlook of Rattlesnake Rapids and an interpretive sign. The trail swings left and takes you down a short, rocky section for about 50 yards to a doubletrack road. Turn left on the doubletrack road, a multi-use route where you may meet mountain bikers and equestrians.

Trail Options: If you and your hound still feel energetic, turn right and follow the doubletrack road 15 more miles as it follows the Deschutes.

See the trail map at the trailhead for other trails. You can take your dog mountain biking on the multi-use trail. This park has a campground (see *Campgrounds* on page 73) if you want to spend a few days. Summertime temperatures can exceed 100°F during July and August. If you visit then, hike early in the morning. Also, be on the lookout for rattlesnakes and check your dog for ticks after your hike.

Riverfront Hike

Contact: The Dalles Parks and Recreation, 541-296-9533, www.thedalleschamber.com

Paw-Approval Rating: 2 paws

Leashes Required? Yes

Length: 2.6 miles out and back

Difficulty: Easy

Fees/Permits: None

Season: Year-round

Getting There: From I-84 in The Dalles take exit 82 and follow signs to the Columbia Gorge Discovery Center.

Description: This short paved path begins outside the Columbia Gorge Discovery Center and Wasco County Historical Museum, and heads east along the shores of the Columbia River. At the start of the path, you can view displays of old wagons that traveled the Oregon Trail.

White River Falls State Park

Contact: Oregon State Parks and Recreation, Suite 1, 1115 Commercial St. NE, Salem OR 97301-1002, 1-800-551-6949, www.oregonstateparks.org

Paw-Approval Rating: 2 paws

Leashes Required? Yes

Fees/Permits: None

Season: Year-round

Getting There: From I-84 in The Dalles, take exit 87 toward Dufur and Bend. At the end of the off-ramp, turn south on Highway 197 and travel 29.4 miles to the junction with Highway 216. Turn left (east) on Highway 216 and proceed 4.2 miles to the entrance to White River Falls State Park. Turn right in to the entrance road and go 0.2 mile on a dirt road to a large parking area.

Description: This state park is a shady oasis during the hot summer months. A large, grassy picnic area with shade trees provides a great place for you and your dog to take a break from your travels. Restrooms and water are also available next to the picnic area. The highlight of this park is the roaring falls that plunge 90 feet over a basalt ledge into the canyon. You can walk to a cliff side viewpoint and view the falls or walk down a rough 0.25-mile trail to the canyon floor, where you'll find the historic Tygh Valley Power Plant built in 1901 by the Wasco Warehouse Milling Company. Originally built to power a flour mill, in 1910 the plant was purchased by Pacific Power and Light, and provided power to Sherman and Wasco counties until 1969. Its now-abandoned hulk makes for great exploring.

CANINE COMFORT ACCOMMODATIONS

$$ Quality Inn

2114 W. 6th St., 541-298-5161

This hotel has pet-friendly, non-smoking rooms, a hot tub, pool, and laundry facilities.

Dog Policy

A $10 fee per dog is charged per night.

$$ Shilo Inn Suites – The Dalles

3223 Bret Clodfelter Way, 1-800-222-2244 or 541-298-5502, www.shiloinns.com

This dog-friendly hotel features 112 guest rooms equipped with a microwave, refrigerator, hair dryer, cable TV, and free Showtime. Some rooms have a river view and outdoor deck. Additional amenities include a guest Laundromat, outdoor seasonal pool, exercise room, indoor spa, sauna, and fitness center.

Dog Policy

The hotel charges $10 per dog per night.

CANINE-APPROVED SHOPPING

Feed Shack

2315 East 2nd St., 541-298-4937

The Feed Shack has been in business twelve years and welcomes you and Fido to browse the aisles. This store carries dog coats, beds, houses, kennels, toys, grooming supplies, and premium diets. Open 9 A.M.–5:30 P.M., Monday to Friday; 9 A.M.–4 P.M., Saturday.

DOGGIE DAYCARE

Columbia Gorge Veterinary Clinic

1208 Belmont, 541-386-7773

Board your dog for the day for $6. Open 8 A.M.–5 P.M., Monday to Friday; 8:30 A.M.–12 P.M., Saturday.

CANINE ER

The Dalles Veterinary Hospital

408 West 3rd Place, 541-296-9191

This mixed animal practice will see your dog on a walk-in basis. The clinic also offers after-hours emergency care. Call the regular office number and the doctor on duty will be paged.

Open 8 A.M.–5:30 P.M., Monday to Friday; 8 A.M.–12 P.M., Saturday.

LOST AND FOUND (ANIMAL SHELTERS)

Wasco County Animal Shelter

200 River Rd, 541-296-5189, www.PetShelter.net

Open 10 A.M.–12 P.M. and 1 P.M.–4 P.M., Monday to Friday.

Central Oregon

*T*he mountains, lakes, canyons, and high desert plateaus of Central Oregon offer adventure and plenty of open space for dogs panting to get away from it all. Central Oregon is geographically separated from Western Oregon by the Cascade Mountains, whose striking volcanic peaks create a rain shadow, causing Central Oregon to be much drier and sunnier, and with vastly different vegetation than Western Oregon. At lower elevations, sagebrush and western juniper cover plateaus, valleys, and deep rimrock canyons. As you climb, the landscape's hills and volcanic peaks become thickly forested with ponderosa pine, Douglas fir, blue spruce, lodgepole pine, mountain hemlock, and whitebark pine.

Doggie Rest Stops

For a shady oasis when traveling through Bend, stop at Drake Park, off Franklin Avenue. In Sisters, check out Village Green Park, between Washington and Jefferson Streets, or Sisters City Park on Jefferson St. just off Highway 20. In Redmond, visit Ray Johnson Park at Fifth and Highland Streets (off U.S. 97) on the south end of town. If you are traveling north from Redmond, stop by the Peter Skene Ogden State Wayside, 11.5 miles north of Redmond on the left side of Highway 97. Prineville's Pioneer Park on E. Third Street and Madras' Friendship Park on the corner of 4th and E Streets are also great leg-stretchers.

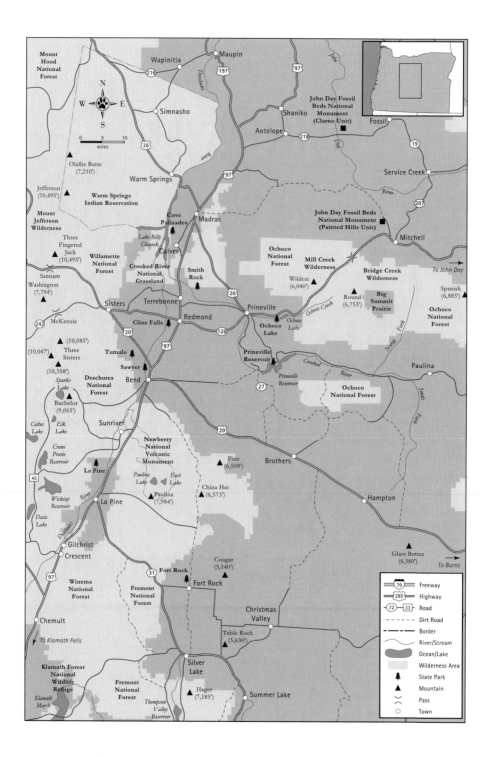

Bend

THE BIG SCOOP

As the largest city in Central Oregon, Bend is a great place to set up a base camp to explore this dog-friendly part of the state. A century ago, Bend was known as "Farewell Bend," named after two wide bends in the Deschutes River, two of the few places where immigrants could safely cross. Bend's 3,600-feet elevation at the foot of the Central Cascades makes it a canine paradise, with its nearby forested trails—some within minutes of downtown, mountain streams, and alpine lakes. Eight major peaks between 7,800 and 10,500 feet dominate Bend's western horizon: Mount Bachelor, Broken Top, North, Middle and South Sister, Mount Washington, Three Fingered Jack, and Mount Jefferson. The Three Sisters Wilderness and Deschutes National Forest are right out Bend's back door and the moody Deschutes River flows through Drake Park in the center of downtown.

Bend is home to dozens of parks that allow dogs on a leash. Currently, there are no designated leash-free parks, although community dog lovers are working with park officials to plan designated sites. Future leash-free areas may be in Hollinshead Park and Harmon Park.

Canine travelers may want to begin exploring Bend on the First Street Rapids hike, which parallels the Deschutes on the northwest side of town. This multi-use trail offers plenty of opportunities for cooling off in the river. Buff dogs may want to tackle the short but steep hike to the summit of Pilot Butte in Pilot Butte State Park on the east side of town. Another beautiful river trail that water dogs will wag their tails for is the Deschutes River Trail, just west of town off the Cascade Lakes Highway. Drake Park is a shady oasis along the banks of the Deschutes River in downtown Bend and is host to Ruff Wear Dog Days the second Saturday in September. Adjacent to Drake Park is Bend's downtown core, with plenty of window-shopping and people watching for leashed canines. Dogs wanting to scratch their shopping itch can check out Biscuits of Bend (1033 NW Brooks St.), which carries locally made Ruff Wear canine gear, toys, and delicious treats.

The Cascade Lakes Highway heads west out of Bend and leads to dozens of hiking, mountain biking, and skiing trails in the Deschutes National Forest and the Three Sisters Wilderness. Many campgrounds are located along this scenic stretch of highway. Cycling canines may want to check out the Phil's Trail-Kent's Trail loop or the Cultus Lake-Deer Lake Trail. Due to popularity and over-use, many trails in the Three Sisters Wilderness will not allow dogs in the near future. Two trails that may soon be restricted are the South Sister Summit Trail and the Green Lakes Trail.

You and your traveling partner can experience the volcanic history of this part of Oregon by hiking the Paulina Lake Trail in the Newberry National Volcanic Monument. Created in 1990, this monument boasts over 50,000 acres of high alpine lakes, lava flows, and mountain peaks. Its most dramatic feature is the 500-square mile Newberry Crater caldera, home to Paulina and East Lakes. Stop by the visitor center to find out about Newberry's many spectacular trails. The national monument is 35 miles southeast of Bend, off U.S. Highway 97. Your best friend must be leashed on all monument trails.

PAW-APPROVED HIKES AND PARKS

Benham Falls Hike

Contact: Deschutes National Forest, 1645 Highway 20 East, Bend, OR 97701, 541-383-5300, www.fs.fed.us
Paw-Approval Rating: 4 paws
Leashes Required? Yes
Length: 4.6 miles out and back
Difficulty: Easy
Fees/Permits: $5 Northwest Forest Pass. Purchase at 1-800-270-7504 or www.naturenw.org
Season: Year-round. Snow may be present during winter.
Getting There: From the intersection of NW Franklin and Highway 97 in Bend, travel 11.2 miles south on Highway 97 to a sign, "Lava Lands Visitor Center." Turn right (west) onto the entrance road and then take an immediate left onto Forest Road 9702 to a sign, "Deschutes River 4/Benham Falls 4." Continue 4 miles to a gravel parking area at the Benham Falls Day-use Area.
Description: This trail travels along the shores of the Deschutes River through a towering ponderosa pine forest. At the Benham Falls day-use area, picnic tables are nestled under the shady canopy of old growth ponderosa pine. If Fido wants to cool off before the hike, show him the great swimming hole at the trailhead. Start hiking on the trail next to the river's edge, where a sign indicates "Deschutes River Trail No. 2.1." After 0.1 mile, you'll cross a long wood bridge. After 0.8 mile, you'll arrive at a viewpoint of Benham Falls. The river rushes through a dramatic lava channel, creating spectacular rapids. From here, continue on the trail as it winds next to the river's edge next to a lava flow, until you reach Slough Meadow at 2.3 miles. Once

you reach this day-use area, turn around and retrace the route back to your starting point. The trail continues along the Deschutes River for another 6.2 miles past Slough Meadow.

Deschutes River Hike

Contact: Deschutes National Forest, 1645 Highway 20 East, Bend, OR 97701, 541-383-5300, www.fs.fed.us
Paw-Approval Rating: 4 paws
Leashes Required? Yes
Length: 4.4 miles out and back (with longer options)
Difficulty: Easy. (Moderate if you are hiking the entire length of the Deschutes River Trail)
Fees/Permits: None. This trailhead does not require a user fee. All other trailheads along this trail do require a $5 Northwest Forest Pass.
Season: Year-round. Snow may be present during winter.
Getting There: The Deschutes River Trail has many trailheads. To reach the closest trailhead to downtown Bend, head west on the Cascade Lakes Highway (Oregon Highway 46) about 6 miles. Turn left on Forest Road 100 at the Meadow Picnic Area sign. Drive 1.4 miles to the parking area and trailhead. Restrooms are available at the trailhead (no water).
Description: The Deschutes River Trail carves its way through dramatic lava-strewn canyons and quiet grassy meadows. This singletrack trail, one of the premier hiking trails in Bend, is part of a multi-user trail system designed for hikers, runners, mountain bikers, and equestrians. It twists and turns along the banks of the Deschutes past waterfalls, boiling rapids, and everything in between. Begin at the trail sign that states, "Deschutes River Trails/Lava Island Rock Shelter 1/Lava Island Falls 1.2/Dillon Falls 4.5/Benham Falls 8.5." Follow the singletrack trail as it heads up a short hill and then winds around lava outcrops above the river

through a gorgeous ponderosa pine forest. At 0.5 mile, arrive at a large pond. Look for a small hiker symbol and take a sharp left. Follow the dirt path as it crosses the pond on a built-up dike. Continue on the trail as it follows the contours of the river. At the 1-mile mark, you and your pal will reach the Lava Island Shelter. Go about 100 yards and keep following the main trail as it parallels the riverbank. At 2.2 miles, you'll arrive at Big Eddy Rapids, your turnaround point. Retrace the route back to the starting point, for a total of 4.4 miles.

Trail Option: For an all-day adventure, continue on to Benham Falls East Day-use Area and back to the Meadow Picnic Area for a total out and back mileage of 17 miles, with 300 feet of elevation gain.

Drake Park

Contact: Bend Metro Park & Recreation District, 200 NW Pacific Park Lane, Bend, OR 97701, 541-389-7275, www.bendparksandrec.org
Paw-Approval Rating: 3 paws
Leashes Required? Yes
Fees/Permits: None
Season: Year-round
Getting There: At the intersection of U.S Highway 97 and Franklin Ave. in downtown Bend, turn west on Franklin Ave. Go 0.8 mile on Franklin Ave. to a public parking area on the right side of the road adjacent to Drake Park.
Description: This beautiful 13-acre park borders Mirror Pond for a half mile in downtown Bend. Towering ponderosa pine, a large grassy lawn, and lots of water make this a favorite canine hangout. Dogs and their people usually congregate near the west end of the park by the footbridge, where canines can cool off and play fetch in the cool waters of Mirror Pond. Plastic bags are provided to encourage owners to clean up after their hounds in this popular park. Be sure to check out the annual Ruff Wear Days held the second Saturday in September in the park (see *Dog Events*).

Dry River Gorge Hike

Contact: Bureau of Land Management, Prineville District Office, 3050 NE Third St., Prineville, OR 97754, 541-416-6700, www.or.blm.gov/Prineville/
Paw-Approval Rating: 3 paws
Leashes Required? Yes
Length: 6 miles out and back
Difficulty: Easy
Fees/Permits: None
Season: Year-round
Getting There: From Bend, head east on Highway 20 to milepost 17. From milepost 17 continue 0.5 mile and turn right onto an unsigned doubletrack dirt road. Cross a cattle guard and continue straight (right) on a doubletrack road that goes between two large gravel piles. Go 0.8 mile on this doubletrack road (you'll have to weave around some rocks) to a primitive campsite on the right. Turn right into the campsite and park. If you have a high clearance vehicle, you have the option of continuing 0.3 mile further on this road. Passenger vehicles should not try this, due to several large rocks in the road.
Description: This desert hike promises plenty of solitude for you and your traveling companion. The route passes through an ancient river gorge filled with a beautiful old growth juniper forest. To begin, walk back out to the doubletrack road and turn right. Follow the doubletrack road 0.3 mile and then start hiking on the singletrack trail that takes you deep into a dramatic basalt canyon past thick groves of juniper and sagebrush. After 2.5 miles, the trail seems to end. To continue, scramble over some very large boulders on the right side of the trail; you'll then see a rocky trail that skirts the right side of the canyon for 0.1 mile and then descends to the canyon floor. From this point, continue another 0.4 mile on a sandy singletrack trail to your turnaround point at the end of the canyon. On this last section, look for raptor and raven nests high on the cliff walls. Avoid this hike during July

and August when temperatures can exceed 100°F. Be sure to bring plenty of water. If you don't mind primitive camping, you can stay overnight at the trailhead.

First Street Rapids Hike
Contact: Bend Metro Park & Recreation District, 200 NW Pacific Park Lane, Bend, OR 97701, 541-389-7275, www.bendparksandrec.org
Paw-Approval Rating: 3 paws
Leashes Required? Yes
Length: 6 miles out and back
Difficulty: Easy
Fees/Permits: None
Season: Year-round
Getting There: From Highway 97 in Bend, turn right on Division St. Proceed 0.8 mile and turn right on Revere Ave. Continue 0.2 mile and turn left on Hill Ave. Go 0.2 mile and turn right on Portland Ave. Proceed 0.2 mile and turn right on First St. Continue 0.3 mile to the street dead-end at First Street Rapids Park.
Description: This popular multi-use trail heads north, paralleling the Deschutes River and then climbing to the top of a ridge high above the river. From First Street Rapids Park, begin walking north on the wood chip trail paralleling the Deschutes. Here's a good place for Rover to get his nose wet. After 0.7 mile, stay to the left on the wood chip trail (don't go right toward the golf course). The trail then intersects the paved Mount Washington Dr. Turn right and follow the wood chip trail downhill as it parallels Mount Washington Dr. (look for the small Deschutes River Trail signs marking the trail). After 0.8 mile, turn left and cross Mount Washington Dr. Pick up the wood chip trail on the other side. The trail parallels a paved trail a short distance but then turns back to wood chip only. The trail continues to parallel the golf course and enters a forest corridor that passes through several residential areas. At 2 miles, cross Archie Briggs Road and continue hiking on the wood chip trail on the other side. At

A high-mountain meadow in the Three Sisters Wilderness.

2.3 miles, the trail crosses another paved road in a residential area and then hugs the ridgeline high above the Deschutes River. From here, you'll have grand views of Mount Washington, Black Butte, and other Central Cascade peaks. At 3 miles, you'll reach your turnaround point at the trail's end. Head back on the same route to your starting point for a total of 6 miles.

Green Lakes Loop Hike
Contact: Deschutes National Forest, 1645 Highway 20 East, Bend, OR 97701, 541-383-5300, www.fs.fed.us
Paw-Approval Rating: 4 paws
Leashes Required? Yes
Length: 11.6-mile loop
Difficulty: Difficult
Fees/Permits: Free wilderness permits are required. Obtain a permit at the trailhead.
Season: Late June through October
Getting There: From the intersection of Highway 97 and Franklin Ave. in downtown Bend, turn west on Franklin Ave. Proceed 1.2 miles (Franklin Ave. turns into Riverside Blvd.) to the intersection

with Tumalo Ave. Turn right on Tumalo Ave. (which turns into Galveston Ave.). Go 0.5 mile and turn left on 14th St. This street soon turns into Century Drive, also known as the Cascade Lakes Highway (OR Highway 46). Continue about 27 miles on the highway to the Green Lakes trailhead parking area on the right side of the road.

Description: This popular route travels uphill for over 1,175 feet, paralleling enchanting Fall Creek and then entering the Green Lakes Basin. The return loop takes you on the Soda Creek Trail through the even more gorgeous Three Sisters Wilderness. Start on Trail 17 that parallels Fall Creek. A sign indicates "Moraine Lake 2 miles/Green Lakes 4.5 miles/Park Meadow 9 miles/Scott Pass 21 miles." At 2 miles, continue straight (right) on the smooth track as it parallels Fall Creek. (The trail that goes left at this junction heads toward Moraine Lake.) At 4.3 miles, turn right toward "Park Meadow/Soda Creek." Continue 10 yards and then take another quick right turn toward "Soda Creek/Broken Top." Continue on the trail as it skirts the south edge of 9,175-foot Broken Top. Along this section, you'll have grand views of the Green Lakes to the north. At 7.1 miles, turn right toward "Soda Creek/Todd Lake." (The Broken Top Trail continues left at this junction) At 7.9 miles, turn right where a sign indicates "Soda Creek." (The trail that goes left heads toward Todd Lake.) From here, you'll continue downhill. Be ready to negotiate water crossings at Crater Creek and Soda Creek. At 11.6 miles, you'll arrive back at the Green Lakes Trailhead. Due to this trail's popularity, dogs may be restricted in the near future. Mosquitoes can be a problem during late June and July. Nearby campgrounds are Devils Lake and Todd Lake (see *Campgrounds*).

Harmon Park

Contact: Bend Metro Park & Recreation District, 200 NW Pacific Park Lane, Bend, OR 97701, 541-389-7275, www.bendparksandrec.org
Paw-Approval Rating: 3 paws
Leashes Required? Yes
Fees/Permits: None
Season: Year-round
Getting There: The park is at the intersection of NW Harmon Blvd. and Nashville Ave. in downtown Bend.
Description: This small 3.7-acre park is located along the banks of the Deschutes River opposite Drake Park in downtown Bend, and is popular with the canine crowd. It features large, open grassy fields used for softball and soccer. It also has a playground and restrooms. Harmon Park may be designated a leash-free park in the future.

Hollinshead Park

Contact: Bend Metro Park & Recreation District, 200 NW Pacific Park Lane, Bend, OR 97701, 541-389-7275, www.bendparksandrec.org
Paw-Approval Rating: 3 paws
Leashes Required? Yes
Fees/Permits: None
Season: Year-round
Getting There: The park is at 1235 NE Jones Road in Bend.
Description: This 16.5-acre neighborhood park in northeast Bend, once a working ranch, boasts a paved bike path, hiking trail, and playground. The park features a rolling grassy landscape, shade trees, and orchards. Tour its historical buildings, including the renovated Hollinshead Barn and the Share Croppers House museum. This park may be a designated a leash-free park in the future. Restrooms and water are available.

McKay Park

Contact: Bend Metro Park & Recreation District, 200 NW Pacific Park Lane, Bend, OR 97701, 541-389-7275, www.bendparksandrec.org
Paw-Approval Rating: 3 paws
Leashes Required? Yes
Fees/Permits: None

Season: Year-round
Getting There: This park is at 166 Shevlin Hixon Dr. in Bend.
Description: This 7-acre riverside park features access to the Deschutes, a large grassy lawn, shade trees, picnic tables, and park benches. Canine water sports are a popular attraction.

 **Pilot Butte
State Park Hike**
Contact: Oregon State Parks and Recreation, Suite 1, 1115 Commercial St. NE, Salem OR 97301-1002, 1-800-551-6949, www.oregonstateparks.org
Paw-Approval Rating: 3 paws
Leashes Required? Yes
Length: 1.7 miles out and back
Difficulty: Moderate
Fees/Permits: None
Season: Year-round
Getting There: From Highway 97 in the center of Bend, turn east on Greenwood Ave. Go 1.5 miles east and turn left at the Pilot Butte trailhead sign. Continue to a large parking area at the trailhead.
Description: Trail hounds will enjoy this short, steep trail that climbs 480 feet to the summit of Pilot Butte. At the summit, you and your best friend will be rewarded with views to the west of Mount Bachelor, Broken Top, North, Middle, and South Sister, Mount Washington, and Mount Jefferson. Begin by walking on the paved path adjacent to the parking area. At 0.1 mile, turn right on the signed "Nature Trail." Continue hiking as the trail ascends steeply. At 0.7 mile, reach the paved summit circle. Walk around it and enjoy the far-reaching views of downtown Bend and the Central Cascades. Head downhill on the same route.

 **Pioneer Park**
Contact: Bend Metro Park & Recreation District, 200 NW Pacific Park Lane, Bend, OR 97701, 541-389-7275, www.bendparksandrec.org
Paw-Approval Rating: 2 paws

Leashes Required? Yes
Fees/Permits: None
Season: Year-round
Getting There: This park is at 1525 NW Hill St. in Bend.
Description: This 6-acre park features large, open, grassy spaces and other natural areas for you and Rover to explore.

 **Ponderosa Park**
Contact: Bend Metro Park & Recreation District, 200 NW Pacific Park Lane, Bend, OR 97701, 541-389-7275, www.bendparksandrec.org
Paw-Approval Rating: 2 paws
Leashes Required? Yes
Fees/Permits: None
Season: Year-round
Getting There: This park is at the intersection of SE 15th St. and Wilson St. in Bend.
Description: This 18.6-acre park has plenty of natural open space to explore, as well as a fitness trail and large soccer fields. Restrooms and water are available.

**Ray Atkeson
Memorial Loop Hike**
Contact: Deschutes National Forest, 1645 Highway 20 East, Bend, OR 97701, 541-383-5300, www.fs.fed.us
Paw-Approval Rating: 3 paws
Leashes Required? Yes
Length: 2.5-mile loop
Difficulty: Easy
Fees/Permits: $5 Northwest Forest Pass. Purchase at 1-800-270-7504 or www.naturenw.org
Season: Late June through October
Getting There: From Bend, travel 26 miles west on the Cascade Lakes Highway (Oregon Highway 46) to the turnoff for Forest Road 400 at the Sparks Lakes Recreation Area sign. Turn left (south) on Forest Road 400 and drive 0.1 mile to a road junction. Stay left on Forest Road 100 toward the signed Sparks Lake Boat Ramp and Trailheads. Go 1.7 miles and turn left into the signed Ray Atkeson Memorial Trailhead parking area.

Description: This picturesque hike, named for the famed nature photographer, takes you and your pup along the shore of Sparks Lake and travels through a thick lodgepole pine forest and past interesting lava flows. Along the way, you'll have wonderful views of the Central Cascades. If you want to spend a few days, camp at nearby Soda Creek campground (see *Campgrounds*). Mosquitoes can be a problem during late June and July.

Robert Sawyer Park
Contact: Bend Metro Park & Recreation District, 200 NW Pacific Park Lane, Bend, OR 97701, 541-389-7275, www.bendparksandrec.org
Paw-Approval Rating: 2 paws
Leashes Required? Yes
Fees/Permits: None
Season: Year-round
Getting There: This park is at 62999 O.B. Riley Road in Bend.
Description: This 61.5-acre park has a hiking trail, picnic tables, and a playground.

Shevlin Park Hike
Contact: Bend Metro Park & Recreation District, 200 NW Pacific Park Lane, Bend, OR 97701, 541-389-7275, www.bendparksandrec.org
Paw-Approval Rating: 4 paws
Leashes Required? Yes
Length: 4.9-mile loop
Difficulty: Easy
Fees/Permits: None
Season: Year-round
Getting There: From the intersection of NW Newport and NW 5th St. in downtown Bend, go 3.7 miles west on Newport Ave. (which turns into Shevlin Park Road after 1.9 miles) to the Shevlin Park entrance. Turn left at the park entrance; park in the paved parking area by the wood trail sign.
Description: Your dog will enjoy the abundant water and shade on this loop hike. This route is also excellent for trail running. From the parking area, walk

around a metal gate. Start hiking on the singletrack trail, which starts to the left of the trailhead sign. This section of the trail is virtually flat and takes you through a thick grove of aspens. After 0.1 mile, arrive at a trail junction. Turn left and follow the singletrack trail about 100 yards until you reach a wood bridge across Tumalo Creek. Your pooch will enjoy wading here. After crossing the bridge, turn right and follow the singletrack trail about 25 yards upstream. The trail then curves sharply left and switchbacks steeply uphill. At 0.2 mile, arrive at a T-intersection and turn right.

At 0.3 mile, arrive at a trail fork. Stay right and continue hiking through a clear-cut area on a high ridge lined with brushy manzanita above Tumalo Creek. At 0.8 mile, arrive at a trail fork. Stay left and ignore the spur trail that heads downhill to the creek. After 0.9 mile, arrive at a T-intersection. Turn right onto a double-track road. At 1.2 miles, bear right on the singletrack trail. After 1.9 miles, arrive at a trail fork. Stay left and continue on the singletrack trail along the ridge above the creek. Ignore the singletrack trail that heads downhill to the right.

After 2 miles, turn right onto a double-track road and begin descending toward the creek. Continue walking on the road as it crosses the creek over a drainage pipe. After crossing the creek, the trail begins climbing. After 2.1 miles, arrive at a T-intersection. Turn right onto a doubletrack road. Go about 25 yards and arrive at a T-intersection. Turn left onto a singletrack trail. At 2.4 miles, the trail descends toward the creek. After 2.5 miles, you'll arrive at the creek and a bridge crossing. You may want to stop for another swimming session. Cross the narrow wood bridge over Tumalo Creek and then continue on the singletrack trail as it heads downstream. After 2.7 miles, you'll arrive at a 5-way intersection. Go left onto a singletrack trail that heads slightly uphill. After 4 miles, arrive at a trail junction. Turn right on the singletrack trail. At 4.1 miles, cross a doubletrack road and continue walking on the singletrack trail. At 4.7 miles, turn left onto the paved park entrance road. At 4.9 miles, arrive back at the trailhead.

South Twin Lake Hike

Contact: Deschutes National Forest, 1645 Highway 20 East, Bend, OR 97701, 541-383-5300, www.fs.fed.us
Paw-Approval Rating: 4 paws
Leashes Required? Yes
Length: 1.4-mile loop
Difficulty: Easy
Fees/Permits: None
Season: Late June through October
Getting There: From Bend, head west and then south on the Cascade Lakes Highway (Oregon 46) about 54 miles to the junction with Forest Road 42 signed for La Pine/Twin Lakes/Crane Prairie. Turn left and drive 4.7 miles on Forest Road 42 to the junction with Forest Road 4260. Turn right on Forest Road 42 toward Twin Lakes Resort/Twin Lakes/Wickiup Reservoir. Go 2 miles on Forest Road 42 and turn left toward the sign, "Campground/Boat Ramps/South Twin Lake Resort." Follow the paved road (ignore the turnoff to the resort store on the right) as it curves left for 0.1 mile to a large Day-use Parking Area.
Description: This short loop circles pretty South Twin Lake and offers water-loving canines plenty of chances for dog-paddling. Start the hike from the day-use area, which has picnic tables, restrooms, and water. Follow South Twin Lake Trail No. 5 in a clockwise direction through towering ponderosa and lodgepole pine. Trail hounds will be distracted by chattering squirrels as you trek on this smooth forest path. At 0.2 mile, arrive at the junction with North Twin Lake Trail that heads left and reaches North Twin Lake in 1 mile. Continue straight on South Twin Lake Trail, which is lined with manzanita and bitterbrush. At 0.8 mile, you'll pass an inviting sandy beach—a great spot for Fido to dip into the lake. Just be sure no one is fishing nearby in case your rambunctious canine scares all the fish away! After 1.2 miles, pass the resort cabins and store and arrive back at your starting point. The resort rents canoes and rowboats. South Twin Lake Campground (see *Campgrounds*) is a great place to spend the night. Mosquitoes can be a problem during late June and July.

Newberry Crater National Monument and Area

Fall River Hike
(See *Cycling for Canines*)

La Pine State Park

Contact: Oregon State Parks and Recreation, Suite 1, 1115 Commercial St. NE, Salem, OR 97301-1002, 1-800-551-6949, www.oregonstateparks.org
Paw-Approval Rating: 3 paws
Leashes Required? Yes
Fees/Permits: None
Season: Year-round
Getting There: From Bend, head 23 miles south on Highway 97 and turn right onto State Park Road at the La Pine State Park sign. Proceed 4.2 miles to a road junction. Turn right and follow signs for the Camping and Day-use Areas.
Description: In a forested setting along the banks of the Deschutes and Fall Rivers, this quiet state park is off the beaten path. You and your hound can explore over 14 miles of trails through ponderosa and lodgepole pine forest and along the banks of these beautiful rivers. This park is home to what is thought to be Oregon's largest ponderosa pine. It also features a large campground (see *Campgrounds*).

Paulina Lake Hike

Contact: Newberry National Volcanic Monument, Deschutes National Forest, 1645 Highway 20 East, Bend, OR 97701, 541-383-5300, www.fs.fed.us

Paw-Approval Rating: 4 paws
Leashes Required? Yes
Length: 7.5-mile loop
Difficulty: Moderate
Fees/Permits: $5 Northwest Forest Pass. Purchase at 1-800-270-7504 or www.naturenw.org
Season: Late June through October
Getting There: At the intersection of Greenwood Ave. and Highway 97 in Bend travel south on Highway 97 for 23.1 miles. Turn left (east) on Forest Road 21 (Paulina Lake Road). After 11.6 miles, you'll pass the entrance booth to the Newberry National Volcanic Monument on your left. Go 1.6 miles past it to the Paulina Lake trailhead on the left.
Description: This beautiful hike circles the shores of Paulina Lake, one of two alpine lakes in the massive Newberry Caldera and has 230 feet of elevation gain.. Swimming opportunities abound for your hound. From the parking area, start hiking in a counter-clockwise direction on the Paulina Lakeshore Trail. After 2.2 miles, a sign states "Paulina Lakeshore Loop Trail follows road." Follow the paved road past a boat ramp and through Little Crater Campground. At the end of the campground, follow the singletrack trail that heads left and continue following the trail as it parallels the lakeshore. At 7 miles, turn right on a gravel road next to the Paulina Lake Resort general store. After 7.2 miles, turn left on the unsigned, dirt singletrack trail. After 7.3 miles, turn left on a paved road and then cross a concrete bridge over Paulina Creek. Immediately after crossing the bridge, turn left and pick up the unsigned dirt trail. After 7.5 miles you'll arrive at the trailhead. This national monument also features campgrounds (see *Campgrounds*) where you can set up base camp and explore the many other trails in the area.

Paulina Peak Hike
Contact: Newberry National Volcanic Monument, Deschutes National Forest, 1645 Highway 20 East, Bend, OR 97701, 541-383-5300, www.fs.fed.us
Paw-Approval Rating: 3 paws
Leashes Required? Yes
Length: 6 miles out and back
Difficulty: Difficult
Fees/Permits: $5 Northwest Forest Pass. Purchase at 1-800-270-7504 or www.naturenw.org.
Season: Year-round
Getting There: At the intersection of Greenwood Ave. and Highway 97 in Bend travel south on Highway 97 for 23.1 miles to a sign for Newberry National Monument and Paulina and East Lakes. Turn left on Paulina Lake Road (Forest Service 21) and continue 14 miles to the visitor center on the right side of the road. The trailhead is on the right, 50 feet before the visitor center.
Description: This tough hike promises a good workout for you and your dog as you climb over 1,300 feet through a lodgepole pine forest to the summit of 7,984-foot Paulina Peak. Spectacular views of Paulina Lake, East Lake, the Newberry Caldera, and the Big Obsidian lava flow await you at the summit. This hike is open only from mid-June through October. You can also reach the summit via car on Forest Road 500.

CYCLING FOR CANINES

Cultus Lake to Deer Lake
Contact: Deschutes National Forest, 1645 Highway 20 East, Bend, OR 97701, 541-383-5300, www.fs.fed.us
Paw-Approval Rating: 4 paws
Leashes Required? No
Length: 12.4 miles out and back
Difficulty: Easy
Fees/Permits: $5 Northwest Forest Pass. Purchase at 1-800-270-7504 or www.naturenw.org.
Season: June through October
Getting There: From Highway 97 in Bend, turn west on Franklin Ave. toward

Mount Bachelor and the Cascade Lakes. Continue 1.2 miles until you reach a stop sign. Turn right on Tumalo Ave. (which soon turns into NW Galveston). Proceed 0.5 mile and turn left on 14th St. Follow signs for the Cascade Lakes Highway and Mount Bachelor. Go about 46 miles west on the Cascade Lakes Highway to the turnoff for Forest Road 4635 at the Cultus Lake Resort sign. Turn right on Forest Road 4635 and go 2 miles to a junction. Turn right onto Forest Road 4635-100 (the road going left heads to Cultus Lake Resort). Continue 0.3 mile and park in the gravel parking lot on the left side of the road in the day-use area.

Description: This shady singletrack lake trail will keep your dog's tail wagging! Start riding on Forest Road 4635-100. After 0.4 mile, turn right. After 0.6 mile, you'll arrive at the Winopee Lake Trailhead. (It's a good idea to keep your dog leashed until you start riding on the singletrack trail.) Begin riding on the Winopee Lake Trail as it heads around the north side of Cultus Lake. At 3.2 miles, continue straight (Corral Swamp Trail heads right). At 3.4 miles, head left toward Deer Lake and keep riding on the shady singletrack around Cultus Lake. At 4 miles, cross a wood bridge and turn right at the next trail junction. At 4.8 miles, turn right toward Deer Lake. At 5.9 miles, turn left at the trail junction and start riding on the Deer Lake Trail. After 6.2 miles, turn right and arrive at scenic Deer Lake. Hop off your bike and cool off in the lake with your hound! Head back on the same route to your starting point.

Fall River

Contact: Deschutes National Forest, 1645 Highway 20 East, Bend, OR 97701, 541-383-5300, www.fs.fed.us
Paw-Approval Rating: 4 paws
Leashes Required? No
Length: 6.2 miles out and back
Difficulty: Easy

Fees/Permits: None
Season: May through November
Getting There: From the intersection of Greenwood Ave. and Highway 97 in Bend, travel 16.7 miles south on Highway 97. Turn right (west) onto Vandevert Road at the Vandevert Road/Fall River sign. Continue 1 mile on Vandevert Road to the junction with South Century Dr. Turn left onto South Century Dr. and go 1 mile to the junction with Cascade Lakes Highway (Forest Road 42). Turn right (west) and continue 10.4 miles (you'll pass Fall River Campground on the left after 9.7 miles) on the Cascade Lakes Highway to an unsigned gravel circular parking area on the left side of the road. A green forest service building is located adjacent to the parking area.

Description: This trail follows the crystal clear waters of Fall River. This spring-fed river is home to abundant wildlife. Be on the lookout for Canada geese, osprey, and mallard ducks. Your dog has plenty of opportunities to swim on this route that travels through immense groves of ponderosa pine and cool thickets of lodgepole pine.

To begin the ride, look to your left and begin pedaling on a doubletrack road that

Levi leading the way on the Fall River Trail.

begins adjacent to a wood pole fence. Go 75 yards and then bear left on a smaller doubletrack road. This road soon turns into a wide singletrack trail that takes you through a corridor of large ponderosa pine. After 0.5 mile, arrive at a sign (facing the other way) that states "End of Trail/Parking on Road 42." Ignore the sign and continue heading east as the trail parallels Fall River. At 0.6 mile, bear right at the brown hiker sign. Just past this junction, you'll pass a picturesque wood bridge spanning Fall Creek. Be sure to take a side trip to check out the bridge and the creek. At 0.7 mile, arrive at Fall River Campground and Day-use Area. Restrooms are available. Hook up with the gravel campground loop road; continue pedaling through the campground to its far end. (This campground is a great place to set up base camp—see *Campgrounds*).

At 0.8 mile, bear right onto the unsigned singletrack Fall River Trail that begins just to the left of campsite 8. The trail continues through a thick lodgepole pine forest near the river's edge. At 1.2 miles, the trail intersects a red cinder road. Turn right, ride on this road 0.3 mile, and then turn right onto an unsigned doubletrack dirt road. Ride 0.1 mile on it, then take a sharp right and continue on an unsigned singletrack trail. After 3 miles you'll arrive at a red cinder parking area. Ride straight across the parking area and continue riding on the signed Fall River Trail. Continue another 0.2 mile to the trail's end at a rock dam and a sign that indicates "End of Trail." Retrace the route back to your starting point.

Phil's Trail— Kent's Trail Loop

Contact: Deschutes National Forest, 1645 Highway 20 East, Bend, OR 97701, 541-383-5300, www.fs.fed.us

Paw-Approval Rating: 3 paws
Leashes Required? No
Length: 8.5-mile loop

Difficulty: Moderate
Fees/Permits: $5 Northwest Forest Pass. Purchase at 1-800-270-7504 or www.naturenw.org.
Season: May through November
Getting There: From Highway 97 in Bend, head west on NW Franklin Ave. (which turns into NW Riverside Blvd.) and travel 1.2 miles to the junction with NW Tumalo Ave. Turn right onto Tumalo Ave. (which turns into NW Galveston Ave. and then into Skyliners Road) and go 3.3 miles west. Turn left onto Forest Road 220 and go 0.5 mile to the trailhead parking area on the right.
Description: This zippy, forested loop with 500 feet of elevation gain is close to downtown Bend and offers a good workout for you and your pooch. Start on the singletrack trail that heads into the woods from the parking area. At 0.3 mile, bear left. At 0.4 mile, turn left onto the signed Phil's Connect Trail/H Trail. Continue cruising through a thick lodgepole pine and ponderosa pine forest. At 1.1 miles, turn right on a doubletrack road where a sign indicates "Phil's Connect/Phil's Trail/H Trail." At 1.7 miles, continue straight on the signed Phil's Connect/H Trail. After 2 miles, continue straight at the four-way junction. After 3.6 miles, cross a doubletrack road and continue on the signed Phil's Trail. At 4.3 miles, you'll arrive at a trail fork. This is the trail's halfway point and a good spot to give your pup some water.

After taking a break, turn right on the signed Kent's Trail. At 4.9 miles, take a sharp right on the signed Kent's Trail and crank up a steep hill. As you ascend, ignore a spur trail that heads left. At 5.6 miles, cross a doubletrack road and continue riding on the singletrack trail. At 6.1 miles, continue straight on the signed Kent's Trail (the KGB Trail heads right). At 6.3 miles, continue straight on the signed Kent's Trail. At 6.7 miles, continue straight on the signed Kent's Trail (The Sandista Trail goes left). At 7.9 miles, turn right where a sign indicates "Kent's Trail–To Trailhead." At 8 miles, you'll end the loop portion of the route. Continue straight (left) where a sign indicates "Trailhead." At 8.2 miles, bear right. After 8.5 miles you'll arrive back at the trailhead.

Swampy Lakes— Swede Ridge Loop

Contact: Deschutes National Forest, 1645 Highway 20 East, Bend, OR 97701, 541-383-5300, www.fs.fed.us
Paw-Approval Rating: 4 Paws
Leashes Required? No
Length: 8.2-mile loop
Difficulty: Moderate
Fees/Permits: $5 Northwest Forest Pass. Purchase at 1-800-270-7504 or www.naturenw.org.
Season: June through October
Getting There: From Bend, travel 16.5 miles west on the Cascade Lakes Highway (Oregon Highway 46) to the Swampy Lakes Sno-Park located on the right side of the road. Turn right and go 0.2 mile to the parking area and trailhead.
Description: The route follows a popular cross-country skiing route and twists and turns through lodgepole and cedar forest to the Swampy Lakes Shelter. Then it traverses a ridge to the Swede Ridge Shelter where you'll have grand views of Broken Top. You'll complete the loop by a series of ups and downs and then get one last cardio rush on an intense hill climb back to the Swampy Lakes Sno-Park. Dogs are not allowed on these trails in the winter, but during the summer your canine is welcome.

Begin riding on the signed Swampy Lakes Trail 23 located on the right side of the restrooms. Pedal a short distance to a trail fork. Turn right toward Swampy Lakes and Swede Ridge. At 0.1 mile, turn left toward the Swampy Lakes Shelter and begin a gradual ascent. At 0.7 mile, continue straight where a sign indicates "Swampy Shelter 1.5/Ridge and Swampy Loops." At 0.9 mile, continue straight on the signed Swampy Loop toward Swampy Lakes Shelter. After 1.5 miles, continue straight and ignore the trail that heads right. Begin a fun downhill toward the Swampy Lakes Shelter. At 1.9 miles, cross a wobbly wood bridge over a small creek lined with wildflowers. This is a good spot to let Rover cool off. From the creek, go 10 yards and turn right at the trail junction toward the signed Swampy Shelter (The Flagline Trail heads left). After 2.1 miles, arrive at Swampy Lakes Shelter. Turn right at the trail fork toward the Swampy Sno-Park. From here, begin a fast descent on tight, curvy switchbacks. At 2.3 miles, arrive at a bouldery creek crossing. Bold riders may attempt to ride across but others may want to walk. This is your last chance on the route to let your dog cool off. After 2.6 miles, turn left toward the signed Swede Ridge Shelter. Begin a fun roller coaster ride. At 3.4 miles, step over a large log crossing the trail. At 4 miles, the route traverses a ridge lined with manzanita with good views looking west to the Bridge Creek Burn and the jagged pinnacles of 9,175-foot Broken Top. At 4.5 miles, turn right on Forest Road 100 toward the signed Swampy Sno-Park. (Note: the Swede Ridge Shelter is located 50 yards from this intersection on the left.) At 5.2 miles, ride around a yellow metal gate and turn right (west) onto Forest Road 140 where a sign indicates "Swampy Sno-Park 2 3/4." At 5.4 miles turn left onto an unsigned singletrack trail. From here you'll begin climbing. At 7.2 miles turn left at the four-way intersection toward the Swampy Sno-Park. At 7.3 miles, ride around a metal gate and continue straight on a doubletrack road. Begin a fun descent. At 8 miles, turn right onto the singletrack trail at the 4-way intersection toward the Swampy Sno-Park. At 8.1 miles, continue straight. At 8.2 miles, arrive at the trailhead at Swampy Sno-Park.

POWDERHOUNDS

To avoid user conflicts during the snowy season, dogs are not allowed at some of

Bend's congested winter recreation areas, including Dutchman Flat, Swampy Lakes, and the Meissner and Vista Butte trail systems. The area south of the Cascade Lakes Highway (except Mount Bachelor Ski Area) is open to dogs. Edison Sno-Park and Skyliner Sno-Park area and trails are open to dogs.

The only exception is for working dogs in harness (with a permit), who are allowed on groomed snowmobile trails only. Free permits are available at the Bend-Fort Rock Ranger Station (1230 NE 3rd St., Suite A-262, Bend, OR 97701, 541-383-4000).

Listed below are a few areas to check out with your snow dog. For additional information, contact the Deschutes National Forest, 1645 Highway 20 East, Bend, OR 97701, 541-383-5300, www.fs.fed.us.

Levi with a prize stick near Mount Bachelor.

Dog Days of Winter

Mount Bachelor Nordic Ski Area, 1-800-829-2442 or 541-382-2442, www.mtbachelor.com

The Mount Bachelor Nordic Ski Area welcomes you and your hound on its groomed cross-country ski trails during two Sundays in mid-March, from 12:30 P.M.–4 P.M. All skiers and canines must have trail passes, which are $10 for skiers and $5 for each dog. All dogs must be on a leash or harness and under control of the skier. Trails open to dogs include all beginner trails, including Oval and Blue Jay's Way.

Edison Butte Sno-Park

Contact: Deschutes National Forest, 1645 Highway 20 East, Bend, OR 97701, 541-383-5300, www.fs.fed.us
Paw-Approval Rating: 4 paws
Leashes Required? No
Fees/Permits: Requires a $3 Sno-Park Pass.
Getting There: From Bend, travel about 18 miles west on the Cascade Lakes Highway to the turnoff for Forest Road 45 toward Sunriver. Turn south on Forest Road 45 and continue about 4 miles to the Edison Butte Sno-Park.

Description: Your pup will love heading out on over 24 miles of trails that begin from this snow park east of Mount Bachelor.

Skyliner Sno-Park

Contact: Deschutes National Forest, 1645 Highway 20 East, Bend, OR 97701, 541-383-5300, www.fs.fed.us
Paw-Approval Rating: 3 paws
Leashes Required? No
Fees/Permits: Requires a $3 Sno-Park Pass.
Getting There: From Bend, head west on Skyliner Road 11 miles to the Sno-Park.
Description: Skyliner Sno-Park is the starting point for a 6-mile trail system, with trails ranging from easy to moderate.

PADDLEHOUNDS

In Bend, for a short warm-up paddle, launch your canoe or kayak on Mirror Pond in downtown's Drake Park.

The Cascade Lakes provide canines dozens of opportunities to get a lungful of fresh mountain air, enjoy awesome mountain views, and romp in the water. Some of our favorite lakes, all west of Bend off the Cascade Lakes Highway, are Todd

Lake (24 miles west; no motorized boats allowed), Devils Lake (29 miles west; no motorized boats allowed), Sparks Lake (26 miles west), Hosmer Lake (36 miles west; boats with electric motors only allowed), Lava Lake (39.5 miles west), and Little Cultus Lake (50 miles west).

South Twin Lake is another idyllic lake where no motorized boats are allowed. From Bend, travel about 54 miles west and then south on the Cascade Lakes Highway (Oregon 46) to the junction with Forest Road 42 signed for La Pine/Twin Lakes/ Crane Prairie. Turn left and continue 4.7 miles on Forest Road 42 to the junction with Forest Road 4260. Turn right on Forest Road 42 toward Twin Lakes Resort/Twin Lakes/Wickiup Reservoir. Go 2 miles on Forest Road 42 and turn left toward the sign for "Campground/Boat Ramps/South Twin Lake Resort." Follow the paved road (ignore the turnoff to the resort store on the right) as it curves left for 0.1 mile to a large day-use parking area and boat ramp. You can rent a boat at the lake.

Three Creek Lake (16 miles south of Sisters off Forest Road 16; no motorized boats allowed) is also an idyllic high mountain lake for dog paddling.

CANINE COMFORT ACCOMMODATIONS

Unless otherwise stated, dogs should not be left unattended in the room and must be leashed on hotel property.

$ Chalet Motel
510 SE Third, 541-317-4916

This budget motel welcomes dogs. Rooms come equipped with a microwave, mini-fridge, and TV with Showtime.
Dog Policy
This motel charges $6 per dog per night.

$-$$ Best Western Entrada Lodge
19221 Century Dr., 541-382-4080

This resort in a forested setting welcomes your canine pal. It is located minutes from the Deschutes River, the Deschutes National Forest, skiing at Mount Bachelor, and the Cascade high lakes. The hotel has a heated pool and hot tub; continental breakfast is included.
Dog Policy
The charge for your dog is $5 per night.

$-$$ East Lake Resort
Newberry National Volcanic Monument, OR 97701, 541-536-2230, www.eastlake resort.com

This resort rents dog-friendly cabins and camping rooms. All cabins are furnished with a stove, refrigerator, coffeemaker, pots, pans, dishes, utensils, stall showers, and linens. Camping rooms are furnished with a sink, toilet, coffeemaker, a shared deck, and a picnic table. Pay showers are available in the RV Park, and you can cook your meals outside on the picnic table. The resort has a well-stocked grocery store.
Dog Policy
$5 per night or $20 per week is charged for each dog.

$-$$ Rodeway Inn
3705 N. Hwy 97, 541-382-2211

This pet-friendly hotel on Highway 97 features rooms with air conditioning, cable TV, iron and ironing board, data port, microwave, and refrigerator. The hotel also has a seasonal heated pool, a hot tub, and offers a complimentary continental breakfast.
Dog Policy
The hotel charges $5 per dog per night.

$-$$$ Bend Riverside Motel Suites
1565 NW Hill St., 1-800-284-2363 or 541-389-2363, www.bendriversidemotel. com

This motel has twenty dog-friendly, individually owned condominium suites, some with fireplaces and kitchens. The motel has a heated indoor pool, hot tub, and sauna. It is adjacent to a forested, riverside park with easy access to downtown Bend.

Dog Policy

A $10 fee per dog per night is charged.

$-$$$ Sonoma Lodge

450 SE Third, 541-382-4891, www.sonomalodge.com

This small hotel features affordable comfort in its seventeen pet-friendly rooms. All rooms are equipped with microwave and small refrigerator. A small picnic area is also present on hotel grounds. A complimentary continental breakfast is included.

Dog Policy

The hotel charges $5 per night per dog. Management asks that you walk your dog directly behind the motel on the side street, and not on the grassy areas on the hotel grounds.

$$ Holiday Inn Express Hotel & Suites

20615 Grandview Dr., 541-317-8500

This hotel on the north end of Bend has some rooms with Cascade Mountain views; all rooms include HBO and data ports. Indoor pool, spa and fitness room.

Dog Policy:

A fee of $5 per dog per night is charged.

$$ Motel 6

201 NE 3rd St., 541-382-8282

This motel near the Factory Outlet Mall and downtown Bend features sixty pet-friendly rooms.

Dog Policy:

Fido stays for free.

$$ Red Lion Inn

1415 N.E. Third St., 541-382-7011, 1-800-RED-LION, www.redlion.com

This hotel is close to downtown and welcomes your furry friend. It has a heated pool and hot tub, and rooms with cable TV and data ports.

Dog Policy

Dogs stay free.

$$ Sleep Inn

600 NE Bellevue St., 541-330-0050, www.sleepinn.com

This dog-friendly hotel, on the east side of Bend off Highway 20, is near Pilot Butte State Park (see *Paw-Approved Hikes and Parks*) and a large shopping center. Some rooms come equipped with microwave and refrigerator. Additional amenities include a heated pool and spa and complimentary continental breakfast.

Dog Policy

The hotel charges $8 per night for one or more dogs.

$$-$$$ Best Western Inn and Suites of Bend

721 NE Third St., 541-382-1515

This hotel just off Highway 97 is convenient to outdoor activities. Some rooms come equipped with refrigerators and microwaves.

Dog Policy

A $5 fee is charged per dog per night.

$$-$$$ Hampton Inn

15 NE Butler Market Rd., 541-388-4114

This hotel on the north end of Bend off Highway 97 offers pet-friendly rooms that include cable TV, HBO, data ports, irons, and ironing boards. Outdoor heated pool and spa.

Dog Policy

Fido gets to stay free.

$$-$$$$ Shilo Inn Suites Hotel

3105 O.B. Riley Rd., 1-800-222-2244, www.shiloinns.com

This hotel's 151 rooms come equipped with a microwave, mini-fridge, in-room coffee, and ironing board. Some rooms have a fireplace and view of the Deschutes River. The hotel is sited on seven acres and has a restaurant, indoor and outdoor pools, three hot tubs (indoor and outdoor), a steam room, sauna, fitness center, and guest laundry. All rooms are dog-friendly except the Jacuzzi rooms.

Dog Policy

A $10 fee per dog per night is charged. The hotel has a pet walking area and asks that you use this area to walk your dog instead of the other lawns on the property.

$$-$$$$ The Riverhouse

3075 N. Highway 97, 1-800-547-3928, www.riverhouse.com

Angie Wirtz, the Riverhouse's marketing manager, says, "Central Oregon is a recreational paradise, and pets enjoy romping and playing just as much as we humans do. We invite pets and humans alike to our outdoor haven!" Nestled along the Deschutes River and under towering ponderosa pines, the Riverhouse has 220 rooms, some with a river view, fireplace, spa, and kitchen. The hotel also features indoor and outdoor pools with Jacuzzis, an exercise room, premium steakhouse, music, and dancing. Take your dog walking next to the river on a nature trail. Your stay includes a free continental breakfast.

Dog Policy

Your furry friend stays for free. However, at check-in you need to sign a Pet Agreement that states you won't leave your dog unattended in your room.

Sunriver

$$-$$$$ Sunray Vacation Rentals

P.O. Box 4518, 1-800-531-1130

This rental agency has over 200 homes and condos for rent in Sunriver, a planned resort community south of Bend. Many rentals allow pets.

Dog Policy

Call for details about the pet policy for each rental unit.

CAMPGROUNDS

Devil's Lake

Contact: Deschutes National Forest, 1645 Highway 20 East, Bend, OR 97701, 541-383-5300, www.fs.fed.us

Season: Late June through October

Facilities: 9 walk-in campsites, picnic tables, fire rings, vault toilets, no water

Getting There: From Bend, head 29 miles west on the Cascade Lakes Highway (Oregon Highway 46) to the Devils Lake Trails sign on the left side of the road. The campground is marked by a small sign in the parking area.

Description: The sites in this campground are on the lakeshore and in the forest surrounding pretty Devil's Lake. The Moraine Lake/South Sister Trailhead begins from the campground's parking area. The Green Lakes Trailhead is also nearby (see *Paw-Approved Hikes and Parks*). Dogs may be restricted from these popular trails in the near future. For a shorter hike, try the 6.2-mile out and back Katsuk Pond Trail 13 that travels south through a shady lodgepole forest, past interesting lava formations, and by the headwater springs of Quinn Creek. The trail's turnaround is at Quinn Meadow Horse Camp. This trailhead can be accessed from the campground parking lot. Mosquitoes can be a problem in early summer.

Fall River

Contact: Deschutes National Forest, 1645 Highway 20 East, Bend, OR 97701, 541-383-5300, www.fs.fed.us

Season: April through October

Facilities: 10 RV/tent campsites (no electrical hook-ups), vault toilets, no water

Getting There: From the intersection of Greenwood Ave. and Highway 97 in Bend, travel 16.7 miles south on Highway 97. Turn right (west) onto Vandevert Road at the Vandevert Road/Fall River sign. Drive 1 mile on Vandevert Road to the junction with South Century Dr. Turn left onto South Century Dr. and go 1 mile to the junction with Forest Road 42. Turn right (west) onto Forest Road 42 and continue 9.7 miles to the campground on your left.

Description: This small campground is sited along the crystal clear waters of Fall River in a forest of stately ponderosa and lodgepole pine. Be sure to hike or mountain bike the Fall River trail that can be accessed on the left side of campsite 8 (see *Cycling for Canines*).

La Pine State Park

Contact: Oregon State Parks and Recreation, Suite 1, 1115 Commercial St. NE, Salem, OR 97301-1002, 1-800-551-6949 (information), 1-800-452-5687 (reservations), www.oregonstateparks.org

Season: Year-round

Facilities: 87 full-hook-up campsites, 50 electrical campsites, 3 yurts, 5 log cabins, picnic tables, fire rings, showers, RV dump station, piped water. Dogs are not allowed in yurts or cabins.

Getting There: From Bend, head 23 miles south on Highway 97 and turn right onto State Park Road at the La Pine State Park sign. Proceed 4.2 miles to a road junction. Turn right and follow signs to the campground.

Description: The large campground has sites in a forested setting and allows you and your dog access to over 14 miles of hiking and mountain biking trails.

Little Crater Campground

Contact: Deschutes National Forest, 1645 Highway 20 East, Bend, OR 97701, 541-383-5300, www.fs.fed.us

Season: June through October

Facilities: 50 RV/tent campsites (no electrical hook-ups), vault toilets, piped water, picnic tables, fire rings, boat launch

Getting There: From Bend, travel 23.5 miles south on Highway 97. Turn left (east) onto Paulina Lake Road (Forest Road 21) and drive 14.5 miles east to the junction with Forest Road 2100-570. Turn north and go 0.5 mile to the campground.

Description: This campground has prime sites with grand views of Paulina Lake. Some of the campsites can be very windy due to the close proximity to the lake. If you feel like hiking, try the Paulina Lake Trail (see *Paw-Approved Hikes and Parks*), or take your friend paddling.

Little Cultus Lake

Contact: Deschutes National Forest, 1645 Highway 20 East, Bend, OR 97701, 541-383-5300, www.fs.fed.us

Season: Late June through October

Facilities: 10 RV/tent campsites (no electrical hook-ups), vault toilets, water, boat launch

Getting There: From Bend, travel 46 miles west and then south on the Cascade Lakes Highway to Forest Road 4635 at the Cultus Lake Resort sign. Turn right on Forest Road 4635 and drive 0.8 mile. At the road junction, turn left on Forest Road 4630 toward Little Cultus Lake/ Taylor Lakes. Continue 1.7 miles until you reach the junction with Forest Road 4636. Turn right and continue 1 mile to the campground on the right side of the road.

Description: This campground is smaller and quieter than its bigger cousin (Cultus Lake) to the north. Sites ring the lakeshore and serve as an excellent base camp for prime mountain biking, hiking, and paddling opportunities. Mosquitoes can be a problem in early summer.

McKay Crossing

Contact: Deschutes National Forest, 1645 Highway 20 East, Bend, OR 97701, 541-383-5300, www.fs.fed.us

Season: April through September

Facilities: 10 RV/tent sites (no electrical hook-ups), vault toilets, no water

Getting There: From Bend, travel 23.5 miles south on Highway 97. Turn left (east) onto Paulina Lake Road (Forest Road 21) and drive 3.2 miles east to the junction with Forest Road 2120. Turn north onto Forest Road 2120 and go 2.7 miles to the campground.

Description: Campsites are located along picturesque Paulina Creek in a shady forest. The Peter Skene Ogden hiking and mountain biking trail passes by the campground and follows the creek uphill for 6 miles. (You are allowed to mountain bike uphill only on this trail.)

Paulina Lake

Contact: Deschutes National Forest, 1645 Highway 20 East, Bend, OR 97701, 541-383-5300, www.fs.fed.us

Season: June through October

Facilities: 69 RV/tent campsites, vault and flush toilets, piped water, picnic tables, fire rings, and a boat launch. An RV dump station is nearby.

Getting There: From Bend, travel 23.5 miles south on Highway. 97. Turn left (east) onto Paulina Lake Road (Forest Road 21) and drive 13.4 miles to the campground on the left side of the road.

Description: This popular campground has some sites right on the lake. It is also notorious for black bears who will boldly walk into your campsite to steal your dinner! Be sure your dog is tied up to avoid any bear chase scenes. You can access the Paulina Lake Loop trail from the campground (see *Paw-Approved Hikes and Parks*). This easy hike is one Rover will love due to the many opportunities to swim in this clear, cold lake.

Point

Contact: Deschutes National Forest, 1645 Highway 20 East, Bend, OR 97701, 541-383-5300, www.fs.fed.us

Season: Late June through October

Facilities: 10 RV/tent campsites (no electrical hook-ups), picnic tables, fire rings, restrooms, piped water, boat launch

Getting There: From Bend, travel 34 miles west on the Cascade Lakes Highway (Oregon Highway 46) to the campground.

Description: This campground on the shores of Elk Lake offers views of South Sister, Mount Bachelor, and Broken Top. The lake is prime for kayaking and canoeing. Mosquitoes can be a problem in early summer.

Rock Creek

Contact: Deschutes National Forest, 1645 Highway 20 East, Bend, OR 97701, 541-383-5300, www.fs.fed.us

Season: Late May through October

Facilities: 31 RV/tent campsites (no electrical hook-ups), fire rings, picnic tables, vault toilets, piped water, boat launch

Getting There: From Bend, travel 49.8 miles southwest on the Cascade Lakes Highway to the campground entrance.

Description: This campground is located on the shores of Crane Prairie Reservoir; many sites have a grand view of South Sister, Broken Top, and Mount Bachelor. This area is a prime feeding ground for osprey. Mosquitoes can be a problem in early summer.

Soda Creek

Contact: Deschutes National Forest, 1645 Highway 20 East, Bend, OR 97701, 541-383-5300, www.fs.fed.us

Season: Late June through October

Facilities: 10 RV/tent sites (no electrical hook-ups), vault toilets, picnic tables, fire rings, no drinking water, boat launch

Getting There: From Bend, travel 26.2 miles west on Cascade Lakes Highway (Oregon 46) to the campground.

Description: This campground has sites along Soda Creek and is adjacent to Sparks Lake. Your pooch will enjoy the 2.5-mile Ray Atkeson Memorial Loop Trail (see *Paw-Approved Hikes and Parks*) that skirts the lake's edge and has wonderful views of South Sister and Broken Top. The trail also passes through jumbled lava flows along the lake's edge. Sparks Lake offers some of the best paddling in the Cascade Lakes area—it has supreme views of South Sister, Broken Top, and Mount Bachelor. Mosquitoes can be a problem in early summer.

South

Contact: Deschutes National Forest, 1645 Highway 20 East, Bend, OR 97701, 541-383-5300, www.fs.fed.us

Season: Late June through October

Facilities: 23 Tent/RV campsites (no electrical hook-ups), picnic tables, fire rings, restrooms, boat launch, no water

Getting There: From Bend, head west and then south on the Cascade Lakes Highway (Oregon Highway 46) 35.5 miles to the junction with Forest Road 4625. Turn left (east) onto Forest Road 4625 and travel 1.2 miles to the campground entrance.

Description: This campground is located in a forested setting on the edge of Hosmer Lake. This idyllic lake has spectacular views of Mount Bachelor and is a wonderful place to canoe or kayak with your traveling buddy. Mosquitoes can be a problem in early summer.

South Twin Lake

Contact: Deschutes National Forest, 1645 Highway 20 East, Bend, OR 97701, 541-383-5300, www.fs.fed.us

Season: May through October

Facilities: 24 RV/tent campsites (no electrical hook-ups), picnic tables, fire rings, vault toilets, water, boat launch

Getting There: From Bend head west and then south on the Cascade Lakes Highway (Oregon 46) about 54 miles to the junction with Forest Road 42 signed for "La Pine/Twin Lakes/Crane Prairie." Turn left and continue 4.7 miles on Forest Road 42 to the junction with Forest Road 4260. Turn right on Forest Road 42 toward "Twin Lakes Resort/Twin Lakes/Wickiup Reservoir." Go 2 miles on Forest Road 42 and turn left toward the signed "Campground/Boat Ramps/South Twin Lake Resort." Follow the paved road to the campground.

Description: Campsites are in a forested setting on the shores of South Twin Lake, where canoeing and kayaking are enjoyable because no motorboats are allowed. If you don't have your own boat, rent one from the resort store. You and your pooch can hike on a 1.4-mile trail around South Twin Lake or hike or mountain bike 1.2 miles to neighboring North Twin Lake on Twin Lakes Trail 5.1. Mosquitoes can be a problem in early summer.

Todd Lake

Contact: Deschutes National Forest, 1645 Highway 20 East, Bend, OR 97701, 541-383-5300, www.fs.fed.us

Season: July through October

Facilities: 11 hike-in sites, vault toilets, picnic tables, no water

Getting There: From Bend, travel 24 miles west on the Cascade Lakes Highway (Oregon 46). Turn right on Forest Road 4600-370. Continue 0.5 mile north to the parking area.

Description: Pretty Todd Lake is ringed with 11 premium campsites. You have to hike 0.5 mile from the parking area to the lake and camping area. Todd Lake is a good base camp for many Three Sisters Wilderness trails. If you have the fortitude to haul your canoe to the lake, it's also a great place to paddle. This campground is at 6,150-feet elevation; bring warm clothes for the often-chilly nights. Mosquitoes can be a problem in early summer.

Tumalo State Park

Contact: Oregon State Parks and Recreation, Suite 1, 1115 Commercial St. NE, Salem, OR 97301-1002, 1-800-551-6949 (information), 1-800-452-5687 (reservations), www.oregonstateparks.org

Season: Year-round

Facilities: 23 full-hook-up sites, 58 tent sites, 2 tepees, 4 yurts, 2 group tents, hiker/biker camp, picnic tables, fire rings, hot showers, restrooms, playground, piped water, ADA site

Getting There: From Highway 97 in north Bend, turn northwest onto O.B. Riley Road and travel 4 miles to Tumalo State Park and the campground.

Description: Travel hounds will appreciate cooling off in the Deschutes River, adjacent to the campground. Dogs are not allowed to stay in yurts or tepees.

DOG EVENTS

Chemult Annual Sled Dog Races

Chemult Ranger District, Chemult, OR, 541-365-7001

This annual race, part of the national sled dog racing circuit, is held the last weekend in January at the Miller Lake Road Sno-Park Area off U.S. 97 on the north end of Chemult (35 miles south of La Pine on U.S. 97). Watch 70 or more dog teams and their drivers compete for several thousand dollars of prize money in multiple races.

Ruff Wear Dog Days

Drake Park, Bend, OR, 1-888-783-3932, www.ruffwear.com

This annual event is held in mid-September at Drake Park in downtown Bend. It features events such as a 5K dog run for humans and their dogs, agility demonstrations, a disc dog competition, a water fetching contest, and a silent auction. Vendors sell dog gear and dog-related services. Be sure to check out the food and drink available from local businesses. The entry fee for your dog is $10; T-shirts are $15. Proceeds benefit the Central Oregon Humane Society and Softdawgs, a local canine advocacy club (see *Canine Clubs*).

CANINE-APPROVED SHOPPING

Bend Pet Express

2525 NE Twin Knolls Dr., 541-385-5298

Your pooch is welcome to check out the wide variety of premium dog food, supplements, collars, leashes, toys, footwear, coats, kennels, and other canine gear at this pet store. Open 9 A.M.–6 P.M., Monday to Friday; 10 A.M.–5 P.M., Saturday.

Biscuits of Bend

1033 NW Brooks St., 541-318-3333

Lisa Joy, owner, says, "I owned a bookstore for two years and wanted my next business to be one where my own dogs and other dogs were welcome and happy." The store carries treats, toys, all natural biscuits, and a full line of Ruff Wear outdoor gear for the discerning canine. Lisa says, "Dogs are encouraged to come and

A future Hover Craft™ champion at Ruff Wear Dog Days in Bend.

shop and be fitted for gear." The store will prepare gift baskets for special occasions. Open 10 A.M.–5 P.M., Monday to Saturday.

Petco

3197 North Highway 97, 541-382-0510, www.petco.com

Rover is welcome to browse the aisles of the warehouse-style pet store that stocks food, vitamins, toys, grooming supplies, and gear for dogs, cats, and other pets. Open 9 A.M.–9 P.M., Monday to Saturday; 10 A.M.–7 P.M., Sunday.

DOGGIE DAYCARE

Bend Pet Resort

60909 SE 27th St., 541-388-0435

This facility provides daycare from 7:30 A.M.–6 P.M. Monday to Friday. The resort has indoor kennels and an indoor play area for dogs to socialize. The daycare fee is $8 per day per dog; overnight boarding rates are $10.50 to $14.50, based on your dog's weight. Your dog must be current on his vaccinations.

Dancin' Woofs Compassionate Dog Training & Day Care Center

541-312-3766, www.dancinwoofs.com

This daycare features 7,000 square feet of indoor space and a fenced outdoor 1-acre play yard. During your dog's stay, he will be involved in supervised play sessions where he can have fun playing on agility equipment, in cool pools of water, or with other dogs and toys. Mare Shey, owner, asks that you call for an appointment the first time you bring your dog. Before your dog can attend the daycare, he must undergo a behavior evaluation, for a $20 fee. Your dog's vaccinations must be current, and he must be older than sixteen weeks and spayed or neutered if he/she is older than six months (there are some exceptions to this rule). Rates are $25 per day per dog; a second dog from the same family is $22.50 per day. This price includes pick-up and drop-off service in the Bend area. Obedience classes are also offered. Open 8 A.M.–4 P.M., Tuesday and Thursday.

For Paws Inn
Bend, OR 541-318-5962 (information) 541-504-5916 (reservations)

This inn's motto is "Where Friends Can Play." Day and overnight boarding for canines and felines is available. During the day, your dog can interact with other dogs in a large supervised play area and then retire to his private luxury suite at night to watch his own TV/VCR. The facility also offers traditional kennel boarding runs. Vaccinations must be current. Open 8 A.M.–1 P.M. Monday to Friday; 8 A.M.–1 P.M., Saturday; 4 P.M.–7 P.M., Sunday. After hours pickup is also available. Call for current rates.

DOG WASHES

U-Wash Pets & Grooming
3405 North Highway 97, Bend, OR 97701, 541-318-1602

This dog wash has been open two years and the owner says, "Dogs are more at ease when they are being groomed [washed] by their owner." When you bring your pup to be beautified, you'll be glad to find raised tubs with ramps for easy loading and unloading. The shop supplies tearless shampoo and conditioner, towels, forced air dryers, brushes, aprons, and holding crates. Full-service grooming and pick-up and drop-off services are available. The fee for a small dog is $11, medium dog $13, and large dog $16. Open 10 A.M.–5 P.M., Satur-day, Sunday, Monday and Thursday; 10 A.M.–6 P.M., Tuesday, Wednesday, and Friday.

DOG MEDIA

The Printed Paw News, The Newsletter of Softdawgs
1137 NW Federal, Bend, OR, 97701, 541-312-3766

This quarterly newsletter provides news and articles about dog-related issues in Bend and Central Oregon. Also included are articles on where to go and what to do with your dog, training tips, and a calendar of dog events and seminars. Call to get on the mailing list.

Canine Clubs

Bend Area Agility Dogs (BAAD)
22806 McGrath Rd., Bend, OR 97701, 541-389-7535, www.agilitydogs.org

This club hosts practice sessions and offers lessons; members compete in agility competitions in the Northwest.

Cascade Skijoring Alliance
P.O. Box 7876, Bend, OR 97708, 541-549-4044, www.cascadeskijoring.com

This club promotes the sport of skijoring (one or more dogs in harness pulling a cross-country skier) and provides education, dog care, equipment, and training. The club focuses on dog control and trail manners and encourages the positive growth of the relationship between dog and owner. Membership includes skiers and their dogs from Oregon, Washington, Idaho, and northern California.

Softdawgs

Central Oregon Environmental Center, 16 NW Kansas, Bend, OR, 541-312-3766,

The goal of this all-volunteer club is to educate dog owners about responsible dog ownership by focusing on dog training and health care, enhancing the dog/owner bond through outdoor activities, and community participation in dog related issues and events. The club helps the community by participating in monthly park cleanups, planning and participating in dog events, and working with park managers and law enforcement agencies. Members meet the fourth Thursday of each month at 7 P.M. at the Central Oregon Environmental Center in Bend. The club publishes a quarterly newsletter filled with information about the local canine scene, training tips, and recommended places to explore with your dog.

CANINE ER

Bend

Cascade Animal Emergency Center

425 NE Windy Knolls Dr., 541-318-5829

This clinic is dedicated to treating pet emergencies after-hours.

Open 6 P.M.–8 A.M., Monday to Friday; 12 P.M. Saturday to 8 A.M. Monday.

La Pine

La Pine Animal Hospital

51693 S. Huntington Rd., 541-536-2001

This full-service small animal hospital takes walk-in appointments. It also carries dog and cat supplies and prescription dog foods.

Open 8 A.M.–6 P.M., Monday to Friday; 9 A.M.–12 P.M. Saturday.

LOST AND FOUND (ANIMAL SHELTERS)

Humane Society of Central Oregon

61170 27th St., Bend, 541-382-3537, www.hsco.org

Open 10 A.M.–5:30 P.M., Monday to Friday; 10 A.M.–5 P.M., Saturday.

Sisters

THE BIG SCOOP

As you expand your exploration of Central Oregon, you and your trail hound may want to travel thirty miles northwest of Bend on Highway 20 to the small western-style town of Sisters. Open, sunny, ponderosa pine forests, dramatic volcanic peaks, high lakes and mountain streams, and the wild and scenic Metolius River characterize the landscape in this area.

Leashed dogs are welcome in this touristy western-style town, and people watching is prime. If you crave java, stop by Sisters Coffee Company (273 W. Hood St.) and sip a steaming mocha while your dog lolls under the canopy of a huge ponderosa pine. If you need to stock up on trail snacks, stop by the Sisters Bakery (251 East Cascade Ave.). For canine snacks, head to Sisters Feed & Supply (192 E. Main).

Sisters is a gateway to the Deschutes National Forest, the Three Sisters Wilderness and the Mount Washington Wilderness. West of town, the Three Sisters stand as sentinels with 6,436-foot Black Butte—one of the state's tallest cinder cones—brooding next door. Buff dogs may want to trek to the top of this awesome volcanic relic on the Black Butte Summit Trail.

Another mountain trail that will test Rover's stamina is the Tam McArthur Rim Trail, which leads you and your pup to a dramatic windswept ridge with unsurpassed views of the Central Cascades and the Three Creeks Lake Basin. If you have a water dog, don't miss the West Metolius River Trail, which saunters along the always-icy, crystal clear waters of the Metolius River. For an enjoyable lake hike, try the Suttle Lake Trail, which circles the lake and offers multiple opportunities to swim in its cool waters. A short and fun mountain bike trail is the Eagle Rock Loop, at Sisters' city limits. For a longer cycling opportunity, try the Peterson Ridge Loop, which begins at the same trailhead as the Eagle Rock Loop (see *Cycling for Canines*).

PAW-APPROVED HIKES AND PARKS

Benson Lake Hike

Contact: Deschutes National Forest, Sisters Ranger District, P.O. Box 249, Sisters, OR 97759, 541-549-7700, www.fs.fed.us
Paw-Approval Rating: 4 paws
Leashes Required? No
Length: 2.8 miles out and back
Difficulty: Easy
Fees/Permits: $5 Northwest Forest Pass. Purchase at 1-800-270-7504 or www.naturenw.org
Season: July through October
Getting There: From Sisters, turn west onto the McKenzie Highway, Oregon 242. Travel west 20.2 miles and turn right (north) onto a gravel road signed for Scott Lake. Continue 1.5 miles to a parking area and the trailhead.
Description: This short forest path ascends 400 feet through a shady lodgepole pine forest to a trail junction at 1.4 miles. Turn left and walk on a side trail to the lakeshore. Let Fido take a soothing swim in the cool waters. After exploring the lake, retrace the route to the trailhead. Mosquitoes are thick during July.
Trail Option: If you want to check out another high lake, head back to the main

trail, turn left, and continue another 1.1 miles to a side trail to Tenas Lakes.

Black Butte Hike

Contact: Deschutes National Forest, Sisters Ranger District, P.O. Box 249, Sisters, OR 97759, 541-549-7700, www.fs.fed.us
Paw-Approval Rating: 3 paws
Leashes Required? Yes
Length: 3.8 miles out and back
Difficulty: Difficult
Fees/Permits: $5 Northwest Forest Pass. Purchase at 1-800-270-7504 or www. naturenw.org
Season: May through October
Getting There: Head 6 miles west of Sisters on Highway 20 and turn right on Green Ridge Road (Forest Road 11). Go 3.8 miles to Forest Road 1110. Turn left and travel 4.2 miles to the junction with Forest Road 700. Turn right and continue 1.1 miles to a large parking area and the trailhead.
Description: If you and your dog love the challenge of steep mountain climbs and gorgeous summit views, you'll dig this 1,585-foot leg burner to the top of 6,436-foot Black Butte. At the top, check out the historic fire lookout and enjoy the spectacular views of the Three Sisters mountains and other Central Cascade peaks. Be sure to carry plenty of water with you. The hike to the summit can be very hot and dusty during the middle of the summer.

Black Crater Hike

Contact: Deschutes National Forest, Sisters Ranger District, P.O. Box 249, Sisters, OR 97759, 541-549-7700, www.fs.fed.us
Paw-Approval Rating: 3 paws
Leashes Required? Yes
Length: 8.2 miles out and back
Difficulty: Difficult
Fees/Permits: $5 Northwest Forest Pass. Purchase at 1-800-270-7504 or www. naturenw.org
Season: Late June through October

Getting There: From Sisters, drive 11.5 miles west on the McKenzie Highway (Oregon 242) to the Black Crater trailhead on the left side of the road.
Description: If your dog is a peak-bagger, he'll love this challenging hike to the craggy summit of 7,251-foot Black Crater. From the trailhead the route winds 2,500 feet up the north side of Black Crater through thickets of mountain hemlock and sunny slopes scattered with purple lupine and fiery Indian paintbrush. At the summit, two prominent pinnacles rise above the crater of an extinct volcano. You'll have fantastic views of the Three Sisters mountains to the south and Belknap Crater, Mount Washington, Mount Jefferson, and Mount Hood to the north. Be sure to bring plenty of water for you and your pooch.

Hand Lake Hike

Contact: Deschutes National Forest, Sisters Ranger District, P.O. Box 249, Sisters, OR 97759, 541-549-7700, www.fs.fed.us
Paw-Approval Rating: 4 paws
Leashes Required? No
Length: 1 mile out and back
Difficulty: Easy
Fees/Permits: A free self-issue wilderness permit available at the trailhead.
Season: July through October
Getting There: From Sisters, turn west onto the McKenzie Highway, Oregon 242 and travel 19.3 miles to a gravel pullout on the left side of the road marked by a brown hiker symbol.
Description: This short hike promises wading opportunities for your pooch in Hand Lake and offers breathtaking views of the pointy summit of Mount Washington and of the Three Sisters. Begin by crossing the highway (use caution here!) to the signed trailhead. Begin walking on the trail as it descends through a thick lodgepole pine forest dotted with bunches of purple lupine. At 0.5 mile, emerge from the forest into a scenic high alpine meadow.

Sage and Levi coolinig off in Hand Lake.

You can explore an old three-sided wood shelter. From here a side trail leads down to the lakeshore. Retrace the route back to the trailhead. Expect armies of mosquitoes in July.

Park Meadow Hike

Contact: Deschutes National Forest, Sisters Ranger District, P.O. Box 249, Sisters, OR 97759, 541-549-7700, www.fs.fed.us
Paw-Approval Rating: 4 paws
Leashes Required? No
Length: 7.2 miles out and back
Difficulty: Moderate
Fees/Permits: $5 Northwest Forest Pass. Purchase at 1-800-270-7504 or www.naturenw.org
Season: Late June through October
Getting There: From Highway 20 in Sisters, turn south on Elm St. (which turns into Forest Road 16) and travel 14 miles to the Park Meadow trailhead on the right side of the road. Turn right at the trailhead sign onto a rough, rocky, and rutted gravel road. If you are in a passenger car, travel 1 mile and park beside the road. Walk the remaining 0.1 mile to the trailhead. If you have a high clearance vehicle, drive 1.1 miles to the trailhead.

Description: This forest walk ascends 700 feet as it winds through the heart of the Three Sisters Wilderness, where your best friend will have fun splashing through creeks and romping in a high alpine meadow with awesome views of Broken Top and South Sister. Your hound will also appreciate multiple opportunities to munch on the horse snacks that are common on this popular equestrian trail. Wear mosquito repellent if you are hiking this trail in early summer. Also, bring water; this trail can be very hot and dusty and no water is available at the trailhead.

Patjens Lakes Hike

Contact: Deschutes National Forest, Sisters Ranger District, P.O. Box 249, Sisters, OR 97759, 541-549-7700, www.fs.fed.us
Paw-Approval Rating: 3 paws
Leashes Required? No
Length: 6.2-mile loop
Difficulty: Easy
Fees/Permits: A free self-issue wilderness permit, available at the trailhead, is required.
Season: Late June through October
Getting There: From Sisters, travel west on Highway 20 to the turnoff for Hoodoo Ski Bowl. Turn left (south) on Big Lake Road and continue 4 miles to a dirt pull-out on the right side of the road and the trailhead.

From Salem, follow Highway 22 east 82 miles to the junction with Highway 20. Stay left on Highway 20 toward Sisters and continue 6 miles to the turnoff for Hoodoo Ski Bowl. Turn right (south) on Big Lake Road and continue 4 miles to a dirt pullout on the right side of the road and the trailhead.
Description: This hike promises plenty of lake swimming and views of the Three Sisters, Belknap Crater, and Mount Washington. Mosquitoes are thick in early summer. At the trailhead, fill out a wilderness permit before you enter the Mount Washington Wilderness. Begin hiking on the

Patjens Lake Trail 3395. At the first trail fork, at 0.1 mile, stay right to begin the lake loop. The trail passes through a pine forest carpeted with clumps of bear grass and lupine. Early in the season, you'll pass small snowmelt ponds beginning at 0.8 mile. At 1.2 miles, you and your pup will ford a small creek with excellent wading pools. At 1.5 miles, stay left and continue on the main trail as it begins climbing over a low pass. As you ascend, you'll have views over the trees of the Three Sisters and Belknap Crater. At 3 miles, you'll arrive at a small lake on the right. A side trail leads to the lake's edge. Your hound may enjoy washing off the trail dust in this shallow, warm lake. As you continue, you'll pass another lake on the left at 3.5 miles. A side trail heads down to it on the left. Continue to the right. At 5 miles, the trail forks; stay left. At 5.2 miles, you'll arrive at scenic Big Lake. Enjoy the views of Hayrick Butte and the jagged summit of Mount Washington. Play fetch with Fido and float in the cool waters of the lake. At 5.6 miles, go left at the trail fork. (The trail that heads right leads to Big Lake Campground.) At 6.1 miles, you'll end the loop portion of the hike. Turn right and continue 0.1 mile to the trailhead. If you want to explore this area more, you can set up camp at Big Lake Campground (see *Campgrounds*). Mosquitoes swarm on this trail during late June through July.

Sisters City Park

Contact: Sisters Chamber of Commerce, 164 N. Elm St., Sisters, OR 97759, 541-549-0251, www.sisters-chamber.com
Paw-Approval Rating: 3 paws
Leashes Required? Yes
Fees/Permits: None
Season: Year-round
Getting There: This park is on Jefferson St., off Highway 20 at the east end of Sisters.
Description: This park is set in a shady pine grove next to Squaw Creek. A day-use area has picnic tables and barbecue pits. This park also has overnight camping sites.

Squaw Creek Falls Hike

Contact: Deschutes National Forest, Sisters Ranger District, P.O. Box 249, Sisters, OR 97759, 541-549-7700, www.fs.fed.us
Paw-Approval Rating: 3 paws
Leashes Required? Yes
Length: 1.8 miles out and back
Difficulty: Easy
Fees/Permits: $5 Northwest Forest Pass. Purchase at 1-800-270-7504 or www.naturenw.org
Season: June through October
Getting There: From Highway 20 in Sisters, turn south on Elm St. (Forest Road 16) and travel 7.5 miles south. Turn right on Forest Road 1514 (a gravel, washboard road) where a sign indicates "Squaw Creek 5 miles." Continue 5.1 miles to the junction with Forest Road 1514-600; turn left. Use caution, as this road is very rough. Continue 2.3 miles to the junction with Forest Road 1514-680; turn left (south). Caution: this is another rough road. Go 0.4 mile to the trailhead.
Description: This trail takes you through thick lodgepole pine to a spectacular viewpoint of the roaring cascade of Squaw Creek Falls in the Three Sisters Wilderness. Not far from the trailhead, you'll cross a small creek where Rover can cool off. The trail heads upstream until you reach a viewpoint of the falls after 0.9 mile. An unofficial trail heads 0.1 mile down to the creek's edge if you want an even better view. Return on the same route back to the trailhead.

Suttle Lake Hike

Contact: Deschutes National Forest, Sisters Ranger District. P.O. Box 249, Sisters, OR 97759, 541-549-7700, www.fs.fed.us
Paw-Approval Rating: 4 paws
Leashes Required? Yes
Length: 3.6-mile loop

Difficulty: Easy
Fees/Permits: $5 Northwest Forest Pass. Purchase at 1-800-270-7504 or www. naturenw.org
Season: May through November
Getting There: From Sisters, head 12.5 miles west on Highway 20. Turn left at the Suttle Lake-Marina & Resort sign onto the Suttle Lake entrance road. Take the first right turn, signed for Cinder Beach. Go 0.3 mile to a parking lot next to the lake and the trailhead.
Description: This route circles pictur-esque Suttle Lake. This hike features opportunities to swim and a phenomenal view of the snow-covered crest of 7,749-foot Mount Washington. Begin on the signed Shoreline Trail. Follow the trail as it circles the lake through lodgepole and ponderosa pine forest. A campground is also present at this lake.

Tam McArthur Rim Hike

Contact: Deschutes National Forest, Sisters Ranger District, P.O. Box 249, Sisters, OR 97759, 541-549-7700, www.fs.fed.us
Paw-Approval Rating: 3 paws
Leashes Required? Yes
Length: 5 miles out and back
Difficulty: Difficult
Fees/Permits: $5 Northwest Forest Pass. Purchase at 1-800-270-7504 or www. naturenw.org
Season: Late June through October
Getting There: From Highway 20 in Sisters turn south on Elm St. (Forest Road 16). Head 15.6 miles south (the road turns to gravel after 14 miles) to the trailhead parking area on the left side of the road at Three Creeks Lake.
Description: This strenuous route climbs over 1,200 feet to the top of Tam McArthur Rim—a vast windswept ridge in the Three Sisters Wilderness. Twisted whitebark pine, delicate high alpine wildflowers, and endless mountain views are your reward after your steep climb to the spectacular rim viewpoint.

The wood trailhead sign for Tam McArthur Rim 4078 indicates it is 2.5 miles to the summit viewpoint. The trail begins here and climbs very steeply the first 0.8 mile through a high alpine forest. Open meadows, old tree logs, and purple lupine line the trail, which leads you and your pup to the top of the wide-open windswept ridge where whitebark pine thrive. Follow the trail west along the ridgeline. Along the way, spur trails head off the trail. Continue on the main trail as it heads west along the ridge. After 2.3 miles, stay right at an unmarked intersection. At 2.5 miles, you'll arrive at a spectacular viewpoint from a lofty rocky escarpment overlooking the Three Creeks Lake Basin to the east, Broken Top and the Three Sisters to the west, Mount Washington and Mount Jefferson to the northwest, and Mount Bachelor to the south. Keep less experi-enced trail hounds on a leash at this view-point. After enjoying the mesmerizing view, head back the way you came to your starting point at 5 miles.

After the hike, drive up the road to Three Creeks Lake for a swim or paddle session. This hike is open mid-June through October. You can set up a base camp at the Three Creeks Lake Camp-ground or the Three Creeks Meadow Campground (see *Campgrounds*).

Village Green Park

Contact: Sisters Chamber of Commerce, 164 N. Elm St., Sisters, OR 97759, 541-549-0251, www.sisters-chamber.com
Paw-Approval Rating: 3 paws
Leashes Required? Yes
Fees/Permits: None
Season: Year-round
Getting There: This park is on Elm St. between Washington and Jefferson streets in downtown Sisters. From U.S. 20 in Sisters turn south on Elm St. and continue 0.1 mile to the park.
Description: This picturesque park is a great place for a break during a long road

trip. A grassy lawn, picnic tables, and plenty of water and shade make this a nice oasis.

 **West Metolius River Hike**
Contact: Deschutes National Forest, Sisters Ranger District, P.O. Box 249, Sisters, OR 97759, 541-549-7700, www.fs.fed.us
Paw-Approval Rating: 4 paws
Leashes Required? No (except at Wizard Falls Fish Hatchery)
Length: 5 miles out and back, with longer options
Difficulty: Easy
Fees/Permits: None
Season: May through November
Getting There: From Sisters head 10 miles west on Highway 20 to Camp Sherman Road (Forest Road 14). Turn right (north) and travel 2.7 miles to the junction with Forest Road 1419. Turn left and go 2.3 miles to a road junction and stop sign. Continue straight (you're now on Forest Road 1420) another 3.4 miles to the junction with Forest Road 400. Turn right on Forest Road 400 toward Lower Canyon Creek Campground and go 0.9 mile through the campground to the road's end and trailhead.
Description: This magical riverside trail takes you and your dog along the banks of the spring-fed Metolius River. Clear rushing water and swimming holes await your trail hound. Be forewarned: this river is frigid! Follow the singletrack trail as it winds along the river's edge through large ponderosa pine and Douglas fir until the turnaround point at the Wizard Falls Fish Hatchery at 2.5 miles.
Option: You have the option of crossing the bridge over the river and continuing on the river trail for about another 5 miles. Lower Canyon Creek Campground is a great place to set up base camp to explore this area further (see *Campgrounds*).

Great singletrack riding on the Eagle Rock Loop in Sisters. Photograph by Ken Skeen

CYCLING FOR CANINES

 Eagle Rock Loop
Contact: Deschutes National Forest, Sisters Ranger District, P.O. Box 249, Sisters, OR 97759, 541-549-7700, www.fs.fed.us
Paw-Approval Rating: 4 paws
Leashes Required? No
Length: 5.6-mile loop
Difficulty: Easy
Fees/Permits: None
Season: Year-round. Snow can be present during winter.
Getting There: From downtown Sisters, head west on Highway 20. At the city limits, turn left (south) on Elm St. Travel 0.5 mile, turn left on Tyee Dr., and park on the right side of the road. Immediately on the right is a trail sign that marks the start of this route.
Description: This mountain bike loop is a fun romp for your dog, as the trail sails through pine-scented forest and then takes you along the edge of the Squaw Creek irrigation ditch, with its many opportunities for hot hounds to cool off. Other distractions include plenty of sticks to fetch.
Trail Option: For a longer route, check out the 16-mile Peterson Ridge Loop that is part of this trail system.

Upper Black Butte Loop

Contact: Deschutes National Forest, Sisters Ranger District, P.O. Box 249, Sisters, OR 97759, 541-549-7700, www.fs.fed.us
Paw-Approval Rating: 2 paws
Leashes Required? No
Length: 14.3-mile loop
Difficulty: Moderate
Fees/Permits: None
Season: May through October
Getting There: From Sisters travel 6 miles west to Green Ridge Road (Forest Road 11). Turn right (north) onto Green Ridge Road and continue 3.8 miles to the junction with Forest Road 1110. Turn left on Forest Road 1110 and continue 1 mile to a dirt pullout on the left side of the road.
Description: This route circles the base of Black Butte through a picturesque ponderosa pine forest. A combination of doubletrack and singletrack, the route has 550 feet of elevation gain and can be hot and dusty in summer. The Lower Black Butte Loop is another trail you may want to explore.

POWDERHOUNDS

Corbett Sno-Park

Contact: Deschutes National Forest, Sisters Ranger District, P.O. Box 249, Sisters, OR 97759, 541-549-7700, www.fs.fed.us
Paw-Approval Rating: 4 paws
Leashes Required? No
Fees/Permits: Requires a $3 Sno-Park Pass.
Getting There: From Sisters, drive 16.8 miles northwest on Highway 20 to the snow park.
Description: A system of over 70 miles of trails can be accessed from this snow park. Connecting trails give you and your pup access to the Suttle Lake, Three Creek, and McKenzie Pass areas.

Upper Three Creek Sno-Park

Contact: Deschutes National Forest, Sisters Ranger District,

P.O. Box 249, Sisters, OR 97759, 541-549-7700, www.fs.fed.us
Paw-Approval Rating: 4 paws
Leashes Required? No
Fees/Permits: Requires a $3 Sno-Park Pass.
Getting There: From Sisters, turn south onto Elm St. (which turns into Forest Road 16) and continue south 11 miles to the Upper Three Creek Sno-Park.
Description: This snow park gives you access to 9 miles of cross-country ski trails in the Three Creek Lake Basin. To gain access to this system of trails, ski south on Forest Road 16, and hook up with the Three Creek Lake Trail. This trail climbs 1,200 feet in over 6 miles to Three Creek Lake. Along the way, you have options to hook up with other loop trails in this beautiful area.

CANINE COMFORT ACCOMMODATIONS

Unless otherwise stated, dogs should not be left unattended in the room and must be leashed on hotel property.

$$ Sisters Motor Lodge

511 W. Cascade Ave., 541-549-2551

This non-smoking motel is located in the heart of downtown Sisters and welcomes dogs in its pet-friendly rooms.
Dog Policy
A $5 fee is charged per day per dog.

$$-$$$ Best Western Ponderosa Lodge

505 Highway 20, 541-549-1200

This hotel, located in a ponderosa pine forest on the edge of Sisters, has a few dog-friendly rooms. Rooms are decorated with a western motif. Amenities include a pool and outdoor spa.
Dog Policy
A $5 fee per day per dog is charged.

$$-$$$ Comfort Inn

540 Highway 20 West, 541-549-7829 or 1-800-228-5150

This hotel features fifty deluxe rooms in a quiet forested setting. Ground floor rooms are pet-friendly. The hotel also features an indoor and outdoor pool and Jacuzzi.

Dog Policy

Fido gets to stay for free.

CAMPGROUNDS

Allen Springs

Contact: Deschutes National Forest, Sisters Ranger District, P.O. Box 249, Sisters, OR 97759, 541-549-7700, www.fs.fed.us

Season: April through October

Facilities: 13 RV/tent campsites (no electrical hookups), 4 tent-only campsites, piped water, vault toilets. No reservations accepted.

Getting There: From Sisters, travel 9.6 miles northwest on Highway 20 and then 11.1 miles north on Forest Road 14.

Description: This is a wonderful campground adjacent to the Metolius River. Campsites are under the shady canopy of ponderosa pines, and you and your dog also have access to the beautiful Metolius River Trail.

Big Lake

Contact: Willamette National Forest, McKenzie Ranger District, 57600 McKenzie Highway, McKenzie Bridge, OR 97413, 541-822-3381, www.fs.fed.us

Season: Late June through October

Facilities: 49 RV/tent campsites (no electrical hook-ups), fire pits, picnic tables, piped water, restrooms, boat launch. Fourteen sites can be reserved.

Getting There: From Sisters head west on Highway 20 to the Hoodoo Ski Bowl turnoff at Santiam Pass. Turn left on Big Lake Road and travel 3.6 miles to the campground entrance on the left.

Description: This popular campground is situated on the scenic shores of Big Lake. Views of Mount Washington are phenomenal and the campgrounds serves as a good base camp for the many hiking trails into the Mount Washington Wilderness. The Pacific Crest Trail can be accessed from the campground. The 6-mile Patjens

Lake Loop hike can also be accessed from here (see *Paw-Approved Hikes and Parks*).

Cold Springs

Contact: Deschutes National Forest, Sisters Ranger District, P.O. Box 249, Sisters, OR 97759, 541-549-7700, www.fs.fed.us

Facilities: 23 RV/tent campsites (no electrical hook-ups), vault toilets, hand-pumped water. No reservations are accepted.

Season: May through October

Getting There: From Sisters, travel 4.2 miles west on Highway 242 to the campground.

Description: This campground is set in a thick ponderosa pine forest just outside of Sisters. It is a good base camp for exploring Sisters-area trails, and is near the Black Crater hike (see *Paw-Approved Hikes and Parks*).

Lower Canyon Creek

Contact: Deschutes National Forest, Sisters Ranger District, P.O. Box 249, Sisters, OR 97759, 541-549-7700, www.fs.fed.us

Season: May through October

Facilities: 4 RV/tent campsites (no electrical hook-ups), vault toilets, no water. No reservations are accepted.

Getting There: From Sisters, head 10 miles west on Highway 20 to Camp Sherman Road (Forest Road 14). Turn right (north) and travel 2.7 miles to the junction with Forest Road 1419. Turn left and go 2.3 miles to another road junction and stop sign. Continue straight (you're now on Forest Road 1420) another 3.4 miles to the junction with Forest Road 400. Turn right on Forest Road 400 toward Lower Canyon Creek Campground and go 0.6 mile to the campground.

Description: This campground has sites along Lower Canyon Creek, against a backdrop of towering ponderosa pine trees, and is adjacent to the Metolius River and the West Metolius River Trail (see *Paw-Approved Hikes and Parks*).

Three Creek Lake

Contact: Deschutes National Forest, Sisters Ranger District, P.O. Box 249, Sisters, OR 97759, 541-549-7700, www.fs.fed.us
Facilities: 10 RV/tent campsites (no electrical hook-ups), vault toilets, no drinking water. No reservations are accepted.
Season: Late June through October
Getting There: From downtown Sisters, turn south on Elm St. (which soon turns into Forest Road 16) and drive 17 miles to the campground.
Description: This picturesque campground is adjacent to Three Creek Lake in the Three Sisters Wilderness. The lake is a great place to paddle and the campground is near the Tam McArthur Rim hike and the Park Meadow hike (see *Paw-Approved Hikes and Parks*). This campground is at an elevation of 6,600 feet, and may not open until late June. A 3-mile hiking trail that takes you to Little Three Creek Lake starts across from the trailhead for Tam McArthur Rim. Beware of mosquitoes in June and July.

Three Creek Meadow

Contact: Deschutes National Forest, Sisters Ranger District, P.O. Box 249, Sisters, OR 97759, 541-549-7700, www.fs.fed.us
Season: Late June through October
Facilities: 11 RV/tent campsites (no electrical hook-ups), vault toilets, no drinking water. No reservations are accepted.
Getting There: From downtown Sisters, turn south on Elm St. (which soon turns into Forest Road 16) and go 15.2 miles to the campground.

Description: Campsites are ringed around a beautiful alpine meadow near the Tam McArthur Rim hike and the Park Meadow hike (see *Paw-Approved Hikes and Parks*). This campground is not far from Three Creek Lake with its paddling opportunities. Mosquitoes are a problem in June and July.

CANINE-APPROVED SHOPPING

Sisters Feed & Supply

192 E. Main, 541-549-4151
This store carries all the gear and food your pooch will need for your travels. Open 9 A.M.–5:30 P.M., Monday to Friday; 10 A.M.–5 P.M., Saturday.

CANINE ER

Sisters Veterinary Clinic

371 E. Cascade Ave., 541-549-6961
This full-service small animal clinic has been serving dogs and cats for over 25 years. The clinic offers twenty-four hour veterinary care, overnight boarding, and grooming. Boarded dogs are walked three times daily and fed Hills Science Diet dog food. Rates are $11 per dog per day. The doctors are also happy to treat walk-in cases. The clinic carries a wide variety of pet care products, including medicated shampoos, conditioners, vitamins, flea and tick protection, parasite control products, toys, treats, and Hills Science Diet dog and cat foods.

Redmond

THE BIG SCOOP

Redmond, Bend's sister city, is 15 miles north on Highway 97. This smaller community, set amidst a spectacular juniper and sage landscape, is not far from world-class rock climbing at Smith Rock State Park, thousands of acres of BLM land, and the Crooked River National Grasslands.

If you are looking for a perfect cup of coffee, stop by the drive-through at Heavenly Grounds Espresso (255 SW 5th St.). In addition to your great cup of coffee, your dog will get a yummy dog treat. Stock up on food and gear for your dog at the Feed Barn, at 2215 N. Highway 97. At this friendly store, you can help yourself to free popcorn and coffee.

High desert scenery doesn't get any better than at Smith Rock State Park, six miles northeast of Redmond off Highway 97. Hikes here (see *Paw-Approved Hikes*) take you and your dog into the dramatic Crooked River Canyon, with its 400-foot high cliffs. While leash laws are strictly enforced in this park, you'll find many happy dogs accompanying their partners as they hike and rock climb. Another trail to make your dog's tail wag is the Gray Butte Hike in the Crooked River National Grassland. This singletrack trail wanders through a sage-scented high desert landscape and offers spectacular mountain views of the Central Cascades. An added bonus is your pal can be unleashed. The Crooked River National Grassland also offers hundreds of miles of doubletrack roads for you and your dog to explore by bike as well as numerous camping opportunities. Your dog does not have to be leashed in the Crooked River Grasslands or BLM lands.

PAW-APPROVED HIKES AND PARKS

Dry Canyon Hike
Contact: City of Redmond Public Works, Redmond, OR 541-504-2000, www.redmond.or.us
Paw-Approval Rating: 2 paws
Leashes Required? Yes
Length: 3 miles
Difficulty: Easy
Fees/Permits: None
Season: Year-round
Getting There: Access the trail at NW Pershall Way or at West Fir St. in Redmond.
Description: This 3-mile paved trail within Redmond's city limits takes you through the landscape of a rimrock canyon. You may have to dodge cyclists and in-line skaters but this short hike is a great in-town getaway your pooch will love.

Gray Butte Hike
Contact: Ochoco National Forest, Crooked River National Grassland, 813 SW Highway 97, Madras, OR 97741, 541-475-9272, www. fs.fed.us
Paw-Approval Rating: 3 Paws
Leashes Required? No
Length: 3.9 miles out and back (with longer options)
Difficulty: Moderate
Permits/Fees: None
Season: Year-round
Getting There: From Redmond, travel 4.5 miles north on Highway 97 to Terrebonne. At the flashing yellow light, turn east on B Ave. (which soon turns into Smith Rock Way). Continue 4.9 miles on

Smith Rock Way to the junction with Lone Pine Road Turn left and continue 4.4 miles north to the junction with Forest Road 5710. Turn left on Forest Road 5710 (you'll pass Skull Hollow Campground on your left), travel 2.6 miles, and then bear left on Forest Road 57. Continue 0.6 mile to the trailhead on the left side of the road.

Description: This route skirts the northwest edge of 5,108-foot Gray Butte in the high desert of the Crooked River National Grassland. You and your pup will possibly share the trail with the bovine species, and your best friend will enjoy lunching on the trail snacks they have left behind. The trail weaves through a sage and juniper-scented landscape around the base of Gray Butte to the Austin Creson Viewpoint at 1.9 miles (your turnaround point). From it, you'll have spectacular views to the west of the Three Sisters volcanoes, Broken Top, Black Butte, and Mount Jefferson.

Trail Option: Continue on this trail all the way to Smith Rock State Park. (You'll reach the park's boundaries in about another 4 miles.) If you decide to pursue this option, your dog must be leashed within the park's boundaries. You may camp free anywhere in the Crooked River National Grassland or for a small fee at the Smith Rock State Park Bivouac Area (see *Campgrounds*). Be sure to carry plenty of water on this hike. Summertime temperatures can soar into the 90s and there isn't any water available at the trailhead.

Smith Rock State Park Hike

Contact: Oregon State Parks and Recreation, Suite 1, 1115 Commercial St. NE, Salem OR 97301-1002, 1 800-551-6949, www.oregonstateparks.org
Paw-Approval Rating: 4 paws
Leashes Required? Yes
Length: 3.6-mile loop
Difficulty: Difficult

Fees/Permits: $3 state park pass fee required. You can purchase a day-use permit from the self-pay station in the main parking area.
Season: Year-round
Getting There: From Redmond, drive approximately 4.5 miles north on Highway 97 to the small town of Terrebonne. At the flashing yellow light, turn right onto B Ave. (which turns into Smith Rock Way after the first stop sign). Drive 3.3 miles northeast, following the signs to Smith Rock State Park. Water and restrooms are available at the trailhead.
Description: This beautiful hike takes you and your canine pal through a desert canyon along the meandering Crooked River and under towering volcanic spires. As you hike, watch the world-class climbers testing their moves on the canyon walls. On a hot summer day your pal may want to cool off in the Crooked River. You are also likely to see Canada geese, ducks, hawks, and otters fishing for trout in the river.

To begin, head toward the canyon and take a right onto an asphalt trail. Follow this to the canyon rim where it begins a steep descent into the Crooked River Canyon. After about 50 yards, turn right onto a foot trail. Head down this steep and slick trail to the canyon floor. At 0.2 mile, cross a footbridge over the Crooked River. After you cross the bridge, turn left at a sign indicating Morning Glory Wall is .25 mile, and Monkey Face is 1.5 miles. Follow the wide dirt path as it parallels the river. Look for a great swimming hole after about 0.25 mile, on the left side of the trail. A side trail leads down to a sandy beach, a great spot to let your dog get wet before you tackle the tough climb later in the hike.

At 1.4 miles, take a right at a trail intersection near the base of Monkey Face. This amazing rock pillar offers some of the most difficult rock climbs in the world. Begin hiking up steep switchbacks for 700 feet to the top of the ridge. Near the top, the trail splits. Stay right and continue your upward climb. You'll reach the ridge top at about

2 miles. Once at the top the trail becomes faint in some spots. Be on the lookout for wood trail markers that are signed "P" for the parking area to help guide your way. Many side trails spin off the route at the top of the ridge. Stay on the main trail. Look west to view several prominent Cascade volcanoes, including Mount Bachelor, North Sister, Middle Sister, South Sister, Mount Washington, Mount Jefferson and, to the far north, Mount Hood. Hike along the ridge 0.2 mile until you begin descending a very steep, loose trail known as Misery Ridge. Watch your footing as you head down switchbacks and multiple stairs. At 3 miles, you'll reach the canyon floor. Continue straight and cross the bridge over the Crooked River. After you cross the bridge, the trail forks. Stay right and walk on the wide dirt track that parallels the river. At 3.1 miles, take a right on a smaller foot trail as the main trail switchbacks left up the hill. Continue walking through a burn area from the mid-1990s.

After 3.2 miles, turn left at the base of a large basalt rock called Rope De Dope Block, and climb the stairs at its left side. At the next T-intersection, stay left and continue climbing to the top of the ridge. Go about another 30 feet and at 3.4 miles you'll reach the top of the ridge and a T-intersection. Turn left onto a gravel trail that parallels the edge of the rim and offers awesome views in every direction of the park and the Crooked River Gorge. After about 50 yards, turn left onto the path back to the main parking area, which you'll reach at about 3.6 miles. Be sure to carry plenty of water with you on this hike—summertime temperatures can soar into the nineties. You can camp at Smith Rock State Park's Bivouac area (see *Campgrounds*). The leash law is strictly enforced in this park by the resident ranger.

CANINE COMFORT ACCOMMODATIONS

Unless otherwise stated, dogs should not be left unattended in the room and must be leashed on hotel property.

$ Hub Motel
1128 N. Highway 97, 541-548-2101

This motel has pet-friendly rooms but allows only one dog per room.
Dog Policy
A $5 fee is charged for your dog.

$ Motel 6
2247 S. Highway 97, 541-923-2100, www.motel6.com

This budget motel has clean, pet-friendly rooms with cable TV.
Dog Policy
No extra fees are charged for dogs.

$-$$ Redmond Inn
1545 Highway 97 S., 1-800-833-3259, redmondinn.net

This hotel has 46 dog-friendly rooms furnished with kitchenette, microwave, refrigerator, and cable TV. The hotel has a seasonal heated pool and serves a complimentary continental breakfast.
Dog Policy
A $5 fee per dog per day is charged.

$$ Super 8 Motel
3629 21st Place, 541-548-8881

This motel has pet-friendly rooms at an affordable price. It features a heated swimming pool and a complimentary breakfast bar.
Dog Policy
The motel requires a $25 refundable pet deposit if you pay with cash. If you pay with a credit card no deposit is required.

CAMPGROUNDS

Skull Hollow and the Crooked River National Grasslands
Contact: Ochoco National Forest, Crooked River National Grassland, 813 SW Highway 97, Madras, OR 97741, 541-475-9272, www.fs.fed.us
Season: Year-round
Facilities: 40 primitive campsites (no electrical hook-ups), no water, vault toilets. No reservations accepted.

Getting There: From Redmond, travel 4.5 miles north on Highway 97 to Terrebonne. At the flashing yellow light, turn east on B Ave. (which soon turns into Smith Rock Way). Drive 4.9 miles on Smith Rock Way to the junction with Lone Pine Road Turn left on Lone Pine Road and drive 4.4 miles north to the junction with Forest Road 5710. Turn left on Forest Road 5710 and drive a short distance to the campground on the left.

Description: This campground is where climbers and their canine friends hang out after a long day of rock climbing at Smith Rock State Park. Amenities are sparse but the canine camaraderie is great. If this campground is a little too congested for you (and you don't mind camping in the wild), head up Forest Road 5710. You can camp anywhere you please in the Crooked River Grasslands. There are some great primitive campsites off this road, and, unlike in the park, your dog does not have to be leashed while you camp. Be sure to check out the Gray Butte hike (see *Paw-Approved Hikes and Parks*).

Smith Rock State Park

Contact: Oregon State Parks and Recreation, Suite 1, 1115 Commercial St. NE, Salem OR 97301-1002, 1 800-551-6949, www.oregonstateparks.org

Season: Year-round

Facilities: A small number of walk-in tent campsites, restrooms, water, and solar showers. No reservations are accepted.

Getting There: From Redmond, travel approximately 4.5 miles north on Highway 97 to the small town of Terrebonne. At the flashing yellow light, turn right onto B Ave. (which turns into Smith Rock Way after the first stop sign). Continue 3.3 miles northeast, following signs to Smith Rock State Park. Once you reach the park, look on the left side of the road for the small wooden Bivouac Area sign, which marks the campground entrance.

Description: This small, walk-in bivouac area is set against a backdrop of towering cliffs. The campsites are along the edge of the rimrock among fragrant juniper trees, with grand views of the Crooked River far below. This is a great spot to spend a few days—climbing, hiking, and mountain biking opportunities in the park and adjoining Crooked River Grasslands are endless. See the Smith Rock State Park hike and the Gray Butte Hike in *Paw-Approved Hikes and Parks*. Also, keep your pooch on a leash in the campground and park—the ranger here is very fierce when it comes to enforcing the leash law.

DOG EVENTS

Mount Bachelor Dog Show

Deschutes County Fairgrounds, 918 W. Highland Ave., Redmond, 541-385-5537

This annual event sponsored by the American Kennel Club features over 1,200 dogs representing 150 breeds. Your dog can earn a Canine Good Citizen award. The show is held the last weekend in June.

Pet Photos with Santa

Humane Society of Redmond Thrift Store, 339 SW 6th, 541-548-2270, www.redmond humane.org

Sadie guarding our backpacks at Smith Rock State Park.

Have a picture of your dog taken with Santa. This annual event is the last weekend in November; for $10, you receive prints and negatives. Proceeds benefit the Humane Society of Redmond.

Run For Their Lives
2-Mile Dog Walk & 5K Fun Run

Humane Society of Redmond, 1317 NE Hemlock, 541-923-0882, www.redmond-humane.org

Held the second weekend in May, this event allows you to walk your dog on a fun, two-mile course or participate in a 5K run. The event starts at 9 A.M. at the Redmond Shelter. Prizes and ribbons are awarded to top finishers. The cost is $10 if you sign up early and $12 the day of event. Proceeds benefit the Humane Society of Redmond.

World of Animals
Education Fair

Humane Society of Redmond, 1317 NE Hemlock, 541-923-0882, www.redmond-humane.org

Talk to experts about animal nutrition, pet careers, pet training, tips on raising pets, and pet grooming, and participate in canine good citizen trials. Of course your best friend is welcome (as long as he is leashed). This annual event is held the first weekend in May at the Deschutes County Fair and Expo Center, 3800 SW Airport Way in Redmond, from 10 A.M.–4 P.M.

CANINE-APPROVED SHOPPING

Big R

3141 S. Highway 97, Redmond 541-548-4095

This large ranch supply store carries dog vaccines, veterinary supplies, collars, leashes, dishes, toys, treats, and premium dog foods. The store also carries a huge selection of farm and ranch supplies. Open 8 A.M.–6 P.M., Monday to Saturday; 9 A.M.–5 P.M., Sunday.

Central Oregon
Ranch Supply

1726 South Highway 97, Redmond, 1-800-235-1623 or 541-548-5195, www.centormall.com

This friendly store carries premium dog foods, doghouses, leashes, collars, hay and straw, livestock protein supplements, tack and show supplies, and horse and livestock handling equipment.

The Feed Barn

2215 N. Highway 97, Redmond, 541-923-3333, www.feedbarn.net

Maryann Abbajay, owner, says, "Leashed or unleashed dogs are welcome in our business. We have been in the current location seven years. It is a typical old-fashioned feed store. There's always free popcorn, candy, and coffee for our customers. Most people say it's a friendly, comfortable place to shop. We carry a complete line of dog products including houses, crates, leashes, collars, supplements, treats, and toys. We carry dog food from Tri Pro, Science Diet, Nutro, Sensible Choice, Diamond, Premium Edge, Pro Plan, Wysong, Canidae, Eagle, Nature's Recipe and Kasco." Open 8 A.M.–5:30 P.M., Monday to Saturday; 10 A.M.–4 P.M., Sunday.

DOGGIE DAYCARE

Deschutes Pet Lodge

6335 SW Canal Blvd., Redmond, 541-504-1903, www.deschutespetlodge.com

CANINE ER

Redmond

Redmond Veterinary Clinic

1785 N. Highway 97, 541-548-1048

This large, mixed animal practice offers emergency services after-hours.

Open 8 A.M.–5 P.M., Monday to Saturday.

Terrebonne

Terrebonne Veterinary Clinic
8485 North Highway 97, 541-923-0232

Open 8:30–5:30, Monday to Friday; 9 A.M.–11 A.M., Saturday.

LOST AND FOUND (ANIMAL SHELTERS)

Humane Society of Redmond
925 SE Sisters Ave., 541-923-0882, www.redmondhumane.org

Open 10 A.M.–5 P.M., Monday to Friday; 10 A.M.–4 P.M., Saturday.

Prineville

THE BIG SCOOP

More off the beaten track in Central Oregon is the Ochoco National Forest and the Mill Creek Wilderness. Both are east of Prineville, a no-nonsense ranching town 35 miles northeast of Bend. Recommended area hikes are Chimney Rock, Steins Pillar, and Twin Pillars. Further east, another destination that should not be missed is the Painted Hills Unit of the John Day Fossil Beds National Monument. Located about 50 miles northeast of Prineville off U.S. 26, its trails will take you and your dog past fascinating multi-colored hills and ancient fossils.

Dogs must be leashed within Prineville's city limits and in the John Day Fossil Beds National Monument. Your dog can be unleashed in the Ochoco National Forest and BLM lands as long as he is under voice control.

PAW-APPROVED HIKES AND PARKS

Chimney Rock Hike
Contact: Bureau of Land Management, Prineville District Office, 3050 NE Third St., Prineville, OR 97754, 541-416-6700, www.or.blm.gov/Prineville
Paw-Approval Rating: 3 paws
Length: 2.8 miles out and back
Difficulty: Moderate
Fees/Permits: None
Season: Year-round
Getting There: From Prineville, travel 16.6 miles south on Highway 27 to a parking area on the left, signed "Rim Trail Trailhead."
Description: This route winds uphill for 500 feet through a sage and juniper landscape to a spectacular viewpoint on Chimney Rock. The trail is near Chimney Rock Campground (see *Campgrounds*), located on the banks of the scenic Crooked River. Be sure to go for a swim after your hike. Note that summertime temperatures can soar into the 100s during July and August. Also, be on the lookout for rattlesnakes and check your dog for ticks after this hike.

Painted Hills Unit of the John Day Fossil Beds Hikes
Contact: John Day Fossil Beds National Monument HCR 82, Box 126, Kimberly, OR 97848-9701, 541-987-2333, www.nps.gov/joda
Paw-Approval Rating: 4 paws
Leashes Required? Yes
Fees/Permits: None
Season: Year-round
Getting There: From Prineville, travel 45.2 miles east on U.S. Highway 26 to the junction with Burnt Ranch Road to a sign for John Day Fossil Beds National Monument-Painted Hills Unit. Turn left (north) and go 5.7 miles. Turn left on Bear Creek Road and go 0.3 mile to the entrance road for the day-use area on the left side of the road.
Description: You will be amazed at the brightly colored hills in the John Day Fossil Beds, where your dog is welcome as long as he is leashed. Several trails explore this unique national monument. These multi-colored hills are composed of

layers of ash deposited over 30 million years ago. Over the years, erosion has exposed the layers, the varying colors of which result from different combinations of minerals such as calcium, titanium, sodium, iron, silicon, aluminum, manganese, and magnesium. When it rains, the colors of the hills change because as the clay absorbs water it reflects more light, changing the soil's colors from red to pink and light brown to yellow-gold. When the clay begins to dry, it contracts, causing surface cracking that diffuses the light and makes the color of the hills deepen. Plants don't grow on these hills because the clay is nutritionally poor and the dense soil cannot absorb much moisture.

For starters, stock up on water and information at the day-use area. From there, head back out to Bear Creek Road and turn left. Go 0.5 mile to the Carroll Rim parking area on the left side of the road. From it, you can hike the 1-mile out and back Painted Hills Overlook Trail, which provides a sweeping view of the multi-colored hills. Just across the road is the trailhead for the 1.5-mile, out and back Carroll Rim Trail. Carroll Rim is a high ridge consisting of John Day ignimbrite, better known as "welded tuff." From the top of rim you'll be able to see Sutton Mountain, which rises prominently to the east.

Options: Two other trails to explore are the 0.25-mile Painted Cove Loop Trail and the 0.25-mile Leaf Hill Trail. To get to these two trails, turn left from the Carroll Rim trailhead onto Bear Creek Road and follow the signs.

Steins Pillar Hike

Contact: Ochoco National Forest, 3160 N.E. 3rd St., Prineville, OR 97754, 541-416-6500, www.fs.fed.us
Paw-Approval Rating: 3 paws
Leashes Required? No
Length: 5.2 miles out and back
Difficulty: Moderate
Fees/Permits: None

Season: May through October
Getting There: From Prineville, travel 9.1 miles east on U.S. 26 to Mill Creek Road (Forest Road 33). Turn left (north) and drive 6.7 miles to the junction with Forest Road 500. Turn right on Forest Road 500 and continue 2.1 miles to the trailhead on the left side of the road.
Description: This hike takes you away from it all, in the diverse landscapes of the Ochoco National Forest, to the base of the stunning Steins Pillar, a 350-foot tall rock outcrop. The trail starts by climbing 680 feet along a ridge and then heading down the other side to Steins Pillar (your turn-around point). A good place to set up camp is at nearby Wildcat Campground (see *Campgrounds*).

Twin Pillars Hike

Contact: Ochoco National Forest, 3160 N.E. 3rd St., Prineville, OR 97754, 541-416-6500, www.fs.fed.us
Paw-Approval Rating: 4 paws
Leashes Required? No
Length: 10.6 miles out and back
Difficulty: Difficult
Fees/Permits: None
Season: May through October
Getting There: From Prineville travel 9.1 miles east on U.S. 26 to Mill Creek Road (Forest Road 33). Turn left (north) and drive 10.6 miles to a road junction. Turn right at a sign for Wildcat Campground. Continue 0.1 mile and turn right into a gravel parking area and the trailhead.
Description: The 17,000-acre Mill Creek Wilderness is a peaceful and beautiful place to hike with your dog. This hike takes you along the banks of Mill Creek through a gorgeous ponderosa pine forest, to the base of Twin Pillars—an unusual rock formation. Multiple creek crossings allow plenty of paddle time.

Start by hiking on Twin Pillars Trail 380. Hike along as the trail zigzags across the creek to a trail junction at 2.4 miles with Belknap Trail 832A. Stay left at this junction and continue along the creek another 0.5 mile. At this point, the trail turns away from the creek and heads uphill through ponderosa pine. At 5.3 miles, you'll arrive at the base of the Twin Pillars rock formation (your turn-around point). You can complete this hike as an overnight backpack trip. Many informal campsites along the creek are idyllic settings to commune with your pooch. For a more established place to camp, stay at Wildcat Campground (see *Campgrounds*). This hike promises a good workout with over 1,900 feet of elevation gain.

CAMPGROUNDS

Chimney Rock

Contact: Bureau of Land Management, Prineville District Office, 3050 NE Third St., Prineville, OR 97754, 541-416-6700, www.or.blm.gov
Season: Year-round
Facilities: 8 RV sites (no electrical hook-ups), 12 tent sites, picnic tables, fire rings, vault toilets, piped water, and wheelchair-accessible fishing ramps and fishing dock
Getting There: Travel 16.4 miles south of Prineville on Highway 27 to the campground.
Description: This campground gives access to the Crooked River and the 2.8-miles out and back Chimney Rock hike (see *Paw-Approved Hikes and Parks*).

Devil's Post Pile

Contact: Bureau of Land Management, Prineville District Office, 3050 NE Third St., Prineville, OR 97754, 541-416-6700, www.or.blm.gov
Season: Year-round
Facilities: 7 RV/tent sites (no electrical hook-ups), picnic tables, fire rings, vault toilets, no drinking water
Getting There: Travel 18 miles south of Prineville on Highway 27 to the campground.

Description: Sites are situated in a sage and juniper landscape adjacent to the Crooked River. If you want to get away from the crowds, this campground is sure to please. Keep a watch for rattlesnakes.

Walton Lake

Contact: Ochoco National Forest, Lookout Mountain Ranger District, 3160 N.E. 3rd St., Prineville, OR 97754, 541-416-6500, www.fs.fed.us
Season: May through October
Facilities: 30 RV/tent campsites, 1 group site, picnic tables, fire rings, vault toilets, level parking, boat launch (no motorized boats are allowed)
Getting There: From Prineville, travel 17 miles east on Highway 26. Turn right at an Ochoco Creek sign and go 8.3 miles to the junction with Forest Road 22. Turn left onto Forest Road 22 and drive 7 miles to Walton Lake.
Description: This campground on the shores of 25-acre Walton Lake is a great place to swim and paddle. You and your dog can also explore the 1-mile trail that circles the lake, which takes you through old growth ponderosa pine.

Wildcat Campground

Contact: Ochoco National Forest, Lookout Mountain Ranger District, 3160 N.E. 3rd St., Prineville, OR 97754, 541-416-6500, www.fs.fed.us
Season: May through October
Facilities: 17 RV/tent campsites (no electrical hook-ups), water, picnic tables, fire rings, vault toilets, picnic area
Getting There: From Prineville, travel 9 miles northeast on Highway 26 to Mill Creek Road (Forest Road 33). Turn left on Mill Creek Road and drive approximately 10 miles to the campground.
Description: This forested campground is a great base camp for exploring the Mill Creek Wilderness on the Twin Pillars Trail (see *Paw-Approved Hikes and Parks*). Another nearby trail is Steins Pillar.

CANINE COMFORT ACCOMMODATIONS

Unless otherwise stated, dogs should not be left unattended in the room and must be leashed on hotel property.

$$ Best Western Prineville Inn

1475 E. Third St., Prineville 541-447-8080

This hotel's large rooms are furnished with a southwest flair. The hotel has pet-friendly rooms (some are non-smoking), an indoor pool and year-round spa.

Dog Policy

A one-time fee of $10 is charged for your dog.

CANINE ER

Prineville Veterinary Clinic

1555 NE 3rd St., 541-447-2179

This full-service large and small animal hospital provides twenty-four hour emergency service and will see walk-ins, but prefers you make an appointment. In an emergency, call the office number and the answering service will page the doctor on duty.

Open 7:30 A.M.–5:30 P.M., Monday to Friday; 9 A.M.–4 P.M., Saturday.

LOST AND FOUND (ANIMAL SHELTERS)

Humane Society of the Ochocos

394 N. Belknap, Prineville, 541-447-7178

Open 10 A.M.–5 P.M., Tuesday through Friday.

Madras

THE BIG SCOOP

Madras, a small agricultural community, is 42 miles north of Bend on Highway 97. This city is the gateway to Cove Palisades State Park and Lake Billy Chinook. Camping, hiking, paddling, and swimming opportunities abound at Cove Palisades, which hosts a leash free area where your pup can run off his extra energy. Be sure to check out the Tam-a-lau Hike, which explores the rich geology of this area. A short hike in town you may want to explore is the Willow Creek Hike.

PAW-APPROVED
HIKES AND PARKS

Tam-a-lau Hike
Contact: Oregon State Parks and Recreation, Suite 1, 1115 Commercial St. NE, Salem OR 97301-1002, 1-800-551-6949, www.oregonstateparks.org
Paw-Approval Rating: 3 paws
Leashes Required? Yes
Length: 6.8-mile loop
Difficulty: Moderate
Fees/Permits: $3 day-use fee
Season: Year-round
Getting There: From Redmond, travel 19 miles north on U.S. 97 to a turnoff for Cove Palisades State Park and Culver/Round Butte Dam. Turn left (west) onto the Culver Highway and follow the state park signs 6 miles to the park entrance. (From Madras, travel 15 miles southwest on U.S. 97, following signs to the park.) Follow the entrance road down into the canyon to a road junction. At the bottom of the canyon, turn left toward Deschutes

Campground and Day-use Areas. Continue 3.7 miles to another road junction. Turn left toward the signed Deschutes Campground. Proceed 0.6 mile to a sign, "Tam-a-lau Trail." Turn right, go 0.3 mile, and turn right into the "Single Car Parking Area."

Description: This loop trail takes you and Rover over 600 feet to the top of a high peninsula above Lake Billy Chinook in Cove Palisades State Park. From there, you have grand views of the vast reservoir below and the snow-capped Central Cascade peaks, including Mount Hood, Mount Jefferson, Broken Top, Mount Bachelor, and the Three Sisters. The Crooked, Deschutes, and Metolius Rivers feed this giant lake, which is popular with boaters.

Begin by walking on the paved path at the northeast corner of the day-use parking area. You'll travel a short distance and arrive at a grassy picnic area and swimming beach. Dogs are not allowed on the swimming beach, but if you detour past the beach, you can let Fido take a dip before you continue the hike. From the picnic area, follow a paved path that heads uphill on the right side of the restrooms. At 0.3 mile, turn right at the trail fork and continue, ascending a flight of steps. At 0.4 mile, go left at the trail fork and continue ascending the paved trail. Cross a paved road and walk through an opening in a fence around Deschutes Campground. At 0.5-miles, turn right onto a dirt path adjacent to a large interpretive sign. Over the next 1.1 miles, the trail ascends steeply to a high plateau above the lake. The hillside is blanketed with bunch grass, yellow balsam root, and purple lupine. At 1.4 miles, turn left onto a wide doubletrack road. At 1.6 miles, turn left and begin the loop portion of the hike. Follow the dirt path as it parallels the edge of the rimrock and offers outstanding views of the lake canyon and the Central Cascade peaks. After 2.7 miles, you'll arrive at the tip of the peninsula, which serves as a good lunch spot. At 5.2 miles, you'll end the loop portion of the hike and descend on the same route back to your starting point at 6.8 miles. Avoid this hike during July and August when temperatures can exceed 100°F. If you're visiting during those months, explore the trail in the cooler early morning, and be sure to bring a lot of water.

Willow Creek Hike

Contact: Madras/Jefferson County Chamber of Commerce, P.O. Box 770, Madras, OR 541-475-2350
Paw-Approval Rating: 2 paws
Leashes Required? Yes
Length: 2 miles out and back
Difficulty: Easy
Fees/Permits: None
Season: Year-round
Getting There: The trailhead is at the intersection of NE 7th St. and NE A St. in downtown Madras.
Description: Traveling dogs will love stretching their legs on this paved path along the course of tumbling Willow Creek in the heart of Madras.

CANINE COMFORT ACCOMMODATIONS

Unless otherwise stated, dogs should not be left unattended in the room and must be leashed on hotel property.

$-$$ Sonny's

1539 SW U.S. 97, Madras 1-800-624-6137, www.sonnysmotel.com

This hotel has several dog-friendly rooms, a pool, hot tub, restaurant, bar, and free continental breakfast.

Dog Policy
A one-time fee of $10 is charged for your dog.

CAMPGROUNDS

Cove Palisades State Park

Contact: Oregon State Parks and Recreation, Suite 1, 1115 Commercial St. NE, Salem, OR 97301-1002, 1-800-551-6949 (information), 1-800-452-5687 (reservations), www.oregonstateparks.org
Season: Year-round
Facilities: 87 full-hook-up sites, 91 electrical sites, 94 tent sites, 3 cabins, 3 group-tent areas, picnic tables, fire rings, piped water, restrooms, hot showers, boat launch, RV dump station
Getting There: From Redmond, travel 19 miles north on U.S. 97 to a turnoff for Cove Palisades State Park and Culver/Round Butte Dam. Turn left (west) onto the Culver Highway and follow the state park signs 6 miles to the park and campgrounds. From Madras, travel 15 miles southwest on U.S. 97, following signs to the park and campgrounds.
Description: This state park has two campgrounds, Crooked River and Deschutes, both of which are located adjacent to Lake Billy Chinook, with its prime paddling and swimming. You can also hike the Tam-a-lau Trail (see *Paw-Approved Hikes and Parks*). Hook up with the trail adjacent to campsite B-17 in the Deschutes Campground. Dogs are not allowed to stay in cabins. The park has a leash-free area in the Deschutes River Campground, adjacent to sites B-21 through B-24.

CANINE-APPROVED SHOPPING

Feed Company

316 SW Madison St./Culver Highway, Madras 541-475-7556

This feed store carries a wide selection of dog food and other canine supplies. Open 9 A.M.–5:30 P.M., Monday to Friday; 9 A.M.–4 P.M., Saturday.

CANINE ER

Cascade East Veterinary Clinic
1689 SW Highway 97, Madras, 541-475-7226

This full-service small and large animal practice takes walk-in appointments and offers emergency service after-hours. In an emergency, call the regular clinic number; the doctor will be paged. The clinic carries Science Diet and Waltham pet foods, vitamins, collars and leashes, shampoos, and flea products.

Open 9 A.M.– 5:30 P.M., Monday to Friday; 9 A.M.–5:30 P.M., Saturday. Evening hours are available on Wednesday with an advance appointment.

LOST AND FOUND (ANIMAL SHELTERS)

Jefferson County Animal Shelter
1694 SE McTaggart Rd., Madras, 541-475-6889

Open 8 A.M.–4 P.M., Friday to Tuesday.

Northeast Oregon

*N*ortheast Oregon is an off-the-beaten-track gem, with several significant mountain ranges, deep river gorges, and picturesque canyons filled with fossilized treasures. You and your canine pal can begin exploring by heading east from Prineville on Highway 26 where you'll travel through Dayville, Mount Vernon, John Day, Canyon City, and Prairie City. All of these cities are within the John Day Valley, carved over eons by the wild and scenic John Day River and its tributaries into spectacular canyons, pinnacles, and spires.

This canyon country of sagebrush, juniper, and ponderosa pine is home to the 14,000-acre John Day Fossil Beds National Monument. Established in 1975, this national monument is a storehouse for the fossil remains of animals and plants dating as far back as 54 million years. Leashed dogs are welcome on all trails. Recommended trails in the national monument are Island in Time and Blue Basin Overlook (see Paw-Approved Hikes and Parks).

The far northeast corner of the state is host to more captivating natural wonders, including the Wallowa Mountains and Hells Canyon.

The jagged, granite Wallowas contain some of Oregon's highest peaks, seventeen of which, such as 9,595-foot Eagle Cap and 9,826-foot Matterhorn, are above 9,000 feet. These mountains are within the Eagle Cap Wilderness, which contains hundreds of miles of trails to glacier-carved meadows and high alpine lakes. The Wallowa Mountain range is 80 miles long and 25 miles wide and towers above the sparsely populated farming and ranching country of Wallowa County.

At an average depth of 6,600 feet, Hells Canyon is the deepest river-carved gorge in North America. This rugged canyon carved by the Snake River serves as the dividing line between Oregon and Idaho. The Hells Canyon National Recreation Area preserves this amazing canyon and has miles of trails for exploration.

All of the Northeast Oregon cities featured in the following chapters require that dogs be leashed within city limits. Also, you're in cattle country here. Open-range grazing is a common practice in the national forests. Don't let your dog chase any live-stock! Deer and elk hunting are also popular; the main hunting season begins September 28.

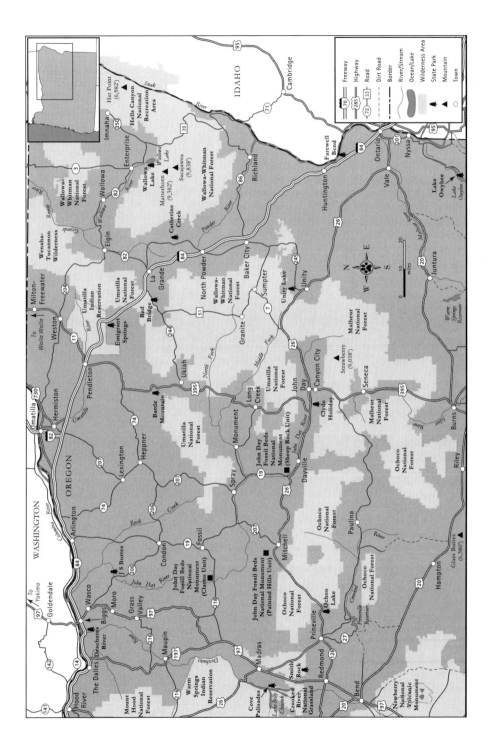

John Day

THE BIG SCOOP

John Day, the largest community along the Highway 26 corridor, is not far from the immense Malheur National Forest, Strawberry Mountain Wilderness, and the North Fork John Day Wilderness. This town has a strong mining, ranching, and logging heritage and is a good place to stock up on supplies before heading out on your Northeast Oregon adventure. Recommended hikes in this area are the Strawberry Lake/Little Strawberry Lake, Reynolds Creek, and North Fork Malheur River.

PAW-APPROVED
HIKES AND PARKS

John Day Fossil Beds Hikes

Contact: John Day Fossil Beds National Monument HCR 82, Box 126, Kimberly, OR 97848-9701, 541-987-2333, www.nps.gov
Paw-Approval Rating: 3 paws
Leashes Required? Yes
Length: Island in Time Trail: 1.4 miles out and back; Blue Basin Overlook Trail: 3-mile loop
Difficulty: Easy
Fees/Permits: None
Season: Year-round
Getting There: From Dayville (31 miles west of the town of John Day on Highway 26) head 6.6 miles west. At the junction with Highway 19, turn right and continue 5.1 miles (you'll pass the Sheep Rock Unit Visitor Center after two miles) to the Blue Basin trailhead and parking area on the right side of the highway.

Description: The Island in Time Trail and Blue Basin Overlook Trail explore the amazing landscape of the Sheep Rock Unit of the John Day Fossil Beds. Both hikes start from the Blue Basin Trailhead.

To explore the Island in Time Trail, head right (the Blue Basin Overlook Loop heads left). This trail's interpretive signs explain that volcanic eruptions millions of years ago covered the native plants and animals with wind-blown silt, and washed them into ash-filled streams and ponds. Subsequent millennia of wind and rain have eroded the greenish clay rock in the basin to expose the fossils of these now extinct plants and animals. At 0.3 mile, you can view a glass-encased fossil of an ancient tortoise; at 0.4 mile is a fossil of an oreodont—a sheep sized leaf-eater that was abundant in this area. At 0.5 mile, gaze at a saber-toothed cat. Continue another 0.2 mile to the trail's end and your turnaround point.
Trail Option: If you and your furry friend want more of a workout, check out the Blue Basin Overlook Trail, which takes you to a viewpoint overlooking the John Day Valley. Hook up with this trail by heading left onto the signed path from the trailhead.

While in this area, visit the park's visitor center 2 miles north of the intersection of Highway 26 and Highway 19. It offers a good introduction to the local geology and contains informative displays about the monument's fossils and the history of the John Day Valley.

The visitor center has outdoor displays that you can explore with your leashed dog, and also has restrooms, water, and a shady picnic area.

North Fork Malheur River Hike

Contact: Malheur National Forest, 431 Patterson Bridge Rd., John Day, Oregon 97845, 541-575-3000, www.fs.fed.us
Paw-Approval Rating: 4 paws
Leashes Required? No
Length: 15.8 miles out and back
Difficulty: Moderate
Fees/Permits: None
Season: April to November. It's not recommended that you hike this trail after September 28, when the main hunting season begins.
Getting There: From Prairie City travel southeast on County Road 62 and then Forest Road 13 for a total of 25 miles. Turn right on Forest Road 16 and continue 2 miles to the intersection of Forest Road 1675. Turn left onto Forest Road 1675 and go 3.5 miles to the North Fork Malheur Trailhead.
Description: You'll begin by crossing a log bridge over the North Fork, and then trekking south on the singletrack trail along the river. The route starts out fairly easy as it winds through a thick ponderosa pine and fir forest. It's common to see deer and elk feeding on the tall grasses lining the shores of the river. After about 2.5 miles, you'll cross a bridge over Crane Creek. Don't be surprised to see hunting camps along this trail.

The scenery along this trail is unsurpassed. The pace of the river changes around every bend—sometimes it's rushing rapids and other times the river slows to eddies and pools that your trail hound will love exploring. After almost 8 miles and a gradual descent of 500 feet, you'll reach a barbed wire fence (your turnaround point). Retrace the route back to the trailhead. This trail is open to mountain bikes. If you want to explore this area further, stay at North Fork Campground.

Reynolds Creek Hike

Contact: Malheur National Forest, 431 Patterson Bridge Rd., John Day, Oregon 97845, 541-575-3000, www.fs.fed.us
Paw-Approval Rating: 4 paws
Leashes Required? No
Length: 2.4 miles out and back
Difficulty: Easy
Fees/Permits: None
Season: April through November
Getting There: From Highway 26 in Prairie City (13 miles east of John Day), turn south at a Depot Park sign. Travel 0.4 mile to a stop sign. Turn left and continue straight (this turns into County Road 62) 7.5 miles to the junction with Forest Road 2635. Turn left onto Forest Road 2635 and go 4.3 miles to the signed trailhead on the right.
Description: Enjoy an easy stroll with 450 feet of elevation gain along tumbling Reynolds Creek. Broad boughs of grand fir keep the trail cool, and huckleberries provide a tasty treat in mid- to late summer. Follow the trail 1.2 miles upstream to a cliff overhang (your turnaround point). If you are feeling adventurous, scramble on a rough trail another 0.2 mile to a small splashing waterfall. Retrace the route back to the trailhead.

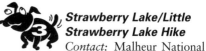

Strawberry Lake/Little Strawberry Lake Hike

Contact: Malheur National Forest, 431 Patterson Bridge Rd., John Day, Oregon 97845, 541-575-3000, www.fs.fed.us
Paw-Approval Rating: 3 paws
Leashes Required? No
Length: 6.8 miles out and back
Difficulty: Difficult
Fees/Permits: Self-issue wilderness permit
Season: July through October
Getting There: From Highway 26 in Prairie City (13 miles east of John Day) turn south onto Bridge St. (County Road 60) and travel about 11.5 miles to Strawberry

Campground (the road turns to gravel after 3.3 miles).

Description: This trail takes you to two high alpine lakes in the Strawberry Mountain Wilderness. Located within the Malheur National Forest, this 68,700-acre wilderness is characterized by its rugged, high-alpine country with jagged mountain peaks, high mountain lakes, and U-shaped glacial valleys. Old and young mountains make up the impressive peaks of the Strawberry Range. More than 200 million years ago, when the North American continent drifted westward, it pushed up a large section of the Pacific seafloor, creating the western half of the Strawberry Range. The eastern half, created only about 16 million years ago, took form when lava erupted from vents and spread east from John Day to Unity. Strawberry Mountain, the forest's tallest peak and star attraction, is the remnant of a much larger stratovolcano that once existed here.

Start the hike on Trail 375, accessed from the Strawberry Lakes Campground (see *Campgrounds*). Follow the forest path as it ascends through a thick pine forest. At 1.3 miles, turn right toward Strawberry Lake (the trail that heads left goes to Slide Lake). After 1.4 miles and 600 feet of climbing, you'll arrive at the lake, which is ringed with shimmering groves of aspen. Turn right and follow the trail as it parallels the lakeshore, allowing plenty of time for Fido to swim. After 2.3 miles, you'll reach the far end of the lake. Turn right toward Little Strawberry Lake. Continue on the quiet forest path a short distance and then arrive at a trail junction. Turn right and continue 0.5 mile to the base of the broad cascade of Strawberry Falls. Continue 0.2 mile and turn left toward Little Strawberry Lake (the trail that heads right leads in 3.2 miles to the summit of Strawberry Mountain). You'll arrive at Little Strawberry Lake after 3.4 miles and 600 more feet of elevation gain. Retrace the route back to the trailhead.

CYCLING FOR CANINES
Prairie City

North Fork of the Malheur River
(See *Paw-Approved Hikes and Parks*)

CAMPGROUNDS

Strawberry Lakes

Contact: Malheur National Forest, 431 Patterson Bridge Rd., John Day, Oregon 97845, 541-575-3000, www.fs.fed.us

Season: Mid-May through October

Facilities: 11 RV/tent campsites (no electrical hook-ups), vault toilets, water, picnic tables, and fire rings. No reservations accepted.

Getting There: From Highway 26 in Prairie City (13 miles east of John Day) turn south onto Bridge St. (County Road 60) and travel about 11.5 miles to the campground (the road turns to gravel after 3.3 miles).

Description: Campsites at this high mountain campground are nestled in a shady forest of fir, spruce, and lodgepole pine. The campground is a good base for exploring the Strawberry Mountain Wilderness. From the trailhead adjacent to the campground, you can hike to Strawberry Lake and Little Strawberry Lake (see *Paw-Approved Hikes and Parks*) as well as many other trails.

CANINE-APPROVED SHOPPING

JD Feed and More
27897-B Wilderness Rd., John Day, 541-575-2572
Open 8:30 A.M.–5 P.M. Monday to Friday

DOGGIE DAYCARE AND CANINE ER

Gambler Veterinary Clinic
59989 Highway 26, John Day, 541-932-4428
This full-service large and small animal clinic will board your dog for $8 per night. The clinic will take walk-in appointments and offers twenty-four hour emergency services.

Open 8 A.M.–5 P.M. Monday to Friday;
8 A.M.–12 P.M. Saturday.

ANIMAL SHELTERS
(LOST AND FOUND)

Fossil

Animal Rescue Foundation
HCR 82, 541-468-2056,
www.arforegon.org

Baker City

THE BIG SCOOP

Baker City is 41 miles south of La Grande off I-84 and also has a rich ranching and mining history. Downtown Baker City is filled with turn-of-the-century architecture; some buildings are listed in the National Register of Historic Places. If you and Rover want to stay in the heart of downtown, check out the Geiser Grand Hotel. Built in 1889, this historic hotel features chandeliers in every room, stunning mahogany woodwork, a stained glass ceiling and ten-foot high windows that offer spectacular views of the snow-capped Blue Mountains (see *Canine Comfort Accommodations*). Hikes in this area that should not be missed are North Fork John Day River to Trout Creek, Anthony Lake/ Hoffer Lake, and Hells Canyon. Pooches who like to paddle will also love to spend the day exploring Anthony Lake or Grande Ronde Lake (see *Paddlehounds*).

PAW-APPROVED HIKES AND PARKS

Anthony Lake/ Hoffer Lakes Hike

Contact: Wallowa-Whitman National Forest, 1550 Dewey, Baker City, Oregon 97814, 541-523-6391, www.fs.fed.us
Paw-Approval Rating: 4 paws
Leashes Required? Yes
Length: 2.2-mile loop
Difficulty: Easy
Fees/Permits: None
Season: July through October
Getting There: From I-84 in Baker City, head 19 miles north and take the North

Powder exit 285. Travel about 21.3 miles west, following signs to the entrance to Anthony Lake Campground. Follow signs to the picnic area and park.
Description: Begin this hike by walking down to the lakeshore and turning left onto the lake trail. Anthony Lake is surrounded by towering granite peaks and is ringed with Douglas fir, white fir, lodgepole pine and tamarack trees. Gunsight Peak shoots skyward and makes a stunning backdrop. While you admire the scenery, let your pup explore the lakeshore and pose for photos that will impress your friends back home. At 0.3 mile, you'll arrive at a boat ramp and a trail junction. Continue to the right on the Hoffer Lakes Trail. The trail continues another 0.3 mile where you'll arrive at another trail junction. Go left along Parker Creek and stroll along it until you reach Hoffer Lake in another 0.6 mile. This smaller lake is dominated by the granite spire of Lees Peak. Retrace the route along Parker Creek for 0.6 mile and when you arrive at a trail junction go left to complete the loop around Anthony Lake. To explore this area further, check out Anthony Lake Campground (see *Campgrounds*).

Hells Canyon Hike

Contact: Wallowa-Whitman National Forest, 1550 Dewey, Baker City, Oregon 97814, 541-523-6391, www.fs.fed.us
Paw-Approval Rating: 3 paws
Leashes Required? Yes
Length: 2.4 miles out and back
Difficulty: Easy
Fees/Permits: None

Season: Year-round

Getting There: From Baker City head 65 miles east on Highway 86 to Oxbow. From Oxbow, follow signs for 24 miles to the visitor center at Hells Canyon Dam.

Description: The Hells Canyon Dam visitor center's displays describe the history of the dam. Start the hike here by heading down a set of stairs to a boat launch area. Pick up the path on the far side of the boat launch. Follow the trail past rugged high-walled cliffs, as it parallels the shores of the impressive Snake River. At 1 mile, you'll reach tumbling Stud Creek. Let your dog explore the creek and then continue another 0.2 mile to the trail's end at a rocky beach next to the river (your turnaround point). Retrace the route back to your car. Watch for poison oak on this trail.

A fun swim session in the John Day River.

splash and play in the rocky, tumbling river. At 2.6 miles you'll arrive at a footbridge crossing lively Trout Creek (your turnaround point). For a longer adventure or backpack, continue on the trail for many more miles. A campground is located at the trailhead.

CYCLING FOR CANINES

 **North Fork
John Day River to
Trout Creek Hike**

Contact: Wallowa-Whitman National Forest, 1550 Dewey, Baker City, Oregon 97814, 541-523-6391, www.fs.fed.us

Paw-Approval Rating: 4 paws

Leashes Required? No

Length: 5.2 miles out and back

Difficulty: Easy

Fees/Permits: None

Season: May through November

Getting There: From Baker City, head north on I-84 for 19 miles; take the North Powder exit 285. Follow Anthony Lake signs for 21 miles to the Anthony Lake Recreation Area. From here continue on Forest Road 73 for 17 miles to a stop sign. Continue straight and enter the North Fork of the John Day Campground. Proceed through the campground to the trailhead on the left.

Description: Your pooch will enjoy exploring this beautiful trail along the North Fork of the John Day River. This hike ascends 350 feet and covers a small section of the 24.6-mile long trail. The trail wanders through a shady Douglas fir forest and provides plenty of opportunities to

Elkhorn Crest Trail
Contact: Wallowa-Whitman National Forest, 1550 Dewey, Baker City, Oregon 97814, 541-523-6391, www.fs.fed.us

Paw-Approval Rating: 3 paws

Leashes Required? No

Length: 5.4 miles out and back

Difficulty: Difficult

Fees/Permits: $5 Northwest Forest Pass. Purchase at 1-800-270-7504 or www. naturenw.org.

Getting There: From Baker City, travel north on Highway 30 for 10 miles to the small town of Haines. Turn left on County Road 1146, following signs for the Elkhorn Scenic Byway and Anthony Lake. Follow signs for about 8 miles (eventually you'll be on Forest Road 73) until you reach the Elkhorn Crest Trailhead on the left.

Description: Cycling canines will enjoy this short, strenuous jaunt that has over 1,200 feet of elevation gain and explores the beautiful Anthony Lake Basin in the Blue Mountains, about 35 miles northwest of Baker City. Begin pedaling on the signed Elkhorn Crest Trail 1611. At 0.5 mile, continue straight (the Shoreline Trail heads right). At the next trail junction, veer left (the trail that goes right heads to Black Lake). Climb steeply on a rough trail until you reach the 2.7-mile mark and the wilderness boundary (bikes are not allowed in the wilderness area). From here, begin an exhilarating downhill descent on the same route back to the trailhead on this technically challenging trail. Be on the lookout for hikers on your descent.

POWDERHOUNDS

Pooches who love to romp in powder an accompany you to the Anthony Lake Recreation Area, where a series of Nordic trails explore Anthony Lake, Lily Pad Lake and Black Lake in a beautiful high mountain basin. To get there from Baker City, take old Highway 30 to Haines (approximately 8 miles). Turn left at Haines and follow Anthony Lake Ski Area signs for about 24 miles.

You can also check out a system of trails in the Phillips Reservoir area. We recommend the Shoreline Trail that circles the reservoir. To get there, from Baker City travel south on State Highway 7 approximately 20 miles to Mason Dam and Forest Road 1145. Turn left and cross Mason Dam; park on the south side of the dam. The Shoreline Trail begins across from the parking area. For more information, contact the Wallowa-Whitman National Forest, 1550 Dewey, Baker City, Oregon 97814, 541-523-6391, www.fs.fed.us.

PADDLEHOUNDS

Paddle enthusiasts should check out picturesque Anthony Lake (no motorized boats allowed). From Baker City, travel 10 miles north on Highway 30 to Haines. In Haines, turn west onto County Road 1146 (the Elkhorn Scenic Byway). Follow signs

for 20 miles (the road eventually turns into Forest Road 73) to the ski resort, Anthony Lake Campground, and the boat launch.

Another nearby lake worth exploring is Grande Ronde Lake—the source for the Grande Ronde River. To get there from Baker City follow the directions for Anthony Lake (described above) and continue 1 mile further on Road 73 to Grande Ronde Lake.

Wallowa Lake is another high mountain lake that should not be missed. To get there, travel 6 miles south of Joseph on Highway 82 to the Wallowa Lake State Park Campground and boat launch.

CANINE COMFORT ACCOMMODATIONS

Unless otherwise stated, dogs should not be left unattended in the room and must be leashed on hotel property.

Baker City

$ Budget Inn
2205 Broadway, 1-800-547-5827
Dog Policy
A $4 fee per dog per night is charged.

$ Oregon Trail Motel
211 Bridge St., 1-800-628-3982
This motel is within walking distance of downtown Baker City and has 54 air-conditioned rooms with microwave, refrigerator, and cable TV. Additional offerings include a seasonal outdoor pool, gift shop, guest laundry, restaurant, and complimentary continental breakfast.
Dog Policy
A $5 fee per dog per night is charged.

$-$$ Baker City Motel & RV Center
880 Elm St., 1-800-931-9229
Dog Policy
A $5 fee per dog per night is charged.

$$ Bridge Street Inn
134 Bridge St. 1-800-932-9220

Dog Policy
A $5 fee per dog per night is charged.

$$ Eldorado Inn
695 Campbell St., 1-800-537-5756

You'll find clean, comfortable, dog-friendly rooms at this friendly inn. Amenities include an indoor pool and Jacuzzi and a 24-hour restaurant.
Dog Policy
A $10 fee per dog per night is charged.

$$-$$$ Geiser Grand Hotel
1996 Main St., 1-888-434-7374

Built in 1889, this historic hotel features chandeliers in every room, mahogany woodwork; a stained glass ceiling and ten-foot high windows that offer spectacular views of the snow-capped Blue Mountains.
Dog Policy
Only one dog per room. A $10 fee is charged per dog per night.

CAMPGROUNDS

Anthony Lake
Contact: Wallowa-Whitman National Forest, 1550 Dewey, Baker City, Oregon 97814, 541-523-6391, www.fs.fed.us
Season: July through September
Facilities: 16 RV/trailer campsites (no electrical hook-ups), 21 tent campsites, picnic tables, vault toilets, fire rings, water, and a boat launch (no motorized boats are allowed on the lake). No reservations accepted.
Getting There: From I-84 in Baker City, head 19 miles north and take the North Powder exit 285. Travel about 21.3 miles west, following signs to the entrance to Anthony Lake Campground.
Description: This campground features forested campsites adjacent to beautiful Anthony Lake. None of the campsites are on the lake but camping here gives you and your dog access to the Anthony Lake/Hoffer Lakes hike (see *Paw-Approved*

Nap time!

Hikes and Parks). Paddling enthusiasts will enjoy an afternoon adventure on the lake and snow hounds can romp during the winter months on the system of trails that surround the lake.

North Fork John Day
Contact: Wallowa-Whitman National Forest, 1550 Dewey, Baker City, Oregon 97814, 541-523-6391, www.fs.fed.us
Season: July through September
Facilities: 15 RV/tent campsites (no electrical hook-ups), picnic tables, vault toilets, grills, horse corrals and ramp, no water. No reservations accepted.
Getting There: From Baker City head north 19 miles on I-84 and take the North Powder exit 285. Follow Anthony Lake signs for 21 miles to the Anthony Lake Recreation Area. From here continue on Forest Road 73 for 17 miles to a stop sign. Continue straight into the campground entrance.
Description: Campsites at this campground are adjacent to the North Fork John Day River in a sunny lodgepole pine forest. This campground is a good staging area for hikes or backpacks on the North Fork John Day National Recreational Trail that begins from the campground (see *North Fork John Day River to Trout Creek Hike* in *Paw-Approved Hikes and Parks*).

DOGGIE DAYCARE & CANINE ER

Baker Veterinary Hospital

3425 10th St., Baker City, 541-523-7772

This hospital offers overnight boarding and emergency services for dogs.

Open 8 A.M.–5:30 P.M. Monday to Friday; 8 A.M.–12 P.M. Saturday.

ANIMAL SHELTERS (LOST AND FOUND)

Baker City Animal Control

11656 1st St., 541-523-3644

La Grande

THE BIG SCOOP

Located on the Grande Ronde River, La Grande is home to Eastern Oregon University and is surrounded by the snow-capped peaks of the Blue Mountains. In the mid-1800s La Grande served as a rest and provisioning stop for pioneers getting ready for the grueling push over the Blue Mountains on their way to the Willamette Valley.

This city sits on the edge of the huge, fertile Grande Ronde River Valley, at the junction of I-84 and Highway 82. It serves as the gateway to the Umatilla Forest to the north and the Wallowa Whitman National Forest to the east and south.

Highway 82 heads northeast from La Grande through the small communities of Wallowa, Lostine, Enterprise, and Joseph. These towns give you access to the Wallowa Mountains, the Eagle Cap Wilderness and the rugged Hells Canyon National Recreation Area. Recommended hikes are the Lakes Basin and Echo/Traverse Lakes. Cycling canines will enjoy exploring the Spring Creek area's many loop trails on doubletrack roads that pass through a great gray owl nesting area.

PAW-APPROVED HIKES AND PARKS

Bear Creek Hike

Contact: Wallowa-Whitman National Forest, 1550 Dewey, Baker City, Oregon 97814, 541-523-6391, www.fs.fed.us
Paw-Approval Rating: 4 paws
Leashes Required? No
Length: 8 miles out and back
Difficulty: Moderate

Fees/Permits: $5 Northwest Forest Pass. Purchase at 1-800-270-7504 or www.naturenw.org.
Season: May through November
Getting There: From I-84 in La Grande take exit 261 and travel northeast on Highway 82 about 46 miles to the small town of Wallowa. As you enter Wallowa, turn right on North Bear Creek Road Travel on North Bear Creek Road (which turns into Forest Road 8250) 8.2 miles to a road junction. Continue straight on Forest Road 040 toward Boundary Campground. Continue 0.9 mile to the road's end and the trailhead.
Description: Your buddy will love this route that ascends 900 feet as it parallels the banks of bouldery Bear Creek as it flows through thick groves of cottonwood and ponderosa pine. Your hound can revel in deep pools, hunt for sticks, and sniff for critters in the creekside shrubbery. Your turnaround point is at 4 miles where the trail crosses Goat Creek.

Echo/Traverse Lakes Hike

Contact: Wallowa-Whitman National Forest, 1550 Dewey, Baker City, Oregon 97814, 541-523-6391, www.fs.fed.us
Paw-Approval Rating: 4 paws
Leashes Required? No
Length: 16.6 miles out and back
Difficulty: Difficult
Fees/Permits: A self-issue permit, available at the trailhead, is required.
Season: July through October
Getting There: From La Grande, head east on 1-84 to Highway 203 (exit 265). Drive southeast on Highway 203 for 11

miles to Union. In Union, take a sharp left and continue following Highway 203 south 13.8 miles to the junction with Forest Road 77 (a gravel road). Turn left on Forest Road 77 and go 15 miles to West Eagle Creek. The trailhead is on the left side of the road. The road becomes rough after 9.6 miles. A sign warns that the road is not suitable for passenger cars; however, if you drive slowly, the road is passable in a passenger car.

Description: This demanding 16.6-mile trail has almost 2,300 feet of elevation gain and blazes through the high country of the Wallowa Mountains to offer stunning views of Echo and Traverse Lakes. Don't start the trail at the wooden trailhead sign; instead, walk up the dirt road at the north end of the parking lot. Follow this dirt road about 0.2 mile as it passes some walk-in campsites. It then turns into a dirt path. At 0.3 mile, cross a wooden bridge. The trail parallels an open, grassy valley where you may see cows grazing (don't let your dog chase them). At 0.5 mile, come to a fork and stay left. (Going right puts you on Fake Creek Trail 1914.) After another 1.2 miles, cross a stream where your dog can cool off before the trail begins climbing. At 1.3 miles, you'll have to cross a stream (ignore the trail

that continues along the stream bank). After crossing, continue on the trail on the other side. After 1.4 miles, you'll enter the Eagle Cap Wilderness. Continue another 3 miles and cross rumbling Eagle Creek. The trail begins climbing steeply an enormous granite canyon on a long series of switchbacks. At 3.8 miles, go right toward Trail Creek. At 6.1 miles, cross Eagle Creek again. At 6.3 miles you'll have a fantastic view of Echo Lake, housed in a deep granite bowl. From here continue another 2 miles to Traverse Lake, your turnaround point. Retrace the route back to the trailhead.

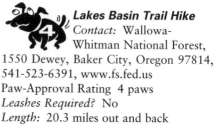

Lakes Basin Trail Hike

Contact: Wallowa-Whitman National Forest, 1550 Dewey, Baker City, Oregon 97814, 541-523-6391, www.fs.fed.us

Paw-Approval Rating 4 paws
Leashes Required? No
Length: 20.3 miles out and back
Difficulty: Difficult
Fees/Permits: $5 Northwest Forest Pass. Purchase at 1-800-270-7504 or www.naturenw.org. A self-issue permit, available at the trailhead, is also required.
Season: July through October
Getting There: Head east from La Grande on Highway 82 to Lostine, and turn south onto Lostine River Road (Forest Road 8210). Travel 17.8 miles (the road turns to gravel after 7 miles) to the Two Pan Trailhead.

Description: This incredibly beautiful and strenuous hike ascends over 2,000 feet; complete it as a super-long day hike or as an overnight backpack trip. Start hiking at the signed Two Pan Trailhead. At 0.1 mile, turn right toward the signed East Fork Lostine Trail 1662. Cross a creek and enter the Eagle Cap Wilderness. Follow the trail as it switchbacks steeply up the Lostine River canyon. At 3 miles, you'll enter a high, rock-strewn glacial valley. The trail skirts the western edge of the valley for the next 4 miles, where you

Sage leading the way on the Lakes Basin Trail in the Eagle Cap Wilderness.
Photograph by Ken Skeen

can view Eagle Cap peak to the south. At 7.3 miles, you'll arrive at a trail fork. Turn left toward Lakes Basin Trail 1810. At this point you'll pass Mirror Lake on the right. At 7.6 miles, turn right at the trail fork onto the signed Moccasin Trail 1810A. After this intersection you'll pass the shallow pool of Moccasin Lake. At 8.3 miles turn left where a sign indicates "West Fork of the Wallowa River." (The trail that heads right is signed for Glacier Pass.) Continue through the high tundra-like landscape of the gorgeous lakes basin. At 10.1 miles Douglas Lake comes into view and then you'll arrive at a trail junction. Turn left toward Hurricane Creek. (The trail that heads right is signed for the West Fork of the Wallowa River.) At 11.5 miles, go left on the Lakes Basin Trail 1810. At 12.4 miles admire Sunshine Lake on your left. After 12.7 miles you'll complete the loop portion of the hike. Turn right on the East Fork Lostine Trail and trek 7.6 miles back to the trailhead.

CYCLING FOR CANINES

La Grande

Spring Creek

Contact: Wallowa-Whitman National Forest, La Grande Ranger District, 3502 Hwy. 30, La Grande, Oregon 97850, 541-963-7186, www.fs.fed.us

Paw-Approval Rating: 2 paws
Leashes Required? No
Length: 7.6-mile loop
Difficulty: Easy
Fees/Permits: None
Getting There: From La Grande, travel 13 miles west on Interstate 84. Take the Spring Creek exit 248. Turn left (south) on Spring Creek Road (Forest Road 21). Go 3.4 miles to the junction of Forest Road 2155. Turn left on Forest Service Road 2155 and park your vehicle in the dirt pullout on the left.

Description: The 7.6-mile Spring Creek Loop begins as a fast doubletrack, eventually sending you careening down a ridge on a rocky, deeply rutted road with great views of the gently-curving Grande Ronde River and a picturesque valley dotted with farms. Before you attempt this ride, it is highly recommended that you stop by the La Grande Ranger District office and pick up a map. The many roads and unsigned junctions make it very easy to get lost. While you are riding, look for great gray owls. As many as eight pairs of great gray owls can be found per square mile in the Spring Creek area, most of whom have nested here since 1982. The owls originally nested on goshawk nests and in dead trees. Over time, the goshawk nests disintegrated, and many of the snags burned in a fire in August 1986. Now the owls primarily nest on two-foot square nesting platforms provided by the La Grande Ranger District and the Forest Service.

Begin the ride at the dirt pullout on Forest Service Road 2155. Turn left on Forest Service Road 100 from Forest Service Road 2155. At 0.4 mile, turn left onto Forest Road 500. At 1.2 miles turn right onto unsigned Forest Road 105. At 2.2 miles, continue straight across a grassy meadow (the trail is hard to distinguish here). At 2.7 miles, admire views of the Grande Ronde River. At 3 miles, test your technical skills on a steep, rocky descent. At 3.8 miles, arrive at a creek crossing. Stop and let your pup cool off and play in the creek. After taking a break, cross the creek, crank up a short, steep hill, and turn right on a doubletrack road. At 4 miles, turn left at the road fork. At 4.8 miles, turn right onto unsigned Forest Road 034. At 5.6 miles, turn right and continue riding on Forest Road 034. At 6.4 miles, turn right on Forest Service Road 2155. At 7.6 miles, arrive back at your starting point. Avoid this area after September 28 when the main hunting season begins.

Joseph

Windy Ridge
Contact: Hells Canyon National Recreation Area, Route 1, Box 270A, Enterprise, OR 97828
Paw-Approval Rating: 3 paws
Leashes Required? No
Length: 17.8 miles out and back
Difficulty: Difficult
Fees/Permits: $5 Northwest Forest Pass. Purchase at 1-800-270-7504 or www. naturenw.org.
Getting There: From Imnaha (29 miles northeast of Joseph on Highway 350) follow Hat Point Road (Forest Road 4240), a gravel winding road, for 21 miles to the junction with Forest Road 315. Turn left and continue on Forest Road 4240 another 4.2 miles to Warnock Corrals.
Description: This challenging ride has 1,680 feet of elevation gain and offers spectacular views of Hells Canyon, the Snake River, and the Seven Devils Mountains. Start by heading north on Summit Ridge Trail 1774. Ignore the Sleepy Ridge Trail that heads left. At the next trail junction turn left onto Windy Ridge Trail 1782. Follow this trail until you reach the 8.9-mile mark (your turn-around point). This trail is in a very remote, dry area. Be sure to carry enough water for you and your pooch.

POWDERHOUNDS
La Grande and Pendleton

For snow adventures in the La Grande or Pendleton areas, head to the Meacham Divide Nordic Trail System—the second largest Nordic area in Oregon. This area is 19 miles west of La Grande and 37 miles east of Pendleton. From I-84, take Summit Road exit 243 and go north 1.7 miles to the Emily Sno-Park. For more information, contact the Umatilla National Forest, 2517 SW Hailey Ave. Pendleton, Oregon 97801, 541-278-3716, www.fs.fed.us.

CANINE COMFORT ACCOMMODATIONS

Unless otherwise stated, dogs should not be left unattended in the room and must be leashed on hotel property.

La Grande

$-$$ Travelodge
2215 Adams Ave., 541-963-7116 or 1-800-578-7878, www.travelodge.com
You and your traveling partner have your choice of five rooms with queen bed, cable TV, in-room coffee, microwave, and refrigerator. Additional amenities include an indoor pool and fitness center and complimentary continental breakfast.
Dog Policy
A one-time $10 pet fee is required.

$$ Super 8 Motel
2407 East R Ave., 541-963-8080
Dog Policy
A one-time $10 pet fee is charged.

Enterprise

$$ Ponderosa Motel
102 E. Greenwood St., 541-426-3186
Dog Policy
$5 fee per night for small dogs; $10 per night for large dogs.

$$ Wilderness Inn
301 W. North St., 1-800-965-1205
All 28 rooms are dog-friendly. The inn is within walking distance of a park and the fairgrounds.
Dog Policy
A $5 fee per dog per night is charged.

Joseph

$$ Indian Lodge Motel
201 S. Main, 541-432-2651
This rustic motel has dog-friendly rooms that are air-conditioned, with cable TV, coffeemaker and refrigerator. The hotel is one mile from Wallowa Lake.

Dog Policy
The motel charges $10 for small dogs, $15 for large dogs, and $20 for two dogs.

$$-$$$ Collett's Cabins and Fine Arts
84681 Ponderosa Lane, Wallowa Lake Highway, 541-432-2391

You and your furry friend can enjoy one of ten cabins equipped with a gas log fireplace, kitchenette, private bath, linens, and cable TV/VCR. The cabins are a ten-minute walk to Wallowa Lake.

Dog Policy
A $6 fee per dog per night is charged.

CAMPGROUNDS

Red Bridge
Contact: Oregon State Parks and Recreation, Suite 1, 1115 Commercial St. NE, Salem, OR 97301-1002, 1-800-551-6949, www.oregonstateparks.org
Season: March through November
Facilities: 20 primitive campsites (no electrical hook-ups), water, restrooms, picnic tables, and fire rings. No reservations accepted.
Getting There: Travel 10 miles west of La Grande on I-84 to exit 252. Travel on Highway 244 southwest about 8 miles to the campground and park.
Description: This campground is part of Red Bridge State Park and features campsites surrounded by grassy lawn and shade trees. From the campground you have access to the Grande Ronde River which promises plenty of fishing and swimming opportunities.

Wallowa Lake State Park
Contact: Oregon State Parks and Recreation, Suite 1, 1115 Commercial St. NE, Salem, OR 97301-1002, 1-800-551-6949 (information), 1-800-452-5687 (reservations), www.oregonstateparks.org
Season: Year-round
Facilities: 121 full-hook-up campsites, 89 tent campsites, 3 group-tent areas 1 cabin, 2 yurts, water restrooms, hot showers, picnic tables, fire rings, playground, ADA campsites, RV dump station, and boat launch
Getting There: Travel 6 miles south of Joseph on Highway 82 to the campground.
Description: This huge campground on gorgeous Wallowa Lake attracts crowds of people. If you can look past the throngs, the scenery of this high mountain lake will astound you. Escape it all by paddling on the lake or checking out the many trails into the Eagle Cap Wilderness.

CANINE-APPROVED SHOPPING

Pisces Pet & Supply
1424 Jefferson Ave., La Grande, 541-975-1411. Open 11 A.M.–6 P.M. Tuesday to Friday; 11 A.M.–4 P.M. Saturday.

DOGGIE DAYCARE

La Grande Small Animal Clinic
1807 Cove Ave., La Grande, 541-963-8002

This clinic's overnight boarding fees are based on the size of your dog and range from $12.50 to $14.50 per night.

Open 8 A.M.–5:30 P.M. Monday to Friday; 8 A.M.–12 P.M. Saturday.

CANINE ER

La Grande

La Grande Small Animal Clinic
1807 Cove Ave., 541-963-8002
This clinic will see walk-ins and offers emergency care after-hours. Call the regular clinic number and the doctor on call will be paged.

Open 8 A.M.–5:30 P.M. Monday to Friday; 8 A.M.–12 P.M. Saturday.

Enterprise

Double Arrow Veterinary Clinic
66260 Lewiston Highway, 541-426-4470

This full-service mixed animal practice accepts walk-ins and offers twenty-four hour emergency services. The clinic stocks Science Diet dog food, flea and tick products, and grooming supplies. This clinic does not offer overnight boarding.

Open 8 A.M.–5:15 P.M. Monday to Friday; 8 A.M.–12 P.M. Saturday.

ANIMAL SHELTERS (LOST AND FOUND)

La Grande

Blue Mountain Humane Association
3212 Highway 30, 541-963-0807

Enterprise

Wallowa County Humane Society
207 E Garfield St., 541-426-4170

Pendleton

THE BIG SCOOP

Pendleton is renowned for its Pendleton Roundup—a four-day, foot-stompin' rodeo held in September. Pendleton Woolen Mills (1307 SE Court Ave; 541-276-6911) is world famous for its wool products, especially its gorgeous Native American blankets. Tour the factory; Fido may appreciate a wool blanket to take home as a souvenir. From Pendleton, I-84 heads southeast toward La Grande; and Highway 395 heads south toward Burns and north toward Spokane, Washington. In Pendleton, check out the Umatilla River Parkway, which follows the course of the Umatilla River right through the heart of downtown.

PAW-APPROVED HIKES AND PARKS

Emigrant Springs State Park

Contact: Oregon State Parks and Recreation, Suite 1, 1115 Commercial St. NE, Salem OR 97301-1002, www.oregonstateparks.org
Paw-Approval Rating: 2 paws
Leashes Required? Yes
Season: April through November
Fees/Permits: None
Getting There: The park is 26 miles southeast of Pendleton at exit 234 off I-84.
Description: Covering 23 acres, this state park features a picnic area under towering ponderosa and lodgepole pine trees. You and Rover can explore a short, self-guided nature trail (accessed near the registration booth) that explores this sunny pine forest ecosystem. A campground is also present if you want to stay overnight.

Pendleton

Umatilla River Parkway

Contact: Pendleton Parks and Recreation, Pendleton, OR 541-276-8100, www.pendleton-oregon.org
Paw-Approval Rating: 2 paws
Leashes Required? Yes
Length: 5 miles out and back
Difficulty: Easy
Fees/Permits: None
Season: Year-round
Getting There: From I-84 in Pendleton, take exit 207 and travel approximately 2 miles east on Highway 30 to a boat ramp where the highway crosses the Umatilla River. Park there.
Description: This paved path is a great place to take a leisurely stroll. The path along the south side of the Umatilla River follows the river through downtown Pendleton.

Umatilla

Hat Rock State Park

Contact: Oregon State Parks and Recreation, Suite 1, 1115 Commercial St. NE, Salem OR 97301-1002, www.oregonstateparks.org
Paw-Approval Rating: 2 paws
Leashes Required? Yes
Fees/Permits: None
Season: Year-round
Getting There: From I-84, take exit 179 and head north on U.S. Highway 82 to Umatilla. Hat Rock State Park is on the Columbia River, 9 miles east of Umatilla off Highway 730.

Description: The namesake of this park is the flat-topped, rocky promontory that Lewis and Clark saw in October 1805. This uniquely shaped rock is the remnant of a 12-million year old basalt flow. Weather and time have created its hat-like shape. The park covers 756 acres along the shores of Lake Wallulu, a lake on the Columbia formed by McNary Dam, and features shady cottonwood and black locust trees, an inviting picnic area, a large pond stocked with rainbow trout, and opportunities to paddle with your canine. Hike to the base of Hat Rock through sweet scented sagebrush on several primitive footpaths.

POWDERHOUNDS

La Grande and Pendleton

For snow adventures in the La Grande or Pendleton areas, head to the Meacham Divide Nordic Trail System—the second largest Nordic area in Oregon. This area is 19 miles west of La Grande and 37 miles east of Pendleton. From I-84, take Summit Road exit 243 and go north 1.7 miles to the Emily Sno-Park. For more information, contact the Umatilla National Forest, 2517 SW Hailey Ave. Pendleton, Oregon 97801, 541-278-3716, www.fs.fed.us.

CANINE COMFORT ACCOMMODATIONS

Unless otherwise stated, dogs should not be left unattended in the room and must be leashed on hotel property.

$ Motel 6

325 SE Nye Ave., 541-276-3160
Dog Policy
Fido gets to stay for free.

$$ Best Western Pendleton Inn

400 SE Nye Ave., 541-276-2135
Dog Policy
A $10 pet fee is charged per night for one or more dogs.

$$ Red Lion

304 SE Nye Ave., 541-276-6111, www.redlion.com
Dog Policy
A one-time $20 refundable deposit is charged.

$$ Super 8 Motel

601 SE Nye Ave., 541-276-8881
Dog Policy
A one time $10 non-refundable pet fee is charged.

$$ Wildhorse Resort & Casino Hotel

72779 Highway 331, 1-800-654-9453, www.wildhorseresort.com
Dog Policy
A one-time $10 pet fee is charged.

$$-$$$ Holiday Inn Express

600 SE Nye Ave., 541-966-6520
Dog Policy
A one time $10 pet fee is charged.

DOGGIE DAYCARE AND CANINE ER

Pendleton Veterinary Clinic

1901 SW Court Place, 541-276-3141

This clinic's overnight boarding fees, based on the size of the dog, range from $12 to $15 per night. For emergency care after-hours, call the regular clinic number to reach the answering service; the doctor on call will be paged.

Open 8 A.M.–5:30 P.M. Monday to Friday; 8 A.M.–12 P.M. Saturday.

Southeast Oregon

Southeast Oregon, the least-populated region in the state, is characterized by wide-open spaces and geologic marvels. This land of extremes is home to large lakes located on the Pacific flyway, hot springs, mountains, and vast sagebrush valleys. Almost two-thirds of Southeast Oregon is managed by the Bureau of Land Management. Cattle outnumber people; open-range cattle grazing is the norm. When you visit, be sure Rover doesn't chase cattle or serious consequences can result, such as being stomped by a cow or shot by a rancher.

Dogs can be off leash on BLM lands and on many trails in the Winema and Fremont National Forests. However, Southeast Oregon is home to many wildlife refuges; on these dogs must be leashed. The only exception is when you are paddling with your canine on refuge lakes. BLM officials say that dogs do not have to be leashed while in a boat but must be leashed at all launch sites.

Many of the destinations in Southeast Oregon are in isolated areas. Before you head out on your outback adventure, be sure you have a full tank of gas and plenty of water and food.

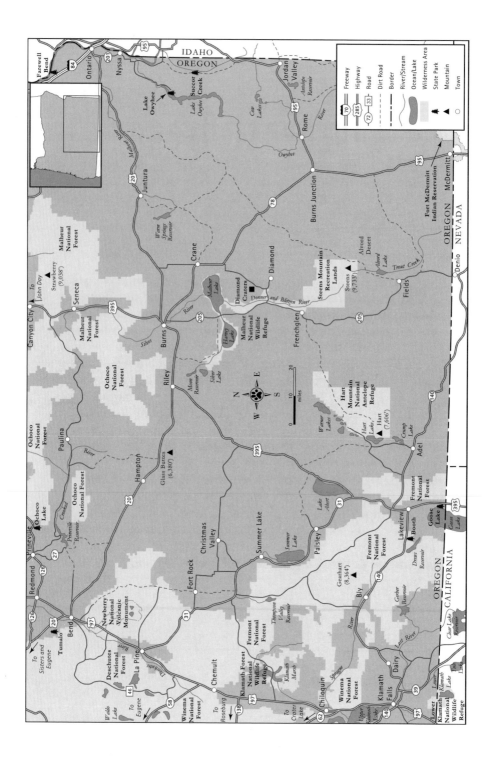

Klamath Falls

THE BIG SCOOP

This farming and ranching community lies at the base of Upper Klamath Lake, east of the Cascade Mountains near the California border. Highway 97 runs north-south through Klamath Falls and Highway 66 heads west over the Cascade Mountains to Ashland. The Klamath Basin is home to six wildlife refuges, from Klamath Lake in the north to Tule Lake in California. Paddle enthusiasts can explore two of the refuges on the Upper Klamath Canoe Trail and the Klamath Marsh Canoe Trail (see *Paddlehounds*), which bring you close to the region's abundant bird life, including American white pelicans, Canada geese, blue herons, egrets, and pintail, mallard and canvasback ducks. Bald eagles, osprey, grebes, and black terns thrive here.

Klamath Falls is also gateway to the Klamath National Forest, Winema National Forest, and the Sky Lakes Wilderness to the west, and the Fremont National Forest to the east.

Two recommended hikes around town are the Link River Nature Trail and Wingwatchers Nature Trail. These short trails along the Link River and Lake Ewauna offer easy opportunities to view the abundant bird life. The OC&E Woods Line State Trail offers cycling canines a chance to run off extra energy as it travels through the ranch and farmland in the Klamath Basin (see *Cycling for Canines*). Recommended hikes in the Sky Lakes Wilderness include Squaw Lake and Summit Lake and Long Lake/Woodpecker Lake/Badger Lake (see *Paw-Approved Hikes and Parks*).

PAW-APPROVED HIKES AND PARKS

 Collier Memorial State Park
Contact: Oregon State Parks and Recreation, Suite 1, 1115 Commercial St. NE, Salem OR 97301-1002, www.oregonstateparks.org
Paw-Approval Rating: 3 paws
Leashes Required? Yes
Season: Year-round
Getting There: This park is 30 miles north of Klamath Falls on Highway 97.
Description: This state park at the confluence of Spring Creek and the Williamson River is a unique place to take a road break. You can tour an outdoor logging museum, take a hike along the Williamson River, or stay overnight at the park's campground (see *Campgrounds*).

 **Jackson F. Kimball State Park**
Contact: Oregon State Parks and Recreation, Suite 1, 1115 Commercial St. NE, Salem OR 97301-1002, www.oregonstateparks.org
Paw-Approval Rating: 3 paws
Leashes Required? Yes
Season: Year-round
Getting There: From Klamath Falls head 25 miles north on U.S. Highway 97. Turn northwest onto Highway 62 and travel about 10 miles to Fort Klamath. From Fort Klamath continue 3 miles north on Highway 62 and follow signs to the park.
Description: Located at the headwaters of the Wood River, this park is filled with

shimmering aspen, lodgepole pine, and beautiful meadows. The park has a small campground with a hiking trail that leads to a viewpoint of the springs that feed the Wood River.

Link River Nature Trail and Wingwatchers Nature Trail Hike

Contact: Klamath County Department of Tourism, Klamath Falls, OR 1-800-445-6728, www.klamathcounty.net
Paw-Approval Rating: 3 paws
Leashes Required? Yes
Length: 4.8 miles out and back
Difficulty: Easy
Fees/Permits: None
Season: Year-round
Getting There: From downtown Klamath Falls head north on Highway 97 to the Lakeshore Dr. exit. Take this exit and follow signs for Lakeshore Dr. for about 0.9 mile. Turn left into the Link River Nature Trail parking area.
Description: Follow the gravel path as it parallels the meandering Link River for 1.7 miles to a parking area. From here, cross Main St. and continue on the gravel Wingwatchers Nature Trail. Follow this trail as it skirts the shore of Lake Ewauna and completes a short loop through a natural marsh where you may see blue herons, white pelicans, mallard ducks, and red winged blackbirds. Return to the trailhead on the same route.

Long Lake/Woodpecker Lake/Badger Lake Hike

Contact: Winema National Forest, 2819 Dahlia St., Klamath Falls, OR 97601, 541-883-6714, www.fs.fed.us
Paw-Approval Rating: 4 paws
Leashes Required? No
Length: 7.4 miles out and back
Difficulty: Moderate
Fees/Permits: Self-issue wilderness permit.
Season: July through October
Getting There: From Klamath Falls travel west on Highway 140 for 36.1 miles.

Turn right onto Forest Road 3661 and continue 5.7 miles to the trailhead parking area on the left.
Description: Start the hike by turning left on the trail toward Fourmile Lake. The first 1.8 miles of the trail skirts the edge of Fourmile Lake Campground (see *Campgrounds*) and then travels along the smooth shoreline of Fourmile Lake. From here you can enjoy stunning views of 9,495-foot Mount McLoughlin—Southern Oregon's highest peak. Look for good swimming holes along this stretch of the trail. The trail continues through lodgepole pine forest until you reach Woodpecker Lake on the left and then Badger Lake on the right at the 1.8-mile mark. From here continue another 1.6 miles through lodgepole pine forest and past a high alpine meadow dotted with bright wildflowers to the idyllic shores of Long Lake (your turnaround point). This hike has a total elevation gain of 360 feet.

OC&E Woods Line State Trail
(See *Cycling for Canines*)

Squaw Lake and Summit Lake Hike

Contact: Winema National Forest, 2819 Dahlia St., Klamath Falls, OR 97601, 541-883-6714, www.fs.fed.us
Paw-Approval Rating: 4 paws
Leashes Required? No
Length: 5.8 miles out and back
Difficulty: Easy
Fees/Permits: Self-issue wilderness permit.
Season: July through October
Getting There: From Klamath Falls, travel west on Highway 140 for 36.1 miles. Turn right onto Forest Road 3661 and continue 5.7 miles to the Fourmile Trailhead parking area on the left.
Description: This short trail leads you and your trail hound into the beautiful Sky Lakes Wilderness. Start the hike by turning right (west) and following the forest path through a thick lodgepole pine forest. Stay right at the next trail fork. At

1.8 miles you have the option of turning right on a side trail that leads to inviting Squaw Lake. This is a good place to let your pup wash off any trail dust. Continue 0.7 mile on the main trail as it ascends to the summit of a small pass and meets up with the Pacific Crest Trail. Continue straight and descend 0.4 mile to scenic Summit Lake (your turnaround point). Retrace the route back to the trailhead. Be prepared for mosquitoes during July and the first part of August.

CYCLING FOR CANINES

OC&E Woods Line State Trail

Contact: Oregon State Parks and Recreation, Suite 1, 1115 Commercial St. NE, Salem OR 97301-1002, www.oregonstateparks.org
Paw-Approval Rating: 2 paws
Leashes Required? Yes
Length: 14.2 miles out-and back (with longer options)
Difficulty: Easy
Fees/Permits: None
Season: Year-round. Snow may be present during winter.
Getting There: From Highway 39 in Klamath Falls, turn south on Washburn Way. Continue to Crosby St.. Turn left on Crosby St.. The trailhead is on the left side of Crosby St. at the junction with Avalon St.
Description: This 100-mile rail trail is open to mountain biking, hiking, and horseback riding. It begins in Klamath Falls and extends east to Bly and then north to Sycan Marsh. The route described here begins at the Klamath Falls Trailhead at Washburn Way and heads east and then north to the Olene Trailhead. The route travels through ranch and farmland in the Klamath Basin and offers stunning views of snow-capped Mount Shasta to the south. This 14.2-mile out and back section is paved; a wood chip trail parallels the paved trail if your dog prefers to run on a softer surface.

Trail Options: From Olene, you have the option of continuing on the trail for many more miles to Bly or its ending point at Sycan Marsh. This trail is popular for cross-country skiing.

PADDLEHOUNDS

Paddle enthusiasts will enjoy the Klamath Marsh Canoe Trail (open July 1 through September 30) that takes you through a vast marsh filled with abundant bird life. To get there, travel 45 miles north of Klamath Falls on Highway 97. Turn right onto Silver Lake Road and travel 9.5 miles east. Turn right onto Forest Road 690 and travel about 4 miles south to the canoe launch area.

You can also paddle with your dog on the 9.5-mile Upper Klamath Wildlife Refuge Canoe Trail. This canoe trail is marked and takes you through open lake and marsh where you can see ducks, geese, swans and other migrating birds. You may also see beaver, muskrat, and river otter. Spring is the best time to visit. Be sure to bring plenty of mosquito repellant! Launch your boat from the Rocky Point Boat Launch.

To get there from Klamath Falls, travel 25 miles west on Highway 140. Turn north on the Rocky Point turnoff to Rocky Point Resort, where you can rent a canoe. Leash your dog at the boat launches. The resort rents cabins and rooms that welcome canines (see *Canine Comfort Accommodations*). For more information about these canoe trails, contact Klamath Basin National Wildlife Refuges, 4009 Hill Road, Tulelake, CA 96134, 530-667-2231, www.klamathnwr.org.

CANINE COMFORT ACCOMMODATIONS

Unless otherwise stated, dogs should not be left unattended in the room and must be leashed on hotel property.

$-$$$ Rocky Point Resort

28121 Rocky Point Rd., 541-356-2287, www.rockypointoregon.com

This resort rents cozy cabins that have a fully equipped kitchen and private bath as well as tent campsites with water and fire rings. Canoes are available for rent to those wanting to explore the Upper Klamath Wildlife Refuge Canoe Trail (see *Paddlehounds*).

Dog Policy
A $2 fee per night per dog is charged. In addition, a $50 refundable cleaning/damage deposit is required on cabin rentals. Dogs are not allowed in the lodge rooms but are welcome in the cabins.

$$ Best Western Klamath Inn
4061 S. Sixth St., 541-882-1200, www. bestwestern.com

This inn features dog-friendly rooms equipped with data port, microwave, refrigerator, and cable TV.

Dog Policy
Fido gets to stay free at this inn.

$$ Red Lion Inn
3612 S. 6th St., 541-882-8864
Dog Policy
A $50 refundable deposit is required.

$-$$ Motel 6
5136 6th St., 541-884-2110
Dog Policy
The motel accepts one well-behaved dog per room.

$$-$$$ Holiday Inn Express
2500 S. 6th St., 541-884-9999
Dog Policy
A $20 refundable pet deposit is required.

$$-$$$ Quality Inn & Suites
100 Main St., 541-882-4666 or 1-800-228-5151

All the rooms are dog-friendly. Rooms are equipped with refrigerator, microwave, coffeemaker, data port, and cable TV. Additional amenities are a seasonal heated pool, spa, meeting rooms, and a complimentary continental breakfast.

Dog Policy
Your dog gets to stay free.

$$$ Shilo Inn
2500 Almond St., 541-885-7980, www. shiloinns.com

This inn offers fresh coffee, fruit, and popcorn in the lobby; twenty-four hour indoor pool, spa, sauna, steam room and fitness center, free local calls, voice mail and data port, guest laundry, in-room microwave, refrigerator, coffeemaker and ironing unit, and satellite TV with free HBO. The hotel also has a restaurant and lounge.

Dog Policy
A $10.60 fee is charged per dog per night.

$$$-$$$$ Crystalwood Lodge
38625 Westside Rd., 1-866-381-2322, www.crystalwoodlodge.com

This non-smoking lodge features dog-friendly rooms with private baths, and a combination of twin, double, or queen sized beds. Included are a gourmet dinner and a continental breakfast. This lodge also offers a one-day mushing boot camp where you can learn to teach your dog to pull for carting, scootering, or skijoring (dog pulling a cross-country skier). Three-day intensive boot camps are also available. Call the lodge for details.

Dog Policy
Your dog gets to stay free at this lodge.

CAMPGROUNDS

Collier Memorial State Park
Contact: Oregon State Parks and Recreation, Suite 1, 1115 Commercial St. NE, Salem OR 97301-1002, www.oregonstateparks.org
Season: April through October
Facilities: 50 full-hook-up campsites, 18 tent campsites, 4-corral primitive horse campsites, hot showers, restrooms, water, picnic tables, fire rings, playground, RV dumping station, logging museum, and playground. No reservations accepted.

Getting There: The park is 30 miles north of Klamath Falls on Highway 97.

Description: The main attraction at this campground is the Collier Logging Museum's displays of antique logging equipment and a pioneer village. On summer weekends you can watch movies about logging and other topics at 9 P.M. The campground is located at the confluence of Spring Creek and the Williamson River, a setting that provides many hiking opportunities for you and your dog.

Fourmile Lake

Contact: Winema National Forest, 2819 Dahlia St., Klamath Falls, OR 97601, 541-883-6714, www.fs.fed.us

Season: June through October

Facilities: 25 RV/tent campsites (no electrical hook-ups), water, picnic tables, restrooms, and a boat launch. No reservations accepted.

Getting There: Travel 35 miles northwest of Klamath Falls on Highway 140 to Forest Road 3661. Turn north on Forest Road 3661 and continue 6 miles to the campground.

Description: Located on the shores of Fourmile Lake, this campground is a good place to stay if you plan on exploring the Sky Lakes Wilderness. Hikes to try are Squaw Lake/Summit Lake and Long Lake/Woodpecker Lake/Badger Lake (see *Paw-Approved Hikes and Parks*). You can paddle with your pooch on the glassy lake with magnificent Mount McLoughlin rising prominently to the southwest. Mosquitoes can be a problem in early summer.

DOG EVENTS

Dog Mushing Bootcamp

Crystalwood Lodge, 38625 Westside Rd., Klamath Falls, OR 866-381-2322 or visit www.mushingbootcamp.com

During the first two weeks in May, Crystalwood Lodge hosts two one-day pull clinics for those who want to teach a single dog to pull for carting, sledding, scootering, or skijoring (dog pulling a cross-country skier). For those with more than one dog, three-day intensive boot camps teach you all the basics you need to teach your dogs to pull. For information on dates and prices, contact the lodge.

CANINE-APPROVED SHOPPING

American Feed & Farm Supply

2225 Washburn Way, 541-884-7733

This farm supply store stocks many different types of dog food, toys and treats, leashes, collars, kennels, grooming supplies, and dog sweaters. Open 8 A.M.–6 P.M. Monday to Saturday.

DOGGIE DAYCARE

Everett Veterinary Hospital

632 Oak Ave., 541-884-2926

This clinic offers overnight boarding for $9 per night.

Open 7:30 A.M.–5:30 P.M., Monday to Friday; 9 A.M.–12 P.M. Saturday.

CANINE ER

Companion Pet Clinic

2343 Gettle St., 541-882-7674

This clinic will take walk-ins. It does not offer overnight boarding.

Open 7 A.M.–6 P.M., Monday to Friday.

Everett Veterinary Hospital

632 Oak Ave., 541-884-2926

This clinic does not see walk-ins.

Open 7:30 A.M.–5:30 P.M., Monday to Friday; 9 A.M.–12 P.M. Saturday.

LOST AND FOUND (ANIMAL SHELTERS)

Klamath Falls Humane Society

500 Miller Island Rd., 541-882-1119, www.klamathhumanesociety.com

Open 10 A.M.–2 P.M., Monday to Thursday; 10 A.M.–2 P.M., Friday and Saturday.

Lakeview

THE BIG SCOOP

Oregon's highest town at 4,800 feet, Lakeview is about 95 miles east of Klamath Falls off Highway 140. This high desert community at the foot of the Warner Mountains is a good place to stock up on supplies before you and your outback hound begin exploring the wild open spaces of the Southeast Oregon desert.

Plan on visiting the nearby Hart Mountain National Antelope Refuge (see *Cycling for Canines*), about 50 miles northeast of Lakeview. The refuge, 430 square miles of sagebrush desert, aspen-covered valleys, steep canyons, and ridges, supports large herds of pronghorn antelope, mule deer, and bighorn sheep. If you stay overnight at the Hot Springs Campground (see *Campgrounds*) in the refuge, be sure to soak in the soothing springs. Many informal creek trails surround this campground.

The Fremont National Forest, both east and west of Lakeview, also has many idyllic trails that offer shade and water for your canine partner and plenty of outstanding scenery for you. Recommended hikes include Gearhart Mountain, Crooked Creek, Cottonwood Creek, and Cougar Peak.

PAW-APPROVED HIKES AND PARKS

Lakeview

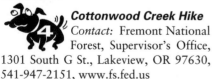

Cottonwood Creek Hike

Contact: Fremont National Forest, Supervisor's Office, 1301 South G St., Lakeview, OR 97630, 541-947-2151, www.fs.fed.us

Paw-Approval Rating: 4 paws
Leashes Required? No
Length: 10 miles out and back
Difficulty: Easy
Fees/Permits: None
Season: May through October
Getting There: From Lakeview, drive west on Highway 140 for 11 miles. Turn right on County Road 2-20. Continue on County Road 2-20 for 6 miles (it turns into Forest Road 3870). Continue on Forest Road 3870 for 3 miles and then turn right onto Forest Road 014. Follow the signs on Forest Road 014 for 1 mile to the trailhead parking area.
Description: This peaceful route follows Cottonwood Creek through shady cottonwood and conifer trees from the Cottonwood Meadows Lake recreation area to Forest Road 3870/014 (your turnaround point). Your trail hound will have plenty of opportunities to pounce on sticks and wallow in the creek. A bonus is your hound can be untethered on this beautiful creek trail. If you want to camp overnight, check out the nearby Cottonwood Meadows Campground (see *Campgrounds*). This route is also open to mountain bikes.

Cougar Peak Hike

Contact: Fremont National Forest, Supervisor's Office, 1301 South G St., Lakeview, OR 97630, 541-947-2151
Paw-Approval Rating: 3 paws
Leashes Required? No
Length: 7.6 miles out and back
Difficulty: Difficult
Fees/Permits: None
Season: June through November

Getting There: Head 74 miles east of Klamath Falls (or 17 miles west of Lakeview) on Highway 140. Turn north onto Forest Road 3870 at a Cottonwood Meadow sign. Continue about 6 miles to the Cottonwood Trailhead on the left side of the road.

Description: Begin hiking through an open ponderosa pine forest. At 0.2 mile your pup can take a plunge at a creek crossing. Continue as the trail passes through more forest and open meadows. After 1.0 mile, cross Cougar Creek and turn left onto a doubletrack road. Trek on this road as it parallels Cougar Creek for 1.5 miles and then arrives at the upper trailhead for Cougar Peak. From the Cougar Peak Trailhead, follow the doubletrack road 0.2 mile and then turn left onto a singletrack trail. Continue another 1.1 miles on a steep ascent to the 7,919 summit of Cougar Peak. From the summit, you'll have first-rate views of Upper Klamath Lake to the west and Goose Lake and Mount Shasta to the south. Return to the trailhead on the same route. This hike has a total elevation gain of 1,820 feet.

Crooked Creek Hike

Contact: Fremont National Forest, Supervisor's Office, 1301 South G St., Lakeview, OR 97630, 541-947-2151, www.fs.fed.us

Paw-Approval Rating: 4 paws
Leashes Required? No
Length: 5 miles out and back
Difficulty: Moderate
Fees/Permits: None
Season: May through October
Getting There: From downtown Lakeview head north on Highway 395 for 11 miles and turn right onto County Road 2-13 at a sign that indicates "Mill Trailhead." Follow this road (it soon turns into Forest Road 012) for 0.2 mile and turn right at a road fork. Continue 1.3 miles to the end of the road and the trailhead.

Description: Your trail hound will love this route that follows the course of rambling Crooked Creek through a striking rimrock gorge shaded with aspen and ponderosa pine. Begin the hike by crossing the creek and heading upstream on a doubletrack road. Continue upstream about 2.6 miles to your turnaround point. Retrace the route back to the trailhead. This trail is open to mountain bikes.

Gearhart Mountain Hike

Contact: Fremont National Forest, Supervisor's Office, 1301 South G St., Lakeview, OR 97630, 541-947-2151, www.fs.fed.us

Paw-Approval Rating: 4 paws
Leashes Required? No
Length: 11 miles out and back (with a longer backpacking option to Blue Lake)
Difficulty: Difficult
Fees/Permits: None
Season: July through October
Getting There: From Bly (54 miles east of Klamath Falls and 42 miles west of Lakeview on Highway 140) head 1.3 miles east on Highway 140 to Campbell Road. Turn left and travel 0.5 mile. Turn right onto Forest Road 34, where a sign indicates "Gearhart Wilderness 17 miles." Drive 14.3 miles on Forest Road 34. At the road fork, stay left. Continue another 0.2 mile and then turn left onto Corral Creek Road (Forest Road 012), a rough narrow dirt road. Continue 1.4 miles to Gearhart Mountain Trail 100 (you'll pass Corral Creek Campground in 0.3 mile).

Description: This intriguing trail leads you through the heart of the little known 22,823-acre Gearhart Mountain Wilderness, protected for its glacier-carved valleys, craggy cliffs, and 8,364-foot Gearhart Mountain. Begin hiking on Gearhart Mountain Trail 100 as it ascends through a sunny, old-growth ponderosa pine forest. At 0.7 mile you'll pass through an area known as the Palisades that is filled with large, stacked rocks of unusual shapes. The route passes by these oddly shaped rocks for about 0.3 mile and then descends on some short switchbacks to a creek crossing at 3.4 miles. At 3.6 miles, you'll pass an impressive rock tower called "The Dome." At 4.9 miles, turn right at the trail fork. At 5.5 miles, you'll arrive at an overlook with magnificent views of California's Mount Lassen to the south, Steens Mountain to the east, and the Three Sisters to the north. You can turn around here and retrace the route to the trailhead. *Trail Option:* If you are backpacking, you can continue another 3.4 miles to Blue Lake—the only lake in this wilderness area. This hike has a total elevation gain of just over 1,900 feet.

Hart Mountain National Wildlife Refuge
(See *Cycling for Canines*)

Paisley

Dead Horse Lake Hike
(See *Campbell Lake* in *Campgrounds*)

Silver Lake

 **Fort Rock State Natural Area**
Contact: Oregon State Parks and Recreation, Suite 1, 1115 Commercial St. NE, Salem OR 97301-1002, www.oregonstateparks.org
Paw-Approval Rating: 2 paws
Leashes Required? Yes
Fees/Permits: None
Season: Year-round
Getting There: From Silver Lake on Oregon Highway 31, head 17 miles north on Highway 31. Watch for signs to turn right (east) to the small hamlet of Fort Rock and then 2 miles to the natural area.
Description: The centerpiece of this natural area is the striking basalt cliffs of a volcanic crater. A mile-long hiking trail leads you into the area for a close up of the protruding remains of this rock monolith. These cliffs and open sagebrush country are haven for golden eagle, red tail hawk, and prairie falcon. After the hike, cool off in the shady picnic area.

National Fremont Recreational Trail
(See *Silver Creek Marsh* in *Campgrounds*)

CYCLING FOR CANINES

Lakeview

Cottonwood Creek
(See *Paw-Approved Hikes and Parks*)

Cougar Peak
(See *Paw-Approved Hikes and Parks*)

Crooked Creek
(See *Paw-Approved Hikes and Parks*)

 **Hart Mountain National Antelope Refuge**
Contact: Hart Mountain National Antelope Refuge, 541-947-3315
Paw-Approval Rating: 3 paws
Leashes Required? Yes
Length: 24.2-mile loop
Difficulty: Difficult
Fees/Permits: None
Season: April through November
Getting There: From Lakeview, travel 4.6 miles north on U.S. 395 to the Oregon Highway 140 junction. Turn right and drive 15.6 miles on Highway 140 to the junction with Plush Cutoff Road (CR 3-13). Turn left and travel 18.5 miles to the town of Plush. Continue through town for about a mile and turn right on Hart Mountain Road (CR 3-12). Follow this road approximately 26 miles to the refuge headquarters. From there, proceed south another 1.7 miles. Turn right at the road fork and continue another 2.5 miles to the Hot Springs Campground on your right.
Description: Wide open spaces blanketed with sagebrush and bunch grass, beveled fault-block mountains, and alkaline lakes characterize the vastness of Southeast Oregon's Warner Valley. Jutting up from this lowland is the well-known landmark, Hart Mountain (the name "Hart" is from the cattle brand used by the Wilson ranch in the 1880s).

DeGarmo, Potter, and Hart Canyons surround Hart Mountain, further accentuating its towering elevation of 8,017 feet. At the base of this massive ridge lies the Warner Basin. A 500-square-mile lake filled this basin at the end of the last ice age. Now those waters have receded, leaving three separate lakes—Pelican, Crump, and Hart. These lakes support a multitude of migrating birds, such as Canada geese, pied-billed grebes, snowy egrets, and an assortment of ducks. Pelican Lake proves itself aptly named with its numerous white pelicans, which feed and nest around the lake.

The centerpiece of the Warner Basin is the Hart Mountain National Antelope Refuge, 430 square miles of sagebrush desert, hot springs, aspen-covered valleys, steep canyons, and ridges that support large herds of pronghorn antelope, mule deer, and bighorn sheep, as well as other animals.

Very fit mountain biking dogs may want to tackle the strenuous 24.2-mile mountain bike ride that starts and ends at Hot Springs Campground (see *Campgrounds*). This route has over 1,000 feet of elevation gain and is on dirt/gravel roads that wind through a sagebrush plateau, looping back through a canyon with aspen groves, creeks, and grassy meadows. For an easier ride, opt for a shorter out and back trip.

Start by turning left out of the Hot Springs Campground parking area and ride back toward refuge headquarters. At 2.5 miles, turn right and go through a metal gate. After 9.1 miles, turn left and ride 0.1 mile to Lookout Point. Watch for pronghorn antelope. After enjoying the view, turn around and ride 0.1 mile back to the main road. At 16.6 miles, turn right at the road fork. At 17.6 miles, ride over Guano Creek on a concrete bridge. This is a great spot to take a break from the saddle and let your dog play in the creek. At 18 miles, pass Blue Sky Hotel Camp on your left, then go around a wooden gate that reads "Road closed December 1–August

1." At 20.4 miles, turn left at the road fork. At 23 miles, turn right at the road fork. At 24.2 miles, arrive back at your starting point.

There are several cattle guards on this route. If your dog isn't familiar with crossing cattle guards you may want to make sure he detours around these metal devices. Paw protection is highly recommended on this route due to the many miles of gravel roads. Also be on the lookout for the occasional car.

Due to the remote location of the ride, plan on camping at Hot Spring Campground, 4.2 miles from refuge headquarters. This camping area offers primitive campsites situated along a beautiful aspen-lined creek. Many informal hiking trails along the creek can lead you to beaver and other wildlife.

After negotiating the trail, you may be in the mood for some well-earned relaxation. There is a bathhouse at the Hot Springs Campground (sorry no dogs!). An ugly concrete building surrounds the hot springs, and the wooden ladder leading into the water is a bit slimy, but if you look past these man-made blunders, you'll enjoy a hot, soothing soak after your ride. The only drawback to this idyllic setting is the swarms of mosquitoes in the early spring and summer. Also be on the lookout for rattlesnakes and check your dog for ticks after your day of adventure.

Paisley

Dead Horse Lake
(See *Campbell Lake* in *Campgrounds*)

Silver Lake

National Fremont Recreational Trail
(See *Silver Creek Marsh* in *Campgrounds*)

POWDERHOUNDS
Snow hounds may want to accompany you at a 21-mile system of cross-country

Snow can be a dog's best friend.

ski trails accessed from the Quartz Mountain Sno-Park, 25 miles west of Lakeview off Highway 140. For more information contact the Lakeview Ranger District, 1301 South G St., Lakeview, OR 97630, 541-947-2151, www.fs.fed.us.

In the Silver Lake area (northwest of Lakeview on Highway 31), check out an 8-mile cross-country trail that starts from the Pole-Butte Sno-Park. From Silver Lake, head south on County Road 4-12 for 6 miles. (After 6 miles the road turns into Forest Road 28.) Continue on Road 28 for 9 miles to the junction with Forest Road 3142. Turn left and continue on Forest Road 28 about 4.5 miles to Forest Road 2916. Turn left and go 2.5 miles to thesnow park. For more information, contact the Silver Lake Ranger District, Highway 31, Silver Lake, OR 97638, 541-576-2107, www.fs.fed.us.

PADDLEHOUNDS

Cottonwood Meadows Lake (electric motors only), northwest of Lakeview,

offers hours of fun on the water. To get there, travel 24 miles west of Lakeview on Highway 140 to the junction with Forest Road 3870. Turn north onto Forest Road 3870 and drive 8 miles to the campground and boat ramp.

You can also enjoy a paddle adventure on Campbell Reservoir (electric motors only) in the Fremont National Forest. To get there from Lakeview, travel west on Highway 140 for 3 miles and turn right onto County Road 2-16. Continue on County Road 2-16 for 5 miles. Turn left onto County Road 2-16A (the road turns into Forest Road 28 after 2 miles) and travel 28 miles and turn left onto Forest Road 033. Continue 2 miles to the campground and boat ramp.

CANINE COMFORT ACCOMMODATIONS

Unless otherwise stated, dogs should not be left unattended in the room and must be leashed on hotel property.

Lakeview

$-$$ Interstate 8 Motel
354 N. K St., 541-947-3341
This motel has six dog-friendly rooms equipped with cable TV and HBO.
Dog Policy
Dogs must be less than 50 pounds.

$-$$ Lakeview Lodge Motel
301 N. G St., 541-947-2181
Dog Policy
Your dog gets to stay for free.

Summer Lake

$$$-$$$$ Summer Lake Inn
31501 Highway 31, 1-800-261-2778, www.summerlakeinn.com
Dog Policy
Dogs are allowed for a one-time charge of $10 per dog. The inn allows a maximum of two dogs per cabin.

CAMPGROUNDS

Cottonwood Meadows

Contact: Fremont National Forest, Supervisor's Office, 1301 South G St., Lakeview, OR 97630, 541-947-2151, www.fs.fed.us

Season: June through mid-October

Facilities: 12 RV/trailer campsites (no electrical hook-ups), 9 tent campsites, picnic tables, fire grates, water, and a boat launch. No reservations accepted.

Getting There: From Lakeview travel 24 miles west on Highway 140 to the junction with Forest Road 3870. Turn north onto Forest Road 3870 and drive 8 miles to the campground.

Description: This campground has campsites right on Cottonwood Lake. This lake is ringed with aspen and towering ponderosa pine. Paddle on its smooth, quiet waters or hike to the high summit of Cougar Peak (see *Paw-Approved Hikes and Parks*). For a more leisurely hike where Rover can play in the lake, explore the lakeshore trail.

Hot Springs

Contact: Hart Mountain National Antelope Refuge, 541-947-3315

Season: Year-round

Facilities: 14 RV/tent campsites (no electrical hook-ups), some picnic tables and fire rings, no water. No reservations accepted.

Getting There: From Lakeview travel 4.6 miles north on U.S. 95 to the OR 140 junction. Turn right and drive 15.6 miles on Highway 140 to the junction with Plush Cutoff Road (CR 3-13). Turn left and travel 18.5 miles to the town of Plush. Continue through town for about a mile and turn right on Hart Mountain Road (CR 3-12). Follow this road approximately 26 miles to the refuge headquarters. From refuge headquarters, proceed south another 1.7 miles. Turn right at the road fork and continue another 2.5 miles to the Hot Springs Campground on your right.

Description: Here you'll find idyllic campsites next to aspen-lined Rock Creek. The

Hanging out at the Hot Springs Campground in the Hart Mountain National Antelope Refuge.
Photograph by Ken Skeen

campground is also host to a hot spring pool housed in a not very appealing concrete building. You can explore many game trails that lead along the creek through the aspens and willows that are haven to beaver and other wildlife. The remoteness of this campground means that it is usually not crowded and you can explore with your dog without worry. See *Cycling for Canines* for a recommended mountain bike route through the refuge.

Paisley

Campbell Lake

Contact: Fremont National Forest, Supervisor's Office, 1301 South G St., Lakeview, OR 97630, 541-947-2151, www.fs.fed.us

Season: July through October

Facilities: 16 RV/tent campsites (no electrical hook-ups), picnic tables, grills, water, vault toilets, and a boat launch (electric motors only)

Getting There: From Paisley (northwest of Lakeview on Highway 31), head 0.5 mile north on Highway 31, and turn left on Mill St., which turns into Forest Road 33 at a road fork. Stay left and continue on Forest Road 33 for 20 miles. At the T-intersection with paved Forest Road 28 turn right.

Travel on Forest Road 28 for 11 miles. Turn left at the junction with Forest Road 033. Continue 2 miles to the campground.

From Lakeview, travel west on Highway 140 for 3 miles and turn right onto County Road 2-16. Drive on County Road 2-16 for 5 miles. Turn left onto County Road 2-16A (the road turns into Forest Road 28 after 2 miles), travel 28 miles, and turn left onto Forest Road 033. Continue 2 miles to the campground.

Description: Located on the shores of Campbell Lake, campsites at this campground are nestled in a thick lodgepole pine forest. Your pooch can play along the lakeshore or you can paddle around the lake. You can also hike or mountain bike 1.7 miles to Deadhorse Lake from the campground (look for the trailhead near campsite 14). There are also many loop options on this trail system. This campground is popular and fills up fast on summer weekends.

Silver Lake

Silver Creek Marsh

Contact: Silver Lake Ranger District, Highway 31, P.O. Box 129, Silver Lake, OR 97638, 541-576-2107, www.fs.fed.us
Season: May through November 15
Facilities: 17 RV/tent campsites (no electrical hook-ups), picnic tables, fire grates, vault toilets, drinking water, and horse corrals with hitching rails. No reservations accepted.
Getting There: From Silver Lake go 1 mile northwest on Highway 31 to the junction with County Road 4-11 (this turns into Forest Road 27). Turn left and follow Forest Road 27 for 10 miles to the campground.

Description: Located on the West Fork of Silver Creek, this beautiful campground is shaded by stately ponderosa pine trees. Although the creek is not large, your hound will love to wallow in its deep, rocky pools. The campground is adjacent to the Fremont National Recreation Trail, which can be accessed at the end of the campground loop. A good 4.4-mile out and back hike (or mountain bike) your dog will love travels through a shady ponderosa pine forest and then along the West Fork of Silver Creek to a wood bridge at 2.2 miles. You have the option of turning around here or continuing to the Antler Trailhead which you'll reach in another 2.3 miles. From the Antler Trailhead the trail continues to the 8,196-foot summit of Yamsey Mountain. Mosquitoes can be a problem in spring and early summer.

DOGGIE DAYCARE AND CANINE ER

Lakeview Animal Hospital
1733 N. 4th St., 541-947-3383

This full-service small animal hospital will take walk-ins (but prefers that you make an appointment). The hospital offers twenty-four hour emergency service and stocks Science Diet prescription dog foods, pet care products, flea and tick products, collars, and leashes. Overnight boarding rates are $7 for small dogs, $8 for medium dogs, and $9 for large dogs.

Open 8 A.M.–5:30 P.M., Monday to Friday; 9 A.M.–12 P.M. Saturday.

Burns

THE BIG SCOOP

The small ranching community of Burns is the county seat of Harney County—Oregon's largest county at over 10,000 square miles. Here, sagebrush desert stretches far into a cloudless horizon. Hidden in this vast desert landscape is the Malheur Wildlife Refuge, 187,000 acres of vast marshes, ponds, and sagebrush desert that is a haven to over 320 bird species. The refuge lies 32 miles south of Burns off Highway 205. Leashed dogs are welcome at the Malheur Refuge; try hiking or mountain biking with your friend on Center Patrol Road, which travels through the heart of the refuge.

Other don't-miss destinations in Harney County are the Steens Mountain Recreation Lands, Diamond Craters Outstanding Natural Area, and the Peter French Round Barn Historic Site.

At 9,773 feet, Steens Mountain is a fault block mountain supporting several eco-zones. Wild mustangs and bighorn sheep roam its glaciated slopes and golden eagles soar above. The Steens Mountain Loop Road (open July through October) takes you past scenic viewpoints, trails, and campgrounds where you can soak in the beauty and immensity of the vast, open landscape. Before you begin your trip up Steens Mountain, stock up on supplies and gas at the Frenchglen Mercantile in Frenchglen. This store is the only show in town; it has everything you need for your outback adventure.

Frenchglen was named after Dr. Hugh James Glen and Peter French. Glen was known as the "Wheat King" in California's Sacramento Valley because of his vast land holdings. In 1872, Glen sent Peter French to purchase land in Southeast Oregon in order to increase the size of his land empire. French ended up purchasing thousands of acres and became a partner with Glen. The town's name honors not only the two individuals, but their enterprising partnership as well.

The Diamond Craters Outstanding Natural Area (see *Cycling for Canines*) is home to many of the area's geologic gems; a ride through this volcanic discovery zone takes you on a tour of lava formations, volcanic craters, and cinder cones.

The Peter French Round Barn (see *Paw-Approved Hikes and Parks*) is just down the road from Diamond Craters. It features a historic barn built in the 1880s that was used to break horses on the 200,000-acre P Ranch, at one time the largest single cattle ranch in the United States.

PAW-APPROVED HIKES AND PARKS

 Arizona Creek to Stergen Meadow Hikes
Contact: Bureau of Land Management, Burns District Office, 28910 Hwy 20 West, Hines, Oregon 97738, 541-573-4400, www.or.blm.gov
Paw-Approval Rating: 2 paws
Leashes Required? No
Length: 11.4 miles out and back
Difficulty: Moderate
Fees/Permits: None
Season: Year-round
Getting There: From Fields (Fields is about 110 miles south of Burns on Highway 205) travel 9.5 miles south (toward

Winnemucca) to an unsigned dirt road on the right side of the road.

Description: This hike explores the fascinating rocky outcrops and pinnacles of Arizona Creek Canyon and ends at Stergen Meadow. While you are looking at the canyon scenery, your dog can explore off-leash in this expansive high desert area. Hike along the doubletrack road about 2.2 miles to a road fork. Continue straight (left) and trek through the canyon for another mile to a T-junction. Turn right and continue your high desert journey for another 2.5 miles to Stergen Meadow (your turnaround point).

Big Indian Gorge Hike

Contact: Bureau of Land Management, Burns District Office, 28910 Hwy 20 West, Hines, Oregon 97738, 541-573-4400, www.or.blm.gov

Paw-Approval Rating: 4 paws

Leashes Required? No

Length: 6.2 miles out and back

Difficulty: Easy

Fees/Permits: None

Season: July through October

Getting There: From Burns travel about 62 miles south on Highway 205 to Frenchglen. From Frenchglen, continue south 10 miles toward Fields until you arrive at the junction with Steens Mountain Loop Road. Turn left onto Steens Mountain Loop Road and travel 19.5 miles to South Steens Campground (see *Campgrounds*), located on the right side of the road. Continue to the second campground entrance. The trailhead is on the left side of the road beyond the group camping area.

Description: Go around a gate and begin hiking on a doubletrack road for 1.9 miles through a sage-scented canyon filled with fragrant juniper trees, to the junction with Big Indian Creek. Cross the creek (there is no bridge) and pick up the trail on the other side. Continue up a scenic canyon for 0.2 mile to the junction with Little Indian Creek. Ford the creek, taking time

to let your hound wallow, and continue on the trail on the other side. Continue another mile upstream through gorgeous canyon country to another crossing of Big Indian Creek. This is your turnaround point. Retrace the route back to the trailhead. This route has a total elevation gain of 500 feet.

Diamond Craters Outstanding Natural Area

(See *Cycling for Canines*)

Malheur Wildlife Refuge

Contact: Malheur National Wildlife Refuge, HC 72 Box 245, Princeton, OR 97721, 541-493-2612, www.pacific.fws.gov

Paw-Approval Rating: 2 paws

Leashes Required? Yes

Fees/Permits: None

Season: Year-round, though the best times to visit are spring and fall.

Getting There: From Burns, head south on Highway 205 for 32 miles. Turn left and go 6 miles to the Malheur Wildlife Refuge Headquarters. Turn left into the visitor parking lot.

Description: The Malheur Wildlife Refuge is one of Southeast Oregon's greatest treasures. The refuge's 187,000 acres are busiest during spring when over 130 species of birds nest there. Northern pintails, tundra swans, snow geese, white-fronted geese, and sandhill cranes arrive on the scene in February. Waterfowl species arrive in April, shorebirds in May, and songbirds in June. Young pronghorn and mule deer fawns can also be seen during May and June. In the fall, great flocks of sandhill cranes can be seen gathering in the southern end of the Blitzen Valley for their migration south to the Central Valley in California. Canada geese and large flocks of ducks can also be seen migrating south.

You can hike or mountain bike with your dog on Center Patrol Road through the heart of the refuge. Be sure to stop by the visitor center and museum to find out more about the refuge. The refuge and museum are open daily from dawn to dusk. The office and visitor center at the refuge headquarters are open 7 A.M.–4:30 P.M., Monday through Thursday, 7 A.M.–3:30 P.M., Friday. The visitor center is open most weekends during spring and summer. Be armed for mosquitoes during spring and early summer.

Page Springs Campground Hikes

Contact: Bureau of Land Management, Burns District Office, 28910 Hwy 20 West, Hines, Oregon 97738, 541-573-4400, www.or.blm.gov
Paw-Approval Rating: 4 paws
Leashes Required? Yes
Length: Nature trail: 1.4 miles; Donner und Blitzen River Trail: 1.4 miles out and back
Difficulty: Easy
Fees/Permits: None
Season: Year-round
Getting There: From Frenchglen (about 62 miles south of Burns on Highway 205), head south on Highway 205 and turn left onto Steens Mountain Loop Road. Continue 3 miles to a T-intersection and turn right toward Page Springs Campground. Continue 1 mile to the campground entrance. From there, drive to the end of the campground and the trailhead.
Description: Page Springs Campground is a good base camp for exploring both the trails described here as well as the Steens Mountain Hikes.

The river trail parallels the meandering Donner und Blitzen River through a rimrock canyon. This river was named by George B. Curry of the U.S. Army who crossed the river with his troops in a thunderstorm during the Snake War of 1864. *Donner und Blitzen* is German for "thunder and lightning." This short trail begins at the far end of the parking lot and passes through several marshy areas filled with the soft, brown cattail plumes that are a favorite perch for red-winged blackbirds.

Deer feed on streamside grasses and swallows swoop over the river, catching insects, with impressive acrobatic moves. Canines will enjoy the many bogs where they can wallow and hunt for sticks. You may also catch a rare glimpse of the fun-loving river otter who feed on trout in the river. In the early 1900s otter were abundant, but their sleek, luxurious hides made them valuable to fur traders who eventually over-trapped the area. By the 1930s, they were completely absent from the river and Malheur Basin. Oregon Fish and Wildlife re-introduced the otter in the early 1980s.

Continue on the trail until it fades out at 0.7 mile. Retrace the route back to the parking area. Once your trail hound has cooled off, get ready to explore the nature trail that is accessed from the same parking area. This loop trail treks through a small juniper and sagebrush canyon to a viewpoint of the campground and surrounding valley. Look for the start of this trail on the left side of the road as you enter the trailhead parking area.

Peter French Round Barn

Contact: Oregon State Parks Trust, P.O. Box 581, Bend, OR 97709, 1-800-497-2757, www.orparkstrust.org
Paw-Approval Rating: 3 paws
Leashes Required? Yes
Fees/Permits: None
Season: Year-round
Getting There: From Frenchglen (62 miles south of Burns on Highway 205) travel 18 miles north on Highway 205 to the junction with Diamond Grain Camp Road Turn right where a sign indicates "Diamond Craters/French Round Barn 17/Diamond 13." Go 7 miles and turn left onto Lava Beds Road where a sign indicates "Diamond Craters 2." Continue 10.1 miles on Lava Beds Road and turn right onto a dirt road where a sign indicates "Welcome to Pete French Round Barn State Heritage Site." Continue 1 mile on a well-graded dirt road to a parking area at the road's end.

Description: This historic site marks a fascinating barn built by Peter French in 1880. This structure is the sole remaining round barn left of only three built in the U.S. during that period. French was a cattle baron who ran the P Ranch in the Blitzen Valley. Over a 28-year period, the P Ranch became the largest cattle ranch in the United States, covering 200,000 acres. This barn was used during the winter months to break the 300 head of horses and mules that were foaled on the ranch each year. The barn houses a 60-foot-wide circular stone corral supported by sturdy juniper posts. This 9-foot-high corral is constructed of 250 tons of lava rock hauled from over eight miles away. An outer 20-foot-wide circular paddock completes the barn's dimensions. The barn's unique shape was designed to more easily break horses, because its round contours do not have corners that could force a horse to stop its natural gait.

Interpretive signs explain the barn's construction and the history of Peter French and the P Ranch. You can walk inside and explore the inner corral and the outer round pen. No doubt your furry sidekick will amuse himself with scents spanning the last century.

Steens Mountain Hikes

Contact: Bureau of Land Management, Burns District Office, 28910 Hwy 20 West, Hines, Oregon 97738, 541-573-4400, www.or.blm.gov

Paw-Approval Rating: 4 paws

Leashes Required? No

Length: Kiger Gorge Viewpoint: 0.4-mile out and back; East Rim Viewpoint: 0.1-mile out and back; Steens Summit Trail: 1 mile out and back; Wildhorse Lake Trail: 3 miles out and back

Difficulty: Easy to Moderate

Fees/Permits: None

Season: July through October. Call ahead to make sure the road is open.

Getting There: From Frenchglen (about 62 miles south of Burns on Highway 205), go south on Highway 205 and turn left onto Steens Mountain Loop Road. Drive 3 miles to a T-intersection and turn left. (If you turn right here, you'll arrive at Page Spring Campground in 1 mile.) Travel 19.2 miles, turn left at the Kiger Gorge Viewpoint and go 0.5 mile to a parking area.

To continue, head back to Steens Mountain Road, turn left, and continue 2.7 miles to a three-way road junction. Turn left at the junction and go 0.5 mile to the East Rim Viewpoint.

When you're finished exploring the East Rim, head back to the three-way junction and take the middle fork where a sign indicates "Wildhorse Lake 2 1/4—Steens Summit 2". Continue to the parking area and trailheads for the Wildhorse Lake Trail and the Steens Summit Trail.

Description: You and your dog will be impressed by 9,733-foot Steens Mountain—Oregon's ninth tallest peak. This fault block mountain range rises 5,500 feet in less than 3 miles from the valley floor of the Alvord Desert on its east side. At 30 miles wide and 60 miles long, this mountain is a store of startling geologic diversity.

The 66-mile Steens Mountain Loop Road gives you access to many trails, viewpoints, and campgrounds. The route travels through several ecological zones that support a wide variety of animal and

Heading to the summit of Steens Mountain.

plant life. Western juniper, mountain mahogany, and a sagebrush steppe grace the lower slopes of the mountain between 4,000 and 6,000 feet. As the road continues higher, groves of quaking aspen stand sentinel over high mountain lakes and provide shelter for mule deer and pronghorn antelope. As the road reaches its high point, fragile and rocky tundra covers the landscape.

At the start of the loop, you'll pass the historic P Ranch, headquarters of cattle baron Peter French, and Page Springs Campground (see *Campgrounds*). At the Kiger Gorge Viewpoint you'll gaze at the U-shaped Kiger Gorge, a 0.5-mile deep valley carved by glaciers. Its U-shape is typical of glacier-carved valleys; river-carved valleys are usually V-shaped.

At the East Rim Viewpoint you'll have a commanding view of Mann Lake, the Sheepheads Mountains, Owyhee Uplands, and the vast Alvord Desert. The Wildhorse Lake Trail descends 1.5 miles into a scenic rock amphitheater that surrounds Wildhorse Lake, which was carved by an enormous glacier. The lake bottom is rich in pollens from ancient plants.

Another short trail worth exploring is the Steens Summit Trail, which takes you to the windblown 9,733-foot summit. From there, you'll have a commanding view of Winter Rim, Summer Lake, Lake Abert, Abert Rim, the Warner Basin, Hart Mountain, and the Alvord Basin.

CYCLING FOR CANINES

Diamond Craters Outstanding Natural Area

Contact: Bureau of Land Management, Burns District Office, 28910 Hwy 20 West, Hines, Oregon 97738, 541-573-4400, www.or.blm.gov
Paw-Approval Rating: 2 Paws
Leashes Required? No
Length: 9.8 miles out and back
Difficulty: Easy
Fees/Permits: None
Season: Year-round

Getting There: From Burns, head 1.6 miles east on Highway 78. Turn right onto Highway 205. Drive 40 miles south on Highway 205 to the Diamond Craters Junction. Turn left and drive 7.1 miles on Diamond Grain Camp Road/CR 409. Turn left on Lava Beds Road/CR 404 and continue 3.4 miles to a cinder pullout on the left side of the road.

Description: Diamond Craters Outstanding Natural Area is a 17,000-acre geologic site in the heart of Oregon's cattle country. Geologists surmise that this area was formed about 25,000 years ago, when lava oozed from fissures, forming a six-mile, molten pool. As this original lava hardened, additional lava flowed under this top layer, uplifting the hardened bed to create lava domes. While your dog may not be intrigued by these geologic gems, he can get a good leash-free workout while you inspect these volcanic formations.

This route explores trail markers 5 through 10, which correspond to different volcanic formations.

Big Bomb Crater, seen at trail marker 5, has a multitude of cored bombs, which began as dollops of molten rock thrown into the air by a volcanic explosion and then cooled into their present form when brought into contact with water.

Lava Pit Crater (trail marker 6) is a large circular hole in the ground. The pit appears to be the result of a large explosion; however, it actually owes its shape to the destructive power of water and erosion. Rain erodes lava edges, which eventually break off, littering the crater floor with a layer of fallen rocks.

Red Bomb Crater (trail marker 7) is nearly 1,000 feet across and is easily distinguished by the bright, reddish-brown cinder earth. The crater was formed when a steam head under the earth's surface exploded, sending magma and rocks shooting into the air. The debris from the explosion landed at the base of the vent, forming a cinder cone.

As you continue riding, you'll see East Twin Crater (trail marker 8), a maar-type explosion crater. A maar-type crater is a shallow depression in the ground, edged with rock fragments hurled from the center of the crater during a large volcanic explosion. You'll see other maar-type craters at West Twin Crater (trail marker 9), and Dry Maar and Malheur Maar, located next to each other at trail marker 10. Dry Maar, as the name suggests, is arid and unexciting. However, six feet of creek water collects in Malheur Maar to form a miniature lake. Studies conducted on the 50 feet of sediment that have accumulated on the crater floor show that it has been filled with water for over 7,000 years! As you approach Malheur Maar, beware of the swarms of mosquitoes that live in this small lake. Be sure to carry plenty of water on this ride and be on the lookout for rattlesnakes.

CANINE COMFORT ACCOMMODATIONS

Unless otherwise stated, dogs should not be left unattended in the room and must be leashed on hotel property.

$ Crystal Crane Hot Springs & Resort

HC 73 2653, Highway 78, 541-493-2312, www.crystalcranehotsprings.com

Located 25 miles southeast of Burns on Highway 78 just west of the town of Crane, this hot springs resort has five rustic cabins, a tent camping area, RV campsites, a horse corral, and a natural spring swimming pool and bathhouse. The dog-friendly one-room cabins are furnished with a double bed, hide-a-beds, bedding, and towels, with a separate restroom outside. Cabins do not have phones or TVs. Dogs are welcome in the camping area but not in the hot springs or bathhouse.

If you just want to stop by to soak in the hot springs or take a private hot tub, the resort is open 9 A.M. TO 9 P.M., seven days a week. Fees for the large communal hot spring pool are $3 for adults and $2.50 for children age 18 and under. For a private hot tub, the charge is $5 per hour per adult,

and $2.50 for children age 12 and under. Use of restrooms and showers are included. If you stay overnight at the campsites or cabins, the hot springs are free.

Dog Policy

Uncrated dogs are $5 per night. Dogs with a crate are $2 per night. A $20 refundable pet damage deposit is required.

$-$$ Best Inn Motel

999 Oregon Ave., Burns, 541-573-1700

This motel has 8 dog-friendly rooms and a pool, spa, and sauna.

Dog Policy

Only dogs that weigh under 50 pounds are allowed. The motel requires a $20 refundable pet deposit and $5 per dog per day.

$-$$ Days Inn

577 W. Monroe, Burns, 541-573-2047, www.daysinn.com

This 52-room inn has dog-friendly rooms, an outdoor pool, and a free continental breakfast.

Dog Policy

A one-time $10 pet fee is charged.

CAMPGROUNDS

Jackman Park

Contact: Bureau of Land Management, Burns District Office, 28910 Hwy 20 West, Hines, Oregon 97738, 541-573-4400, www.or.blm.gov

Season: July through October

Facilities: 6 RV/tent campsites (no electrical hook-ups), picnic tables, fire rings, water, vault toilets. No reservations accepted.

Getting There: From Frenchglen (about 62 miles south of Burns on Highway 205), travel south on Highway 205 and turn left onto Steens Mountain Loop Road. Continue 3 miles to a T-intersection, turn left, and continue about 17 miles to the campground.

Description: This mountain campground is ringed with aspens and prime Steens Mountain scenery; it's a great place to set up base camp for exploring the many trails on Steens Mountain. (See *Steens Mountain Hikes* in *Paw-Approved Hikes and Parks*) From your campsite, watch for golden eagles and other raptors soaring above. The campground is at 7,800 feet; nights can be chilly.

Page Springs Campground

Contact: Bureau of Land Management, Burns District Office, 28910 Hwy 20 West, Hines, Oregon 97738, 541-573-4400, www.or.blm.gov
Season: Year-round
Facilities: 36 RV/tent campsites (no electrical hook-ups), water, picnic tables, fire rings, vault toilets, picnic shelter. No reservations accepted.
Getting There: From Frenchglen (about 62 miles south of Burns on Highway 205), travel south on Highway 205 and turn left onto Steens Mountain Loop Road. Continue 3 miles to a T-intersection and turn right toward Page Springs Campground. Continue 1 mile to the campground entrance.
Description: Located adjacent to the Donner und Blitzen River this campground is filled with wildlife. Campsites are set amongst shady juniper trees next to a sage-filled rimrock canyon. You can hike on a 1.4-mile nature trail or a trail that parallels the river. Water loving hounds will most likely opt for the second trail where they can wallow in bogs and splash in the river. This campground is on the way to the top of Steens Mountain. (See *Steens Mountain Hikes* in *Paw-Approved Hikes and Parks*) Beware of ticks, stinging nettles, and rattlesnakes when camping here.

South Steens Campground

Contact: Bureau of Land Management, Burns District Office, 28910 Hwy 20 West, Hines, Oregon 97738, 541-573-4400, www.or.blm.gov
Season: June through October
Facilities: 36 RV/tent campsites (no electrical hook-ups; 15 of these sites are set up for horses), picnic tables, fire rings, water, vault toilets, and an ADA site. No reservations accepted.
Getting There: From Burns travel about 62 miles south on Highway 205 to Frenchglen. From Frenchglen, continue south 10 miles to the small town of Fields. In Fields, turn left onto Steens Mountain Loop Road and travel 19.5 miles to South Steens Campground on the right side of the road.
Description: This campground is a good staging area for exploring Big Indian Gorge (see *Paw-Approved Hikes and Parks*) or Little Blitzen Gorge. Campsites, nestled in a thick stand of sweet-smelling juniper, make you want to stay a while.

CANINE-APPROVED SHOPPING

Western Big R

13115 Highway 20, Burns, 541-573-2024
This ranch supply store carries Science Diet dog food, toys, dog beds, coats, footwear, leashes, tie-outs, doghouses, pet carriers, shampoos, and treats. Open 7:30 A.M.–6 P.M., Monday to Saturday; 9 A.M.–5 P.M., Sunday.

DOGGIE DAYCARE AND CANINE ER

Harney County Veterinary Clinic

1050 Crane Blvd., 541-573-6450
This full-service small and large animal hospital offers after-hours emergency care and overnight boarding. The clinic stocks Science Diet dog food and carries a large supply of pet care products. Overnight boarding is available.
Open 8:30 A.M.–5:30 P.M. Monday to Friday; 9 A.M.–12 P.M. Saturday.

LOST AND FOUND (ANIMAL SHELTERS)

Humane Society of Harney County

P.O. Box 195, Burns, 541-573-6773

Ontario

THE BIG SCOOP

Agriculture is the center of commerce for this community on the Idaho border, just off I-84. The Payette, Malheur, and Owyhee rivers join the Snake River here, providing a reliable irrigation source in this very dry part of Eastern Oregon. All this water means paddling opportunities on Lake Owyhee, south of Ontario. Recommended desert hikes offering amazing gorge scenery are Juniper Gulch and Timber Gulch (see *Paw-Approved Hikes and Parks*). Paddling enthusiasts will want to visit Lake Owyhee State Park.

PAW-APPROVED HIKES AND PARKS

Coffeepot Crater Hike

Contact: Bureau of Land Management, Vale District, 100 Oregon St., Vale, Oregon 97918-9630, 541-473-3144, www.or.blm.gov
Paw-Approval Rating: 2 paws
Leashes Required? No
Length: 1.1-mile loop
Difficulty: Easy
Fees/Permits: None
Season: Open year-round
Getting There: From Jordan Valley on the Oregon/Idaho border (about 140 miles southeast of Burns via Highway 95) travel north on Highway 95 for 8.3 miles to a gravel road signed for Jordan Craters. Turn left and drive 11.4 miles; stay right at a junction. Go 6.7 miles to another junction and go left (the road becomes rough here). Continue on this rough road about 8.8 miles (staying left at all junctions) to a parking area at the end of the road.

Description: This loop route allows you and Fido to investigate Coffeepot Crater in the Jordan Craters Lava Beds. Here you'll have a chance to explore layered lava flows, lava tubes, spatter cones, and lava bombs. Additional side trails lead you into an immense lava field. Avoid this area in mid-summer when temperatures can soar above 100°F.

Juniper Gulch and Timber Gulch Hikes

Contact: Bureau of Land Management, Vale District, 100 Oregon St., Vale, Oregon 97918-9630, 541-473-3144, www.or.blm.gov
Paw-Approval Rating: 2 paws
Leashes Required? No
Length: Juniper Gulch: 1.6 miles out and back; Timber Gulch 1.2 miles out and back
Difficulty: Easy
Fees/Permits: None
Season: Year-round
Getting There: In Ontario, take exit 374 or 376 off I-84. Take Highway 201/20/26 south to Nyssa. From Nyssa, turn south onto Highway 201 and travel about 20.5 miles to the junction with Succor Creek Road. Turn right on Succor Creek Road, proceed 25 miles, and turn right onto a dirt road signed for Leslie Gulch. Continue 10.6 miles to the signed Juniper Gulch parking area on the right.
Description: Follow the trail as it crosses Leslie Creek and rambles up a canyon with spectacular honeycomb cliffs. These uniquely shaped cliffs and pillars were formed by rain and wind and make a spectacular backdrop for pictures of your photogenic friend. At 0.6 mile, turn right and

ascend to a viewpoint and your turn-around point at 0.8 mile. Return to the trailhead on the same route.

To explore other gulches in the area, turn right out of the parking area and continue 1.2 miles to an unmarked pullout on the right. From the pullout, head up Timber Gulch for 0.6 mile and soak in the view of the magnificent multi-colored spires in the canyon. There isn't a trail here, so you'll have to go cross-country through thick sagebrush. If you want to camp in this area, continue another 2.3 miles up the dirt road to Slocum Campground on the left side of the road.

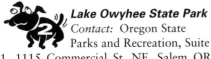 **Lake Owyhee State Park**
Contact: Oregon State Parks and Recreation, Suite 1, 1115 Commercial St. NE, Salem OR 97301-1002, www.oregonstateparks.org
Paw-Approval Rating: 2 paws
Leashes Required? Yes
Season: Open year-round
Getting There: The park is off Highway 201, 33 miles south of Nyssa on the Oregon/Idaho border.
Description: Located along the 53-mile-long Owyhee Reservoir, this state park features campgrounds, picnic areas, and plentiful paddling. The landscape here is arid and features colorful rimrock canyons and rocky promontories. Wildlife includes golden eagle, mule deer, coyote, and wild horses.

PADDLEHOUNDS

In the Ontario area, check out Lake Owyhee State Park. Here you can watch for wildlife as you cruise on the 53-mile-long Owyhee Reservoir. The only distraction at this beautiful desert place is the drone of motorboats. To get there from Ontario, travel 12 miles south on Highway 20/Highway 26 to Nyssa. From Nyssa follow signs to Highway 201 and continue south on 201 for 8 miles to Owyhee. Turn right onto Owyhee Ave. and continue south 4.5 miles to the junction with Owyhee Lake Road. Turn left onto Owyhee Lake Road and go 23 miles south to the state park campground and boat ramp.

CANINE COMFORT ACCOMMODATIONS

Unless otherwise stated, dogs should not be left unattended in the room and must be leashed on hotel property.

$ Motel 6
325 SE Nye Ave., Ontario, 541-889-6617
Dog Policy
Fido gets to stay for free.

$$ Holiday Inn
1249 Tapadera Ave., Ontario, 541-889-8621
Dog Policy
A one-time $10 fee is charged.

$$-$$$ Best Western Inn and Suites
251 Goodfellow St., Ontario 541-889-2600, www.bestwestern.com

Dogs are welcome at this inn, which offers a pool, hot tub, fitness room, and a guest laundry.
Dog Policy
This inn only accepts dogs that weigh 25 pounds or less. A $20 refundable pet deposit is required.

CAMPGROUNDS

Succor Creek State Natural Area
Contact: Oregon State Parks and Recreation, Suite 1, 1115 Commercial St. NE, Salem OR 97301-1002, www.oregonstateparks.org
Season: March through November
Facilities: 19 primitive campsites (no electrical hook-ups; trailers are not recommended), picnic tables, fire rings, vault toilets, no water. No reservations accepted.
Getting There: From Jordan Valley on the Oregon/Idaho border, travel 18 miles north on Highway 95 to the junction with Succor Creek Road. Turn left onto Succor Creek Road and drive 21 miles to the campground.

Description: This remote campground is located in the amazing gorge carved by Succor Creek. A trail leads up the creek where your hound can hunt for the best swimming holes while you admire the gorgeous canyon scenery.

DOGGIE DAYCARE
AND CANINE ER

Four Rivers Veterinary Clinic
2280 SW 4th Ave., Ontario, 541-889-7776

This full-service small animal hospital accepts walk-ins and provides emergency services and grooming services. Overnight boarding rates: (dogs 1 to 25 pounds: $8; 26 to 50 pounds: $9; 50 to 100 pounds: $10; 100 pounds and over: $11). In stock are Waltham and IVD dog foods, shampoos, flea products, dental products, and treats.

Open 8 A.M.–5:30 P.M., Monday, Tuesday, Thursday, and Friday; 8 A.M.–7 P.M., Wednesday.

LOST AND FOUND
(ANIMAL SHELTERS)

Ontario Animal Control
414 SW 4th St., Ontario, 541-889-7266

Southwest Oregon

Southwest Oregon is host to rugged mountains, wild and remote rivers, and its most famous landmark, Crater Lake National Park. The Cascade Mountains form the eastern border for this part of the state and is dominated by three immense national forests: the Umpqua, Rogue, and Siskiyou. These three gorgeous national forests have hundreds of miles of trails that lead to high mountain lakes, to beautiful waterfalls, and through spectacular old-growth forests.

The Rogue River plunges down a steep gorge from its origin at Crater Lake. This world-famous white-water rafting river makes its journey into the Rogue River Valley where Medford and Ashland are settled. These Oregon towns are unique in their customs and culture and both cities boast leash-free parks.

The Klamath and coastal mountains create the western boundaries to this part of the state, while the Siskiyou Mountains are boundaries to the south. Containing some of Oregon's oldest geologic features, the Siskiyou Mountains and its scrub oak, brushy manzanita, and orange-barked madrone forests are a sharp contrast to the fir and pine forests to the north. The Kalmiopsis Wilderness is another gem travel hounds will enjoy visiting. This wilderness area has a unique array of plants and animals that are found nowhere else in Oregon.

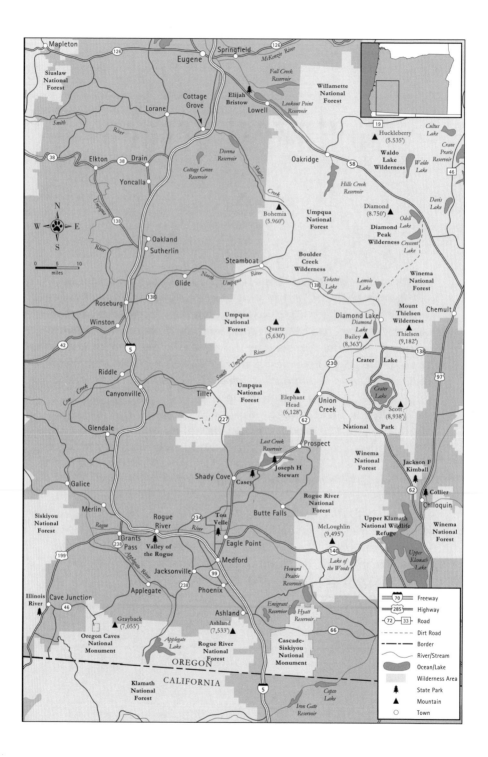

Mapleton
126
Springfield
126
Eugene
McKenzie River
Siuslaw
National
Forest
Fall Creek
Reservoir
Willamette
National
Forest
Cottage
Grove
Elijah
Bristow
Lowell
Lookout Point
Reservoir
Huckleberry
(5.535')
Cultus
Lake
Lorane
Smith
River
Waldo
Lake
Wilderness
Crane
Prairie
Reservoir
Waldo
Lake
38
Elkton
38
Drain
Oakridge
58
46
Yoncalla
Dorena
Reservoir
Hills Creek
Reservoir
Diamond
(8.750')
Davis
Lake
Cottage Grove
Reservoir
Bohemia
(5.960')
Umpqua
National
Forest
Odell
Lake
Diamond
Peak
Wilderness Crescent
Lake
138
N
W   E
S
Oakland
Sutherlin
Steamboat
Boulder
Creek
Wilderness
Winema
National
Forest
0   5   10
miles
Glide
North Umpqua River
138
Toketee
Lake
Lemolo
Lake
Roseburg
138
Umpqua
National
Forest
Quartz
(5,630')
Diamond Lake
Diamond
Lake
Bailey
(8,363')
Mount
Thielsen
Wilderness
Thielsen
(9,182')
Chemult
Winston
5
South Umpqua River
Crater   Lake
138
42
Riddle
Umpqua
National
Forest
Elephant
Head
(6,128')
Crater
Lake
Scott
(8,938')
97
Cow Creek
Canyonville
Tiller
Union
Creek
62
Glendale
227
National   Park
Prospect
Lost Creek
Reservoir
Winema
National
Forest
Jackson F
Kimball
Galice
Shady Cove
Casey
Joseph H
Stewart
62
Collier
Chiloquin
Siskiyou
National
Forest
Merlin
Rogue
River
Rogue
234
Tou
Velle
Butte Falls
Rogue River
National
Forest
McLoughlin
(9,495')
Upper Klamath
National Wildlife
Refuge
Winema
National
Forest
Grants
Pass
238
Valley of
the Rogue
River
Eagle Point
140
Lake of
the Woods
Upper
Klamath
Lake
199
Applegate River
Medford
Jacksonville
99
Howard
Prairie
Reservoir
Illinois
River
Cave Junction
46
Applegate
238
Phoenix
Ashland
Emigrant
Reservoir
Hyatt
Reservoir
66
Grayback
(7,055')
Ashland
(7,533')
Cascade-
Siskiyou
National
Monument
Oregon Caves
National
Monument
Applegate
Lake
Rogue River
National
Forest
OREGON
CALIFORNIA
Klamath
National
Forest
5
Copco
Lake
Iron Gate
Reservoir

70	Freeway	
285	Highway	
72 33	Road	
	Dirt Road	
	Border	
	River/Stream	
	Ocean/Lake	
	Wilderness Area	
▲	State Park	
▲	Mountain	
○	Town	

Roseburg

THE BIG SCOOP

Roseburg is located along I-5 in a large valley at the confluence of the North Forks and South Forks of the Umpqua River. Oregon Highway 138 east of Roseburg provides access to outdoor adventures in the Umpqua National Forest. If you and your traveling partner are waterfall lovers, you'll be glad to know the North Umpqua River has one of the greatest concentrations of waterfalls in the state (see *Paw-Approved Hikes and Parks*).

The North Umpqua Trail, accessible from Highway 138, runs 79 miles along this wild and scenic river. You can hike, mountain bike, or trail-run with your dog along different sections of this trail. Oregon Highway 138 also leads to 3,015-acre Diamond Lake, where paddling is prime and many campgrounds invite you to set up a base for exploring the area. Crater Lake National Park is just 13 miles south of Diamond Lake off Highway 138. Although dogs are not allowed on any of the park's trails, they are allowed at viewpoints and rest areas. So hop in your car, roll down the windows, and tour the lake by auto with your best friend on the 33-mile Rim Drive Loop.

PAW-APPROVED HIKES AND PARKS

Crater Lake National Park
Contact: Crater Lake National Park, P.O. Box 7, Crater Lake, OR 97604-0007, 541-594-2211, www.nps.gov
Paw-Approval: 1 paw

Leashes Required: Yes
Fees/Permits: $10
Season: Late June through October
Getting There: Crater Lake is about 87 miles east of Roseburg off Oregon Highway 138. From Medford, the park is about 72 miles east via Highway 62. From Klamath Falls, the park is about 72 miles via Highway 97 north and Highway 62 west. From Bend, the park is about 90 miles via Highway 97 south and Highway 138 west.
Description: Crater Lake National Park is Oregon's only national park. Like all national parks, it does not allow dogs on hiking trails or in the backcountry. The good news is that you can take your dog on a driving tour around the lake on the 33-mile Rim Drive. This loop road is a cornucopia of spectacular viewpoints where you and your partner can soak in the beauty of this immense sapphire-colored lake. Allow 3 to 4 hours for the full loop.

Crater Lake, at 1,932-feet deep, is the deepest lake in North America. It sits in the immense caldera of the now extinct Mount Mazama, a volcano that once reached a height of 12,000 feet and spewed pumice, cinder, and ash for over half a million years. Catastrophic eruptions beginning approximately 7,700 years ago spread ash deposits over 5,000 square miles. Eventually, the volcano collapsed on itself, creating the deep caldera. Over a period of 5,000 years after the collapse, the lake formed as springs, snow, and rain slowly filled the caldera. Wizard Island, located in the caldera, is a secondary volcano that rises 764 feet above the lake.

If you want to stay overnight in the park, camp at Diamond Lake Campground (see *Campgrounds*). Dogs are not allowed to stay at Crater Lake Lodge, nor are they allowed on the winter skiing trails in the park.

Deadline Falls and Fern Falls

(See *North Umpqua Trail: Swiftwater to Wright Creek* in *Cycling for Canines*)

Fall Creek Falls Hike

Contact: Umpqua National Forest, North Umpqua Ranger District, 18782 North Umpqua Highway, Glide, OR 974443, 541-496-3532, www.fs.fed.us
Paw-Approval Rating: 3 paws
Leashes Required? No (except at the trailhead)
Length: 1.8 miles out and back
Difficulty: Easy
Fees/Permits: None
Season: Year-round
Getting There: From I-5 in Roseburg take exit 124, head 32.2 miles east on Highway 138, and park at the marked trailhead on the left side of the road.
Description: A short climb takes you to the base of the 50-foot fan-shaped cascade of lower Fall Creek Falls and then to a viewpoint of the upper falls.

North Umpqua Trail: Wright Creek to the Mott Trailhead Hike

Contact: Roseburg District Office, Bureau of Land Management, 777 NW Garden Valley Blvd., Roseburg, OR 97470, 541-440-4930, www.or.blm.gov
Paw-Approval Rating: 4 paws
Leashes Required? No (except at the trailheads)
Length: 11 miles out and back (with a shuttle option)
Difficulty: Moderate
Fees/Permits: None
Season: Year-round

Getting There: From I-5 in Roseburg take exit 124 and head 33.5 miles east on Highway 138 to Wright Creek Road. Turn right and drive 0.2 mile to the Wright Creek Trailhead on the left.
Shuttle option: If you want to complete this hike as a shuttle, continue east on Oregon 138 for 5.1 miles, turn right, and drive a short distance to the Mott Trailhead on the right. Leave a bike or car at this upper trailhead, and drive back to the Wright Creek Trailhead to begin the hike.
Description: Head up the road a short distance to the trailhead. Begin walking through towering old-growth Douglas fir and red cedar. After about a mile of pleasant walking, the trail nears the river's edge where you can explore its rocky pools and ripples. Continue on the trail as it meanders along the river gorge until you reach the Mott Creek Trailhead at 5.5 miles, your turnaround point. This section of the trail is open to mountain bikes.

Susan Creek Falls Hike

Contact: Umpqua National Forest, North Umpqua Ranger District, 18782 North Umpqua Highway, Glide, OR 974443, 541-496-3532, www. fs.fed.us
Paw-Approval Rating: 3 paws
Leashes Required? No (except at the trailhead)
Length: 1.4 miles out and back
Difficulty: Easy
Fees/Permits: None
Season: Year-round
Getting There: From I-5 in Roseburg take exit 124 and head 28.3 miles east on Highway 138 to the Susan Creek Picnic Area on the right side of the road.
Description: Start the hike from the picnic area by crossing Highway 138 and picking up the trail on the other side. Continue 0.7 mile through an old-growth Douglas fir, cedar, and hemlock forest to the base of the feathery 70-foot cascade of Susan Creek Falls. After enjoying the view, retrace

the route back to the trailhead. Be on the lookout for poison oak. The Susan Creek Campground (see *Campgrounds*) is nearby if you want to stay overnight.

Tipsoo Peak Hike

Contact: Umpqua National Forest, Diamond Lake Ranger District, 2020 Tokette Ranger Station Rd., Idleyld Park, OR 97447, 541-498-2531, www.fs.fed.us
Paw-Approval Rating: 3 paws
Leashes Required? No
Length: 6.2 miles out and back
Difficulty: Difficult
Fees/Permits: $5 Northwest Forest Pass. Purchase at 1-800-270-7504 or www.naturenw.org.
Season: Late July through October
Getting There: From I-5 in Roseburg take exit 124 and travel 75 miles east on Highway 138 to the junction with Cinnamon Butte Road (Forest Road 4793). Turn east and travel 1.7 miles to the junction with Wits End Road (Forest Road 100). Go straight on Wits End Road and continue 3.2 miles on a rough road to a small, signed trailhead on the right.
Description: Intrepid dogs lured by the challenge of high mountain peaks will enjoy this trek that climbs 1,780 feet to the 8,034-foot summit of Tipsoo Peak in the Mount Thielsen Wilderness.

The trail ascends through a fragrant mountain hemlock forest and skirts the edge of Tipsoo Meadow after 2.8 miles. As you continue, you'll see twisted and bent whitebark pine along the trail. These trees can be found only at high elevations and are a reminder of the area's harsh winter storms. As you near the top, the trail follows a lava-strewn ridgeline until you reach the summit at 3.1 miles. From the top you'll have a commanding view of North, Middle, and South Sister, Mount Thielsen, Mount Bailey, Diamond Lake, and Diamond Peak. Retrace the route back to the trailhead.

Toketee Falls Hike

Contact: Diamond Lake Ranger District, 2020 Toketee Ranger Station Rd., Idleyld Park, OR 97447, 541-498-2531, www.fs.fed.us
Paw-Approval Rating: 3 paws
Leashes Required? Yes
Length: 0.8 mile out and back
Difficulty: Easy
Fees/Permits: None
Getting There: From I-5 in Roseburg take exit 124 and head 58.6 miles east on Highway 138 to Toketee-Rigdon Road. Turn left (north) and go 0.4 mile to the signed trailhead.
Season: Year-round
Description: This short, forested trail is lined with wild rhododendron that bloom in May and June and leads you and your furry friend to a viewing platform for misty 90-foot cascade of Toketee Falls. Good swimming holes abound along this stretch of river.

Twin Lakes Hike

Contact: Umpqua National Forest, North Umpqua Ranger District, 18782 North Umpqua Highway, Glide, OR 974443, 541-496-3532, www.fs.fed.us
Paw-Approval Rating: 4 paws
Leashes Required? No
Length: 3.3-mile loop (with a longer 2.2-mile round trip option to the summit of Twin Lakes Mountain)
Difficulty: Easy/Moderate to the summit of Twin Lakes Mountain
Fees/Permits: None
Season: Mid-June through November
Getting There: From I-5 in Roseburg take exit 124 and travel 49 miles east on Highway 138. Turn right onto Wilson Creek Road (Forest Road 4770). Drive on this narrow gravel road 9 miles to the road's end and trailhead.
Description: This easy, smooth trail traipses through a shady Douglas fir forest with logs and sticks that will keep your dog occupied for hours. At 0.3 mile, enjoy

the phenomenal views of Mount Bailey, Diamond Peak, and Mount Thielsen. At 0.6 mile, turn right at a trail junction. (You have the *option* of turning left and heading on a 2.2-mile roundtrip trek to the summit of 5,580 Twin Mountain.) At the next trail junction, turn left and enjoy the profusion of color as you walk through a high alpine wildflower meadow. At 0.9 mile, you'll arrive at a wood-sided shelter on the shores of the first Twin Lake. Continue to the right, walk through a picturesque campground, and follow the trail around the lake's edge. (This campground promises solitude if you want to backpack in and stay a few days.) Take your time as you continue around the lake so your trail hound can have fun swimming. At 1.3 miles, bear right on a trail that leads to the smaller Twin Lake. Circle this lake for 0.7 mile and then retrace the route back to the trailhead. Beware of mosquitoes during July and the first few weeks in August.

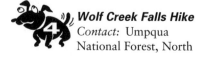

Watson Falls Hike

Contact: Diamond Lake Ranger District, 2020 Toketee Ranger Station Rd., Idleyld Park, OR 97447, 541-498-2531, www.fs.fed.us
Paw-Approval Rating: 3 paws
Leashes Required? Yes
Length: 0.8-mile loop
Difficulty: Easy
Fees/Permits: None
Season: Year-round
Getting There: From I-5 in Roseburg take exit 124 and head 60.8 miles east on Highway 138 to Fish Creek Road. Turn right (south) and continue to a signed picnic area on the right.
Description: This quick loop trail takes you to a viewpoint of the 272-foot cascade of Watson Falls, the highest waterfall in Southern Oregon.

Wolf Creek Falls Hike

Contact: Umpqua National Forest, North

Umpqua Ranger District, 18782 North Umpqua Highway, Glide, OR 974443, 541-496-3532, www.fs.fed.us
Paw-Approval Rating: 4 paws
Leashes Required? No
Length: 2.6 miles
Difficulty: Easy
Fees/Permits: None
Season: Year-round
Getting There: From I-5 in Roseburg, take exit 124 and head 16 miles east on Highway 138 to the junction with Little River Road. Turn right on Little River Road and drive 10.4 miles to the signed Wolf Creek Falls trailhead on the right side of the road.
Description: This trail starts by crossing a bridge over the Little River, with its many deep, inviting rocky pools. Continue on the trail as it heads into a cool Douglas fir and big leaf maple forest. At 1.3 miles, you'll reach the 20-foot lower cascade of Wolf Creek Falls and after walking a short distance you'll arrive at the sweeping 70-foot upper cascade. From here, retrace the route back to the trailhead. Be on the lookout for poison oak.

CYCLING FOR CANINES

North Umpqua Trail: Swiftwater to Wright Creek

Contact: Roseburg District Office, Bureau of Land Management, 777 NW Garden Valley Blvd., Roseburg, OR 97470, 541-440-4930, www.or.blm.gov
Paw-Approval Rating: 4 paws
Leashes Required? No (except at the trailheads)
Length: 15.3 miles one way (with shorter options)
Difficulty: Difficult
Fees/Permits: None
Season: Year-round
Getting There: From I-5 in Roseburg head east on Oregon 138 for 22 miles to Swiftwater County Park, located on the right side of the road. Turn into the park

entrance, cross a bridge over the North Umpqua River, and then turn left into the Tioga Trailhead parking area on the left.

Shuttle option: If you want to complete this ride as a shuttle, continue east on Oregon 138 for 11.5 miles. Turn right onto Forest Road 4711 and continue 0.2 mile to the Wright Creek Trailhead on the left. Leave a bike or car at this upper trailhead.

Description: Get ready to crank on this awesome 15.3-mile section of the North Umpqua Trail as it parallels the swift-flowing North Umpqua River. This national scenic trail is over 79 miles long and took 20 years to build.

Begin riding through a maze of green in a spectacular old-growth forest. At 0.2-miles, the 8-foot cascade of Deadline Falls comes into view. After 1.7 miles, you'll reach a bridge and a viewpoint for the shimmering cascade of Fern Falls. From here, continue on the trail over easy rolling hills through mossy forest. After about 3 miles, you'll begin a tough climb on a series of switchbacks that traverse Bob Butte. This may be a good turnaround point if your dog is only up for an easy afternoon outing. Or continue on this demanding route until you reach Forest Road 4711 at the Wright Creek Trailhead (your turnaround point at 15.3 miles). Tailor your mileage to your dog's fitness level.

The BLM asks that you keep your dog leashed at the trailheads and to ride carefully the first few miles because this section of the trail has many hikers. If you want to explore the next section of the trail, see the *North Umpqua Trail: Wright Creek to the Mott Trailhead* in *Paw-Approved Hikes and Parks.*

POWDERHOUNDS

Many skiing trails can be found in the Diamond Lake Recreation Area in the Umpqua National Forest and are accessible via Howlock, Thielsen, South Diamond, and Three Lakes Sno-Parks. Reach Diamond Lake by heading 80 miles east of Roseburg on Highway 138 to the intersection with Highway 230.

For more information on specific trails, contact the Umpqua National Forest, Diamond Lake Ranger District, 2020 Toketee Ranger Station Road, Idleyld Park, OR 97447, 541-498-2531, www.fs.fed.us. Another great resource is *Cross-Country Ski Routes: Oregon* by Klindt Vielbig. Dogs are not allowed on any of the winter skiing trails in Crater Lake National Park.

PADDLEHOUNDS

You can paddle with your dog on a 6.5-mile, class 2 section of the North Umpqua River that begins at Amacher County Park in Winchester, just north of Roseburg, and ends at River Forks Park. Near the end of the run, you'll have to contend with the class 2+ Burkhardt Rapids (Canoes are not recommended). The takeout point is at a nice beach at River Forks Park, where the North Umpqua meets the South Umpqua. To get to Amacher County Park, head 5 miles north of Roseburg on I-5 to exit 129 in Winchester. After you exit, follow signs to the park, which is located beneath the I-5 bridge. To get to the takeout, head west on Winchester Road 5 miles. (It turns into Wilbur-Garden Valley Rd.) Continue 2 more miles and then turn left (south) and go 1 mile to River Forks Park.

If you and your pooch prefer lake paddling, check out Lemolo Lake or Diamond Lake. Launch your boat on Lemolo Lake from the Poole Creek Campground on the west shore of the lake. To get there from Roseburg, head east on Highway 138 for 72 miles to the junction with Bird's Point Road (Forest Road 2610). Turn left (north) onto Bird's Point Road and travel 4 miles to the signed campground.

Diamond Lake is another scenic high lake. To get there, travel 80 miles east of Roseburg on Highway 138 to the intersection with Highway 230. Turn right on Highway 230 toward Diamond Lake South Shore/Medford. Drive 0.1 mile on Highway 230 and turn right on Forest Service

Road 4795 where a sign indicates "Diamond Lake Recreation Area." Drive 0.7 mile on Forest Service Road 4795 toward Thielsen View Campground/Broken Arrow Campground. At the next junction, turn left and drive 0.2 mile on Forest Service Road 4795 (unsigned) to the South Shore Picnic Area and boat ramp on the right side of the road. This picnic area/boat ramp requires a $5 Northwest Forest Pass. You can also launch your boat from Diamond Lake Campground (see *Campgrounds*).

CANINE COMFORT ACCOMMODATIONS

Unless otherwise stated, dogs should not be left unattended in the room and must be leashed on hotel property.

Roseburg

$ Motel 6

3100 NW Aviation, 541-464-8000

This clean, budget motel has 82 pet-friendly rooms.

Dog Policy

Fido gets to stay for free.

$$ Best Western Douglas Inn Motel

511 SE Stephens, 1-877-368-4466, www. bestwestern.com

This hotel has 52 dog-friendly rooms. Amenities include a complimentary continental breakfast, coffee and tea in lobby, free morning newspaper, fitness center, sauna, hot tub, and guest laundry.

Dog Policy

A $6 fee per dog per night is charged.

$$ Best Western Garden Villa Motel

760 NW Garden Valley Blvd., 1-800-547-3446, www.bestwestern.com

You and Rover can stay in one of this hotel's 120 air-conditioned rooms equipped with cable television with HBO and ESPN, data port, and coffeemaker. Some rooms have a refrigerator. Enjoy a complimentary continental breakfast with coffee and a free newspaper. Cool off in one of the two seasonal pools, get a workout in the well-equipped exercise room and then relax in the Jacuzzi. There is a walking path across the street where you can walk your dog.

Dog Policy

Only dogs that weigh 10 pounds or less are allowed. A one-time $10 fee is charged per dog.

$$ Windmill Inn

1450 Mulholland Dr., 1-800-547-4747, www.windmillinns.com

You'll find deluxe rooms and suites with cable TV, data port, microwave, and refrigerator. You'll also receive a complimentary newspaper and continental breakfast of orange juice, coffee, and muffin delivered to your door. This hotel offers free hot coffee and beverages in the lobby twenty-four hours per day, and has a guest laundry, guest bicycles, a pool, hot tub, sauna, and exercise room.

Dog Policy

Dogs get to stay for free.

$$-$$$ Holiday Inn Express

375 W. Harvard Blvd., 1-800-898-7666,

This hotel on the South Umpqua River has 22 dog-friendly non-smoking rooms with river views. All rooms have a private balcony/patio, hairdryer, iron and ironing board, coffeemaker, and TV. Refrigerators are available by request. You can take a plunge in the indoor swimming pool, soak in the outdoor Jacuzzi, or work off your road stress in the fitness center. The hotel also has a family suite that allows Rover. This suite is equipped with 2 queen size beds, a sitting area with two overstuffed chairs, a sofa, microwave, refrigerator, sink, coffeemaker, and two televisions. Other amenities are a business center with Internet access, guest laundry, and complimentary full continental breakfast. A grassy pet area is available. Adjacent to the hotel are walking paths that parallel the river and lead to parks.

Dog Policy

The hotel charges $5 fee per dog per night. Management asks that you walk your dog in the pet area. If you do leave your dog alone in your room, management asks that you leave a phone number so they can contact you if there is a problem.

Diamond Lake

$$-$$$$ Diamond Lake Resort

350 Resort Dr., 1-800-733-7593, www.diamondlake.net

This resort along the shores of Diamond Lake is just 5 miles from the north entrance to Crater Lake National Park. It features a 40-room lodge, 10 studio rooms, and 42 cabins. Lodge rooms can accommodate four people and have a queen bed, double bed, TV, coffeemaker, electric heat, and bathroom. The studio units can accommodate two people and have a queen bed, TV, electric heat, kitchen, coffeemaker, bathroom, and shower. The cabins can accommodate six people and have two bedrooms, a full-service kitchen, a living room with a TV, wood stove (or fireplace), a bathroom and shower, and electric heat. The lodge has a family restaurant, grocery store, laundry, marina, and kayak, canoe, fishing boat, and mountain bike rentals. Hike the lake's perimeter on a paved bike trail that begins to the right of the beach in front of the lodge.

Dog Policy

A $5 fee per dog per night is charged.

Elkton

$$$$ The Big K Guest Ranch

20029 Highway 138, 541-584-2395 or 1-800-390-2445, www.big-k.com

This 2,500 working ranch is northwest of Roseburg, along the shores of the Umpqua River in the Coast Range. The ranch has 20 private cabins and a 12,000-square-foot log lodge with a recreation/game room, big screen TV, pool table, and Ping-Pong. Hike and bike with your dog on over 20 miles of trails. The ranch has bicycle rentals and offers guided fishing and rafting tours on the lower Umpqua

River. All meals are included with the price of your stay.

Dog Policy

A fee of $10 per dog per day is charged. Dogs are allowed in cabins but not in the main lodge. This is a working ranch and the owners ask that you be responsible for your dog around their livestock.

Glide

$$ Steelhead Run B&B

23049 N. Umpqua Highway, 1-800-348-0563, www.steelheadrun.com

This resort-style bed and breakfast is 20 minutes east of Roseburg on five forested acres on the wild and scenic North Umpqua River. Stay with your dog in the Shiloh Room, a non-smoking studio apartment decorated in a Civil War theme, and furnished with a private bath and shower, fully equipped kitchen, queen bed and two full bunk bed sets. The Shilo Room has a private entrance, a lower deck with an old fashioned patio swing, and a great view of the North Umpqua just outside the door. Additional amenities at this B&B include a video and book library, game room with pool table, fine art gallery, and guided fishing trips. You'll also have access to the North Umpqua Trail (see *Paw-Approved Hikes and Parks*), waterfalls, and hot springs. A homemade breakfast (be sure to save some for Fido) is included with your stay.

Dog Policy

Trained, obedient and house-broken dogs are welcome in the Shilo Room for $15 per night plus a refundable security deposit of $20.00.

Sutherlin

$-$$ Sutherlin Inn

1400 Hospitality Place (I-5 exit 136), 1-800-635-5425, www.cloud9inns.com

This hotel is located off I-5, 10 miles north of Roseburg. Smoking and non-smoking pet-friendly rooms are equipped with TV with HBO, and data ports. A complimentary continental breakfast of bagels and gourmet coffee, tea, and cocoa is available. The hotel has a guest laundry.

Dog Policy
A $10 fee per dog per day is charged.

CAMPGROUNDS

Diamond Lake
Contact: Contact: Diamond Lake Ranger District, 2020 Toketee Ranger Station Rd., Idleyld Park, OR 97447, 541-498-2531, www.fs.fed.us
Season: Mid-May to October
Facilities: 238 RV/tent campsites (160 with electrical hook-ups), water, hot showers, restrooms, picnic tables, fire rings, RV dump station, ADA campsites, and a boat launch
Getting There: From Roseburg head east on Highway 38 for 80 miles to the junction with Diamond Lake Road (Forest Road 4795). Turn right onto Diamond Lake Road and travel 2.5 miles to the campground.
Description: This busy campground has large lakeshores campsites with grand views of snowy Mount Bailey. You can paddle on the lake with your dog, check out some of the area hikes (see *Paw-Approved Hikes and Parks*), or take a driving tour around nearby Crater Lake (see *Paw-Approved Hikes and Parks*).

Horseshoe Bend
Contact: Umpqua National Forest, North Umpqua Ranger District, 18782 North Umpqua Highway, Glide, OR 974443, 541-496-3532, www.fs.fed.us
Season: Late May through September
Facilities: 24 RV/tent campsites (no electrical hook-ups), water, restrooms, fire rings, ADA campsites, and a boat launch
Getting There: Head about 47 miles east of Roseburg on Highway 138. Turn right (south) on Forest Road 4750 and follow signs to the campground.

Description: This campground is nestled in a mature grove of Douglas fir and sugar pine adjacent to the North Fork of the Umpqua River. Its large campsites give you and Rover some breathing room. Hike on the North Fork of the Umpqua River Trail by crossing a bridge over the river to the Calf Creek Trailhead.

Poole Creek at Lemolo Lake
Contact: Contact: Diamond Lake Ranger District, 2020 Toketee Ranger Station Rd., Idleyld Park, OR 97447, 541-498-2531, www.fs.fed.us
Season: Late May to October
Facilities: 59 RV/tent campsites (no electrical hook-ups), water, vault toilets, picnic tables, fire rings, and a boat launch
Getting There: From Roseburg, head east on Highway 38 for 72 miles to the junction with Bird's Point Road (Forest Road 2610). Turn left (north) onto Bird's Point Road and travel 4 miles to the signed campground.
Description: This campground has campsites on the shores of Lemolo Lake (actually a reservoir on the North Umpqua River). This is a good spot to launch your boat and take an afternoon paddle.

Susan Creek
Contact: Roseburg District Office, Bureau of Land Management, 777 NW Garden Valley Blvd., Roseburg, OR 97470, 541-440-4930, www.or.blm.gov
Season: May to October
Facilities: 31 RV/tent campsites (no electrical hook-ups), restrooms, hot showers, water, fire pits, picnic tables, and ADA campsites
Getting There: The campground is 29.5 miles east of Roseburg, (12.5 miles east of Glide) on Highway 138.
Description: This beautiful forested campground along the banks of the North Fork of the Umpqua River gives you access to the Susan Creek Falls Trail, accessible from the picnic area.

CANINE-APPROVED SHOPPING

Mini Pet Mart

2820 NE Stephens St., Roseburg, 541-957-8130

Rover will find all the toys and food he needs at this friendly pet mart. Open 9 A.M.–7 P.M., Monday to Saturday; 10 A.M.–6 P.M., Sunday.

CANINE ER

Bailey Veterinary Clinic

248 NW Garden Valley Blvd., Roseburg, 541-673-4403

This clinic will see walk-ins.

Open 8 A.M.–5:30 P.M., Monday to Friday; 9 A.M.–4 P.M., Saturday.

LOST AND FOUND (ANIMAL SHELTERS)

Umpqua Valley Humane Society

943 Del Rio Rd., Roseburg, 97470, 541-672-3907

Open 12 P.M.–7 P.M., Tuesday to Friday; 12 P.M.–5 P.M., Saturday and Sunday.

Grants Pass

THE BIG SCOOP

Grants Pass is 70 miles south of Roseburg on I-5, on the banks of the mighty Rogue River. The city's fifteen parks and green spaces welcome leashed dogs. If you want a break from the road, check out Riverside Park, at the intersection of 6th St. and East Park St. This park, adjacent to the Rogue River, has a picnic area, Frisbee golf course, and a rose garden.

From Grants Pass, travel southwest on the Redwood Highway, U.S. 199, to the Siskiyou National Forest and the Kalmiopsis Wilderness. This 179,655-acre wilderness of deep river gorges and rocky ridges is home to many rare plant species. One of the Kalmiopsis' star attractions is the 27-mile-long Illinois River Trail. Highway 199 also leads to Oregon Caves National Monument. Dogs are not allowed on any of the monument trails but are allowed at viewpoints, rest areas, and picnic areas.

PAW-APPROVED HIKES AND PARKS

 Babyfoot Lake Hike
Contact: Siskiyou National Forest, Galice Ranger District, 200 NE Greenfield Rd., Grants Pass, OR 97528, 541-471-6500, www.fs.fed.us
Paw-Approval Rating: 4 paws
Leashes Required? No
Length: 2 miles out and back
Difficulty: Easy
Fees/Permits: $5 Northwest Forest Pass. Purchase at 1-800-270-7504 or www.naturenw.org. A free self-issue wilderness

permit (available at the trailhead) is also required.
Season: June through October
Getting There: Drive about 28 miles south of Grants Pass on the Redwood Highway, U.S. 199, to Eight Dollar Road (just south of Selma). Turn right, or west, on Eight Dollar Road (this turns into Forest Road 4201 after you enter the Siskiyou National Forest). Continue on Forest Road 4201 for 11.3 miles to the intersection with Forest Road 140. Turn left onto Forest Road 140 and travel 0.3 mile to the trailhead on the right.
Description: This hike takes you to Babyfoot Lake, located in a glacial cirque surrounded by forested hills and rocky

Checking out Babyfoot Lake in the Kalmiopsis Wilderness.

bluffs. This high lake is part of the 352-acre Babyfoot Lake Botanical Area, established in 1963 to protect the Brewers spruce and other rare plant species.

The route begins by winding through an immense old-growth forest of Brewers spruce, Douglas fir, Shasta red fir, sugar pine, Port Orford cedar, and incense cedar. At 0.3 mile, turn right at the trail fork (the trail that heads left goes toward Ridge Trail). After 1 mile, you'll arrive at Babyfoot Lake where you and your best friend can swim or just hang by the lakeshore. Retrace the route back to the trailhead.

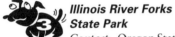

Illinois River Forks State Park

Contact: Oregon State Parks and Recreation, Suite 1, 1115 Commercial St. NE, Salem OR 97301-1002, www.oregonstateparks.org

Paw-Approval Rating: 3 paws

Leashes Required? Yes

Fees/Permits: None.

Season: Open year-round.

Getting There: Drive 32 miles south of Grants Pass on Highway 199 to the town of Cave Junction. The park is located one mile south of Cave Junction off Highway 199.

Description: This day-use park is along the east and west forks of the Illinois River. Stop and play with your dog by the river or take a short hike.

Illinois River Hike

Contact: Siskiyou National Forest, Galice Ranger District, 200 NE Greenfield Rd., Grants Pass, OR 97528, 541-471-6500, www.fs.fed.us

Paw-Approval Rating: 4 paws

Leashes Required? No

Length: 8 miles out and back (with longer options)

Difficulty: Moderate

Fees/Permits: $5 Northwest Forest Pass. Purchase at 1-800-270-7504 or www.naturenw.org. A free self-issue wilderness permit, available at the trailhead, is also required.

Season: May through November

Getting There: From Grants Pass take exit 55, Oregon Caves and Crescent City. Turn south on Highway 199 (the Redwood Highway) and travel 21.6 miles to Selma. From U.S. 199 in Selma, turn right on Forest Road 4103 (Illinois River Road) at the flashing yellow light. The pavement ends and the road turns rough and rocky after 11 miles. At mile 17.8, head left at the road fork. At mile 18, go right at the road fork. A sign here indicates that this road is not recommended for low clearance vehicles. If you are driving a passenger car, park here and walk the remaining mile to the trailhead.

Description: This beautiful trail traverses high above the Illinois River and through the heart of the Kalmiopsis Wilderness. You'll start by hiking on a trail that crosses Briggs Creek and slowly ascends through a forest of Douglas fir, canyon live oak, and orange madrone trees (identified by their rusty orange-colored, papery bark). Along the way you'll see the low-growing, bushy manzanita and chinquapin. Also be on the lookout for poison oak.

When you see the Illinois River, notice its dark green color, which is due to serpentinite rock along the river's course. As you ascend the trail you'll pass rough, rocky outcrops of lava that offer viewpoints of the river and the river gorge. Continue on the trail 4 miles to Clear Creek (your turn-around point). This bubbling creek has deep rocky pools that are perfect for your pup to wade in. If you want to backpack further into the wilderness, you can continue on the trail for many more miles.

Oregon Caves National Monument

Contact: National Park Service, Oregon Caves National Monument, 19000 Caves Highway, Cave Junction, OR 97523, www.nps.gov

Paw-Approval Rating: 1 paw

Leashes Required? Yes

Fees/Permits: None unless you want to go on a cave tour ($7.50 for adults and $5 for children 16 and under). Dogs are not allowed on cave tours.

Season: March through November

Getting There: From I-5 in Grants Pass, drive south on Highway 199 about 32 miles to the town of Cave Junction. Turn left on Highway 46. The monument is 20 miles east of Cave Junction at the end of Highway 46.

Description: The main attraction at this 488-acre national monument is an intricately-carved cave that contains three known miles of chambers and the fast flowing River Styx, which runs the length of the cave. This cave began as limestone deposits in a shallow sea about 200 million years ago. As the continental crust shifted, the limestone layers were lifted up, compressed, and metamorphosed into marble. As the Siskiyou Mountains continued to rumble and shake, the marble formations became exposed and water began to erode the soft rock, creating tunnels and caves.

Explore these magnificent caves by taking a tour through more than a half-mile of gleaming marble passageways filled with stalactites, columns, cave popcorn, pearls, and moon milk. Tours are given March through November.

Other activities include 5 miles of trails that wind through a predominantly Douglas fir forest that is home to 80 species of birds, 35 species of mammals, and more than 110 unique species of plants. The lodge is worth a peek, as it is curiously and precariously perched on the sides of a steep valley, atop the spring that originates in the cave. Dogs are not allowed on any of the trails in the monument. However, as long as your dog is leashed he is welcome at picnic areas, rest areas, and viewpoints.

Valley of the Rogue State Park

Contact: Oregon State Parks and Recreation, Suite 1, 1115 Commercial St. NE, Salem, OR 97301-1002, www.oregonstateparks.org

Paw-Approval Rating: 3 paws

Leashes Required? Yes

Fees/Permits: None.

Season: Open year-round.

Getting There: This park is 12 miles east of Grants Pass, off I-5 exit 45B.

Description: This state park on the banks of the Rogue River has a campground and a 1.25-mile long nature trail you can explore with your traveling buddy.

CANINE COMFORT ACCOMMODATIONS

Unless otherwise stated, dogs should not be left unattended in the room and must be leashed on hotel property.

$ Motel 6

1800 NE 7th St., 541-474-1331

This budget motel has clean, comfortable rooms for you and your traveling partner.

Dog Policy

Dogs get to stay for free.

$-$$ Comfort Inn

1889 NE Sixth St., 541-479-8301, www.comfortinn.com

This hotel has rooms with refrigerator, microwave, and cable TV. Amenities include an outdoor seasonal pool, free morning newspaper, and complimentary continental breakfast.

Dog Policy

The hotel charges a $100 refundable pet deposit.

$$ Best Western Inn at the Rogue

8959 Rogue River Highway, 541-582-2200

This inn, adjacent to the Rogue River, has four dog-friendly rooms. It is located near exit 48 off I-5. Amenities include a heated pool, hot tub, guest laundry, and complimentary continental breakfast.

Dog Policy

Dogs under 50 pounds are welcome. A $10 nightly fee per dog is charged for small dogs; $20 for large dogs.

$$ Holiday Inn Express
105 NE Agness Ave., 541-471-6144
Dog Policy
The inn charges a $5 nightly fee per dog.

$$ La Quinta Inn & Suites
243 NE Morgan Lane, 541-472-1808,
www.lq.com
Dog Policy
Your dog gets to stay for free at this inn.

$$ Shilo Inn
1880 NW Sixth St., 541-479-8391, www.
shiloinns.com
You'll enjoy the large, comfortable rooms at this pet-friendly inn. Rooms are equipped with a hair dryer, coffeemaker, and cable TV with free Showtime. The inn also features a seasonal outdoor pool, steam room, and a free complimentary breakfast.
Dog Policy
The hotel charges $10 per dog per night.

CANINE-APPROVED SHOPPING

American Feed & Farm Supply Inc.
870 Redwood Ave., 541-479-3335
This store carries dog leashes, collars, grooming supplies, and high-quality dog foods. Open 8 A.M.–5:30 P.M., Monday to Friday; 8 A.M.–5 P.M., Saturday.

Mini Pet Mart
876 NW 6th St., 541-479-3141
Rover will find all the toys and food he needs at this friendly pet mart. Open 9 A.M.–7 P.M., Monday to Saturday; 10 A.M.–6 P.M., Sunday.

DOGGIE DAYCARE AND CANINE ER

Grants Pass Veterinary Clinic
585 SW Lincoln Rd., 541-476-7769
This clinic offers boarding services and will see walk-in appointments. For an after-hours emergency, call the regular office number and the doctor will be paged.
Open 8 A.M.–5 P.M., Monday to Friday.

LOST AND FOUND (ANIMAL SHELTERS)

Rogue Valley Humane Society Animal Shelter
429 NW Scenic Dr., 541-479-5154, www.grantspass.net
Open 12 P.M.–4:30 P.M., Monday, Tuesday, Thursday, and Friday; 12 P.M.–3 P.M., Saturday.

Medford

THE BIG SCOOP

Medford is Southern Oregon's largest city. Located about 30 miles south of Grants Pass on I-5 and 15 miles north of Ashland, this community is well known for its thriving fruit industry. Your dog can run off his extra energy at Medford's off-leash area in Bear Creek Dog Park (see *Paw-Approved Hikes and Parks*). Leashed dogs are allowed at all of Medford's other city parks.

East on Highway 62 from Medford are hiking and mountain biking trails in the Rogue River National Forest. Southwest on Highway 238 is Applegate Reservoir in the foothills of the Siskiyou Mountains, just north of the California border. On your way to the reservoir, you'll pass through the historic town of Jacksonville, one of the oldest settlements in Southern Oregon. Many of its historic buildings have been preserved, and you can learn more about Jacksonville's history at the Jacksonville Museum of Southern Oregon History (206 N. 5th St.). A great place in Jacksonville to get coffee to go is the Pony Espresso Café at 545 N. 5th St.

PAW-APPROVED HIKES AND PARKS

 Bear Creek Dog Park
Contact: Medford Parks and Recreation, 200 South Ivy Lausmann Annex: Room 140, Medford, OR 97501, 541-774-2400, www.ci.medford.or.us
Paw-Approval Rating: 4 paws
Leashes Required? No
Fees/Permits: None

Season: Year-round
Getting There: The off-leash area is located in Bear Creek Park at the corner of Highland Dr. and Barnett Road, near I-5 exit 27 in Medford.
Description: Let Rover enjoy running on this 2-acre, fenced, off-leash area equipped with water, a covered picnic table, and natural track. From the park you can access the Bear Creek Greenway, a paved bike/pedestrian way which travels north about 6 miles through Medford to Central Point.

 Da-Ku-Be-Te-De Hike
Contact: Rogue River National Forest, Applegate Ranger District, 6941 Upper Applegate Rd., Jacksonville, OR 97530-9314, 541-899-3800, www.fs.fed.us
Paw-Approval Rating: 3 paws
Leashes Required? Yes
Length: 4.8 miles one way
Difficulty: Easy
Fees/Permits: None
Season: Year-round
Getting There: From I-5 South in Medford take exit 27, Medford/Barnett Road. At the end of the off-ramp, turn right on Barnett Road and get into the right lane. Go 0.2 mile and turn right on Riverside Ave./Highway 99 North toward City Center/Jacksonville. Continue 0.9 mile on Main St. through downtown Medford. Turn left on Highway 238 toward Jacksonville. Drive west on Highway 238 about 5.6 miles to downtown Jacksonville. From there, continue 7.4 miles southwest on Highway 238 to Applegate Road Turn left onto Applegate Road and proceed

15.1 miles to the Swayne Viewpoint on the left side of the road.

Description: This unpronounceable hike takes you along the shores of Applegate Lake, a reservoir nestled in the foothills of the Siskiyou Mountains. Start at the south end of the parking lot near the restrooms. The trail follows the lake's contours through a shady oak and pine forest. If you want to explore further, stay at Watkins Campground (see *Campgrounds*) or one of the many other campgrounds surrounding the lake.

Lost Creek Reservoir Hike

Contact: Oregon State Parks and Recreation, Suite 1, 1115 Commercial St. NE, Salem, OR 97301-1002, www.oregonstateparks.org

Paw-Approval Rating: 3 paws
Leashes Required? Yes
Length: 5 miles out and back
Difficulty: Easy
Fees/Permits: None
Season: Year-round
Getting There: From Medford head northeast on Highway 62 for 35.5 miles to the junction with Lewis Road Turn left onto Lewis Road and continue 1 mile to the trailhead on the left side of the road.

Description: This route takes you and your companion through an oak and pine forest along the shores of Lost Creek Lake. Look for good swimming beaches as you follow the path along the lake's edge. At 2.4 miles, bear right at a "Grotto" sign and ascend to a viewpoint. Turning around here or continue on the lakeshore trail. Watch out for poison oak on this route. You can stay overnight at Stewart State Park Campground (see *Campgrounds*).

Mount Bailey Hike

Contact: Diamond Lake Ranger District, 2020 Toketee Ranger Station Rd., Idleyld Park, OR 97447, 541-498-2531, www.fs.fed.us

Paw-Approval Rating: 2 paws

Leashes Required? No
Length: 9.8 miles out and back
Difficulty: Difficult
Fees/Permits: None
Season: July through October
Getting There: From Medford head about 60 miles north on Highway 62 to the junction with Highway 230. Turn left (north) on Highway 230 continue about 24 miles to the Diamond Lake Recreation Area turnoff. Continue on Forest Road 6592 to a South Shore Picnic Area sign. Turn left onto Forest Road 4795, travel 1.7 miles, and turn left onto Forest Road 300. Continue 0.4 mile to the trailhead parking area.

Description: This trail takes you to the 8,368-foot summit of Mount Bailey. This challenging route climbs over 3,100 feet through a lodgepole pine forest lined with manzanita. After 2.2 miles, the trail intersects a dirt road. Cross the road and continue your steep ascent through a mountain hemlock forest that eventually thins to whitebark pine. You'll reach the spectacular summit after another 2.7 miles. Enjoy the views of Diamond Lake, Mount Thielsen, and Mount Scott and return on the same route. This trail has a section of lava scree that can be hard on a dog's feet. Make sure your dog has some foot protection before you attempt this hike.

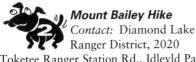

Natural Bridge Hike

Contact: Rogue River National Forest, Prospect Ranger District, 47201 Hwy. 62, Prospect, OR 97536, 541-560-3400, www.fs.fed.us

Paw-Approval Rating: 4 paws
Leashes Required? Yes
Length: 22.4-mile loop
Difficulty: Easy
Fees/Permits: $5 Northwest Forest Pass. Purchase at 1-800-270-7504 or www.naturenw.org.
Season: March through November
Getting There: Head 55 miles northeast of Medford on Highway 62 and turn right at a sign for Natural Bridge Campground (see *Campgrounds*). Drive 0.7 mile (stay

left at the road fork) to the Natural Bridge parking area.

Description: Begin hiking on the paved path that crosses a footbridge over the Rogue River. In 0.2 mile, you'll arrive at an amazing viewpoint of Natural Bridge—the river does a vanishing act as it charges into a lava tube. To complete the loop, turn right after crossing the bridge and head upriver 1 mile to a trail fork. Turn right and cross the river on a footbridge. After crossing the bridge, turn right and head 1.1 miles back to the trailhead. For a longer hiking adventure, turn left at this junction and hike upstream another 1.7 miles to Union Creek Campground (see *Campgrounds*). Return to the trailhead on the same route.

Takelma Gorge Hike
Contact: Rogue River National Forest, Prospect Ranger District, 47201 Hwy. 62, Prospect, OR 97536, 541-560-3400, www.fs.fed.us
Paw-Approval Rating: 3 paws
Leashes Required? Yes
Length: 3.2 miles out and back (with longer options)
Difficulty: Easy
Fees/Permits: $5 Northwest Forest Pass. Purchase at 1-800-270-7504 or www.naturenw.org.
Season: March through November
Getting There: Head northeast of Medford on Highway 62 about 51.5 miles and turn left onto Woodruff Meadows Road. Drive 1.7 miles and turn left into the Woodruff Bridge picnic area.
Description: Begin walking on a forested path that parallels the Rogue River. At 1.6 miles, you'll arrive at a stunning viewpoint of Takelma Gorge. Turn around here or continue another 3 miles. The trail passes many scenic viewpoints of the narrow gorge and churning river and leads to some nice dog-paddling spots. If you decide to continue, your turnaround point is at River Bridge Campground.

Touvelle State Recreation Site
Contact: Oregon State Parks and Recreation, Suite 1, 1115 Commercial St. NE, Salem, OR 97301-1002, www.oregonstateparks.org
Paw-Approval Rating: 3 paws
Leashes Required? Yes
Fees/Permits: $3 day-use fee
Season: Year-round
Getting There: The park is 9 miles north of Medford off Highway 62.
Description: This day-use park and picnic area is on the banks of the Rogue River. Rising prominently above the park is Table Rocks—a well-known geologic landmark. This park is also adjacent to the Denman Wildlife Refuge, which teems with bird life.

Union Creek Hike
Contact: Rogue River National Forest, Prospect Ranger District, 47201 Hwy. 62, Prospect, OR 97536, 541-560-3400, www.fs.sfed.us
Paw-Approval Rating: 4 paws
Leashes Required? No
Length: 8.2 miles out and back
Difficulty: Moderate
Fees/Permits: None
Season: April through November
Getting There: From Medford head 56 miles northeast on Highway 62 and park on the right side of the road at the trail sign.
Description: You and your dog will love this trek along Union Creek. Start hiking on the trail as it heads upstream, and cross the creek on a footbridge. Turn right and continue as the trail travels through a cool Douglas fir forest. The creek escorts you along as it rumbles and rushes over large rocks and through deep channels. At 3.3 miles, you'll arrive at a small 8-foot waterfall, and at 4.1 miles is the miniature 10-foot cascade of Union Creek Falls. From here, retrace the route back to the trailhead.

CYCLING FOR CANINES

Payette Trail #970 at Applegate Reservoir
Contact: Rogue River National Forest, Applegate Ranger District, 6941 Upper Applegate Rd., Jacksonville, OR 97530-9314, 541-899-3800, www.fs.fed.us
Paw-Approval Rating: 3 paws
Leashes Required? No
Length: 13.2 miles out and back
Difficulty: Moderate
Fees/Permits: None
Season: Year-round
Getting There: From I-5 South in Medford, take exit 27, Medford/Barnett Road. At the end of the off-ramp, turn right on Barnett Road and get into the right lane. Go 0.2 mile and turn right on Riverside Ave./Highway 99 North toward City Center/Jacksonville. Continue 0.9 mile on Main St. through downtown Medford. Turn left on Highway 238 toward Jacksonville. Drive west on Highway 238 about 5.6 miles to downtown Jacksonville. From there, continue 7.4 miles southwest on Highway 238 to Applegate Road. Turn left onto Applegate Road and drive 15.5 miles to French Gulch Road. Turn left on French Gulch Road and drive 1.1 miles over the Applegate Dam to the French Gulch Trailhead on the right side of the road. *Description:* This singletrack trail follows the contours of the eastern shore of Applegate Reservoir through a mixed conifer and hardwood forest. Your canine pal will appreciate the fact that he can take a plunge into the lake to cool off. Beware of poison oak, ticks, and rattlesnakes. For more hiking or biking opportunities, check out the Da-Ku-Be-Te-De Trail (see *Paw-Approved Hikes and Parks*). Follow the trail for 6.6 miles until you reach the junction with Trail #947 (your turnaround point).

POWDERHOUNDS

Dogs are not allowed on designated Nordic ski trails on the Rogue River and Winema National Forests. For information on trails where dogs are permitted, contact the Supervisor's Office, Rogue National Forest, 333 W. 8th St., Medford, Oregon 97501-0209, 541-858-2200, www.fs.fed.us.

PADDLEHOUNDS

Your dog will enjoy an afternoon paddling with you at Lost Creek Reservoir, about 35 miles northeast of Medford on Highway 62. Another paddling spot worth checking out is Applegate Reservoir, about 30 miles southwest of Medford. See the directions to Applegate Reservoir in the *Payette Trail #970 at Applegate Reservoir* ride under *Cycling for Canines.*

CANINE COMFORT ACCOMODATIONS

Medford

$ Motel 6
2400 Biddle Rd., 541-779-0550
This motel is located off exit 30 off I-5. Rooms are clean and affordable.
Dog Policy
Fido gets to stay for free.

$-$$ Cedar Lodge
518 N. Riverside, 1-800-282-3419

Exploring trails in the Winema National Forest.

This lodge has 15 dog-friendly rooms equipped with refrigerator, microwave, and color cable TV. A complimentary paper and continental breakfast are included with your stay. A park one block away is a great place for Rover to stretch his legs after a long day on the road.

Dog Policy
The hotel requires a $20 refundable pet deposit and that you sign a Pet Deposit form. The lodge allows dogs that weigh 45 pounds or less.

$$ Red Lion Inn
200 N. Riverside Ave., 541-779-5811, www.redlion.com
Dog Policy
If you pay with cash, a $50 refundable deposit is required. If you pay with a credit card, no deposit is required.

$$ Shilo Inn
2111 Biddle Rd., 541-770-515, www.shiloinns.com

This inn has 48 dog-friendly rooms equipped with a microwave, refrigerator, hair dryer, iron and ironing board, coffeemaker, and cable TV. Additional amenities include a guest laundromat, complimentary USA Today, continental breakfast, exercise room, indoor spa, sauna, and fitness center. When you check in, your pup will receive yummy dog treats. The Deer Creek Bike Trail is nearby if you want to take your friend for a walk.
Dog Policy
The hotel charges $10 per dog per night.

$$-$$$ Windmill Inn of Medford
1950 Biddle Rd., 1-800-547-4747, www.windmillinns.com

This inn is located off exit 30 on I-5. All rooms are dog-friendly and are equipped with a microwave, refrigerator, hair dryer, iron and ironing board, and cable TV. You'll receive a complimentary newspaper and continental breakfast delivered to your door. Amenities include free hot coffee and beverages in the lobby twenty-four hours per day, a guest laundry, guest bicycles, a seasonal pool, hot tub, sauna, and exercise room. Bear Creek Park's leash-free area is about 3 miles south of the hotel. Petsmart (see *Canine-Approved Shopping*) is also nearby.
Dog Policy
There are no additional charges for dogs. Dogs are not allowed in the pool area.

Prospect

$-$$ Prospect Historical B&B and Motel
391 Mill Creek Dr., 1-800-944-6490, www.prospecthotel.com

This B&B and motel, on five partially wooded acres in the small town of Prospect, is a completely refurbished stagecoach inn originally built in 1890, and is one of the oldest operating hotels in southern Oregon. Prospect is southwest of Crater Lake off Highway 62. The property has hiking trails and adjoins Mill Creek, where you can fish for rainbow trout. Dogs cannot stay in the B&B's 10 rooms but are welcome in the 14 dog-friendly rooms in the motel. Some rooms can sleep up to six and some have kitchenettes.
Dog Policy
Your dog stays for free.

CAMPGROUNDS

Farewell Bend
Contact: Rogue River National Forest, Prospect Ranger District, 47201 Highway 62, Prospect, OR 97536-9724, 541-560-3400, www.fs.fed.us
Season: May to mid-October
Facilities: 61 RV/tent campsites (no electrical hook-ups), water, restrooms, picnic tables, fire rings, ADA campsites, and a playground.
Getting There: Travel 12 miles north of Prospect on Highway 62 to the campground.
Description: This forested campground is adjacent to the Rogue River and the Upper Rogue River Trail.

Natural Bridge

Contact: Rogue River National Forest, Prospect Ranger District, 47201 Highway 62, Prospect, Oregon 97536-9724, 541-560-3400, www.fs.fed.us

Season: May to October

Facilities: 17 RV/tent campsites (no electrical hook-ups), no water, vault toilets, fire rings, picnic tables

Getting There: This campground is 11 miles north of Prospect on Highway 62.

Description: This campground has some large campsites along the Rogue River. You also have access to the Rogue Gorge Trail, which heads downstream 3 miles along the river to a viewpoint of Natural Bridge.

Stewart State Park

Contact: Oregon State Parks and Recreation, Suite 1, 1115 Commercial St. NE, Salem OR 97301-1002, www.oregon-stateparks.org

Season: March through November

Facilities: 148 electrical campsites, 49 tent campsites, 2 group-tent areas, restrooms, hot showers, water, picnic tables, and fire rings

Getting There: This campground is 35 miles northeast of Medford off Highway 62.

Description: This campground is surrounded by a shady pine forest and mountains. Campsites overlook Lost Creek Reservoir. Explore the park on several miles of hiking and biking trails. This is also a great place to take your furry friend paddling.

Union Creek

Contact: Rogue River National Forest, Prospect Ranger District, 47201 Highway 62, Prospect, Oregon 97536-9724, 541-560-3400, www.fs.fed.us

Season: Mid-May to mid-October

Facilities: 99 RV/tent campsites (no electrical hook-ups), vault toilets, water, fire rings, and picnic tables

Getting There: This campground is 11 miles north of Prospect on Highway 62.

Description: This thickly forested campground is off Highway 62, adjacent to the roaring Rogue River and Union Creek. Be sure to check out the Union Creek Hike (see *Paw-Approved Hikes and Parks*).

Watkins

Contact: Rogue River National Forest, Applegate Ranger District, 6941 Upper Applegate Rd., Jacksonville, OR 97530-9314, 541-899-3800, www.fs.fed.us

Season: April 30 to November 30

Facilities: 14 RV/tent campsites (no electrical hook-ups), water, vault toilets, and ADA sites

Getting There: From I-5 South in Medford, take exit 27, Medford/Barnett Road. At the end of the off-ramp, turn right on Barnett Road and get into the right lane. Go 0.2 mile and turn right on Riverside Ave./Highway 99 North toward City Center/Jacksonville. Drive 0.9 mile on Main St. through downtown Medford. Turn left on Highway 238 toward Jacksonville. Drive west on Highway 238 about 5.6 miles to downtown Jacksonville. From there, continue 7.4 miles southwest on Highway 238 to Applegate Road Turn left and proceed 18.6 miles to the campground on the left side of the road.

Description: This forested campground on the shores of Applegate Reservoir provides access to the Da-Ku-Be-Te-De Trail (see *Paw-Approved Hikes and Parks*) where you can hike or mountain bike with your canine pal.

CANINE-APPROVED SHOPPING

Mini Pet Mart

1081 Stewart Ave., Medford, 541-779-8410

Open 9 A.M.–7 P.M., Monday to Saturday; 10 A.M.–6 P.M., Sunday.

Petsmart

3279 Crater Lake Highway, Medford, 541-772-5564, www.petsmart.com

Open 9 A.M.–9 P.M., Monday to Saturday; 10 A.M.–6 P.M., Sunday.

DOGGIE DAYCARE

Rogue Animal Hospital
1455 North Riverside, Medford, 541-779-4414

Prices for overnight boarding range from $10.25 to $15.40, based on your dog's weight. Open 8 A.M.–5:30 P.M., Monday to Friday; 8 A.M.–12 P.M., Saturday.

CANINE ER

Banfield the Pet Hospital
3279 Crater Lake Highway, Medford, 541-858-9686

This is a full-service veterinary hospital located near I-5 and next to Petsmart. The hospital does not offer overnight boarding.

Open 9 A.M.–7 P.M., Monday to Saturday.

Rogue Animal Hospital
1455 North Riverside, 541-779-4414

The clinic offers emergency services after-hours. Call the regular hospital number and the doctor will be paged.

Open 8 A.M.–5:30 P.M., Monday to Friday; 8 A.M.–12 P.M., Saturday.

LOST AND FOUND (ANIMAL SHELTERS)

Medford Humane Society
2910 Table Rock Rd, 541-779-3215

Open 11 A.M.–6 P.M., Monday to Friday; 10 A.M.–5 P.M., Saturday.

Ashland

THE BIG SCOOP

Ashland is 16 miles south of Medford and about 15 miles north of the Oregon/California border. This beautiful city is home to Southern Oregon University and is well known for its Oregon Shakespeare Festival. While your dog may think this is much ado about nothing, it is worth checking out a play while in the area (Oregon Shakespeare Festival, 541-482-4331, www.osfashland.com).

In downtown Ashland, visit the Ashland Dog Park. Not only is this park leash-free, it is the only park in Ashland where dogs are allowed. Luckily, Ashland is not far from many dog-friendly hiking and biking trails in the Rogue National Forest. Head into the Rogue National Forest by heading east on Highway 66.

PAW-APPROVED HIKES AND PARKS

Ashland Dog Park

Contact: Ashland Parks and Recreation, 340 S. Pioneer St., Ashland, OR 97520, 541-488-5340, www.ashland.or.us
Paw-Approval Rating: 4 paws
Leashes Required? No
Fees/Permits: None
Season: Year-round
Getting There: This park is just off West Nevada St. behind the Ashland Greenhouse and Nursery.
Description: This off-leash park is a two-acre canine paradise. The area is fenced and has a picnic shelter, shade trees, and water. If your dog is too timid or small to roughhouse with the big dogs, lead him to the smaller, 0.25-acre fenced enclosure where he can roam off leash with pooches his own size. The park is open dawn to dusk, seven days a week.

Brown Mountain Hike

Contact: Rogue River National Forest, 645 Washington St., Ashland, OR 97520, 541-482-3333, www.fs.fed.us
Paw-Approval Rating: 3 paws
Leashes Required? No
Length: 10.8 miles out and back
Difficulty: Moderate
Fees/Permits: $5 Northwest Forest Pass. Purchase at 1-800-270-7504 or www.naturenw.org
Season: June through October
Getting There: From I-5 in Ashland, take exit 14. Turn east on Highway 66 and proceed 0.8 mile to Dead Indian Memorial Road. Turn left and drive 22.5 miles to Forest Service Road 37 (Big Elk Road).

Levi on the Mount McLoughlin Trail.
Photograph by Ken Skeen

Turn left and travel 6.1 miles to F.S. Road 3705. Turn right and drive 3.4 miles to the Brown Mountain Trailhead on the left. Park in the gravel lot opposite the trailhead. *Description:* Follow the trail along the contours of the South Fork of Little Butte Creek through old-growth forest. Let your trail hound wallow in the creek, so he'll stay cool for the rest of the hike. At 1.7 miles, you'll arrive at Forest Road 500. Cross it and pick up the singletrack trail on the other side. At 2.7 miles, cross Forest Road 560 and continue through fern-filled forest on the singletrack Brown Mountain Trail. At 3.2 miles, you'll reach the intersection with the Pacific Crest Trail. Continue straight on the Brown Mountain Trail. On this section of the trail you'll be able to see Brown Mountain and its jumbled lava flows through the trees. Geologists believe this mountain erupted as recently as 2,000 years ago. At 4.5 miles, your pooch can pounce for sticks in Scott Creek. At 5.4 miles, you'll come to a trail junction and your turnaround point. *Option:* You have the option of turning left and hooking up with the High Lakes Trail. This trail is also open to mountain bikes. Mountain bikes are not allowed on the Pacific Crest Trail. To camp in this area, check out the North Fork Campground (see *Campgrounds*).

Fish Lake Hike

Contact: Rogue River National Forest, 645 Washington St., Ashland, OR 97520, 541-482-3333, www.fs.fed.us
Paw-Approval Rating: 4 paws
Leashes Required? No
Length: 4.6 miles out and back (with longer options)
Difficulty: Easy
Fees/Permits: $5 Northwest Forest Pass. Purchase at 1-800-270-7504 or www.naturenw.org.
Season: June through October
Getting There: From Ashland, head east on Highway 66 to the Dead Indian Memorial Highway. Turn left and drive 22 miles to the junction with Forest Road 37 (Big Elk Road). Turn left onto Forest Road 37 and proceed 8 miles to the North Fork campground. Turn right into the trailhead parking area on the right side of the road (opposite the campground).
Description: Your trail hound will appreciate the pristine creek filled with rocky boulders and cool swimming holes at the start of this hike. At 0.6 mile, go left as the path turns away from the creek. At 1.4 miles, you'll arrive at Fish Lake. Continue on the path as it follows the lake contours. At 2.3 miles, you'll arrive at the Fish Lake Resort. To continue, hook up with the High Lakes Trail and follow it another 6 miles as it heads through scenic forest, and past a large lava flow to its ending point at Lake of the Woods. These trails are open to mountain bikes.

Pacific Crest Trail— Mount Ashland Hike

Contact: Rogue River National Forest, 645 Washington St., Ashland, OR 97520, 541-482-3333, www.fs.fed.us
Paw-Approval Rating: 3 paws
Leashes Required? No
Length: 6.8 miles out and back (with longer options)
Difficulty: Moderate
Fees/Permits: None
Season: Late June through November
Getting There: From I-5 in Ashland take exit 6, Mount Ashland. Follow signs for Mount Ashland and turn right on Mount Ashland Rd. Drive 7.2 miles on Mount Ashland Rd. to a dirt parking area on the right.
Description: This trek follows the Pacific Crest Trail through large wildflower meadows and pockets of cool Shasta red fir and grand fir. Take the perfect picture of your pooch in one of these brilliant meadows or against the backdrop of 7,531-foot Mount Ashland. Your turnaround point is at 3.4 miles at a gravel road that leads to Grouse Gap shelter. To stay overnight,

head to Mount Ashland Campground (see *Campgrounds*).

CYCLING FOR CANINES

The Brown Mountain Hike and the Fish Lake Hike are great cycling trails to explore. See *Paw-Approved Hikes and Parks* for more information.

Another popular trail in the Ashland area is the Siskiyou Crest Mountain Bike Trail. This route begins at the Mount Ashland Ski Area parking lot and follows Forest Road 20 for 14 miles along the crest of the Siskiyou Mountains to Jackson Gap. From Jackson Gap, Forest Road 800 ascends on the right about 1.5 miles to the 7,418-foot summit of Dutchman Peak. Total distance from the parking lot to Dutchman Peak and back is about 31 miles. This is a challenging route, and roads are rocky and rough in many spots. Be sure your dog has foot protection, and carry plenty of water.

There are many shorter, out-and-back options along this route. At 2 miles, you can head left to the Grouse Gap Shelter, which offers nice views of Mount Shasta. A longer option is to head 11 miles out on Forest Road 20 to the junction with Forest Road 2030. Head right and arrive at Wrangle Camp in 0.5 mile. Wrangle Camp has vault toilets, water, picnic tables, and shade, which makes it a good spot to rest up before your return trip. This route is open late June through October. For more information, contact the Rogue River National Forest, 645 Washington St., Ashland, OR 97520, 541-482-3333 www.fs.fed.us.

POWDERHOUNDS

Dogs are not allowed on designated Nordic ski trails in the Rogue River and Winema National Forests. To find out about trails where dogs are permitted, contact the Rogue River National Forest, Ashland Ranger District, 645 Washington St., Ashland, OR 97520, 541-482-3333 www.fs.fed.us.

PADDLEHOUNDS

Take your dog paddling at Howard Prairie Reservoir, east of Ashland. You can launch your boat from Willow Point Campground. From Ashland, travel east on Highway 66 for 17 miles. Turn left (north) onto East Hyatt Road and proceed about 3 miles to Howard Prairie Dam Road Turn right onto Howard Prairie Dam Road and continue 0.5 mile to the campground. You can also take a cruise on Fish Lake, 35 miles east of Medford off Oregon 140. Launch your boat from Doe Point Campground (see *Campgrounds*).

CANINE COMFORT ACCOMMODATIONS

Unless otherwise stated, dogs should not be left unattended in the room and must be leashed on hotel property.

$-$$ Ashland Motel
1145 Siskiyou Blvd., 541-482-2561

This motel is across from Southern Oregon University and has 6 dog-friendly rooms. A heated pool is also available.
Dog Policy
A $5 nightly fee per dog is charged.

$-$$ Knights Inn Motel
2359 Ashland St., 1-800-547-4566

This hotel's comfortable pet-friendly rooms have air conditioning with cable TV. The hotel also has a heated pool and spa.
Dog Policy
A $10 fee per dog per night is charged.

$$ Ashland Super 8 Motel
2350 Ashland St., 541-482-8887, www.super8.com

This motel is located off I-5, exit 14, and has dog-friendly rooms.
Dog Policy
A $25 refundable deposit is required as well as a one-time $10 pet fee.

$$-$$$ Ashland Patterson House
639 N. Main St., 1-888-482-9171 www.patterson-house.com

This B&B has a separate, dog-friendly cottage equipped with a queen size bed, fireplace, full bath, and private deck. A homemade vegetarian breakfast is included with your stay. Talk to the owners about pet sitting services if you can't take Rover with you.

Dog Policy

A one time $10 fee is charged for your dog.

$$-$$$ Windmill Inn of Ashland

2525 Ashland St., 1-800-547-4747, www.windmillinns.com

This inn is located off I-5, exit 14. You'll find deluxe rooms and suites with cable TV, data port, microwave, and refrigerator. Amenities include a complimentary newspaper and continental breakfast delivered to your door each day, free hot coffee and beverages in the lobby twenty-four hours per day, a guest laundry, guest bicycles, a seasonal outdoor heated pool, spa, fitness room, and tennis court.

Dog Policy

Your dog is welcome at no additional charge.

CAMPGROUNDS

Doe Point

Contact: Rogue River National Forest, Ashland Ranger District, 645 Washington St., Ashland, OR 97520, 541-482-3333 www.fs.fed.us
Season: Mid-May through October
Facilities: 25 RV/tent campsites (no electrical hook-ups), 5 walk-in tent sites, water, restrooms, picnic tables, fire rings, and boat launch
Getting There: From Medford head 35 miles east on Highway 140 to the campground entrance.
Description: Doe Point is located along the shores of Fish Lake. You can hike along the lake, go swimming, or take a leisurely paddle with your best friend.

Mount Ashland

Contact: Klamath National Forest, Scott River Ranger District, 11263 N. Highway 3, Fort Jones, CA 96032-9702, 530-468-5351
Season: May through October
Facilities: 2 RV/tent campsites (no electrical hook-ups), 7 walk-in campsites, vault toilets, picnic tables, fire rings, no water
Getting There: From Ashland, travel south on I-5 and take exit 6. Go 11 miles to the campground entrance.
Description: This campground is only a mile down the road from the Mount Ashland Ski Area. It will surprise you with its stunning northern views of the Rogue Valley and the Oregon Cascades, and its southern views of Mount Shasta, the Shasta Valley, and the Marble Mountain Wilderness. Mountain bike, hike, and lounge all you want at this great campground. See the *Pacific Crest Trail—Mount Ashland Hike* in *Paw-Approved Hikes and Parks* for a great hike along the Pacific Crest Trail.

North Fork

Contact: Rogue River National Forest, Ashland Ranger District, 645 Washington St., Ashland, OR 97520, 541-482-3333 www.fs.fed.us
Season: April 30 to November 15
Facilities: 9 RV/tent campsites (no electrical hook-ups), water, vault toilets
Getting There: From Ashland, travel east on Dead Indian Memorial Road 22 miles to the junction with Forest Road 37. Turn north on Forest Service Road 37 and drive 8 miles to the campground.
Description: This pretty, forested campground promises solitude, and is not far from the Brown Mountain Trailhead (see *Paw-Approved Hikes and Parks*).

Willow Point

Contact: Jackson County Parks, 400 Antelope Rd., White City, OR 97503, 541-774-8183, www.jacksoncountyparks.com
Season: Mid-April through October
Facilities: 41 RV/tent campsites (no electrical hook-ups), water, restrooms, picnic tables, fire rings, and boat launch

Getting There: From Ashland, travel east on Highway 66 for 17 miles. Turn left (north) onto East Hyatt Road and proceed about 3 miles to Howard Prairie Dam Road Turn right onto Howard Prairie Dam Road and drive 0.5 mile to the campground.

Description: This forested campground is on Howard Prairie Lake. Fido will enjoy opportunities for an afternoon of swimming or paddling around the lake's 1.6 miles of lakeshore.

CANINE-APPROVED SHOPPING

Ray's Garden & Pet Center
1679 Jackson Rd., Ashland, 541-482-1100
Open 9 A.M.–5:30 P.M., Monday to Saturday; 10 A.M.–5 P.M., Sunday.

DOGGIE DAYCARE AND CANINE ER

Bear Creek Animal Clinic
1955 Ashland St., Ashland, 541-488-0120
This clinic offers complete small animal veterinary services and overnight boarding. The boarding fee is $12 per night.
Open 9 A.M.–5 P.M., Monday to Friday; 9:30 A.M.–12 P.M., Saturday.

LOST AND FOUND (ANIMAL SHELTERS)

Friends of The Animal Shelter
P.O. Box 3412, Ashland, 541-772-5600

Oregon Coast

*T*he Oregon Coast stretches over 360 miles from Astoria at the mouth of the Columbia River to Brookings on the California border. This magical stretch of coast with its dunes, coastal cliffs, headlands, waterfalls, and tide pools, is a wonderland of fun for you and your dog. There are more than eighty state parks along the Oregon Coast, and national forest land covers a majority of the Coast Range.

The only thoroughfare on the Oregon Coast is U.S. Highway 101. This windy road hugs the coastline from Astoria to Brookings, with only two inland jaunts, and offers plenty of opportunities to stop and enjoy spectacular ocean vistas from its many roadside viewpoints. You and your dog can hike on endless sandy beaches, walk through old-growth forests, stand under beautiful waterfalls, explore amazing estuaries, and wander forever through some of the world's largest continuous sand dunes, the Oregon Dunes National Recreation Area on the South Coast. If your pooch loves to paddle, the Oregon Coast has dozens of rivers, creeks, freshwater lakes, and bays that offer spectacular scenery and wildlife.

Tired of all this nature? Check out the tourist scene in the many dog-friendly coastal towns. For hiking gear, treats, or food for your pooch, stop by Brim's Farm and Garden (34963 Business Highway 101) in Astoria, Paws on the Sand (1640 NE Highway 101) in Lincoln City, Pet Project (195 NW Highway 101) in Waldport, or For Pet's Sake, (16340 Lower Harbor Rd.) in Brookings.

In Oregon, all the beaches—every last mile of them—are open to the public. Oregon State Parks, the U.S. Forest Service, and the BLM manage the beaches and forests along the Oregon Coast. In general, these entities require that your dog be leashed in established recreation areas (such as campgrounds, boat ramps, picnic areas, and most established trails). The BLM states, "Dogs are required to be on leash in trails within developed recreation sites. On trails not associated with developed recreation sites, voice command is acceptable, although leash control would be preferable." The majority of city officials in coastal towns told me that dogs are to be leashed in all public areas within city limits.

In only a few places are dogs totally verboten: Cascade Head (north of Lincoln City), Shore Acres State Park (southwest of Coos Bay), and Yaquina Head Outstanding Natural Area in Newport. Also, some trails and beaches are restricted during certain times of year to protect the endangered snowy plover and other sensitive wildlife.

A Word About Weather

Be prepared for wet weather; the Oregon Coast records the highest rainfalls in Oregon. Astoria and Newport receive an annual rainfall of over 80 inches, and Brookings, nicknamed "the banana belt of the Oregon Coast" for its often warm and sunny weather, comes in with an average rainfall of only about ten inches less.

Coastal temperatures range from the low to mid-60s in summer with occasional days in the mid-70s and, rarely, the low 80s. In winter, expect temperatures in the 40s and 50s. The weather on the coast can change in a moment—it can be sunny and bright, cloudy and foggy, rainy and windy, or a combination of the above. Always carry a rain jacket and insulating layers such as polar fleece or a wool sweater as well as sturdy, waterproof shoes and insulating socks. Short-coated dogs will appreciate a waterproof coat with an insulating layer (see Gearing Up Your Pup in the Appendix for dog gear companies).

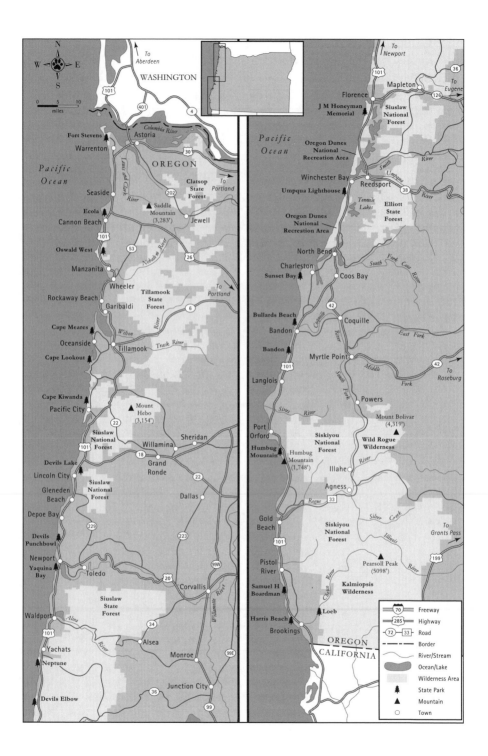

North Coast

PAW-APPROVED HIKES AND PARKS

The hikes and parks in this section are listed in geographical order from north to south.

Astoria

Riverfront Promenade
Contact: Astoria/ Warrenton Chamber of Commerce, 111 W. Marine Dr., Astoria, OR 97103, 1-800-875-6807
Paw-Approval Rating: 3 paws
Leashes Required? Yes
Length: 2.8 miles
Difficulty: Easy
Fees/Permits: None
Season: Year-round
Getting There: Access the promenade from Highway 30 in downtown Astoria by turning north on 17th St.
Description: This 2.8-mile stroll takes you and your faithful friend along the historic Astoria waterfront, passing canneries, shops, and restaurants, and providing outstanding views of the Columbia River. From the 17th St. access point, you can walk west 1.7 miles or east 1.1 miles.

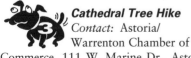

Cathedral Tree Hike
Contact: Astoria/ Warrenton Chamber of Commerce, 111 W. Marine Dr., Astoria, OR 97103, 1-800-875-6807
Paw-Approval Rating: 3 paws
Leashes Required? Yes
Length: 1-mile out and back
Difficulty: Easy
Fees/Permits: None
Season: Year-round
Getting There: From Highway 30 in downtown Astoria, turn south on 16th St. toward the Astoria Column. Continue to the intersection with Irving St. Turn left (east) on Irving St. and park along roadside at 28th St.
Description: This 1-mile round-trip hike provides a great opportunity to take a break from your travels. You'll walk through an impressive coastal forest to a 300-year-old Sitka spruce called the Cathedral Tree.

Fort Stevens State Park
Contact: Oregon State Parks and Recreation, Suite 1, 1115 Commercial St. NE, Salem, OR 97301-1002, 1-800-551-6949, www.oregonstateparks. org
Paw-Approval Rating: 3 paws
Leashes Required? Yes
Fees/Permits: $3 day-use permit required
Season: Year-round
Getting There: From Highway 101/Highway 30 in Astoria, head south on Highway 101 approximately 2.5 miles and turn right (west) onto East Harbor Dr. Drive about 4.5 miles on East Harbor Dr. to Hammond. From Hammond, go south about a mile on Lake Dr. to the state park.
Description: This 3,763-acre park features shallow lakes, wetlands, coastal forest, and sandy beaches. You and your best friend can spend the whole day exploring its 6 miles of hiking trails. For starters, try the 2-mile walk around Coffenbury Lake, a popular lake for canoeing and kayaking.

Option: Another interesting walk is a 1-mile trail from the campground (see *Campgrounds*) to a long, sandy beach where rests the wreck of the *Peter Iredale.* This four-masted British freighter ran aground here on Clatsop Spit in a rough storm in 1906. You and your dog may also want to explore the abandoned gun batteries of the Fort Stevens Military Reservation, which guarded the mouth of the Columbia River from the Civil War until World War II.

Seaside

Del Rey Beach State Recreation Site

Contact: Oregon State Parks and Recreation, Suite 1, 1115 Commercial St. NE, Salem, OR 97301-1002, 503-636-9886 or 1-800-551-6949, www.oregon stateparks.org
Paw-Approval Rating: 2 paws
Leashes Required? Yes
Fees/Permits: None
Season: Year-round
Getting There: Del Rey Beach is located 2 miles north of Gearhart off Highway 101.
Description: You'll find a flat, sandy beach at this day-use site. You and your dog can frolic in the surf or explore the beach to your heart's content.

Seaside Promenade

Contact: Seaside Visitor Bureau, 7 N. Roosevelt, Seaside, OR, 1-888-306-2326
Paw-Approval Rating: 2 paws
Leashes Required? Yes
Fees/Permits: None
Season: Year-round
Getting There: From Highway 101, turn west on A St. in downtown Seaside and head west until you reach Prom St. and the boardwalk.
Description: Seaside's Promenade is a well-known concrete boardwalk that parallels a long sandy beach in downtown Seaside, and has outstanding views of the crashing waves of the Pacific Ocean. This 1.5-mile-long boardwalk is popular with humans and canines alike. After cruising the boardwalk, head to the beach for a run, a game of Frisbee, or fetch.

Cannon Beach

Ecola State Park to Indian Beach Hike

Contact: Oregon State Parks and Recreation, Suite 1, 1115 Commercial St. NE, Salem, OR 97301-1002, 503-636-9886 or 1-800-551-6949, www.oregon stateparks.org
Paw-Approval Rating: 4 paws
Leashes Required? Yes
Length: 3 miles out and back
Difficulty: Easy
Fees/Permits: $3 day-use fee
Season: Year-round
Getting There: From Highway 101 at the north end of Cannon Beach, exit west at the Ecola State Park sign. Travel about 0.25 miles and turn right at a small sign for the park. Go 2.3 miles on a narrow, windy road to a large parking area and the trailhead.
Description: Look for a small trailhead sign on the north side of the parking lot. Pick up the singletrack trail as it winds through a thick coastal forest. Mossy logs and a fern-filled understory create a mystical quality on this beautiful trail. As the route heads north toward Indian Beach, you and your dog will pass cliffside viewpoints that offer premier views of the Pacific. At 1.5 miles, you'll arrive at a trail fork. The left fork will take you to secluded Indian Beach (your turnaround point). Walk along the rocky beach and watch the boogie boarders and surfers catching waves offshore. From here, retrace the same route to the trailhead for a total of 3 miles.

Haystack Rock at Cannon Beach Hike

Contact: Cannon Beach Chamber of Commerce, 207 N. Spruce

St., Cannon Beach, OR 97110, 503-436-2623, www.cannonbeach.org
Paw-Approval Rating: 4 paws
Leashes Required? Yes and No (see *You be the Judge* below)
Length: 4.4 miles out and back
Difficulty: Easy
Fees/Permits: None
Season: Year-round
Getting There: Head about 73 miles west of Portland on Highway 26 to the intersection with Highway 101. Turn south on Highway 101 and take the first Cannon Beach exit. Drive south through downtown Cannon Beach to a public parking area at the intersection of 2nd St. and Spruce St.
Description: This well known North Coast beach trek promises fresh Pacific air, a pristine sandy beach, and spectacular views of Haystack Rock and the ocean. Your canine will also make new friends with the many dogs who frequent this beach.

To get to the beach from the public parking area, turn left on Spruce St. At 0.1 mile, turn left on 1st St. At 0.2 mile, cross Hemlock St. and continue west toward the beach. Cross Laurel St. and then pick up the sandy path to the beach. Once you reach the beach, turn left (south) and enjoy an easy trek on the long, flat, sandy beach. Play in the surf, let your dog chase sticks, or enjoy a game of Frisbee. At 1.1 miles, pass 235-foot Haystack Rock on your right. This dramatic rock formation is the basalt remnant of volcanic eruptions 17 million years ago. It is also part of the Oregon Islands Wildlife Refuge and is an important nesting site for puffins, pelagic cormorants, pigeon guillemots, and Western gulls. At its base are tide pools filled with colorful creatures like sea anemones, starfish, mussels, and hermit crabs. Keep heading south until you reach Tolovana Wayside at 2 miles. This is your turnaround point. Retrace the route back to your starting point for a total of 4 miles.
You be the Judge: The Cannon Beach municipal code states that dogs don't have

to be leashed as long as they are under voice control. State park law conflicts with this municipal code and requires that dogs be leashed. The Cannon Beach police department told me that police do not cite dog owners for having their dog off leash on the beach. They cite owners only when someone has made an official complaint about their dog. So you'll most likely see many dogs on Cannon Beach that are not on a leash.

Saddle Mountain State Park Hike

Contact: Oregon State Parks and Recreation, Suite 1, 1115 Commercial St. NE, Salem, OR 97301-1002, 1-800-551-6949, www.oregonstateparks.org
Paw-Approval Rating: 3 paws
Leashes Required? Yes
Length: 5.2 miles out and back
Difficulty: Difficult
Fees/Permits: None
Season: April through October
Getting There: From Cannon Beach, drive 10 miles east (or 65 miles west of Portland) on Highway 26 to the signed entrance for Saddle Mountain State Park. Turn north onto Saddle Mountain Road and continue to the road's end and campground.
Description: This very strenuous hike climbs 1,620 feet and takes you and your pooch to the summit of 3,283-foot Saddle Mountain—the highest point in the northern Coast Range. The route takes you through a thick alder forest that soon turns to Douglas fir. Near the summit, the landscape becomes open and tundralike, and is dotted with wildflowers. From the summit, you'll have expansive views of Nehalem Bay to the southwest, the Columbia River to the northwest, and the snow capped peaks of Mount Hood and Mount Jefferson to the east. This hike is brutally steep, with some precipitous drops, and is recommended only for experienced trail hounds. This park has a campground if you want to stay overnight (see *Campgrounds*).

Tolovana Beach State Recreation Site

Contact: Oregon State Parks and Recreation, Suite 1, 1115 Commercial St. NE, Salem, OR 97301-1002, 1-800-551-6949, www.oregonstateparks.org

Paw-Approval Rating: 2 paws

Leashes Required? Yes

Fees/Permits: None

Season: Year-round

Getting There: Tolovana Beach is 1 mile south of Cannon Beach off Highway 101.

Description: Tolovana Beach is a flat, sandy beach, ideal for ocean views and Frisbee. If you walk north, you'll get close up views of Haystack Rock (see the *Haystack Rock* hike). Walk south, and you'll find another large coastal rock just offshore, Tunnel Rock, whose tide pools lead into a tunnel that is accessible at extreme low tides. Water and restrooms are available.

Hug Point State Recreation Site

Contact: Oregon State Parks and Recreation, Suite 1, 1115 Commercial St. NE, Salem, OR 97301-1002, 1-800-551-6949, www.oregonstateparks.org

Paw-Approval Rating: 3 paws

Leashes Required? Yes

Fees/Permits: None

Season: Year-round

Getting There: Hug Point is 5 miles south of Cannon Beach off Highway 101.

Description: The beach at Hug Point State Recreation Site is an historic wagon route. Settlers had to "hug" closely to the headland to get around the point at low tide. Hug Point is a pretty beachside cove with two sea caves and a waterfall to explore. If you and your pup feel adventurous, head north on the Oregon Coast Trail 5.2 miles to Third St. in Cannon Beach. If you do, make sure you time the trip for low tide, or you will be stuck at several of the headlands. Local stores and newspapers provide tide information.

Water and restrooms are available at the trailhead.

Oswald West State Park

Contact: Oregon State Parks and Recreation, Suite 1, 1115 Commercial St. NE, Salem, OR 97301-1002, 503-636-9886 or 1-800-551-6949, www.oregonstateparks.org

Paw-Approval Rating: 4 paws

Leashes Required? Yes

Fees/Permits: None

Season: Year-round

Getting There: Drive 10 miles south of Cannon Beach on Highway 101. There are two parking areas—one on the east side of the highway and the other on the west.

Description: This 2,474-acre state park offers breathtaking scenery and many hiking opportunities. Arch Cape, Neahkahnie Mountain, Cape Falcon, and Smuggler's Cove are all located in this park. You and your best friend can camp here but will need to haul your gear to the campground in wheelbarrows and doggie packs (see *Campgrounds*). A 1-mile out and back hiking trail leads to beautiful Short Sands Beach. This beach is nestled in a sheltered cove and is a popular surfing and boogie boarding spot. The Oregon Coast Trail passes through the park; if you head north

Summit views on Neahkahnie Mountain. Photograph by Ken Skeen

on it, you and your dog can hike the 5-mile out and back trail to Cape Falcon with its dizzying views. Or hike south on the Oregon Coast Trail and take a strenuous 7.2-mile round trip trek to the summit of Neahkahnie Mountain. The ocean views from the summit are spectacular.

Manzanita

 ### Nehalem Bay State Park
Contact: Oregon State Parks and Recreation, Suite 1, 1115 Commercial St. NE, Salem, OR 97301-1002, 1-800-551-6949, www.oregonstateparks.org
Paw-Approval Rating: 3 paws
Leashes Required? Yes
Fees/Permits: $3 day-use fee
Season: Year-round
Getting There: From Manzanita, travel 3 miles south on Highway 101 to Carey St. Turn west onto Carey St. and go 1.5 miles to the park entrance.
Description: Your furry friend will love this 890-acre state park, located on a sand spit between Nehalem Bay and the Pacific Ocean. This park features a large campground (see *Campgrounds*) where you and your buddy can set up base camp for a few days-worth of exploring. On one side of the campground is scenic Nehalem Bay and on the other are sand dunes that lead to a 4-mile-long sandy beach that extends to the end of the Nehalem Bay spit. The bay is popular for canoeing and kayaking; rentals are available in nearby Wheeler. You can walk on the 1.5-mile paved path that winds through open dunes adjacent to the bay. While on this path, you and your best friend may see deer, elk, and other wildlife. If you trek along the bay beachfront, you can enjoy prime bird and seal watching.

Tillamook

 ### Cape Meares State Park
Contact: Oregon State Parks and Recreation, Suite 1,
1115 Commercial St. NE, Salem, OR 97301-1002, 1-800-551-6949, www.oregonstateparks.org
Paw-Approval Rating: 4 paws
Leashes Required? Yes
Fees/Permits: None
Season: Year-round
Getting There: From Highway 101 in Tillamook, follow signs for the Three Capes Scenic Highway. Head 10 miles west on the Three Capes Scenic Highway to the Cape Meares State Park sign on the west side of the highway.
Description: A good place to start your tour of this 233-acre park is the 0.4-mile out and back Cape Meares Lighthouse Trail. Viewpoints along this trail let you peek at large colonies of seabirds nesting on the surrounding 200-foot rocky cliffs. After checking out the 40-foot-tall lighthouse, head back to the parking lot and pick up the 0.2-mile out and back path to the oddly shaped Octopus Tree. To view a 400-year-old Sitka spruce, head back out to the park's entrance and park on the north side of the road in a dirt pullout that is the starting point for the 0.4-mile out and back Big Spruce Tree Trail.

 ### Oceanside Beach State Recreation Site
Contact: Oregon State Parks and Recreation, Suite 1, 1115 Commercial St. NE, Salem, OR 97301-1002, 1-800-551-6949, www.oregonstateparks.org
Paw-Approval Rating: 3 paws
Leashes Required? Yes
Fees/Permits: None
Season: Year-round
Getting There: Oceanside Beach is 11 miles west of Tillamook on the Three Capes Scenic Highway.
Description: This secluded state park is next to the small town of Oceanside. You and your dog can walk on the beach and enjoy spectacular views of Three Arch Rocks located a half mile offshore, as well as watch surfers and kayakers playing in the waves.

Cape Lookout Hike

Contact: Oregon State Parks and Recreation, Suite 1, 1115 Commercial St. NE, Salem, OR 97301-1002, 1-800-551-6949, www.oregonstateparks.org
Paw-Approval Rating: 3 paws
Leashes Required? Yes
Length: 5.4 miles out and back
Difficulty: Moderate
Fees/Permits: $3 day-use fee
Season: Year-round. This trail can be muddy during winter.
Getting There: From Highway 101 in Tillamook head 15.5 miles southwest on the Three Capes Scenic Highway to the signed trailhead on the right side of the highway.
Description: Take a ramble through coastal woodlands to a viewpoint at the tip of Cape Lookout on this trail in 2,000-acre Cape Lookout State Park. Along the way, you'll pass spectacular viewpoints of Cape Meares to the north and Cape Kiwanda to the south. When you reach the tip of the cape, your turnaround point, you'll have a grand view of the Pacific Ocean. This is a great vantage point to spot gray whales on their annual migration. There are some steep drop-offs on this trail. Make sure your dog is leashed at all times. Rest up and head back on the same trail as it ascends 400 feet back to the trailhead.

Munson Creek Falls Hike

Contact: Oregon State Parks and Recreation, Suite 1, 1115 Commercial St. NE, Salem, OR 97301-1002, 1-800-551-6949, www.oregonstateparks.org
Paw-Approval Rating: 3 paws
Leashes Required? Yes
Length: 0.6-mile out and back
Difficulty: Easy
Fees/Permits: None
Season: Year-round
Getting There: From the intersection of the Three Capes Scenic Highway and Highway 101 in Tillamook, drive 7.4 miles south on Highway 101 to the signed Munson Falls State Natural Area turnoff on the left side of the road. Turn left and go 1.5 miles to a circular parking lot and the trailhead.
Description: This short but sweet old-growth forest path parallels Munson Creek to the base of 266-foot Munson Creek Falls. Enjoy the views and then head back to your starting point.

Pacific City

Cape Kiwanda State Natural Area

Contact: Oregon State Parks and Recreation, Suite 1, 1115 Commercial St. NE, Salem, OR 97301-1002, 1-800-551-6949, www.oregonstateparks.org
Paw-Approval Rating: 4 paws
Leashes Required? Yes
Fees/Permits: None
Season: Year-round
Getting There: From the intersection of Oregon 18 and Highway 101 in Lincoln City, turn north on Highway 101. Travel 14.6 miles north and turn left (west) on Brooten Road where a sign states "Cape Kiwanda Recreation Area/Pacific City."

A moment of quiet reflection at Cape Kiwanda Beach.

Go 2.8 miles west on Brooten Road and then turn left on Pacific Ave. toward Netarts/Oceanside. Drive 0.3 mile on Pacific Ave. and then turn right on Kiwanda Dr. Go 1 mile and then turn left into the Cape Kiwanda public parking area adjacent to the Pelican Pub and Brewery Restaurant.

From Tillamook travel 25 miles south on Highway 101 and turn right (west) on Brooten Road where a sign states "Cape Kiwanda Recreation Area/Pacific City." Follow the rest of the directions given for Lincoln City in the preceding paragraph.

Description: Your dog will love the sandy beach and gorgeous sand dune at this state natural area. For starters, head north from the parking area and climb to the top of Cape Kiwanda sand dune. From there, you'll have a spectacular ocean view, north and south, as well as views of Haystack Rock, located about a mile offshore. After you catch your breath, you and your pooch will have a grand time running down the dune.

For a longer trek, turn left (south) on to the beach from the parking lot and walk over four miles to the tip of Nestucca Spit. (Be sure to plan this beach trek at low tide.) You may see dory boats being launched in the surf and boogie boarders and surfers catching waves. After your beach adventure, you and your pup can relax on the outdoor patio at the Pelican Brew Pub and enjoy some handcrafted microbrews and great seafood.

Lincoln City

Neskowin Beach State Recreation Site
Contact: Oregon State Parks and Recreation, Suite 1, 1115 Commercial St. NE, Salem, OR 97301-1002, 1-800-551-6949, www.oregonstateparks.org
Paw-Approval Rating: 4 paws
Leashes Required? No
Length: 1.8-miles out and back
Difficulty: Easy
Fees/Permits: None

Having fun at Short Sands Beach.

Season: Year-round
Getting There: From Tillamook, travel 28.5 miles south on Highway 101 (or about 10 miles north of Lincoln City) to the junction with Winema Road. Turn right (west) on Winema Road and go 0.6 mile to the road's end at a beach access sign.
Description: From the trailhead access point, walk north (right) on the long, flat, sandy beach. Look for small mollusk and crab shells while Rover runs in the surf. After 0.4 mile you'll arrive at a large stack of sandstone rocks covered with barnacles. Walk through a narrow passage between the rocks and continue your trek north on the endless beach scattered with driftwood. Watch for brown pelicans fishing offshore and listen for the sharp cry of gulls. At 0.9 mile, arrive at the mouth of the Nestucca River where you may see seals lounging on its sandy shores. This is your turnaround point. Return on the same route back to your starting point.

Roads End State Recreation Area
Contact: Oregon State Parks and Recreation, Suite 1, 1115 Commercial St. NE, Salem, OR 97301-1002, 1-800-551-6949, www.oregonstateparks.org
Paw-Approval Rating: 2 paws

215

Leashes Required? Yes

Fees/Permits: None

Season: Year-round

Getting There: From the intersection of Highway 101 and Oregon 18 in Lincoln City, travel 2.7 miles south on Highway 101 to Logan Road. Continue on Logan Road approximately 1 mile to the parking area.

Description: Play with your pooch at this sheltered beach adjacent to Cascade Head.

Drift Creek Falls Hike

Contact: Siuslaw National Forest, Hebo Ranger District, P.O. Box 235, Hebo, OR 97122, 503-392-3161, www.oregoncoast.com

Paw-Approval Rating: 4 paws

Leashes Required? Yes

Season: Year-round

Length: 3 miles out and back

Difficulty: Easy

Fees/Permits: $5 Northwest Forest Pass. Purchase at 1-800-270-7504 or www.naturenw.org

Getting There: From Highway 101 just past milepost 119 in Lincoln City, turn left (east) on Drift Creek Road. Go 1.6 miles on Drift Creek Road to the junction with South Drift Creek Road and turn right. Go 0.4 mile and turn left on Drift Creek Camp Road. Continue 0.9 mile to another road junction signed for the Drift Creek Falls Trail and turn left. Continue about 9.8 miles (following signs to the Drift Creek Falls Trail) to a parking area on the right side of the road.

Description: This well graded trail descends 340 feet through a fern-filled forest for about a mile and then crosses a creek. After 1.3 miles, hang on tightly to your pal as you cross a high suspension bridge over Drift Creek. From the bridge you'll have a grand view of pretty Drift Creek Falls. After crossing the bridge, continue another 0.2 mile to the base of the falls and your turnaround point. Retrace the route back to the trailhead.

Gleneden Beach State Recreation Site

Contact: Oregon State Parks and Recreation, Suite 1, 1115 Commercial St. NE, Salem, OR 97301-1002, 1-800-551-6949, www.oregonstateparks.org

Paw-Approval Rating: 2 paws

Leashes Required? Yes

Fees/Permits: None

Season: Year-round

Getting There: Gleneden Beach is 7 miles south of Lincoln City off Highway 101. Follow Gleneden Beach State Park signs to the parking area.

Description: This beach is a great place to picnic with your pup and play on the beach. You may see sea lions, surfers, and boogie borders in the surf.

Depoe Bay

Fogarty Creek State Recreation Area

Contact: Oregon State Parks and Recreation, Suite 1, 1115 Commercial St. NE, Salem, OR 97301-1002, 1-800-551-6949, www.oregonstateparks.org

Paw-Approval Rating: 3 paws

Leashes Required? Yes

Fees/Permits: $3 day-use fee

Season: Year-round

Getting There: Fogarty Creek is 2 miles north of Depoe Bay off Highway 101.

Description: Your pal will have fun playing in Fogarty Creek as it runs out of the forest and into the ocean. Picnic tables are scattered across a grassy lawn bordered by a forest of western hemlock, Sitka spruce, and shore pine. A trail leads down to the beach, where you and your dog can wade in the cool Oregon surf.

CYCLING FOR CANINES

Mary's Peak

Contact: Waldport Ranger District, 1094 SW Pacific Highway, Waldport, OR 97394, 541-563-3211, www.fs.fed.us

Paw-Approval Rating: 3 paws
Leashes Required? No
Length: 13 miles out and back
Difficulty: Difficult
Fees/Permits: None
Season: Mid-May through October
Getting There: From Corvallis, drive west on U.S. Highway 20/OR 34 to Philomath. Go through Philomath and stay on Highway 20 toward Toledo/Newport. A mile after you cross Mary's River, turn left on Forest Road 2005 (Woods Creek Road). Travel on Woods Creek Road approximately 7.4 miles. At the intersection of Forest Road 112, park in the pullout on the left.
Description: This demanding singletrack and gravel road route takes you and your pedaling quadruped on a 2,700-foot climb to the summit of Mary's Peak. Begin by going around a gate and pedaling up Forest Road 2005. After about 3.5 miles, you'll reach another gate. Ride around it, and then bear right onto East Ridge Trail. At the next intersection bear left, continuing on East Ridge Trail. Eventually, East Ridge Trail intersects with a gravel road. Turn left on the gravel road and ride to the summit of Mary's Peak. Retrace the route back to the trailhead.

PADDLEHOUNDS

Coffenbury Lake at
Fort Stevens State Park
Contact: Oregon State Parks and Recreation, Suite 1, 1115 Commercial St. NE, Salem OR 97301-1002, 1-800-551-6949, www.oregonstateparks.org
Fees/Permits: $3 day-use fee
Getting There: From Astoria, head south on Highway 101 to Warrenton. From Warrenton, follow signs about 5.5 miles to the state park and lake.
Description: Located in Fort Stevens State Park, 50-acre, freshwater Coffenbury Lake has an average depth of 9 feet and offers leisurely paddling on those dog day afternoons.

OTHER PLACES
TO HOUND AROUND

Cannon Beach

Grain & Sand Baking
1064 S. Hemlock, 503-436-0120
This European style baker features hearty breads and baguettes, croissants, pastries and rich desserts. Since Rover can't come in, order lunch to go—select from quiches, tarts, and homemade soups. For a caffeine jolt, try the espresso bar or the large selection of specialty teas.

Manzanita

Manzanita News and Espresso
500 Laneda, 503-368-7450
This great coffee shop features coffee by the Portland Roasting Company, and cookies, muffins, scones, and other treats. Even better are the 450 magazines for sale here. Hang out with your friend on the outdoor patio while you sip your coffee. This shop is just blocks from a long, sandy beach where you can work off your caffeine buzz.

CANINE COMFORT
ACCOMMODATIONS
Towns in this section are listed geographically, from north to south. Unless otherwise stated, dogs should not be left unattended in the room and must be leashed on hotel property.

Astoria

$-$$ Lamplighter Motel
131 West Marine Dr., 1-800-845-8847, www.lamplighter.com
This motel features 29 dog-friendly rooms furnished with a refrigerator, microwave, and TV. Behind the hotel is a grassy area where you can walk your dog. The Lamplighter is close to many city and state parks.

Dog Policy

A fee of $5 per dog is charged; only one dog per room.

$$-$$$ Astoria Red Lion Inn

400 Industry St., 503-325-7373 or 1-800-RED-LION, www.redlion.com

Dog-friendly rooms at this hotel have private balconies overlooking the Columbia River or the marina, and feature telephone data ports, irons and ironing boards, coffeemakers, microwaves, and refrigerators.

Dog Policy

The hotel charges $10 per dog per day. Dogs can be left unattended in rooms if they are crated.

$$-$$$ Shilo Inn Warrenton/Astoria

1609 E. Harbor Dr., 503-861-2181 or 1-800-222-2244, www.shiloinns.com

Mark Hemstreet, owner of this hotel chain, said, "We understand that pets are a part of your family, and should be included in your travel plans." All rooms are mini-suites with a microwave, refrigerator, hair dryer, ironing unit, and data ports. Smoking and non-smoking units are available, with king beds or two queen beds and kitchenettes. The hotel also has a heated indoor pool, spa, sauna, and twenty-four hour fitness center. Trails in Fort Stevens State Park and ocean beaches are nearby.

Dog Policy

A $10 fee per dog per night is charged.

Seaside

$-$$ Motel 6

2369 S. Roosevelt/Highway 101, 503-738-6269

This clean, pet-friendly motel is four blocks from the beachside promenade and other downtown Seaside activities.

Dog Policy

No extra fees are charged for your dog.

$-$$$$ Best Western Ocean View Resort

414 North Prom, 1-800-234-8439, www.oceanviewresort.com

The hotel is on Seaside's famous mile-long promenade, a great place for a dog walk, as is the wide sandy beach in front of the hotel. The hotel has 104 spacious guest rooms (nineteen of which are dog-friendly), an award-winning restaurant, cozy fireplace lounge, indoor pool and spa, and meeting and banquet facilities. The nineteen dog-friendly rooms are on the hotel's first floor; eleven have an oceanfront view, and four are wheelchair accessible. The resort is an easy walk to Seaside's shops, eateries, and arcades. Factory Outlet Shopping is eight blocks away. Guest rooms feature views of the Pacific Ocean or the Coast Range, complimentary in-room coffee, color remote TV/VCR (videos are available for rent), hair dryer, iron and ironing board, voice mail, and data ports. Most rooms have a kitchenette, gas fireplace, and private balcony, and some have a Jacuzzi with an ocean view.

Dog Policy

There is a pet fee of $15 per night as well as a one-time fee of $15 per dog.

$$-$$$$ Comfort Inn

545 Broadway, 503-738-3011

This hotel is on the Necanicum River three blocks from the beach. The majority of its 65 dog-friendly rooms have balconies or patios overlooking the river. All rooms have a coffeemaker, and you can rent a VCR to watch movies. Rooms with a spa and Jacuzzi are available. Other amenities are a twenty-four hour pool, spa, and sauna. Fresh baked cookies are available in the evening and the hotel has treats for your best friend! A breakfast of fresh bagels and cream cheese, muffins, fruit, toast, hot and cold cereal, coffee, and juice is served every morning.

Dog Policy

You can leave your dog in a room alone as long as he is well behaved.

Cannon Beach

$-$$$$ McBee Hotel Cottages

539 S. Hemlock St., P.O. Box 943, 503-436-2569

Old-fashioned cottages range from simple guest rooms to suites with kitchen and fireplace. Additional amenities include a coffeemaker, refrigerator, and cable TV. The cottages are just blocks from the beach and Cannon Beach shops.

Dog Policy

The motel charges $5 per night per dog.

$$-$$$ Cannon Beach
Ecola Creek Lodge

208 5th St., 503-436-2776 or 1-800-873-2749, www.cannonbeachlodge.com

This quiet lodge is located on the north end of Cannon Beach within easy walking distance to the beach and downtown shops. The property is landscaped with grassy lawns, flower gardens, fountains, and a lily pond. This non-smoking lodge has one and two bedroom apartments with a living room, gas fireplace, TV, VCR and full kitchen. Suites and guest rooms are also available.

Dog Policy

A $10 fee is charged per night per dog.

$$-$$$ Haystack Resort

3339 S. Hemlock St., 503-436-1577 or 1-800-499-2220, www.haystackresort.com

This dog-friendly hotel is in south Cannon Beach, one block from the beach and features rooms with an ocean view, balcony, gas fireplace, TV/VCR, HBO, and some with kitchen suites. In addition, you'll receive complimentary coffee and a daily newspaper delivered to your door. The resort also has an indoor heated pool and spa.

Dog Policy

The hotel charges $10 per dog per night.

$$-$$$$ Surfsand Resort

148 W. Gower, P.O. Box 219, 1-800-547-6100, www.surfsand.com

The Surfsand Resort was built in 1966 and operated by the original owner until 1979. With its rooms in disarray and full of sand, cabinet doors coming off the hinges, and the pool with a large hole in it, Jan and Steve Martin purchased the resort in 1979. A policy of no pets was implemented. The first night, three rooms were rented and fifteen potential guests were lost. It was then the Martins realized the importance of family and the necessity of a family-friendly resort. (We all know that a family is not a family without pets and children!) The Surfsand Resort offers views of Haystack Rock and the Pacific from oceanfront and ocean-view rooms. Continually renovated, its 73 rooms are ideally suited to fit pet traveler needs. The hotel also hosts the annual Dog Show on the Beach, co-sponsored by NUTRO food products, with proceeds going to local animal shelters and charities. (See *Dog Events* for more information.) Your dog is a part of the family; when you check in, he gets a bag of doggie treats.

Dog Policy

The hotel charges $12 per night per dog.

$$$-$$$$ Tolovana Inn

3400 S. Hemlock St., 503-436-2211 or 1-800-333-8890

This oceanside inn offers spacious studios and one and two bedroom suites with living room, full kitchen, dining room set, fireplace, and private balcony. Additional amenities include a spa, sauna, indoor heated pool, on-site Laundromat, on-site masseuse, fitness center, and game room. Your pooch will appreciate the fact that this hotel is just a short walk from the beach.

Dog Policy

A $10 fee per night per dog is charged.

$$$$ Hallmark Resort

1400 S. Hemlock, 503-436-1566 or 1-888-448-4449, www.hallmarkinns.com

This high-end resort features many rooms with ocean views; some are furnished with fireplace, in-room hot tub, kitchenette, and refrigerator. Additional amenities include an exercise area, two pools, a hot tub, a dry sauna, laundry facilities, and business services.

Dog Policy

The hotel charges $12 per night per dog.

$$$$ The Guest House Motel

1016 S. Hemlock, 503-436-0630 or 1-800-585-0630, www.cannon-beach.net

This motel offers two lodging styles that welcome you and your canine. You can rent a four bedroom, two-bath house that sleeps eight to ten, with a family room, gas burning stove, a fully equipped kitchen, and cable TV/VCR. Or check out "The Cottage," which features a double Jacuzzi, gas-burning fireplace, fully equipped kitchen, queen bed, and double rollaway bed. These accommodations are within walking distance of Cannon Beach and shops.

Dog Policy

A $10 nightly fee per dog is charged for the house-style lodging, and a $5 nightly fee per dog is charged for "The Cottage."

Garibaldi

$$ Bayshore Inn

227 Garibaldi Ave., 503-322-2552 or 1-877-537-2121

This hotel features comfortable air-conditioned rooms with microwave, refrigerator, TV, and queen beds.

Dog Policy

A one-time pet fee of $7 is charged.

Tillamook

$$ Western Royal Inn

1125 N. Main (Highway 101), 503-842-8844 or 1-800-624-2912

Dog Policy

The inn charges a $10 a night pet fee.

$$-$$$ Shilo Inn

2515 N. Main St., 503-842-7971, or 1-800-222-2244, www.shiloinns.com

This hotel is on the banks of the Wilson River not far from the Tillamook Cheese Factory. It features rooms with mini-suites with refrigerator, microwave, wet bar, coffeemaker, hair dryer, iron and ironing board, cable TV with free ShowTime, twenty-four hour indoor pool, spa, sauna, steam room and fitness center.

Dog Policy

The hotel charges $10 per dog per night.

Netarts

$-$$ The Terimore

Lodging By the Sea, 5105 Crab Ave., P.O. Box 250, 97143, 503-842-4623, www.oregoncoast.com/Terimore

Ben and Priscilla Nimez, owners of the Terimore, said, "This hotel is an ideal place to come with your pet. We are located at the end of a dead-end street, overlooking the mouth of pristine Netarts Bay and the Pacific Ocean. There are approximately two miles of sandy beach for dogs and their human companions to enjoy. We have lodged dogs of all sizes, pot bellied pigs, cats, and even an iguana." Twelve units are pet-friendly. Some have kitchens, fireplaces, and ocean views. Attractions nearby include Cape Meares State Park (6 miles north) and Cape Lookout State Park and lighthouse (6 miles south).

Dog Policy

A $7 fee per dog per night is charged; $10 for two dogs. Only two dogs per room are allowed.

Pacific City

$-$$ Anchorage Motel

6585 Pacific Ave., 503-965-6773 or 1-800-941-6250

This pet-friendly motel is on a quiet residential street four blocks from the beach. It features cottage style suites with a kitchen and separate living room, as well as smaller rooms with kitchens.

Dog Policy

The motel charges $3 dog per night per dog.

$-$$ Inn at Pacific City

35215 Brooten Rd., 97135, 1-888-722-2489, www.innatpacificcity.com

This dog-friendly inn is five blocks from the beach in Pacific City. Complimentary coffee and tea are always available, as is a picnic area on the hotel grounds. Doug Olson, owner of the hotel, said, "While we accept dogs, cats, and most pets, our most unusual was a llama. The owner tied the llama to a tree in the back yard during a five-day stay. He then continued his journey down the coast. The Oregon Coast has quite a variety of travelers!"

Dog Policy

A $9 fee is charged per dog per night. The hotel has a pet walking area and provides you with clean-up bags at check-in. If your dog is wet and sandy from the beach, ask for towels to clean him up before you head back to your room.

$$-$$$ Inn at
Cape Kiwanda

33105 Cape Kiwanda Dr., 1-888-965-7001, www.innatcapekiwanda.com

All rooms have an ocean view, gas fireplace, full balcony with two deck chairs, mini-bar, coffeemaker with complimentary Starbucks coffee, and TV/VCR. The Nestucca Jacuzzi rooms feature a two-person tub with a view of the fireplace and the ocean. The entire facility is smoke-free; ten pet rooms are available. Nine pet rooms are Kiwanda guest rooms, and one is a Nestucca Jacuzzi room. At check-in, your dog will receive doggie

At the summit of the Cape Kiwanda Dune in Pacific City.

treats, a cozy blanket, and a letter from the house doggie, Ginger P. There is a two-night minimum stay on July and August weekends and for all legal holidays.

Other attractions are a gift shop, mountain bike rental, espresso/book shop, gallery, dory boat charter service, and day spa. The beachfront at Cape Kiwanda is alive with activities including surfing, sea kayaking, fishing, hang gliding, volleyball, and beachcombing. The Pelican Pub & Brewery is across the street from the hotel. With a 180-degree view from Cape Kiwanda to Cascade Head, the Pelican Pub invites guests to settle in and enjoy a great meal and award-winning beers.

One employee said, "Not only are we fond of dogs; one of our employees is a dog—Ginger P Doggie (middle initial P for Puppy), the Night Auditor Dog. She has been working the 11 P.M. to 7 A.M. shift for almost as long as the hotel has been here. Our human night auditor found that shift to be less lonesome with Ginger P's smiling face for company. Ginger P was adopted from an animal shelter. She has no formal education, but she has an amazing natural talent for innkeeping. She has met many guests over the years and won their hearts with her sparkling personality. Many times, guests will ask if Ginger P will be working that night. Some send her Christmas cards. She has someone read them to her (she's a senior and her eyesight isn't what it once was) while she listens solemnly but appreciatively. Ginger P doesn't do too much bookkeeping, but she has penned a chatty letter to other dogs who are checking in, letting them know her 'pet rules' and philosophy in general."

Dog Policy

There is a $15 nightly fee for each pet. The hotel has a warm outdoor shower and asks that after a day of beach adventures you rinse the sand and debris off your dog before returning to your room. Leashed dogs are allowed in any public area of the hotel.

Neskowin

$$-$$$$ The Breakers Condominiums
48060 Breakers Blvd., 503-392-3417, www.breakersoregon.com

The Breakers offers five dog-friendly rental condominiums. All are three bedroom homes with a spectacular ocean view. These homes also feature two full bathrooms, a fully equipped kitchen, fireplace with wood, TV, VCR, stereo, puzzles, games, and videos. You and your dog will enjoy long walks on the beach and the peaceful atmosphere of Neskowin. You can also shop at Paws on the Sand (see *Canine-Approved Shopping*) a local shop that caters to canines. There is a two night minimum stay except holidays when reservations for the full holiday period are required. There is also a one-week minimum stay from mid-June through mid-September.
Dog Policy
A $10 pet fee is charged for your dog.

Lincoln City

$-$$ Budget Inn Motel
1713 NW 21st St., 541-994-5281

This budget motel in downtown Lincoln City has five pet-friendly rooms and is close to many beaches.
Dog Policy
Dog fees range from $5 to $10 per night depending on the number of dogs. Dogs over 40 pounds are not permitted.

$$ Blue Heron Landing Hotel
4006 W. Devils Lake Rd., 541-994-4708

This hotel is on scenic Devils Lake in Lincoln City, and rents boats if you want to go cruising on the lake with your dog.
Dog Policy
This hotel will accept dogs less than 35 pounds. A $10 fee per night per dog is charged.

$$ Coho Inn
1635 NW Harbor Ave., 541-994-3684 or 1-800-848-7006, www.cohoinn.com

This hotel features 14 dog-friendly rooms equipped with a TV/VCR. Other amenities are a sauna and Jacuzzi.
Dog Policy
A pet fee of $7 per night is charged. Only one dog per room. Dogs must weigh less than 25 pounds.

$$ Sea Echo Motel
3510 NE Highway 101, 541-994-2575

This hotel has 12 dog-friendly rooms furnished with queen beds and cable TV.
Dog Policy
The motel charges a one-time $5 fee per dog.

$-$$$ Ester Lee Motel
3803 SW Highway 101, 1-888-996-3606, www.esterlee.com

Paul and Linda Love own this comfy motel with its 25 dog-friendly rooms. A pet walking area and miles of sandy beach are at your doorstep. Each room has a VCR, a video library, refrigerator, and coffee service; some have separate bedrooms, full kitchens, and wood-burning fireplaces. A complimentary newspaper is delivered to your doorstep each morning.
Dog Policy
A fee of $7 per dog per night is charged with a maximum of two dogs per room, and a $50 refundable cleaning deposit is required. Doggie blankets and sheets are available in each pet-friendly unit.

$-$$$$ Sea Horse Oceanfront Lodging and Vacation Rentals
2039 NW Harbor Dr., 1-1-800-662-2101, www.seahorsemotel.com

This charming inn boasts panoramic ocean views with a variety of oceanfront rooms and suites. Dogs are allowed in 34 of the 54 rooms, and 4 of 9 vacation rentals are dog-friendly. Smoking and non-smoking rooms are available. A meeting center and vacation rentals are nearby. An outdoor oceanfront spa and heated indoor pool are also available. All rooms feature a coffeemaker, TV/VCR (video rentals are available), and free local calls. Fido also receives a welcome dog cookie when you check in.

When I asked Jeanne Back, host and manager of the facility, about memorable guests and their canines (and felines) she replied, "We have many repeat doggie guests at the Sea Horse, and right up at the top is 'Queenie' who excitedly wags her tail and leads her owners to her room without the hindrance of having to know the room number. She knows it by heart. Then there is 'Corbin,' a beagle who started visiting us at about four months old. He is getting quite acquainted and is mellower after just a few months of visits (and a few welcoming doggie cookies to make him feel at home). 'Merlin' the Dalmatian sends us Christmas cards. May we also mention 'Lucky,' who rides on his human's car dash and parades around the property on a leash! He is canine at heart, even though his pedigree is feline."

Dog Policy

The hotel charges $8 per dog per night and allows only two dogs per room. Plastic bags are provided for waste pickup.

$$$-$$$$$ Shilo Inn

1501 NW 40th Place, 1-541-994-4708 or 1-800-994-4708, www.shiloinns.com

This oceanfront resort features 247 pet-friendly rooms, including 61 ocean-view suites with fireplaces and balconies. Oceanfront rooms include a microwave, refrigerator, and coffeemaker. The resort offers complimentary coffee, fruit and mints, free local phone calls and voice mail, cable TV with free ShowTime, first-run movies, and entertainment by Lodgenet. A guest Laundromat, indoor pool, spa, two saunas, a steam room, and restaurant and lounge are also available to guests.

Dog Policy

A $15 fee per night is charged for one or more dogs.

Gleneden Beach

$$$-$$$$ Westin Salishan Lodge and Golf Resort

North 7760 Highway 101, 1-888-SALIS-HAN, www.salishan.com

This beautiful resort on 750 forested acres has traditional and deluxe rooms that are dog-friendly. (Fido is not allowed in the suite rooms.) All rooms have a cozy fireplace and balcony. The resort has an 18-hole golf course, indoor recreation center with a pool, sauna and hot tub, indoor and outdoor tennis courts, and boutique shops and galleries. Annette Freed at the Salishan said, "We have a dog program that we like to think is rather unique for resorts. At check-in, the owner will receive a doggie bag that contains dog biscuits, plastic 'mess' pick-up bags, a map of the resort's trails and beaches, and information regarding local vet services. In addition, if the owner forgets the dog's blanket it's just a quick call to Service Express and a clean dog blanket is delivered. Our gift shop, Out of the Woods, stocks leashes, dog bowls, rain boots, and other accessories. Our guests and their pets have access to a private beach and nature trails on the property. Close by are miles of public beaches for romping and swimming."

Dog Policy

The pet rate is $25 per day.

Depoe Bay

$$ Inn at Arch Rock

70 NW Sunset St., 541-765-2560 or 1-800-767-1835, www.innatarchrock.com

This oceanfront inn in downtown Depoe Bay features four pet-friendly units, some with a full kitchen, stove, and coffeemaker. A deluxe continental breakfast is included.

Dog Policy

This inn accepts only well behaved dogs and may not accept unruly or very large dogs; $10 per night per dog.

CAMPGROUNDS

Campgrounds are listed geographically by city, from north to south. All campgrounds listed are leashed-dog-friendly. The only exception is that dogs are not allowed inside yurts, tepees, camper wagons, or cabins.

Astoria

Fort Stevens State Park

Contact: Oregon State Parks and Recreation, Suite 1, 1115 Commercial St. NE, Salem OR 97301-1002, 1-800-551-6949 (information), 1-800-452-5687 (reservations), www.oregonstateparks.org

Season: Year-round

Facilities: 171 full-hook-up sites, 304 electrical sites, 42 tent sites, 15 yurts, 4 group-tent areas, hiker/biker camp sites (by request), picnic tables, barbecue grills, RV dump station, hot showers and restrooms, and a playground

Getting There: From Astoria, head south on Highway 101 to Warrenton. From Warrenton, follow signs about 5.5 miles to the campground and park.

Description: This very popular wooded campground is in Oregon's third largest state park. The park encompasses 3,763 acres of beach, sand dunes, shallow lakes, and coastal forest at the mouth of the Columbia River. Expect crowds, but it is easy to get away on the many paved hiking and biking trails that crisscross the park through a thick coastal forest of western hemlock, red cedar, big leaf maple, and red alder. You and your best friend can also go canoeing or kayaking on Coffenbury Lake. The wreck of the *Peter Iredale* is a popular attraction. This four-masted British freighter was caught in a rough storm in 1906 and wrecked on Clatsop spit.

Cannon Beach

Saddle Mountain State Natural Area

Contact: Oregon State Parks and Recreation, Suite 1, 1115 Commercial St. NE, Salem OR 97301-1002, 1-800-551-6949, www.oregonstateparks.org

Season: April to November

Facilities: 10 walk-in primitive tent sites, picnic tables, barbecue grills, flush toilets, firewood, and piped water. No reservations are accepted.

Getting There: From Cannon Beach, drive 10 miles east (or 65 miles west of Portland) on Highway 26 to the signed entrance for Saddle Mountain State Park. Turn north onto Saddle Mountain Road to the road's end and campground.

Description: This wooded campground's walk-in sites fill up fast during summer. If your pooch doesn't mind hiking on a somewhat steep and precarious trail, check out the 5.2-mile out and back trek to the summit of 3,283-foot Saddle Mountain (see *Paw-Approved Hikes and Parks*). This trail is only for calm and experienced trail hounds. Due to some precipitous sections, it is not recommended for young, excitable pups who haven't earned their hiking badges.

Oswald West State Park

Contact: Oregon State Parks and Recreation, Suite 1, 1115 Commercial St. NE, Salem OR 97301-1002, 1-800-551-6949, www.oregonstateparks.org

Season: March to November

Facilities: 30 walk-in tent sites (wheelbarrows are provided to haul your camping gear to your campsite), picnic tables, barbecue grills, flush toilets, piped water. No reservations are accepted.

Getting There: Travel ten miles south of Cannon Beach on Highway 101. The campground is on the right (west) side of the highway.

Description: This campground is set in a beautiful old-growth forest of Sitka spruce, Douglas fir, and western hemlock, and sites fill up fast during the summer. Several hiking trails lead from the campground through beautiful old growth forest to the Cape Falcon overlook, the summit of Neahkahnie Mountain, and along Short

Sands Creek to Short Sands Beach. (See *Paw-Approved Hikes and Parks*)

Manzanita

Nehalem Bay State Park

Contact: Oregon State Parks and Recreation, Suite 1, 1115 Commercial St. NE, Salem, OR 97301-1002, 1-800-551-6949 (information), 1-800-452-5687 (reservations), www.oregonstateparks.org

Season: Year-round

Facilities: 6 full hook-up sites, 270 electrical sites, 16 yurts, horse camp (17 sites with corrals), hiker/biker camp sites, fly-in camp (adjacent to the air strip), ADA sites, picnic tables, barbecue grills, piped water, flush toilets, hot showers, playground, bike path, boat launch, and a RV dump station

Getting There: From Manzanita, head 3 miles south on Highway 101 to Carey St. Turn west on Carey St. and drive 1.5 miles to the park entrance and campground.

Description: Nehalem Bay State Park campground is located on a sandy spit separating the Pacific Ocean and Nehalem Bay. This is a popular campground for horse enthusiasts; your dog's sniffer may lead him to the horse trails in the park. You and your pup will also love the endless sandy beach that can be accessed from the campground. Kayaking and canoeing in Nehalem Bay is another option.

Tillamook

Cape Lookout State Park

Contact: Oregon State Parks and Recreation, Suite 1, 1115 Commercial St. NE, Salem, OR 97301-1002, 1-800-551-6949 (information), 1-800-452-5687 (reservations), www.oregonstateparks.org

Season: Year-round

Facilities: 38 full-hook-up sites, 1 electric site, 176 tent sites, 10 yurts, 3 cabins (with bathroom, kitchen, and TV/VCR), 4 group tent-camping areas, hiker/biker sites, ADA sites, picnic tables, barbecue grills, piped water, restrooms, hot showers, firewood, and an RV dump station

Getting There: From Tillamook, drive 12 miles southwest on Netarts Highway (the Three Capes Scenic Loop) to the state park entrance.

Description: At this campground, you'll enjoy cozy campsites surrounded by coastal forest. From the campground you can hike to the tip of a long, skinny sand spit where you may see seals and shorebirds. Shorter nature trails can also be accessed from the campground. The Cape Lookout Trailhead (see *Paw-Approved Hikes and Parks*) is about 3 miles south of the campground.

DOG EVENTS

Astoria

Mutt March

Clatsop Animal Assistance, Inc., 89813 Logan Road, 97103, www.dogsncats.org

Join the annual Mutt March the last weekend in September. This dog walk parades down the riverwalk in Astoria and helps raise money for Clatsop Animal Assistance.

Cannon Beach

Dog Show at the Beach

Surfsand Resort, 148 W. Gower, 1-800-547-6100 or 503-436-2274, www.surfsand.com

This community event in mid-October is sponsored by the Surfsand Resort. You and your dog can participate in fourteen events, such as cutest dog, oldest dog, biggest dog, and smallest dog. Others include Frisbee catch, best bark, an obstacle course race, best tail wag, the 25-yard doggy dash, obedience trials, best trick, a "so ugly you're cute!" award, best costume, and a pet/owner lookalike contest. In addition to the events and awards ceremony is the auction/raffle and Parade of Champions at the day's end. Proceeds go to the Clatsop County Animal Shelter.

CANINE-APPROVED SHOPPING

Stores are listed geographically, from north to south.

Astoria

Brim's Farm and Garden

34963 Business Highway 101, 503-325-1562

Established in 1986, Brim's Farm and Garden is a warehouse feed store and garden center that stocks quality pet feeds including Science Diet, Pro Plan, Exclusive, Nutro Max and others. The store has pet toys, treats, leashes, collars, shampoos, flea control, grooming tools, pet beds, and carriers. Leashed dogs are welcomed with a responsible owner attached to the other end. Open 8:30 A.M.–5:30 P.M., Monday to Saturday; 12 P.M.–4 P.M., Sunday.

Seaside

Lyle's Seaside Garden and Pets

725 Ave. J, 503-738-5752

This store carries all the supplies and gear your dog needs. Your leashed dog is allowed to browse the aisles with you. In addition, this store carries supplies for cats, birds, fish, reptiles, and other small pets. Open 9:30 A.M.–6 P.M., Monday to Saturday; 10 A.M.–4 P.M., Sunday.

Lincoln City

Paws on the Sand

1640 NE Highway 101, 541-996-6019, www.pawsonthesand.com
This store features pet-themed cards, jewelry and gifts, such as mouse pads, calendars, picture frames, key chains, and woodcarvings. Open 10 A.M.–6 P.M., Monday to Saturday; 11 A.M.–5 P.M., Sunday.

Dog Media

Bow-Wow! (Dog News for Dog Lovers)

P.O. Box 130, Warrenton, OR 97146, 503-861-3331, bowwow@seasurf.net

Bow-Wow! is a newspaper dedicated to canine owners. It informs readers about dog-related events on the Oregon North Coast and Washington's Long Beach Peninsula, and educates people about responsible dog ownership, including health, nutrition, training and behavior issues. It entertains with articles about local dogs and their people. *Bow-Wow!* is published as a monthly insert in Warrenton's *The Columbia Press* and is distributed free throughout Clatsop and Pacific Counties at dog-friendly businesses and organizations. It is also available by subscription for $24 a year.

CANINE ER

Astoria

Astoria Animal Hospital

35109 Highway 105, 503-325-1581

This full-service veterinary hospital has been at this location since 1953. It offers medical, surgical, and dental care for your furry friend, and carries prescription Science Diet dog food, shampoos, and Advantage flea products. Overnight boarding is offered (includes two daily walks) for $11 per dog per night.

Open 8 A.M.–5:30 P.M., Monday to Friday; 8 A.M.–12 P.M., Saturday

Seaside

Remensnyder Pet Clinic

900 24th Ave., 503-738-8846

This veterinary hospital takes walk-in appointments in the afternoons, Monday to Friday, and on Saturdays. This full-service clinic has been in business 12 years and carries a variety of shampoos, flea products, and Science Diet and Pro Plan dog food. They will board your dog for short stays. Proof of vaccinations is required. Prices vary from $7 to $18, depending on the dog's size. In an emergency, call the office number and you'll be referred to an emergency number.

Open 8:30 A.M.–5:30 P.M., Monday through Friday; 9 A.M.–12 P.M., Saturday.

Tillamook

Pioneer Veterinary Hospital
801 Main Ave., 503-842-8411

Open 8 A.M.–12 P.M., Monday through Friday; 8 A.M.–5 P.M., Saturday

Lincoln City

Oceanlake Veterinary Hospital
3545 NW Highway 101, 541-994-2929

This hospital has served Lincoln City dogs, cats, birds, reptiles, and pocket pets (ferrets, rabbits, guinea pigs, gerbils, rats, etc.) for over five years. It will see walk-ins but prefers appointments. Twenty-four hour emergency service is available; call the regular office number and the doctor on call will be paged. Lynn Aszman, D.V.M., says the hospital staff "often serve as 'animal control' during evenings and weekends when travelers find stray or injured dogs on the beach. Clinic staff treat sick or injured wildlife and assist in transporting them to local rehabilitation facilities." The clinic does not offer overnight boarding unless your animal is being treated for a medical condition. Overnight medical boarding for large dogs is $18, medium dogs $16, and small dogs and cats is $13. Dogs are walked twice daily.

Open 8 A.M.–5:30 P.M., Monday to Friday; 8 A.M.–12 P.M., Saturday.

LOST AND FOUND (ANIMAL SHELTERS)

Astoria/Warrenton

Clatsop Animal Assistance
1315 SE 19th St., Warrenton, OR 97146, 503-861-7387, www.dogsncats.org

Open 10 A.M.–1 P.M., Monday and Friday; 2 P.M.–6 P.M., Tuesday and Thursday; and 10 A.M.–1 P.M. the first Saturday of the month.

Central Coast

PAW-APPROVED
HIKES AND PARKS

The hikes and parks in this section are listed geographically from north to south.

Newport

Beverly Beach State Park
Contact: Oregon State Parks and Recreation, Suite 1, 1115 Commercial St. NE, Salem, OR 97301-1002, 1-800-551-6949, www.oregonstateparks.org
Paw-Approval Rating: 3 paws
Leashes Required? Yes
Fees/Permits: None
Season: Year-round
Getting There: From Newport, travel 7 miles north on Highway 101 to the park entrance.
Description: If you and Rover love the beach, this state park is for you! The beach here stretches for miles, from Yaquina Head in the south to the headlands of Otter Rock up north. This state park has a large campground (see *Campgrounds*) and day-use area with picnic tables in a grassy area surrounded by coastal forest. After checking out the beach, explore the 0.75-mile self-guided nature trail that parallels Spencer Creek. The trail can be accessed between campsites C3 and C5.

Yaquina Bay State Recreation Site
Contact: Oregon State Parks and Recreation, Suite 1, 1115 Commercial St. NE, Salem, OR 97301-1002, 1-800-551-6949, www.oregonstateparks.org

Paw-Approval Rating: 3 paws
Leashes Required? Yes
Fees/Permits: None
Season: Year-round
Getting There: At Highway 101 in Newport, turn west at the north end of the Yaquina Bay Bridge at the state park sign and proceed to the park entrance.
Description: This 32-acre park boasts the 40-foot-tall Yaquina Bay Lighthouse, which was in service from 1871 to 1874. The lighthouse sits atop a high bluff that offers outstanding views of the Pacific Ocean and the Yaquina River. You can also hike through the sand dunes along the jetty or trek 1.3 miles north along the beach to historic Nye Beach.

South Beach State Park
Contact: Oregon State Parks and Recreation, Suite 1, 1115 Commercial St. NE, Salem, OR 97301-1002, 1-800-551-6949, www.oregonstateparks.org
Paw-Approval Rating: 3 paws
Leashes Required? Yes
Fees/Permits: None
Season: Year-round
Getting There: From Newport, travel 2 miles south on Highway 101 to the park entrance.
Description: Located on the south side of Yaquina Bay, this state park covers 434 acres. You and your dog can start exploring on the 1-mile Cooper Ridge Trail, accessed at the hiker/biker camp or at campsite C37. You can also walk on the 1-mile paved pedestrian and bicycle path that connects the park's day-use area to South Jetty Road.

Ona Beach State Park

Contact: Oregon State Parks and Recreation, Suite 1, 1115 Commercial St. NE, Salem, OR 97301-1002, 1-800-551-6949, www.oregonstateparks.org
Paw-Approval Rating: 3 paws
Leashes Required? Yes
Fees/Permits: None
Season: Year-round
Getting There: Drive 8 miles south of Newport on Highway 101 to the signed park entrance.
Description: Ona Beach State Park covers 237 acres and features a glistening sandy beach where you and your dog can play Frisbee or romp in the surf. Paddle or kayak in Beaver Creek, which empties into the ocean at Ona Beach. A boat ramp is located on the east side of Highway 101.

Seal Rock State Recreation Site

Contact: Oregon State Parks and Recreation, Suite 1, 1115 Commercial St. NE, Salem, OR 97301-1002, 1-800-551-6949, www.oregonstateparks.org
Paw-Approval Rating: 3 paws
Leashes Required? Yes
Fees/Permits: None
Season: Year-round
Getting There: From Newport, travel 10 miles south on Highway 101.
Description: This state recreation site has outstanding views of Seal Rock. A short hiking trail down to the beach leads you to closer views of sea lions and sea birds. This is also an excellent spot to inspect the rocky tide pools and their inhabitants that are exposed during low tide. If you decide to explore the tide pools, make sure your pup doesn't fall off the slippery rocks.

Waldport

Horse Creek-Harris Ranch Hike

Contact: Siuslaw National Forest, Waldport Ranger District, 1094 SW Pacific Highway, Waldport, Oregon 97394, 541-563-3211, www.fs.fed.us
Paw-Approval Rating: 4 paws
Leashes Required? No
Length: 9.2 miles out and back
Difficulty: Difficult
Fees/Permits: None
Season: Year-round
Getting There: From Waldport, head 7 miles north on Highway 101. Turn right on North Beaver Creek Road and go 1 mile to a road junction. Go left at the junction and drive 2.7 miles to another road junction. Turn right onto North Elkhorn Road and proceed about another 5.8 miles to the junction with Road 50. Turn left on Road 50 and go 1.4 miles to the junction with Road 5087. Turn right onto Road 5087 and continue another 3.4 miles to the trailhead.
Description: This trail will dazzle you with its pristine, old-growth Douglas fir, western red cedar, and Sitka spruce forest. Start hiking on the Horse Creek Trail located next to a small registration booth. The trail starts off level for the first few miles and then descends rapidly on a series of switchbacks about 1,400 feet until it intersects pretty Drift Creek after 3.6 miles. To continue hiking along the creek, head right onto Harris Ranch Trail, which follows the creek for about another mile. The turnaround point is where this trail fords Drift Creek.

Driftwood Beach State Recreation Site

Contact: Oregon State Parks and Recreation, Suite 1, 1115 Commercial St. NE, Salem, OR 97301-1002, 1-800-551-6949, www.oregonstateparks.org
Paw-Approval Rating: 2 paws
Leashes Required? Yes
Fees/Permits: None
Season: Year-round
Getting There: From Waldport, head 3 miles north on Highway 101 to the recreation area.
Description: Your dog will enjoy a good romp on this scenic, sandy beach. After spending the morning splashing in the

waves, digging up driftwood sticks for a game of fetch, and other canine beach pursuits, take a break in the shaded picnic area and fuel up for an afternoon of more beach fun.

Governor Patterson Memorial State Recreation Site

Contact: Oregon State Parks and Recreation, Suite 1, 1115 Commercial St. NE, Salem, OR 97301-1002, 1-800-551-6949, www.oregonstateparks.org
Paw-Approval Rating: 2 paws
Leashes Required? Yes
Fees/Permits: None
Season: Year-round
Getting There: From Waldport, head 1 mile south on Highway 101 to this recreation site.
Description: Your dog will love running on the long stretch of sandy beach. Hike north to Yaquina John Point, located at the mouth of Alsea Bay. From this spot, you may see seals lounging on the sandy shore and groups of brown pelicans fishing for their next meal. You can also hike south on the beach toward Yachats.

Make a point to stop at the Alsea Bay Bridge Historical Interpretive Center, (541-563-2002), located in Waldport at the south end of the Alsea Bay Bridge. You'll learn about the history of travel routes on the Oregon Coast, from Indian trails to modern highways.

Beachside State Recreation Site

Contact: Oregon State Parks and Recreation, Suite 1, 1115 Commercial St. NE, Salem, OR 97301-1002, 1-800-551-6949, www.oregonstateparks.org
Paw-Approval Rating: 3 paws
Leashes Required? Yes
Fees/Permits: None
Season: Year-round
Getting There: Drive 4 miles south of Waldport on Highway 101 to the state park entrance.

Description: Beach dogs will love to play Frisbee or fetch on the expansive beach here. This state park has campground sites with ocean views (see *Campgrounds*). You may even see migrating gray whales as they pass by from December through June.

Yachats

Smelt Sands State Recreation Area

Contact: Oregon State Parks and Recreation, Suite 1, 1115 Commercial St. NE, Salem, OR 97301-1002, 1-800-551-6949, www.oregonstateparks.org
Paw-Approval Rating: 3 paws
Leashes Required? Yes
Fees/Permits: None
Season: Year-round
Getting There: At the intersection of Highway 101 and Lemwick Ln. on the north edge of Yachats, turn west onto Lemwick Ln. and proceed to the recreation area.
Description: This recreation area is known for its annual smelt run and is also a good location to watch for migrating gray whales. If you and your best friend want to hike, try the 0.75-mile historic 804 Trail. This route heads north from the parking area, takes you past two blowholes, and leads you through a windblown coastal ecosystem. After 0.75-miles, you'll reach the beach. To keep hiking, continue north and you'll reach Vingie Creek in another 0.8 mile and the Tillicum Beach picnic area in another 2.7 miles.

Cape Perpetua Scenic Area

Contact: Cape Perpetua Interpretive Center, Yachats, OR, 541-547-3289, www.newportnet.com
Paw-Approval Rating: 4 paws
Leashes Required? Yes
Fees/Permits: $3 day-use fee
Season: Year-round
Getting There: From Yachats, drive 3 miles south on Highway 101 (or 22.5 miles north of Florence) to the Cape Perpetua

Interpretive Center on the east side of the highway.

Description: This 2,700-acre scenic area's ten trails wind through coastal forest, rocky tide pools, and past spectacular blowholes and the unique narrow rock channel of Devil's Churn. Stop in the visitor center to pick up a trail map and learn more about the area's history and its unique flora and fauna.

Recommended is the 2-mile Giant Spruce Trail that parallels Cape Creek and takes you to the base of a 500-year-old Sitka spruce. Another Fido favorite is the 0.6-mile Captain Cook Trail past blowholes and craggy tide pools filled with colorful sea creatures. For ocean views, try the Saint Perpetua Trail. This 2.6-mile round trip trail climbs 600 feet up a series of switchbacks on the south face of Cape Perpetua. From the top are outstanding views of the Pacific Ocean.

Florence

Carl G. Washburne Memorial State Park

Contact: Oregon State Parks and Recreation, Suite 1, 1115 Commercial St. NE, Salem, OR 97301-1002, 1-800-551-6949, www.oregon stateparks.org

Paw-Approval Rating: 3 paws
Leashes Required? Yes
Fees/Permits: None
Season: Year-round
Getting There: From Florence, travel 12.5 miles north on Highway 101 to the park entrance.
Description: One of the highlights of this park is a 6-mile out and back hike to Heceta Head Lighthouse from the campground (see *Campgrounds*). Start hiking on the Valley Trail, located before the pay station to the campground. The trail follows China Creek and then leads to an open, grassy meadow where you may see Roosevelt elk. The trail then leads through a boggy area, crosses Highway 101, and turns onto Hobbit Trail. Hike a short ways

on this trail to a trail junction. Turn left onto the Heceta Head Trail to the Heceta Head Lighthouse. At the lighthouse, watch for seabirds nesting in the high cliffs.

Heceta Head Lighthouse Hike

Contact: Oregon State Parks and Recreation, Suite 1, 1115 Commercial St. NE, Salem, OR 97301-1002, 1-800-551-6949, www.oregonstateparks.org

Paw-Approval Rating: 3 paws
Leashes Required? Yes
Length: 1-mile out and back
Difficulty: Easy
Fees/Permits: $3 day-use fee
Season: Year-round
Getting There: From Florence, drive 12 miles north on Highway 101 (or 14 miles south of Yachats) to the Heceta Head Lighthouse Scenic Viewpoint on the west side of the road. Go 0.3 mile to a large parking area and the trailhead.
Description: This trail takes you to a scenic viewpoint at the historic Heceta Head Lighthouse. The 56-foot lighthouse, commissioned in 1894, rests on a rocky headland 205 feet above the ocean. Adjacent to the lighthouse is the Heceta House, the original lightkeeper's house built in 1893 and now operated as a bed and breakfast (unfortunately, no canines are allowed to stay at the B&B).

To start the hike, head uphill on the gravel path from the parking lot and walk 0.5 mile through a thick coastal cedar and fir forest dotted with sword fern, wild iris, and salal. Once you reach the lighthouse, you'll have great views of puffins, cormorants, and other sea birds nesting on the offshore cliffs. After checking out the lighthouse, take your best friend to the beach and enjoy exploring tide pools and other beach dog activities.

Sutton Creek Recreation Area

Contact: Siuslaw National Forest, Mapleton Ranger District, 4480

Highway 101 N, Bldg G, Florence, OR 97439, 541-902-8526, www.fs.fed.us

Paw-Approval Rating: 4 paws
Leashes Required? Yes
Fees/Permits: $5 Northwest Forest Pass. Purchase at 1-800-270-7504 or www.naturenw.org.
Season: Year-round. Some areas may be closed to dogs March 15 to September 15 to protect sensitive Snowy Plover nesting sites. These areas are posted. Please respect postings and take your dog to other areas within Sutton Creek.
Getting There: From Florence travel 4.2 miles north on Highway 101 to the junction with Sutton Beach Road. Turn left (west) onto Sutton Beach Road at the Sutton Creek Recreation sign. Go 0.7 mile and turn right into Sutton Creek Campground. At the T-intersection, turn left toward "A Loop." Go 0.2 mile to the Sutton Group Camp parking area between campsites A18 and A19. The trailhead is on the right side of the Sutton Group Camp Parking area.
Description: This 2,700-acre recreation area has 6 miles of trails for your furry friend to explore and features a large campground (see *Campgrounds*). Trails lead through a diverse coastal ecosystem of sand dunes, forest, freshwater lakes, a creek, and a long sandy beach. This area is also rich with wildlife—207 types of birds and nearly 50 types of animals, including deer, osprey, chipmunks, rabbits, opossum, black bear, and deer.

From Sutton Creek Campground, you can hike the 4.5-mile out and back trail (you'll have to ford Sutton Creek) to Baker Beach. You also have the option of hiking 3.5 miles out and back through sand dunes to Alder Dune Campground where you and your best friend can walk around Dune Lake and Alder Lake. View the weird insect-eating cobra lily on the short Bog Trail, located on the right side of the road near the Sutton Creek Campground entrance.

Pawn Old Growth Hike
Contact: Siuslaw National Forest, Mapleton Ranger District, 4480 Highway 101 N, Bldg G, Florence, OR 97439, 541-902-8526, www.fs.fed.us

Paw-Approval Rating: 3 paws
Leashes Required? Yes
Length: 0.8-mile loop
Difficulty: Easy
Fees/Permits: None
Season: Year-round
Getting There: From Florence, head east on Oregon Highway 126. Go 1 mile and turn left onto North Fork Road. Drive 11 miles on North Fork Road to the junction with Upper North Fork Road. Continue straight on Upper North Fork Road for 5.4 miles. Turn right on Elk Tie Road and go a short distance to the trailhead.
Description: This short loop hike takes you and Fido on a tour through magnificent old-growth Douglas fir and Western red cedar. A brochure at the trailhead will provide you with detailed information about this amazing forest.

Sweet Creek Falls Hike
Contact: Siuslaw National Forest, Mapleton Ranger District, 4480 Highway 101 N, Bldg G, Florence, OR 97439, 541-902-8526, www.fs.fed.us

Paw-Approval Rating: 4 paws
Leashes Required? Yes
Length: 2.2 miles out and back
Difficulty: Easy
Fees/Permits: None
Season: Year-round. This trail can be muddy during winter.
Getting There: From Florence, head 15 miles east on Highway 126 to Mapleton, to the junction with Sweet Creek Road. Turn left (south) on Sweet Creek Road and travel 10.2 miles to the Homestead Trailhead on the right.
Description: This forested out and back trail takes you and Rover along the banks of bouldery Sweet Creek. From the

Homestead Trailhead, start walking upstream. You'll pass small waterfalls and after 1.1 miles, you'll reach 20-foot Sweet Creek Falls (your turnaround point). Head up a short side trail to a fantastic viewpoint of the upper falls.

Jessie M. Honeyman Memorial State Park

Contact: Oregon State Parks and Recreation, Suite 1, 1115 Commercial St. NE, Salem, OR 97301-1002, 1-800-551-6949, www.oregonstateparks.org

Paw-Approval Rating: 3 paws
Leashes Required? Yes
Fees/Permits: $3 day-use fee
Season: Year-round
Getting There: From Florence, travel 3 miles south on Highway 101 to the park entrance.
Description: This popular state park is adjacent to sand dunes and provides access to 82-acre Cleawox Lake and 350-acre Woahink Lake. Boat ramps are present on both lakes. If you feel like hiking, a 0.5-mile trail takes you from the Cleawox Lake picnic areas to Lily Lake, which is bordered by colorful rhododendrons. A second nature trail connects the Cleawox day-use area with the group camp on Woahink Lake. If your trail hound is sniffing the sea breezes and wanting to play in the surf, hike over 2 miles of dunes from the Cleawox area to the beach.

Reedsport

Taylor and Carter Dunes Hike

Contact: Oregon Dunes National Recreation Area, 855 Highway Ave., Reedsport, OR, 541-271-3611, www.fs.fed.us

Paw-Approval Rating: 3 paws
Leashes Required? Yes
Length: 2.8 miles out and back
Difficulty: Easy
Season: Year-round

Fees/Permits: $5 Northwest Forest Pass. Purchase at 1-800-270-7504 or www.naturenw.org.
Getting There: From Florence, travel 8 miles south on Highway 101 (or 12.5 miles north of Reedsport) to the Carter Lake Campground turnoff. Turn (west) and drive to the Taylor Dunes Trailhead on the left.
Description: From the Taylor Dunes Trailhead, the trail travels through coastal dunes and past Taylor Lake. At 0.4 mile is a viewpoint of the dune ecosystem. To continue on the trail, follow trail markers through the dunes another 0.5 mile to the intersection with the Carter Dunes Trail. Turn right and you'll reach the beach in another 0.5 mile (your turnaround point).

Oregon Dunes Overlook Hike

Contact: Oregon Dunes National Recreation Area, 855 Highway Ave., Reedsport, OR, 541-271-3611, www.fs.fed.us

Paw-Approval Rating: 3 paws
Leashes Required? Yes
Length: 2.2 miles out and back
Difficulty: Easy
Season: Year-round. Some areas on this trail may be restricted March 15 to September 15 to protect the endangered western snowy plover. Closed areas are posted.
Fees/Permits: $5 Northwest Forest Pass. Purchase at 1-800-270-7504 or www.naturenw.org.
Getting There: From Florence, travel 10 miles south on Highway 101 (or 11 miles north of Reedsport) to the Oregon Dunes Overlook parking area.
Description: The hike starts on a paved path adjacent to the parking area, takes you through pretty, coastal forest and then arrives at the dunes after 0.3 mile. Follow trail markers through the dunes west toward the ocean. You'll reach the beach in a little over a mile. After enjoying the beach scene with your pooch, head back to the trailhead on the same route.

Takenitch Creek Hikes

Contact: Oregon Dunes National Recreation Area, 855 Highway Ave., Reedsport, OR, 541-271-3611, www.fs.fed.us
Paw-Approval Rating: 4 paws
Leashes Required? Yes
Length: Loop options of 1.5 miles, 2.5 miles, and 5 miles
Difficulty: Moderate
Fees/Permits: $5 Northwest Forest Pass. Purchase at 1-800-270-7504 or www.naturenw.org.
Season: Year-round. Some areas may be restricted March 15 to September 15 to protect the endangered western snowy plover. Closed areas are posted.
Getting There: From Florence, travel 12 miles south on Highway 101 (or 9 miles north of Reedsport) to the Takenitch Creek Trailhead.
Description: From the trailhead you can complete three different loops through several different coastal ecosystems including forest, meadow, marsh, deflation plain, and sandy beach. One of the highlights is scenic Takenitch Creek where you may see a variety of shorebirds feeding, as well as otter, mink, and raccoon.

Takenitch Dunes and Three Mile Lake Hike

Contact: Oregon Dunes National Recreation Area, 855 Highway Ave., Reedsport, OR, 541-271-3611, www.fs.fed.us
Paw-Approval Rating: 4 paws
Leashes Required? Yes
Length: 6.5-mile loop
Difficulty: Difficult
Season: Year-round
Fees/Permits: $5 Northwest Forest Pass. Purchase at 1-800-270-7504 or www.naturenw.org.
Getting There: From Florence, travel 12.5 miles south on Highway 101 (or 8 miles north of Reedsport) to Takenitch Campground and the trailhead.

Description: Begin hiking at the signed trailhead (both the Takenitch Dunes and Three Mile Lake Trails begin as the same trail). After hiking 0.25 mile, the trail splits. Go left and continue hiking on the Three Mile Lake Trail through a second-growth conifer forest. After about 2.7 miles, skirt the edge of Three Mile Lake before reaching the beach at 3 miles. Turn right and walk north along the beach about 1.5 miles. Hook up with the Takenitch Dunes Trail on your right and walk 2 miles through dunes and forest back to your starting point. Be ready to climb about 650 feet on this hike, much of it in soft, sandy conditions.

Bolon Island Tideways State Scenic Corridor

Contact: Oregon State Parks and Recreation, Suite 1, 1115 Commercial St. NE, Salem, OR 97301-1002, 1-800-551-6949, www.oregonstateparks.org
Paw-Approval Rating: 2 paws
Leashes Required? Yes
Fees/Permits: None
Season: Year-round
Getting There: From Reedsport, drive 0.5 mile north on Highway 101 to the park entrance.
Description: At this park on an island in the Umpqua River, you can hike on a nature trail that offers opportunities to watch for wildlife and view the Umpqua River.

Kentucky Falls Hike

Contact: Siuslaw National Forest, Mapleton Ranger District, 4480 Highway 101 N, Bldg G, Florence, OR 97439, 541-902-8526, www.fs.fed.us
Paw-Approval Rating: 4 paws
Leashes Required? Yes
Length: 4 miles out and back
Difficulty: Moderate
Fees/Permits: None
Season: Year-round. This trail can be muddy during winter.

Getting There: From Reedsport, head north on Highway 101, cross a bridge over the Umpqua River, and then turn right (northeast) on Smith River Road (Forest Road 48). Go approximately 15 miles on Smith River Road and turn left (north) on North Fork Road. Go about 10 miles on North Fork Road to the intersection with Forest Road 23. Turn right onto Forest Road 23 and follow signs to Kentucky Falls. After another 10 miles you'll arrive at a T-intersection. Turn left on Forest Road 919 and continue 2.6 miles to the trailhead.

Description: This trail descends 760 feet through magnificent old-growth western red cedar and Douglas fir. After about 0.5 mile, you'll arrive at the shimmering double cascade of Upper Kentucky Falls. Continue about another 1.5 miles to a viewpoint of Lower Kentucky Falls and North Fork Falls (your turnaround point).

North Fork of Smith River Hike

Contact: Siuslaw National Forest, Mapleton Ranger District, 4480 Highway 101 N, Bldg G, Florence, OR 97439, 541-902-8526, www.fs.fed.us

Paw-Approval Rating: 4 paws
Leashes Required? Yes
Length: 13 miles out and back
Difficulty: Difficult
Fees/Permits: None
Season: Year-round. This trail can be muddy during winter.

Getting There: From Reedsport, head north on Highway 101, cross a bridge over the Umpqua River, and then turn right (northeast) on Smith River Road (Forest Road 48). After about 15 miles, turn left (north) on North Fork Road After about 23 miles, cross a bridge and bear right (east) at a road junction, following a sign to Mapleton. In less than a mile is another river crossing, then turn right (east) at a T-intersection onto paved Forest Road 23. Continue another 4.3 miles to the trailhead on your left.

Description: This trail takes you through coastal forest along the North Fork of Smith River. Your best friend will love wading in the cool waters of this pristine river on a hot summer day.

Umpqua Lighthouse State Park

Contact: Oregon State Parks and Recreation, Suite 1, 1115 Commercial St. NE, Salem, OR 97301-1002, 1-800-551-6949, www.oregonstateparks.org

Paw-Approval Rating: 4 paws
Leashes Required? Yes
Fees/Permits: None
Season: Year-round

Getting There: From Reedsport, head 6 miles south on Highway 101 (or 16 miles north of Coos Bay). Turn west on Umpqua Lighthouse Road and follow signs to the park.

Description: This state park has it all: oceanfront, riverfront, lakefront and dunes, plus a campground (see *Campgrounds*) and day-use area. Lake Marie offers fishing and non-motorized boating, making canoeing and kayaking a popular activity. Check out the whale viewing platform just north of the lake; its interpretive signs fill you in on the migration and feeding patterns of gray whales. Hike on one of three paths from the campground that take you to the 1.4-mile lakeshore loop around Lake Marie. A short trail off the lakeshore loop leads to a viewpoint of the sand dunes. Explore the mouth of the Umpqua River by canoe or kayak. If you and Fido are feeling energetic, hike over the dunes to the beach. Another attraction here is the 65-foot Umpqua River Lighthouse.

William M. Tugman State Park

Contact: Oregon State Parks and Recreation, Suite 1, 1115 Commercial St. NE, Salem, OR 97301-1002, 1-800-551-6949, www.oregonstateparks.org

Paw-Approval Rating: 3 paws
Leashes Required? Yes

Fees/Permits: None
Season: Year-round
Getting There: From Reedsport, head 8 miles south on Highway 101 to the park entrance.
Description: The star attraction of this state park is 350-acre Eel Lake, popular for canoeing, kayaking, windsurfing, and fishing. A trail around the south end of the lake explores habitat of osprey, eagle, and black-tailed deer. This state park also has a campground (see *Campgrounds*).

Umpqua Dunes Hike

Contact: Oregon Dunes National Recreation Area, 855 Highway Ave., Reedsport, OR, 541-271-3611, www.fs.fed.us
Paw-Approval Rating: 3 paws
Leashes Required? Yes
Length: 1-mile loop (5-mile out and back option)
Difficulty: Moderate
Fees/Permits: $5 Northwest Forest Pass. Purchase at 1-800-270-7504 or www.naturenw.org.
Season: Year-round
Getting There: From Reedsport travel 10.5 miles south on Highway 101 (or 12.5 miles north of North Bend) to the trailhead.
Description: This 1-mile interpretive loop takes you through magnificent coastal dunes. A brochure is available at the trailhead.
Option: If you and your pup are feeling ambitious, hike through the dunes 2.5 miles to the beach. Look for posts with blue bands to guide your way. Be prepared to hike through soft sand.

Blue Bill Hike

Contact: Oregon Dunes National Recreation Area, 855 Highway Ave., Reedsport, OR, 541-271-3611, www.fs.fed.us
Paw-Approval Rating: 3 paws
Leashes Required? Yes
Length: 1.2-mile loop
Difficulty: Easy
Season: Year-round

Fees/Permits: $5 Northwest Forest Pass. Purchase at 1-800-270-7504 or www.naturenw.org.
Getting There: From Reedsport, travel 23 miles south (or 2 miles north of North Bend) on Highway 101. Turn west on Horsfall Road and continue to the signed trailhead.
Description: This trail circles 60-acre Blue Bill Lake and takes you through a shady western hemlock forest with a thick understory of huckleberry and salal. The trail also features a unique wetland ecosystem.

CYCLING FOR CANINES

Siltcoos Lake

Contact: Oregon Dunes National Visitor Center, 855 Highway Ave., Reedsport, OR 541-271-3611, www.fs.fed.us
Paw-Approval Rating: 4 paws
Leashes Required? No
Length: 4.5-mile loop
Difficulty: Easy
Fees/Permits: $5 Northwest Forest Pass. Purchase at 1-800-270-7504 or www.naturenw.org.
Season: Year-round. This trail can be muddy during winter.
Getting There: From Florence, drive 7 miles south on Highway 101. Turn left (east) at the Siltcoos Lake Trail sign. From Reedsport, head north on Highway 101 approximately 13 miles. Turn right (east) into the Siltcoos Lake Trail parking lot.
Description: You and your mountain bike partner will enjoy this singletrack loop trail through a fragrant cedar and spruce forest and along the shores of 3,500-acre Siltcoos Lake. From the parking area, pick up the signed singletrack trail. After 0.8 mile, turn right on the South Fork Trail to begin the loop portion of the ride. After 1.5 miles, turn right toward South Camp to check out the lake, where your friend may want to cool off. After enjoying views of the lake, head back to the main trail and continue the

loop. At 2.6 miles, turn right and head back on the north route to the trailhead.

PADDLEHOUNDS
Newport

Beaver Creek at
Ona Beach State Park
Contact: Oregon State Parks and Recreation, Suite 1, 1115 Commercial St. NE, Salem, OR 97301-1002, 1-800-551-6949, www.oregonstateparks.org
Fees/Permits: None
Getting There: Travel 8 miles south of Newport on Highway 101 to the park entrance.
Description: If you and your pup are paddling fanatics, launch a canoe or kayak in picturesque Beaver Creek. A boat ramp is located on the east side of Highway 101.

Reedsport

Lake Marie at
Umpqua Lighthouse State Park
Contact: Oregon State Parks and Recreation, Suite 1, 1115 Commercial St. NE, Salem, OR 97301-1002, 1-800-551-6949, www.oregonstateparks.org
Fees/Permits: None
Getting There: From Reedsport, head 6 miles south on Highway 101 (or 16 miles north of Coos Bay). Turn west on Umpqua Lighthouse Road and follow signs to the park and lake.
Description: Lake Marie offers easily paddling for dogs who just can't get enough of the water. You can complete an easy paddle around the lake in about an hour.

CANINE COMFORT ACCOMMODATIONS
Towns in this section are listed geographically from north to south. Unless otherwise stated, dogs should not be left unattended in the room and must be leashed on hotel property.

Newport

$$ Waves Motel
820 NW Coast St., 541-265-4661 or 1-800-282-6993

This motel has ocean-view rooms with queen size beds, cable TV with HBO, refrigerators, microwaves, and coffeemakers. Additional amenities include a large grassy area where you can let your dog run, complimentary continental breakfast, and free popcorn. The motel is within walking distance of the beach.
Dog Policy
The motel only accepts dogs that weigh less than 40 pounds. A $5 pet fee is charged per dog per night.

$$-$$$ Best Western Agate Beach Inn
3019 N. Coast Highway, 1-800-547-3310, www.newportbestwestern.com

This hotel features eight pet-friendly rooms, some of which overlook Agate Beach and Yaquina Head Lighthouse. All rooms come with a microwave, refrigerator, data ports, phone, TV, VCR, free HBO, complimentary in-room coffee, hair dryer, iron and ironing board, and dog treats. The hotel features a heated indoor pool, spa, fitness center, arcade, and gift shop. The hotel is 250 feet from Agate Beach and provides a beach access driveway. Nearby are the Oregon Coast Aquarium, Hatfield Marine Science Center, Yaquina Bay State Park and Lighthouse, and many hiking trails.
Dog Policy
A one-time $10 fee is charged per pet. The hotel allows only two dogs per room.

$$-$$$ The Beach House
107 SW Coast St., 1-866-215-6486, www.beachhousebb.com

This friendly B&B is owned by Nel Ward and Sue Hardesty. Its one pet-friendly room, the Coast Room, is a large room on the ground floor with a private entrance, a refrigerator, and a microwave.

Additional amenities include TV/VCR, robes, gourmet coffee, private book and video library, and non-smoking rooms. A continental breakfast is included. The B&B also features an elevated tub with warm water (towels are also available) where you can wash your dog off after a day filled with adventures at the nearby beach.

Dog Policy

Dogs are welcome in the Coast Room. No extra fees are charged.

$$-$$$ The Vikings Cottages

729 NW Coast St., 1-800-480-2477, www.vikingsoregoncoast.com

Dogs are welcome in all cottages at this motel in historic Nye Beach. There are 14 cottages, each with its own floor plan and cozy, cabinlike atmosphere. Most units have a kitchen, fireplace, and ocean view. All have cable TV. The motel has beach access.

Dog Policy

No extra fee is charged for your dog.

$$-$$$$ Best Western Hallmark Resort Newport

744 SW Elizabeth, 541-265-2600 or 1-888-448-4449, hallmarkinns.com

This hotel is a three-diamond destination resort with panoramic oceanfront views from every guestroom. The resort has many styles of rooms, and some have spas, mini-kitchens, and fireplaces. All rooms have a balcony or patio overlooking the ocean, a coffeemaker, refrigerator, and a complimentary newspaper delivered each morning. Other amenities are an indoor pool, spa, sauna, and workout facility. Georgie's Beachside Grill offers fresh Northwest cuisine for breakfast, lunch, and dinner. This resort caters to your canine pal by offering a treat bag, pet sheets, and an exercise area.

Dog Policy

Your pal is welcome in ground floor rooms. A $5 fee is charged per night per dog. Your dog can be left unattended in your room if he is crated.

$$$-$$$$ Shilo Inn Newport Waterfront

536 SW Elizabeth St., 541-265-7701, 1-800-222-2244, www.shiloinns.com

Dog Policy

The inn charges $10 per dog per night.

Waldport

$$-$$$$ Edgewater Cottages

3978 SW Pacific Coast Highway, 541-563-2240, www.coastgraphics.com/edgewater

The theme of the Edgewater Cottages is "A good place for kids and dogs and well-behaved adults." Each cozy beachside cottage features a fireplace, fully stocked kitchen, deck, and ocean view. In addition, eight miles of sandy beach are right out the back door. During July, August, and September, cottages are usually booked on a weekly basis.

Dog Policy

The charge is $5–$10 per night per dog (the rate varies depending on what cottage you stay in). Your dog can be left unattended in your room if he is crated.

Yachats

$-$$ See Vue Motel

95590 Highway 101, 541-547-3227, www.seavue.com

Renee Lachance and her two dogs, Jasmine and Rocky, welcome you to their seven-room motel located on a high bluff above the ocean. Each room has a spectacular ocean view and is decorated with its own theme, reflecting its unique charm. The Salish room has one double bed, a refrigerator, and coffeemaker, and features Northwest Native American murals by Judy Tallwing. The Princess and the Pea room has a queen bed, refrigerator, coffeemaker, and is decorated with velvet and lace, musical instruments, and brass rubbings of a lady and her knight. The Santa Fe room, two full rooms with a double bed and hide-a-bed, is decorated with a southwest theme and boasts a corner fireplace and full kitchen. Granny's room has a queen bed, a full kitchen, and is decorated with handsome antiques. The Mountain Shores room has a queen bed, fireplace, and kitchenette, and is decorated in a rustic mountain theme. The Far Out West rooms are furnished with one double and one single hide-a-bed, a fireplace, and full kitchen, and are decorated in a cowboy theme. The cottage is a self-contained unit with views of the mountains and ocean. It features a queen bed, a double hide-a-bed, and full kitchen.

Dog Policy

There is a $5 charge per night per dog, with a limit of two dogs per room (although more may be allowed if they are well behaved). Pet sheets are provided for bedding. Renee asks that you keep your dog off the beds and furniture.

$-$$ Yachats Inn

331 South Coast Highway 101, 1-888-270-3456, www.yachatsinn.com

This inn, built in 1948, is one of our favorites. Its rustic charm has not diminished through the years. Paul and Kathy Plunk, longtime owners and innkeepers, have made updates and improvements but have kept the ambiance of the original hotel intact. Kathy says, "We are just a short distance from the quaint hamlet of Yachats, out of town far enough to escape the crowds but close enough to be part of it all! We have 19 pet-friendly rooms: 11 standard units with one or two queen beds, six kitchen/fireplace suite rooms, and two kitchen/fireplace oceanfront suites. We have an indoor heated pool and year-round spa. We offer our four-legged friends blankets and towels and have spacious grounds for them to run and play. We are just a few steps from the beach. We offer fresh coffee each morning in our commons area."

Dog Policy

A pet fee of $5 per dog per night is charged. Paul and Kathy say, "We accept all well behaved dogs."

$-$$$ Fireside Motel

1-800-336-3573, www.overleaflodge.com/fireside/

Many of the rooms in this canine-friendly motel have an ocean view and are furnished with a refrigerator, color cable TV, coffeemaker, a direct dial phone, and a balcony where your pooch can sniff the cool sea breezes. Some rooms have a cozy fireplace and Jacuzzi. When you check in, your dog will receive a gift pack that includes a basket with dog treats, dog towels, dog sheets (to cover the furniture), and information on the hotel's pet policy. This motel is near the Cape Perpetua Scenic area (see *Paw-Approved Hikes and Parks*) and many long, sandy beaches.

Dog Policy

The hotel charges $7 per dog per day.

$$-$$$ The Shamrock Lodgettes

105 Highway 101 South, www.shamrock-lodgettes.com, 1-800-845-5028 or 541-547-3312

Nancy Goss, owner of the Shamrock Lodgettes, says, "We have ten dog-friendly units in a four-acre park on the edge of the Yachats River and the Pacific Ocean. Our original six rustic log cabins, built in 1951, are self-contained houses with a delightful corner stone fireplace, separate bedrooms, bath, and fully stocked kitchenette. Each has an ocean view. Two units have two bedrooms. Covered carports are available. The single bedroom cabins have a covered patio area. Our Sherwood House has a full kitchen, two bedrooms, Danish fireplace, and covered parking.

"The newer Redwood Motel units have vaulted ceilings with skylights, Fisher wood-burning stoves, microwave, refrigerator, and coffeemaker. Three of these eight units are dog-friendly.

"Our grass-covered, four-acre property is just feet away from a sandy beach with easy stair access down an approximately 15-foot-high cliff. We are on one of the few sandy beaches in Yachats. Rugged basalt outcroppings add to the beauty and sound of the area, with the waves crashing against them. At the edge of our property are hundreds of-year-old shoals left over by Indian camps as they fished and cleaned shellfish here. Agates are everywhere—from miniscule treasures to the occasional fist-size gem. Guests and locals alike gather agates daily. Yachats is truly the agate capital of the whole coastline.

"We have great lawns and flowerbeds. Over a hundred varieties of rhododendron blossom in the spring. The hydrangeas will still be blooming into the first of every new year. The nasturtiums, geraniums, and chrysanthemums barely stop blooming before the new spring re-awakens their blossoms. Our azalea bushes are varied and beautiful, too.

"We are also a short distance to hiking and walking trails, gourmet quality restaurants, gift shops, and art galleries.

Baby is a 13-year-old Persian cat who quietly oversees the office. We think Waddles the Cat is about four years old. She adopted us two years ago and has been entertaining us ever since. We have signs posted to please not listen to her when she tries to talk you into letting her outside." Additional amenities include a spa with a hot tub, dry sauna, and exercise room.

Dog Policy

The hotel charges $5 per dog per night.

$$-$$$$ Adobe Resort

1555 Highway 101, 541-547-3141, www.adoberesort.com

The premier resort is located along the scenic rocky shore in Yachats and many of its pet-friendly rooms have commanding ocean views. Rooms are equipped with refrigerators, color cable TV/VCR with remote, hair dryers, coffeemakers, and direct dial phones. The hotel has an exercise room, a heated indoor Jacuzzi, and sauna.

Dog Policy

A $5 fee per dog per night is charged.

Florence

$-$$ Lighthouse Inn

155 Highway 101, 541-997-3221, lighthouseinn.tripod.com

This inn has nine dog-friendly rooms. One is a two-room suite; one room has a king bed and the adjoining living room/dining area is furnished with a couch, chairs, VCR, microwave, coffee service, and refrigerator. The hotel is one block from historic Old Town and the Siuslaw Riverfront. While visiting the inn, your dog may want to exchange sniffs with the two resident miniature dachshunds, Hans and Otto.

Dog Policy

The inn charges $5 per dog per night.

$-$$ Park Motel

85034 Highway 101 South, 541-997-2634

This motel is on six acres of wooded parkland and features 15 dog-friendly rooms and family suites that have knotty pine decor. Additional amenities include in-room coffee, TV, and hair dryer. VCR rentals are available. The motel features a large grassy area to exercise your dog.

Dog Policy

A $6 fee is charged per dog per night. Dogs need to be kept on a leash at all times except in the rooms and pet exercise area.

Reedsport

$-$$ Anchor Bay Inn

1821 Highway 101, 1-800-767-1821

This hotel has four pet-friendly rooms (three smoking and one non-smoking). Additional amenities include cable TV and in-room coffee.

Dog Policy

A pet fee of $7 per dog per day is charged.

$$-$$$ Best Western Salbasgeon Inn & Suites

1400 Highway Ave. 101, 541-271-4831 or 1-800-528-1234

This hotel has five dog-friendly rooms. All rooms were remodeled in 1999. All have free high-speed Internet service, coffeemakers, irons, and ironing boards. The hotel has an indoor pool, hot tub, fitness center, and laundry facilities. Included is a continental breakfast.

Dog Policy

The charge is $5 per dog per night. Dogs over 40 pounds are not allowed. Dogs are not permitted in the lobby.

CAMPGROUNDS

Campgrounds are listed geographically by city, from north to south. All campgrounds listed are leashed dog-friendly. The only exception is that dogs are not allowed inside yurts, tepees, camper wagons, or cabins.

Newport

Beverly Beach State Park

Contact: Oregon State Parks and Recreation, Suite 1, 1115 Commercial St. NE, Salem, OR 97301-1002, 1-800-551-6949 (information), 1-800-452-5687 (reservations), www.oregonstateparks.org

Season: Year-round

Facilities: 54 full-hook-up sites, 75 electrical sites, 128 tent sites (no trailers of any type are allowed in the tent sites), 21 yurts (some with cable TV), 5 group-tent areas, hiker/biker camp, meeting hall, picnic tables, barbecue grills, playground, piped water, restrooms, hot showers, gift shop, and an RV dump station

Getting There: From Newport, head 7 miles north on Highway 101 to the park entrance.

Description: You and your canine pal will enjoy campsites tucked into a thick forest adjacent to pebbly Spencer Creek. Explore the campground by taking a short hike on the 0.75-mile, self-guided nature

trail that parallels Spencer Creek, or head to the beach where Frisbee, fetch, and ocean-play await you.

South Beach State Park

Contact: Oregon State Parks and Recreation, Suite 1, 1115 Commercial St. NE, Salem, OR 97301-1002, 1-800-551-6949 (information), 1-800-452-5687 (reservations), www.oregonstateparks.org

Season: Year-round

Facilities: 227 electrical hook-up sites (maximum trailer or RV *Length:* 60 feet), 6 primitive tent sites, 22 yurts, 3 group-tent areas, hiker/biker sites, picnic tables, firewood, barbecue grills, restrooms, hot showers, volleyball and basketball courts, RV dump station

Getting There: From Newport, head 2 miles south on Highway 101 to the park entrance.

Description: The campground is adjacent to a wide expanse of beach. If you and your pooch want to hike, you can explore a nature trail (accessed from the campground) or hike the paved South Jetty Trail that parallels the beach.

Waldport

Mary's Peak Campground

Contact: Siuslaw National Forest, Waldport Ranger District, 1094 SW Pacific Highway, Waldport, OR, 541-563-3211, www.fs.fed.us

Season: Mid-May to mid-October

Facilities: 6 RV/tent sites (no electrical hook-ups; RVs to 18 feet), picnic tables, fire rings, piped water, and restrooms

Getting There: From Highway 101 in Waldport, turn east on Oregon Highway 34. Travel east ten miles to Mary's Peak Road (Forest Road 30). Turn onto Mary's Peak Road and continue about 9 miles to the campground.

Description: This small, forested campground gives access to ten miles of hiking and mountain biking trails surrounding 4,097-foot Mary's Peak.

Beachside State Recreation Site

Contact: Oregon State Parks and Recreation, Suite 1, 1115 Commercial St. NE, Salem, OR 97301-1002, 1-800-551-6949 (information), 1-800-452-5687 (reservations), www.oregonstateparks.org

Season: March 15 to October 31

Facilities: 33 electrical hook-up sites, 45 tent sites, 2 yurts, hiker/biker camp, ADA sites, picnic tables, barbecue grills, firewood, restrooms, hot showers, and a playground

Getting There: Drive 4 miles south of Waldport on Highway 101 to the park entrance.

Description: This beachside campground tempts you with miles of sandy beach that you and Fido can explore.

Yachats

Cape Perpetua

Contact: Siuslaw National Forest, Waldport Ranger District, 1094 SW Pacific Highway, Waldport, OR, 541-563-3211, www.fs.fed.us

Season: Late May to September

Facilities: 38 Tent/RV sites (no electrical hook-ups), fire rings, picnic tables, piped water, and restrooms. No reservations are accepted.

Getting There: From Yachats, drive 2.1 miles south on Highway 101 to the sign marking the campground entrance. Turn left, and then take a sharp right into the campground.

Description: This campground is set in a coastal forest along the shores of Cape Creek in the Cape Perpetua Scenic Area, where 23 miles of trails (see *Paw-Approved Hikes and Parks*) lead you and your pup through old-growth forest to rocky tide pools filled with sea anemones, purple urchins, and sea stars.

Florence

Carl G. Washburne Memorial State Park

Contact: Oregon State Parks and Recreation, Suite 1, 1115 Commercial St. NE, Salem, OR 97301-1002, 1-800-551-6949, www.oregonstateparks.org

Season: Year-round

Facilities: 58 full-hook-up sites, 2 yurts, 6 walk-in tent sites, hiker/biker sites, picnic tables, fire pits, firewood, playground, restrooms, hot showers. No reservations are accepted.

Getting There: From Florence, travel 12.5 miles north on Highway 101 to the park entrance.

Description: Campsites are secluded and surrounded by a green expanse of coastal forest. You and your trail hound will be tempted by trails to the beach and to picturesque Heceta Head Lighthouse (see *Paw-Approved Trails and Parks*).

Tenmile Creek

Contact: Siuslaw National Forest, Waldport Ranger District, 1094 SW Pacific Highway, Waldport, OR, 541-563-3211, www.fs.fed.us

Season: Year-round

Facilities: 4 combined RV and tent sites, restrooms, picnic tables, barbecue grills, no fresh water. No reservations are accepted.

Getting There: From Florence, head north on Highway 101 approximately 20 miles to Forest Road 56. Turn east on Forest Road 56 and drive about 5.5 miles to the campground.

Description: You and your dog will like this off-the-beaten-path campground close to Tenmile Creek. Once you set up base camp, head out to the Cape Perpetua Scenic Area and Heceta Head Lighthouse (see *Paw-Approved Hikes and Parks*).

Alder Dune

Contact: Siuslaw National Forest, Mapleton Ranger District, 4480 Highway 101, Bldg G, Florence, OR, 541-902-8526, www.fs.fed.us

Season: May through September

Facilities: 39 RV/tent sites (no electrical hook-ups), piped water, flush toilets, picnic tables, and fire grills

Getting There: From Florence, travel 4.1 miles north on Highway 101 to the campground entrance on the left (west) side of the road.

Description: This wonderful campground among pine and alder trees is located between 3-acre Alder Lake and 2-acre Dune Lake. You and your best friend can paddle or swim in the lakes, hike around Alder Lake, or take a trail to Sutton Creek Campground through a coastal sand dune ecosystem.

Sutton Creek

Contact: Siuslaw National Forest, Mapleton Ranger District, 4480 Highway 101, Bldg G, Florence, OR, 541-902-8526, www.fs.fed.us

Season: Year-round

Facilities: 81 RV/tent sites (23 with electrical hook-ups), hiker/biker sites, picnic tables, barbecue grills, piped water, restrooms, flush toilets, playground, boat ramp

Getting There: From Florence, travel 4.2 miles north on Highway 101 to Sutton Beach Road and turn west (left) at the "Sutton Recreation" sign. Proceed 0.7 mile and turn right into Sutton Creek Campground.

Description: Plan on staying a few days at this campground with its secluded sites surrounded by cedar, spruce, alder, and wild rhododendron. Once you set up camp, strike out on six miles of trails that explore sand dunes, coastal forest, Sutton Lake, Sutton Creek, and sandy beach (see *Paw-Approved Hikes and Parks*). Paddlehounds will also enjoy cruising around on Sutton Lake.

Jessie M. Honeyman Memorial State Park

Contact: Oregon State Parks and Recreation, Suite 1, 1115 Commercial St. NE, Salem, OR 97301-1002, 1-800-551-6949 (information), 1-800-452-5687 (reservations), www.oregonstateparks.org

Season: Year-round

Facilities: 47 full-hook-up sites, 119 electrical sites, 191 tent sites, 10 yurts, 6 group-tent areas, hiker/biker camp, picnic tables, barbecue grills, restrooms, hot showers, playground, firewood, RV dump station, boat dock and boat launch at Woahink Lake

Getting There: From Florence, head 3 miles south on Highway 101 to the park entrance.

Description: This is the second largest campground in Oregon. Its location next to Cleawox and Woahink Lakes offers great paddling and swimming opportunities. Several interconnected trails lead through a diverse coastal ecosystem of spruce, fir, hemlock, salal, and thimbleberry (see *Paw-Approved Hikes and Parks*).

Carter Lake

Contact: Oregon Dunes National Recreation Area, 855 Highway 101, Reedsport, OR, 541-271-3611, www.fs.fed.us

Season: May through September

Facilities: 24 tent/RV sites, picnic tables, barbecue grills, piped water, restrooms, and hot showers. No reservations are accepted.

Getting There: From Florence, travel 7.5 miles south on Highway 101 to the campground entrance.

Description: This campground is in a coastal sand dune ecosystem adjacent to 28-acre Carter Lake, and sites are surrounded by lush coastal vegetation. Taylor and Carter Dunes Trails are nearby (see *Paw-Approved Hikes and Parks*).

Reedsport

Umpqua Lighthouse State Park

Contact: Oregon State Parks and Recreation, Suite 1, 1115 Commercial St. NE, Salem, OR 97301-1002, 1-800-551-6949 (information), 1-800-452-5687 (reservations), www.oregonstateparks.org

Season: Year-round

Facilities: 20 full-hook-up sites, 24 tent sites, hiker/biker sites, 8 yurts, 2 cabins, picnic tables, barbecue pits, firewood, piped water, restrooms, hot showers, boat launch and docks on the Umpqua River

Getting There: From Reedsport, head 6 miles south on Highway 101 to the park entrance.

Description: This campground is adjacent to Lake Marie. A 1.4-mile trail loops around the lake; you can also hike to the beach from the campground. Paddlehounds will have fun exploring the lake by canoe or kayak.

William M. Tugman State Park
Contact: Oregon State Parks and Recreation, Suite 1, 1115 Commercial St. NE, Salem, OR 97301-1002, 1-800-551-6949 (information), 1-800-452-5687 (reservations), www.oregonstateparks.org
Season: Year-round
Facilities: 100 electrical sites, 13 yurts, hiker/biker sites, piped water, restrooms, hot showers, laundry facilities, picnic tables, fire pits, and a boat launch
Getting There: From Reedsport, travel 8 miles south on Highway 101 to the park entrance.
Description: This quiet campground is ringed with shore pines along the shores of Eel Lake, which is prime for kayaking and canoeing. To explore a more secluded section of the lake, head out on a hiking trail around the south end of the lake. You may see eagles, osprey, or cranes.

DOG EVENTS
Newport

Gleneden Beach Easter Pet Parade
831 NE Yaquina Heights Dr., 541-265-3719, www.centralcoasthumane.org

This event, held the last Saturday in March at Gleneden Beach, features a parade of pets dressed in clever costumes. Money raised from donations and door prizes goes to the Lincoln County Animal Shelter, Central Coast Humane Society, and United Paws of America.

CANINE-APPROVED SHOPPING
Waldport

Pet Project
195 NW Highway 101, 541-563-6101 or 1-877-563-6101 (toll free order line)

Shasta Kirsch, owner, says, "We stock a little bit of everything, with an emphasis on premium foods, non-leather and humane toys, apparel, treats, grooming supplies, collars, leads, books, natural remedies, bedding for dogs, as well as cats, rodents, birds and fish. We carry gift and household items and are proud to be an authorized retailer for Muck Boots, makers of the new 'Pet Lovers' shoe.' We carry quality brands, a surprisingly broad variety given our remote location and limited size, and prices are as good or better as customers will find anywhere. Some hard-to-find/novelty items include dog booties for hot or cold surfaces, life jackets, Harley Davidson logo items, mesh vehicle barriers, truck-bed tethers, seat belts/harnesses and car window vents. We are happy to special order and mail order." Open 9 A.M.–6 P.M., Monday to Saturday; 10 A.M.–5 P.M., Sunday.

CANINE ER
Newport

Animal Medical Care of Newport
159 NE 10th St., 541-265-6671

Florence

Coastal Animal Clinic
87738 Highway 101, 541-997-4416
Open 9 A.M.–5 P.M., Monday through Friday; 9 A.M.–12 P.M., Saturday.

Reedsport

Lower Umpqua Veterinary Clinic
199 Port Dock Rd., 541-271-4696

LOST AND FOUND (ANIMAL SHELTERS)
Newport

Lincoln County Animal Shelter
Animal Control Division, 510 NE Harney St., Newport, OR 97365, 541-265-6610, www.co.lincoln.or.us

Open 10 A.M.–6 P.M., Monday and Friday; 10 A.M.–4 P.M., Tuesday to Thursday; 10 A.M.–2 P.M., Saturday.

Open 11 A.M.–4 P.M., Monday, Tuesday, Thursday, Friday, and Saturday; 1 P.M.–4 P.M., Sunday.

Florence

Humane Society, Florence Area
2840 North Rhododendron Dr., 541-997-4277, florencehumane.org

South Coast

PAW-APPROVED HIKES AND PARKS

The hikes and parks in this section are listed in geographical order from north to south.

Coos Bay

South Slough Estuary

Contact: South Slough National Estuarine Research Reserve, P.O. Box 5417, Charleston, OR 97420, 541-888-5558, www.southsloughestuary.com
Paw-Approval Rating: 3 paws
Leashes Required? Yes
Fees/Permits: None
Season: Year-round. Trails can be muddy during winter.
Getting There: From Coos Bay or North Bend, follow signs to Charleston, Shore Acres State Park and Ocean Beaches. From Charleston, head west on Cape Arago Highway and in 0.1 mile turn left (south) on Seven Devils Road. Follow signs to South Slough Sanctuary and Bandon. Drive 4.5 miles, turn left at the interpretive center, and continue to a parking area. The trailhead is past the interpretive center to the left of a panel entitled "Journey to the Sea."
Description: You and your furry friend can explore a series of trails through a wetland ecosystem at this 4,700-acre Coos Bay estuary. Paths lead through fresh and saltwater marshes, mudflats, and floodplains. Canoeing and kayaking are also popular. If you plan to paddle, be sure to check the tide table before you head out. Because this is a wildlife area, it is vital that your best friend be leashed at all times on the estuary trails. The visitor center is open 8:30 A.M.–4:30 P.M. Monday to Friday during winter and 8:30 A.M.–4:30 P.M. daily during summer.

Sunset Bay State Park Hike

Contact: Oregon State Parks and Recreation, Suite 1, 1115 Commercial St. NE, Salem, OR 97301-1002, 1-800-551-6949, www.oregonstateparks.org
Paw-Approval Rating: 4 paws
Leashes Required? Yes
Length: 4 miles out and back
Difficulty: Easy
Fees/Permits: None
Season: Year-round
Getting There: From Highway 101 in Coos Bay, follow signs for Charleston Harbor and Ocean Beaches. Follow Cape Arago Highway 12 miles southwest to the park. Turn into the day-use picnic area on the west side of the highway.
Description: Sunset Bay State Park is nestled into a scenic cove between sandstone cliffs. Day-use facilities along the bay have picnic tables set along a grassy expanse of lawn. This state park also has a campground (see *Campgrounds*) and a scenic stretch of sandy beach.

From the day-use picnic area, hook up with the Oregon Coast Trail and trek 2 miles south to Shore Acres State Park. To start the hike, look for the Oregon Coast Trail marker on the right side of the restrooms. Follow the well-graded path through coastal forest. At 0.3 mile, you'll reach a good viewpoint of Sunset Bay and dramatic offshore rocks. At 0.6 mile, hang a left as the trail winds up a fern-covered hill to a paved road. Turn right at the road and follow it until you reach a set of wood steps on the right. Walk up the steps over the metal road barrier. At 1.3 miles, bear right at the trail fork. A short distance past this is a good viewpoint of the Cape Arago Lighthouse. After 2 miles, you'll reach the boundary of Shore Acres State Park. Unfortunately, pooches aren't allowed in this park, so turn around here.

Cape Arago State Park
Contact: Oregon State Parks and Recreation, Suite 1, 1115 Commercial St. NE, Salem, OR 97301-1002, 1-800-551-6949, www.oregonstateparks.org
Paw-Approval Rating: 3 paws
Leashes Required? Yes
Fees/Permits: None
Season: Year-round. North Cove is closed March 1 to June 30 while sea lions birth and raise their pups.
Getting There: From Highway 101 in Coos Bay, follow signs for Charleston Harbor and Ocean Beaches. Follow Cape Arago Highway 14 miles southwest to the park.
Description: This state park is located on a rocky headland 200 feet above the Pacific. Picnic tables at scenic viewpoints along the bluff are good venues for whale watching and for spotting nesting sea birds in the spring. Simpson Reef off this cape is home to seals and sea lions. Access the beach at North, Middle, and South Coves. South Cove has numerous tide pools to explore.

 Golden and Silver Falls Hike
Contact: Oregon State Parks and Recreation, Suite 1, 1115 Commercial St. NE, Salem, OR 97301-1002, 1-800-551-6949, www.oregonstateparks.org
Paw-Approval Rating: 4 paws
Leashes Required? Yes
Length: 1.8 miles out and back

Difficulty: Easy
Fees/Permits: None
Season: Year-round. This trail can be muddy during winter.
Getting There: From Highway 101 in Coos Bay, head east on the Coos River Highway, following signs to Allegany. Travel 13.5 miles east on the north side of the Coos River to the town of Allegany. From here, follow state park signs another 9.5 miles to the Golden and Silver Falls State Natural Area.
Description: This spectacular trail takes you on a tour of the shimmering cascades of Golden Falls and Silver Falls. Start by crossing a bridge over Silver Creek. At the trail junction, head left and enjoy the shady canopy of old-growth Douglas fir trees. At 0.4 mile, turn left to view the billowing 160-foot cascade of Silver Falls. After viewing the falls, head back to the main trail and turn left. Continue uphill and hang on tightly to your pooch as the trail follows the edge of a steep cliff to viewpoint of Golden Falls at 0.9 mile (your turnaround point). For a less precipitous view of Golden Falls, take the right fork at the beginning of the hike and walk 0.3 mile to the viewpoint.

Bullards Beach State Park
Contact: Oregon State Parks and Recreation, Suite 1, 1115 Commercial St. NE, Salem, OR 97301-1002, 1-800-551-6949, www.oregonstateparks.org
Paw-Approval Rating: 3 paws
Leashes Required? Yes
Fees/Permits: None
Season: Year-round
Getting There: From Coos Bay, drive approximately 22 miles south on Highway 101 to the park entrance on the west (right) side of the road. From Bandon, drive 2 miles north on Highway 101 to the park.
Description: This state park is between the Coquille River and the Pacific. From the campground, you and your furry

friend can walk on a 1-mile paved path to the beach. Another 3-mile trail takes you to the North Jetty, that is site of the historic Coquille River Lighthouse, built in 1896. Paddlehounds will enjoy exploring the estuary at the mouth of the Coquille River, an area designated as the Bandon Marsh National Wildlife Refuge. To rent a kayak and gear, visit Adventure Kayak, 315 First St., Bandon, 541-347-3480, www.adventurekayak.com.

Port Orford

Cape Blanco State Park

Contact: Oregon State Parks and Recreation, Suite 1, 1115 Commercial St. NE, Salem, OR 97301-1002, 1-800-551-6949, www.oregonstateparks.org
Paw-Approval Rating: 4 paws
Leashes Required? Yes
Fees/Permits: None
Season: Year-round
Getting There: Travel 46 miles south of Coos Bay or 4 miles north of Port Orford on Highway 101 to the junction with Cape Blanco Road. Turn west and drive 5 miles to the park.
Description: Cape Blanco is the westernmost point in the contiguous 48 states. This uncrowded state park is a great place to enjoy the sights and sounds of the South Oregon Coast. Set up a base camp at the scenic campground (see *Campgrounds*) and spend a few days exploring the 8 miles of hiking trails through a diverse coastal ecosystem. Other star attractions are the 59-foot Cape Blanco Lighthouse and the Hughes House Museum.

Humbug Mountain State Park

Contact: Oregon State Parks and Recreation, Suite 1, 1115 Commercial St. NE, Salem, OR 97301-1002, 1-800-551-6949, www.oregonstateparks.org
Paw-Approval Rating: 4 paws
Leashes Required? Yes
Fees/Permits: None
Season: Year-round. This trail can be muddy during winter.
Getting There: From Port Orford, travel 6 miles south on Highway 101 to the park entrance on the left (east) side of the Highway. From Gold Beach, the park is 21 miles north.
Description: This beautiful, quiet state park and campground (see *Campgrounds*) is worth a stop. At 1,761-feet, Humbug Mountain is located at the center of the park. If you and your four-legged friend are feeling ambitious, trek the 5.5-mile loop trail that climbs 1,730 feet to the summit. To reach the trailhead, at the campground cross a bridge over Brush Creek and proceed through the tunnel under Highway 101. The trail passes through maple and myrtle trees and then through old-growth Douglas fir. A junction in about a mile is the start of the loop portion of the trail. If you go right, you'll come to a viewpoint to the north, of Redfish Rocks, Port Orford, and Cape Blanco. Keep following the trail as it loops back around to rejoin the main trail. At this junction, hike up a short, steep trail to a viewpoint looking south toward Gold Beach.

If want to explore the beach pick up the trail that starts near campsite C7.

Gold Beach

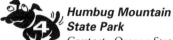

Shrader Old Growth Hike

Contact: Gold Beach Ranger District, 29279 Ellensburg Ave., Gold Beach, OR 97444, 541-247-3600, www.fs.fed.us
Paw-Approval Rating: 3 paws
Leashes Required? Yes
Length: 0.8-mile loop
Difficulty: Easy
Fees/Permits: $5 Northwest Forest Pass. Purchase at 1-800-270-7504 or www.naturenw.org
Season: Year-round. This trail can be muddy during winter.

Getting There: From Gold Beach, drive 11.2 miles east on Jerry's Flat Road (County Road 595) to the junction with Forest Road 3300-090. Turn right on Forest Road 3300-090 and follow signs about 2 miles to the trailhead.

Description: This short loop takes you and your traveling partner through a grove of immense Douglas fir and hardwood trees. While your pal may not be so interested in how tall the trees are, he may enjoy sniffing around their bases.

Rogue River Hike

Contact: Gold Beach Ranger District, 29279 Ellensburg Ave., Gold Beach, OR 97444, 541-247-3600, www.fs.fed.us

Paw-Approval Rating: 4 paws
Leashes Required? Yes
Length: 8.6 miles out and back
Difficulty: Difficult
Fees/Permits: $5 Northwest Forest Pass. Purchase at 1-800-270-7504 or www.naturenw.org.
Season: Year-round. This trail can be muddy during winter.
Getting There: From Highway 101 in Gold Beach, turn east onto Jerry's Flat Road. Go 32 miles to a road junction. Go right toward Illahe and continue 3.5 miles to the trailhead on the right.

Description: This beautiful trail wanders through the wild Rogue River Canyon in the Rogue River Wilderness. From the trailhead, hike 4.3 miles and ascend over 600 feet to pretty Flora Dell Falls, which is your turnaround point. Beware of poison oak and blazing summertime temperatures in August.

Pistol River State Scenic Viewpoint

Contact: Oregon State Parks and Recreation, Suite 1, 1115 Commercial St. NE, Salem, OR 97301-1002, 1-800-551-6949, www.oregonstateparks.org

Paw-Approval Rating: 3 paws
Leashes Required? Yes

Fees/Permits: None
Season: Year-round
Getting There: From Gold Beach, drive 11 miles south on Highway 101 to the signed entrance to the park.

Description: At the north parking area, you'll have access to Myers Beach, which is strewn with huge boulders. From the south parking area, you'll see the Pistol River carving its way to the Pacific through a series of sand dunes. Bring your binoculars to spot birds in the estuary.

Brookings

Cape Ferrelo to Whalehead Beach Hike

Contact: Oregon State Parks and Recreation, Suite 1, 1115 Commercial St. NE, Salem, OR 97301-1002, 1-800-551-6949, www.oregonstateparks.org

Paw-Approval Rating: 4 paws
Leashes Required? Yes
Length: 9.4 miles out and back
Difficulty: Moderate
Fees/Permits: $3 day-use fee
Season: Year-round. This trail can be muddy during winter.
Getting There: From Brookings, travel 4.8 miles north on Highway 101 and turn left (west) at the Cape Ferrelo Viewpoint. Continue 0.2 mile to a parking area.

Description: The 12 miles of rugged and wild coastline in 1,471-acre Samuel H. Boardman State Park is replete with offshore rocks and sea stacks, secluded sandy beaches, and beautiful coastal headlands. This hike follows a section of the Oregon Coast Trail through some of the park's best scenery. Pick up the trail in the northwest corner of the parking area. The trail heads north and takes you and your best pal through a fragrant Sitka spruce forest and past open meadows of purple lupine. After 1.4 miles you'll arrive at House Rock Viewpoint, home to a monument to Samuel H. Boardman, the first superintendent of Oregon Parks. Over the next 1.7 miles, the trail switchbacks down a scenic headland for about 400 feet until you reach Whalehead Beach at 3.1 miles. Walk north on the beach while enjoying views of the offshore sea stacks and Whalehead Island. Rover will have fun in the surf, looking for the perfect stick on this isolated beach. At 4.3 miles, look for an Oregon Coast Trail marker on the right side of the beach. After you reach the marker, continue walking north. Ignore a set of stairs that head left at 4.6 miles. At 4.7 miles, you'll arrive at a picnic area with restrooms. This is your turnaround point.

Riverview and Redwood Hike

Contact: Oregon State Parks and Recreation, Suite 1, 1115 Commercial St. NE, Salem, OR 97301-1002, 1-800-551-6949, www.oregonstateparks.org

Paw-Approval Rating: 3 paws
Leashes Required? Yes
Length: 3.6 miles out and back
Difficulty: Easy
Fees/Permits: $3 day-use fee
Season: Year-round. These trails can be muddy during winter.
Getting There: From Highway 101 in Brookings, turn east on North Bank Chetco River Road and travel 7.5 miles to the park entrance. Turn right onto the park entrance road. At the road fork, turn left. Continue to the picnic area and park in the parking area on the right side of the road.
Description: The Riverview and Redwood Nature Trails are located in Alfred. A. Loeb State Park. This park, adjacent to the salmon-rich Chetco River, features a large campground (see *Campgrounds*) and many hiking opportunities.

The 0.7-mile Riverview Trail takes you along the banks of the Chetco through an old grove of myrtle trees. Your pooch will have plenty of opportunities to cool off in the river on this trail. The Riverview Trail can be accessed from the picnic area adjacent to the campground.

Follow this trail 0.7 mile and cross a paved road, where you'll begin the 1.2-mile Redwood Nature Trail, which loops you through a grove of immense, 300–800-year-old coastal redwoods. Pick up an interpretive brochure with descriptions that corresponds to numbered trail markers.

PADDLEHOUNDS
Bandon

Old Towne Bandon to Rocky Point

Contact: Adventure Kayak, 315 First St., Bandon, OR 541-347-3480, adventure kayak.com
Fees/Permits: None
Getting There: To get to the Bandon Harbor from Highway 101 in Bandon, follow signs to Old Town and the Harbor. To get to the Rocky Point take-out, from Highway 101 just north of Bandon turn east on North Bank Road (just north of the Coquille River). Travel 1 mile to Rocky Point County Park.
Description: This is a scenic 4.5 mile (one way) paddle north along the banks of the Coquille River from Old Town Bandon to Rocky Point. Along this section, you'll see amazing wildlife in the 289-acre Bandon National Wildlife Refuge, a vast salt marsh of the Coquille River watershed. You'll be paddling upriver, so plan your paddle for an incoming tide. For tide tables, pick up the local paper or stop by Adventure Kayak in Old Town Bandon to get tide information as well as information about paddling hot spots in this area. Adventure Kayak also offers guided tours and kayak rentals.

CANINE COMFORT ACCOMMODATIONS

Towns in this section are listed geographically, from north to south. Unless otherwise stated, dogs should not be left unattended in the room and must be leashed on hotel property.

Coos Bay

$ Motel 6

1445 Bayshore Dr., 541-267-7171

This motel features clean, pet-friendly rooms. Amenities include a dry sauna and hot tub/spa room.

Dog Policy

Your pooch gets to stay for free.

$$-$$$ Red Lion Hotel

1313 North Bayshore Dr., 541-267-4141, www.redlion.com

This hotel has 143 rooms equipped with digital satellite TV, Super Nintendo® on-demand movies, complimentary HBO, telephone data ports, room service, laundry, and valet service.

Dog Policy

No extra fees are charged for your dog.

Bandon

$-$$ Table Rock Motel

840 Beach Loop Rd., 1-800-457-9141, www.tablerockmotel.com

This motel features pet-friendly, non-smoking rooms with refrigerator, cable TV/VCR, telephone, in-room coffee, and clock radio. Some rooms have an ocean view.

Dog Policy

Well-behaved canines are welcome for $5 per dog per night.

$-$$$$ Sunset Oceanfront Condominiums

1865 Beach Loop Dr., 1-800-842-2407, www.sunsetmotel.com

This motel features non-smoking, ocean-view rooms and beach access in beautiful Bandon. Additional amenities include an indoor heated pool, spa, and gift shop. Beach house rentals are also available.

Dog Policy

The motel charges $10 per dog per night.

Port Orford

$$ The Holly House Inn

600 Jackson St., 541-332-7100, www.hollyhouseinn.com

The Holly House Inn is owned and managed by Francie MacLeod and her American bulldog Blinky and her cat Midnight. The inn features a two-bedroom upstairs unit with a private entrance, full kitchen, and bath; and a downstairs one-bedroom apartment. Both units are fully furnished, roomy, and comfortable. Additional amenities include TV/VCR, video library, reading library, sitting room, antiques, and a garden. A breakfast of homemade scones, fresh fruit, tea, and Italian coffee is served in the dining room or in your room. The inn is a short walk from a scenic beach and close by many mountain bike trails.

Dog Policy

Well-behaved dogs and cats are welcome for no extra charge. Dogs are not permitted to sleep on the furniture.

Gold Beach

$-$$ Motel 6

94433 Jerry's Flat Rd., 541-247-4533

This motel features clean, pet-friendly rooms.

Dog Policy

No extra fees are charged for your dog.

$-$$ Oregon Trail Lodge

29855 Ellensburg Ave., 541-247-6030

This motel is adjacent to the mouth of the Rogue River in downtown Gold Beach. All rooms are clean, cozy, and have a rustic charm. Rooms have one, two, or three bedrooms and are equipped with a microwave, refrigerator, and kitchen. The motel is within walking distance of the beach, restaurants, and shops.

Dog Policy
A fee of $5 per day is charged for your dog.

$-$$$ Ireland's Rustic Lodges
29330 Ellensburg Ave., 541-247-7718, www.irelandsrusticlodges.com

You and your dog can stay in one of seven cozy log cabins with a wood-burning fireplace. This hotel also has 33 rooms, some with kitchen and fireplace.

Dog Policy
This lodge charges $5 per night for small dogs and $10 per night for large dogs.

Brookings

$-$$ Harbor Inn Motel
15991 Highway 101 South, 1-800-469-8444, www.harborinnmotel.com

Managers Jane and Mike and their 2-year-old chocolate Chihuahua, Scooter, welcome you to their dog-friendly motel. The 30 rooms include queen beds, TV, and direct dial phones. The motel is within walking distance of beaches and trails.

Dog Policy
The motel charges $8 per dog per night.

$$ Sea Dreamer Inn
15167 McVay Lane, 1-800-408-4367

This friendly bed and breakfast inn with four comfortable rooms is owned by Penny Wallace and Don Roy. KC, a friendly lab, is one of the resident canines; he loves other animals and loves to play tug of war with old socks. Two rooms are pet-friendly. Penny says, "Our Victorian house, built in 1912, has a beautiful view of the ocean and overlooks a large lily field. It is a comfortable old house where guests are encouraged to sit by the fire, play the piano, read, play games, or watch Web TV. We also serve cookies and treats in the evening. We are your hosts, local guides, piano teachers (if you've never had a lesson before), admirers of your pet (if he or she is well behaved) ..." A home-made breakfast is included with your stay. The Sea Dreamer does not accept credit cards but does accept cash, personal checks, and traveler's checks.

Dog Policy
Dogs are welcome as long as they are leashed and get along with the resident dogs KC and Scotty and the resident feline Ladycat. After a day of exploring, the inn will provide you with towels to wipe down your dog. A $10 fee is charged per dog.

$$-$$$ Best Western Beach Inn
16008 Boat Basin Rd., 541-469-7779 or 1-800-468-4081

Dog Policy
This inn charges $5 per pet per night.

CAMPGROUNDS
Campgrounds are listed geographically by city, from north to south. All campgrounds listed are leashed dog-friendly. The only exception is that dogs are not allowed inside yurts, tepees, camper wagons, or cabins.

Coos Bay

Bullards Beach State Park
Contact: Oregon State Parks and Recreation, Suite 1, 1115 Commercial St. NE, Salem, OR 97301-1002, 1-800-551-6949 (information), 1-800-452-5687 (reservations), www.oregonstateparks.org
Season: Year-round
Facilities: 102 full-hook-up sites, 83 electrical sites, 13 yurts, horse camp (8 sites with 3 single corrals, 3 double corrals, and two 4-space corrals), hiker/biker camp, picnic tables, barbecue grills, restrooms with hot showers, piped water, boat launch and docks on the Coquille River
Getting There: From Coos Bay, drive approximately 22 miles south on Highway 101 to the park entrance on the west (right) side of the road. From downtown Bandon, the park is two miles north on the left (west) side of Highway 101.
Description: You and your best friend will enjoy the shade of shore pines in this

restful campground. A 1-mile paved trail takes you through coastal forest and a dune environment before it reaches the beach. Another attraction is the Coquille River Lighthouse on the north jetty of the Coquille River. You can reach the lighthouse on a 3-mile trail accessible from the campground.

Sunset Bay State Park

Contact: Oregon State Parks and Recreation, Suite 1, 1115 Commercial St. NE, Salem, OR 97301-1002, 1-800-551-6949 (information), 1-800-452-5687 (reservations), www.oregonstateparks.org
Season: Year-round
Facilities: 29 full-hook-ups sites, 36 electrical sites, 66 tent sites, 8 yurts, 11 group-tent areas, hiker/biker camp area, picnic tables, barbecue grills, firewood, restrooms, and hot showers
Getting There: From Highway 101 in Coos Bay, follow the signs to Charleston Harbor and Ocean Beaches and continue on the Cape Arago Highway 12 miles southwest to Sunset Bay State Park.
Description: This picturesque park is filled with rocky sandstone cliffs, rugged sea stacks, and a protected cove. The campground is on the banks of Big Creek. Be sure to take your furry friend on a beautiful section of the Oregon Coast Trail that travels two miles south to the boundary of Shore Acres State Park (see *Paw-Approved Hikes and Parks*). Dogs are not allowed in Shore Acres State Park.

Port Orford

Cape Blanco State Park

Contact: Oregon State Parks and Recreation, Suite 1, 1115 Commercial St. NE, Salem, OR 97301-1002, 1-800-551-6949 (information), 1-800-452-5687 (reservations), www.oregonstateparks.org
Season: Year-round
Facilities: 58 electrical sites, 4 cabins, 8 horse campsites with 4 double corrals, 4 group-tent areas, hiker/biker camp, picnic

tables, barbecue grills, firewood, piped water, restrooms, and hot showers, RV dump station. All campsites are first-come, first-served (except cabins, horse sites, and group camp sites).
Getting There: Travel 46 miles south of Coos Bay or four miles north of Port Orford on Highway 101 to the junction with Cape Blanco Road. Turn west and drive 5 miles on Cape Blanco Road to Cape Blanco State Park
Description: This secluded campground is protected from coastal winds by sheltering trees and a thick understory of salal, salmonberry, and thimbleberry. This park has 8 miles of trails to explore and a lot of natural beauty, including high, chalky bluffs, a black sand beach, and off-shore sea stacks which are home to herds of sea lions and are nesting sites for sea birds. Explore the Cape Blanco Lighthouse, the oldest lighthouse in Oregon, or the Hughes House Museum.

Humbug Mountain State Park

Contact: Oregon State Parks and Recreation, Suite 1, 1115 Commercial St. NE, Salem, OR 97301-1002, 1-800-551-6949 (information), 1-800-452-5687 (reservations), www.oregonstateparks.org
Season: Year-round
Facilities: 33 electrical sites, 68 tent sites, hiker/biker camp, picnic tables, fire rings, firewood, piped water, restrooms, and hot showers
Getting There: From Port Orford, travel 6 miles south on Highway 101 to the park entrance on the left (east) side of the highway.
Description: This state park in a forested setting features some of the warmest weather on the Oregon Coast. Your trail hound will enjoy the moderate 5.5-mile loop to the summit of 1,756-foot Humbug Mountain (see *Paw-Approved Hikes and Parks*). If the beach beckons, a walkway leads under the highway from the campground to a four-mile stretch of blissfully-peaceful sandy beach.

Brookings

Alfred A. Loeb State Park
Contact: Oregon State Parks and Recreation, Suite 1, 1115 Commercial St. NE, Salem, OR 97301-1002, 1-800-551-6949 (information), 1-800-452-5687 (reservations), www.oregonstateparks.org
Season: Year-round
Facilities: 48 electrical sites, 3 cabins, picnic tables, barbecue grills, restrooms, and piped water. Only cabins can be reserved by phone.
Getting There: From Highway 101 in Brookings, turn east on North Bank Chetco River Road and drive 7.5 miles to the park entrance.
Description: This shady campground on the Chetco River sits in a grove of myrtle and other deciduous trees. Highlights include the Riverview and Redwood Nature Trails (see *Paw-Approved Hikes and Parks*) that take you and Fido along the banks of the Chetco and through old growth myrtle and redwood. Your pooch will enjoy the many swimming holes along the Chetco.

Harris Beach State Park
Contact: Oregon State Parks and Recreation, Suite 1, 1115 Commercial St. NE, Salem, OR 97301-1002, 1-800-551-6949 (information), 1-800-452-5687 (reservations), www.oregonstateparks.org
Season: Year-round
Facilities: 36 full-hook-up sites, 50 electrical sites, 68 tent sites, cable TV hookups at selected campsites, 6 yurts, hiker/biker camp, picnic tables, barbecue grills, firewood, restrooms, hot showers, and a RV dump station
Getting There: From Brookings, travel 2 miles north on Highway 101 to the park entrance on the left (west) side of the highway.
Description: This campground is surrounded by beautiful Oregon Coast scenery. You and your four-legged friend can walk on a long sandy beach. On your beach walk watch for sea birds nesting on Bird Island—the largest offshore island on the Oregon Coast. You may also view sea lions and harbor seals on the offshore rocks or migrating gray whales from December through June.

DOG EVENTS
North Bend
Oregon Dune Mushers Mail Run
Oregon Dune Mushers, P.O. Box 841, www.harborside.com

Held the second weekend in March, this annual 3-day event is a 75-mile endurance mush from North Bend to Florence through the Oregon Dunes National Recreation Area. Dryland dog teams (dogs pulling a cart on wheels) and their owners brave sand dunes, trails, hard packed roads, and sandy beaches. Each participant carries hand-signed commemorative envelopes. Each stamped envelope is cancelled in North Bend, Lakeside, and Florence and is sold after the race to raise money for the club.

Bandon

The Coos Kennel Club's All-Breed Dog Show & Obedience Trials
Bandon High School, 541-347-2171

This annual two-day show is held at the Bandon High School football field the first weekend in July. This American Kennel Club-approved event includes a conformation show and obedience court trials. Over 600 dogs representing 140 breeds attend. Judging starts at 9 A.M. both days. Admission is free; concession stands feature food (human type) and dog products. This dog show is just a few blocks from the ocean and a short walk to restaurants and shopping.

CANINE-APPROVED SHOPPING
Stores are listed geographically, from north to south.

Reedsport

Parent Feed & Farm
1960 Ranch Rd., 541-271-3929

This store has been open 12 years and carries Eagle Pack dog food, Advantage flea products, waterproof dog coats, Sportmix dog biscuits, cedar dog houses, toys, and carriers. The owners ask that you do not bring your dog in the store. Open 10 A.M.–6 P.M., Monday to Friday; 10 A.M.–2 P.M., Saturday.

Coos Bay

Coos Grange Supply
1085 S. 2nd St., 541-267-7051

This store stocks Science Diet, Nutro, Natural Choice, and Canidae dog and cat foods. It also carries Frontline and Advantage flea control products, toys, collars, leashes, and crates. The staff caters to anyone with problems with their pets or anyone looking for something different. Pets are welcome except in the garden area. Open 9 A.M.–5:30 P.M., Monday to Saturday.

Puppy Love Grooming
237 South 7th St., 541-267-4942

This friendly retail store and grooming shop has been in business over 20 years and carries specialty dog foods including Eagle, Nutro, Eukanuba, Pro Plan, Nature's Recipe, Iams, and Science Diet. In addition, the store stocks pet carriers, seat belts, travel dishes, shampoos, flea control products, and more to keep your dog healthy and happy. Open 7:30 A.M.–6 P.M., Monday to Friday; 8 A.M.–5 P.M., Saturday.

Brookings

For Pet's Sake
16340 Lower Harbor Rd., 541-412-3647

You and your best friend will love cruising the aisles in this friendly pet store, which carries a full line of rain gear, boots, packs, and sweaters. Also in stock are homeopathic and herbal remedies, Pro-Biotic natural food lines, Bone-A-Fido biscuit bakery, made-in-Oregon products, and Suzie's Tarter Control liquid. This shop will day-sit well behaved and socialized dogs for $15 per dog per day. Open 10 A.M.–5 P.M., Monday to Saturday; 12 P.M.–5 P.M. Sunday.

DOGGIE DAYCARE
Brookings

For Pet's Sake
16340 Lower Harbor Rd., 541-412-3647

This pet shop will day-sit well behaved and socialized dogs for $15 per day. Hugs, kisses, and treats are included. Open 10 A.M.–5 P.M., Monday to Saturday; 12 P.M.–5 P.M., Sunday.

CANINE ER
North Bend

Harbor Lights Animal Hospital
1710 Virginia Ave., 541-269-4465

This full-service hospital has been in business since 1964. It offers vaccinations, check-ups, surgery, and dentistry services. The hospital will see walk-ins and offers twenty-four hour emergency service. Hills Science Diet prescription dog food, a full line of grooming and flea control products, leashes, and collars are stocked. Overnight boarding is available; rates vary from $11 to $14 per night.

Open 8:30 A.M.–5:30 P.M., Monday to Friday; 9 A.M.–1 P.M., Saturday.

Coos Bay

Hanson Animal Hospital
45 East Lockhart, 541-269-2415

This full-service hospital has been at its current location 28 years; it accepts walk-ins and after-hours emergency calls. The clinic stocks flea control products, shampoos, and special prescription diet dog foods.

Open 9 A.M.–5:30 P.M. Monday, Tuesday, Thursday and Friday; 9 A.M.–11:30 A.M., Wednesday and Saturday.

Gold Beach

Gold Beach Veterinary Clinic
94211 3rd St., 541-247-2513

Brookings

Town and Country Animal Clinic
15740 Highway 101 S., 541-469-4661

This small and large animal clinic has been in business nine years. It takes walk-in appointments and handles after-hours emergencies. The clinic stocks premium foods, toys, shampoos, and flea control products, and offers overnight boarding for $10 per night for dogs, and $8 per night for cats.

Open 8 A.M.–5:30 P.M., Monday to Friday; 8 A.M.–12 P.M., Saturday.

LOST AND FOUND (ANIMAL SHELTERS)

Brookings

South Coast Humane Society
620 Hemlock St., 541-412-0325, www.socoasthumane.com/about.html

Adoption clinics are held the second Saturday of each month, from 1 P.M.–3 P.M. at the Humane Society Thrift Store at 620 Hemlock St.

Appendix: Gearing Up Your Pup

Backpacks

Doggie backpacks allow Fido to carry his own food, water, and toys on the trail. Dogs in good condition can carry up to 25% to 30% of their body weight. Most packs are fitted to a dog's weight and girth measurement; manufacturers generally publish guidelines to help you pick the size that's right for your dog. When purchasing a pack, look for a harness with two padded girth straps, a padded chest strap, leash attachments, removable saddle bags, internal water bladders, and external gear cords.

If your trail-busting is limited to afternoon outings to the park or short hikes, Ruff Wear's (1-888-783-3932, www.ruff wear.com) lightweight and compact Daytripper™ is a good choice. This pack has a full suspension mesh back panel that easily distributes the weight and keeps your pal cool on hot days. It holds toys, treats, and other necessities for short day outings.

Let your dog carry his own gear in a doggie backpack.

If you're going on longer adventures and your buddy needs to carry more gear, check out Ruff Wear's Approach Pack™. Like the Daytripper™ this pack disperses the pack's weight with a full mesh panel but has more room to stow treats, a first aid kit, bowls, food, and toys.

If you're heading into the backcountry for a multi-day trip, check out Ruff Wear's top-of-the-line Palisades Pack™, which features an integrated hydration system, load-stabilizing compression straps, an exterior gear cord, and a webbing handle to assist dogs over streams and other trail obstacles. Packs can be easily removed from the pack harness if Rover wants a break from hauling gear. This pack is the largest of Ruff Wear's doggie packs.

Wolf Packs® (541-482-7669, www.wolfpacks.com) also make high quality packs any canine will appreciate. The Wolf Packs® Reflector™ pack will keep Fido safer at night due to its Scotchlite™ reflective trim. This pack is big enough to carry the essentials for a trip to the park or a long hike. The Banzai™ pack is made of tough Cordura Plus nylon and is Wolf Packs'® top-of-the-line design. One of its best features is the horizontal compression straps that distribute the pack's weight toward the shoulders—the strongest part of a dog's back. Like the Reflector™ pack, this pack features 3M Scotchlite™ reflective trim. Toys and snacks are easily stashed in the handy, zippered outer pockets.

Other canine gear companies that sell high quality packs include Mountainsmith (1-800-551-5889, www.mountainsmith.com), Granite Gear (218-834-6157, www.granitegear.com), Caribou Mountaineering

(1-800-824-4153, www.caribou.com), and Fidogear™ (1-877-FIDO-GEAR, www.fidogear.com).

Water Bowls

There are dozens of collapsible dog water bowls on the market made of lightweight, tough materials. Ruff Wear's bowls (1-888-783-3932, www.ruffwear.com) are made of tough Cordura nylon and come in three different sizes. Two of the larger sizes offer a cinch top option that allows you to stash your dog's dry food right in the bowl by pulling the drawstring closure.

Other clever bowl designs include Fidogear™ (1-888-FIDO-GEAR, www.fido gear.com) Roll Bowls™, which are made of lightweight waterproof material, and roll up and close with a Velcro closure. A clip attaches the bowl to a backpack or belt. Bison Designs™ (www.bisondesigns.com) Fold A Bowl™ is a lightweight, one-liter bowl that can be folded inside itself and then zippered shut. Its exterior ring allows you to clip it to your pack or belt.

An inventive sport bottle made by Cool Pooch (1-877-CLPOOCH, www.coolpooch.com) allows you and your canine to drink from the same bottle. You drink from a plastic straw and your dog drinks out of the cup-shaped lid. To fill up the cup, just bend the straw and squeeze the bottle.

Coats

Keeping your four-legged friend comfortable in Oregon's often wet and cold weather is a top priority. If your dog has a short coat or is not used to cold and bluster, an extra layer will keep him happier when you are hiking, biking, or cross-country skiing. Fidogear's™ (1-888-FIDO-GEAR, www.fidogear.com) Winter Coat will protect him from the cold and rain with its strong, weather-resistant Cordura shell and soft, fleece lining. The K-9 Overcoat by Ruff Wear also protects dogs from the elements, and has a streamlined fit (1-888-783-3932, www.ruffwear.com).

Collapsible bowls are convenient and easy to store when you are traveling and on the trail.

Portable Flotation Device (PFD)

If you paddle with your dog, especially in big water, invest in a high quality flotation vest. Ruff Wear's K-9 Float Coat™ (1-888-783-3932, www.ruffwear.com) has a streamlined fit and a high buoyancy that keeps your dog afloat. It also has a low-profile handle that enables you to lift your dog out of the water and back into the boat. The Extrasport Fido PFD (available at REI, 1-800-426-4840, www.rei.com) is made of nylon covered, closed-cell PVC foam and features high-contoured openings for more freedom of movement. Two non-corrosive, adjustable, side-release buckles allow for a custom fit, and a convenient nylon handle helps you lift your pup out of the water.

First-Aid Kit

Always carry a first aid kit in the car or on the trail so you are prepared to treat your dog's injuries. MediPet (1-888-633-4738, www.medipet.com) and Ruff Wear (1-888-783-3932, www.ruffwear.com) make canine first-aid kits.

Dog Boots

Would you run barefoot on a rocky trail or hot pavement? Well, just imagine what your best friend must go through! When you head into the outdoors with your canine pal, consider protecting his paws from gravel roads, hot asphalt, chemicals, abrasive sand, broken glass, grass stubble, mud, ice, burrs, grass seeds, and other hazards. Dog boots protect your pal's paws from cuts, bruises, and thorns.

Muttluk dog boots (1-888-MUTTLUK, www.muttluks.com) are made of breathable, waterproof, Hydroflex-coated fabric. They offer leather toe protection, 3M Scotchlite™ reflective material, a self-adjusting fastening system to obtain the perfect fit, and a stretchy sleeve that fits over your dog's paw like a sock. Muttluks also come in a polar fleece style.

Ruff Wear's 3D Bark n' Boots feature a flat sole and an articulated cuff, which fits the natural shape of a dog's paw. The boots are made of tough, 500-denier Cordura® uppers and grippy, flexible, Reprotek® soles. For really adventurous canines who love to wear out their dog boots, these boots feature a reinforced toe that will stand up to the rigors of the trail. An easy-to-use hook and loop closure allows you to get a good fit.

Other companies that make high quality dog boots include Duke's Dog Fashions (1-800-880-8969, www.dukesdog.com), Fidogear (1-888-FIDOGEAR, www.fidogear.com), and Cool Paw Productions (1-800-650-PAWS).

Toys

No doubt your pooch carries his favorite toy wherever he goes. Bringing your dog's playthings along is a great way to keep him entertained and exercised on the trail, at rest stops, and in camp. The classic dog toy is a tennis ball. If you dread picking up the slimy, dirty ball, check out Canine Hardware's Chuckit! tennis ball thrower (1-800-660-9033, www.chuckit.com). Its circular, claw-shaped end allows you to pick up the ball without having to touch it with your hands. No more "Yecchh!!!" It also enables throws of up to 140 feet. No more sore, tired arms!

If Rover likes to chase squirrels instead of balls, consider the Flying Squirrel™ by Canine Hardware. It throws like a Frisbee but looks like a flying squirrel. For an alternative to hard plastic Frisbees that are tough on your best friend's mouth, check out Ruff Wear's durable Hover Craft™ (1-888-783-3932, www.ruffwear.com). This soft flying disc is made of tough nylon and soars like an eagle.

If your dog isn't into chasing objects but loves tug of war, he'll dig Ruff Wear's Zoing™ Interactive Dog Toy. This toy is a stretchy tubular assembly you attach to a stationary object; when your pup pulls on the toy, it pulls back, creating a fantastic game of tug of war.

And then there are the old, low-tech standbys. One of Levi's favorite toys is a leather soccer ball found at any sporting goods store. He can spend hours keeping himself entertained with this inexpensive and durable toy.

Trail Snacks

On long, hard hikes, trail runs, or bike rides, Rover needs to refuel just like you do. Zuke's Treats for Dogs (1-866-ZUKE-DOG, www.zukes.com) carries a wide assortment of trail treats including high-energy Power Bones, Trek'n Treats (a lower calorie version of Power Bones), Hip Action Snacks (each treat contains 300 mg of glucosamine and 250 mg of chondroitin, which eases joint soreness in older dogs) and Jerky Natural Treats. For a convenient place to store treats on the trail, check out Canine Hardware's Treat Tote (1-800-660-9033, www.chuckit.com). This small nylon pouch's clip fits onto your belt, making it easy to access your dog's snacks.

Other Cool Gear

To protect your best friend's eyes from harmful ultraviolet rays, check out Ruff

Wear's Doggles (1-888-783-3932, www. ruffwear.com). These protective goggles are designed to fit a dog's head and will protect his eyes in the snow or on the water.

Other handy travel gear is Ruff Wear's Kibble Kaddie. This container of tough Cordura nylon stores up to 14 pounds of dog chow. Its convenient food chute allows you to dispense kibble from the bottom of the bag; an external gear cord holds food bowls and other dog gear.

And for the other end of the food consumption factory known as your dog, you may want to get Bags on Board® by Tame Products (805-495-976, www.tameproducts.com). Bags on Board® is a compact, refillable dispenser that attaches to any type of dog collar. Inside is a roll of doggie clean-up bags. Bag refills snap easily into the dispenser.

Index

About the Author

Photograph by Ken Skeen

LIZANN DUNEGAN is a full-time freelance writer and photographer who specializes in writing about outdoor activities and travel. She has traveled thousands of miles throughout Oregon with her travel partners Levi and Sage, conducting research for her books and articles. She has authored six other guidebooks about Oregon, including *Road Biking Oregon, Hike America Oregon, Mountain Biking Northwest Oregon, Trail Running Northwest Oregon, Hiking the Oregon Coast,* and *Insiders' Guide to the Oregon Coast.*

Lizann is a licensed Veterinary Technician in the state of Oregon and has four years of experience working in the veterinary field. Besides writing and photography, she enjoys trail running, mountain biking, hiking, cross-country skiing, sea kayaking, spinning wool, and playing the violin and cello. She lives in Portland, Oregon, with her two canine best friends.